Essential Guide to Marketing Planning

Marian Burk Wood

Essential Guide to
Marketing Planning

Third edition

PEARSON

Harlow, England • London • New York • Boston • San Francisco • Toronto • Sydney
Auckland • Singapore • Hong Kong • Tokyo • Seoul • Taipei • New Delhi
Cape Town • São Paulo • Mexico City • Madrid • Amsterdam • Munich • Paris • Milan

Pearson Education Limited
Edinburgh Gate
Harlow CM20 2JE
United Kingdom
Tel: +44 (0)1279 623623

Web: www.pearson.com/uk

First published 2007 (print)
Second edition published 2010 (print)
Third edition published 2013 (print and electronic)

ISBN: 978-0-273-77363-4 (print)
       978-0-273-77367-2 (PDF)
       978-0-273-79483-7 (eText)

British Library Cataloguing-in-Publication Data
A catalogue record for the print edition is available from the British Library

Library of Congress Cataloging-in-Publication Data
A catalog record for the print edition is available from the Library of Congress

10 9 8 7 6 5 4 3 2 1
17 16 15 14 13

Print edition typeset in 10/12.5 Palatino LT Std by 35
Print edition printed by Ashford Colour Press Ltd., Gosport

NOTE THAT ANY PAGE CROSS REFERENCES REFER TO THE PRINT EDITION

Brief contents

Contents

Preface

In a world where customers' needs and behaviours are always changing, economic circumstances are unpredictable, competitive pressure is a constant factor and every day brings new technological advances, you'll need careful planning to achieve your objectives. This book is your essential guide to creating a practical, effective marketing plan for achieving financial, marketing and societal objectives. Through clear explanations, real-world examples and hands-on exercises, it will help you to:

- understand what marketing planning is, how it works and why it's important
- complete the seven stages of the marketing planning process
- formulate a marketing plan customised for your situation.

Chapter by chapter, you'll learn the language and basic concepts of planning, gain insights from the experiences of marketers worldwide and put your knowledge to work as you develop a marketing plan of your own. You'll find out how to research your market and marketing situation, set objectives, decide on marketing strategies and document your ideas in a marketing plan similar to the sample plan in the Appendix. Whether you go to work for a major corporation, specialise in consumer or business marketing, start your own business or join a non-governmental organisation, your understanding of the planning process will be a valuable asset.

NEW IN THIS EDITION

You'll find updated coverage of the very latest developments in marketing, including definitions, descriptions and examples of:

- *content marketing* to demonstrate thought leadership and engage customers
- *crowdsourcing* and *co-creation* of new products
- *freemium* pricing strategies for product introductions
- *key performance indicators* and *metrics* for evaluating marketing results
- *multichannel marketing* to allow customers to buy when and where they prefer

- *neuromarketing* for marketing research
- *pop-up shops, showrooming* and other retail trends
- *social media marketing, buzz marketing* and *social gifting*
- *sustainable marketing* and issues concerning *greenwashing*.

In addition, this new edition contains three new checklists to help you with specific aspects of the planning process, for a total of 20 checklists. You'll also learn from dozens of new extended examples and detailed cases showing how manufacturers, retailers, service firms, non-profits and other organisations actually apply the principles of marketing planning. Because the world of marketing is dynamic, every chapter has been thoroughly revised to reflect current marketing thought and practice. And because marketing is increasingly global, this new edition includes new examples examining the role of planning in consumer marketing, business-to-business marketing and non-profit marketing around the world.

YOUR STEP-BY-STEP GUIDE

Each chapter is packed with special features to assist you in understanding and completing the essential steps in formulating a marketing plan:

- *No-nonsense directions.* The 'how to' approach clearly explains the questions to be asked and the decisions to be made as you research and write your marketing plan.

- *Diagram of the planning process.* A diagram at the start of each chapter shows your progress through the seven stages of the marketing planning process.

- *Company examples.* Every chapter opens with an interesting example of marketing in action at a well-known organisation, such as Specsavers, McDonald's and Unilever. Extended examples within each chapter demonstrate how marketers apply planning principles to benefit from opportunities or deal with marketplace challenges. Several of these extended examples take a closer look at contemporary trends and issues such as pricing for rentals, online customer reviews, fast fashion and contingency planning.

- *Practical exercises.* 'Apply your knowledge' exercises challenge you to translate principles into practice by analysing a specific organisation's marketing activities. 'Build your own marketing plan' exercises direct you through the main steps in preparing a strong, relevant marketing plan. Answering the 'marketing plan analysis' question that follows each extended example will help you think through the implications of different marketing situations and strategies.

- *Case studies.* Every chapter closes with a case study of a company facing challenges and opportunities in consumer or business marketing, such as Burberry, Uniqlo, Michelin, Hyundai and Google. Answering the case questions will reinforce your understanding of the concepts and strengthen your planning skills.

- *Definitions.* Key terms defined in each chapter and in the glossary help you master the words and phrases every marketer must know. Every entry in the glossary includes the chapter number in which the definition appears, so you can review the context as you study or prepare for class.

SAMPLE MARKETING PLAN

The Appendix contains a brief sample marketing plan showing how a fictional start-up company, Lost Legends Luxury Chocolatier, plans to launch its first products and compete with established confectionery companies. This sample plan includes background information about market trends and customer characteristics; analyses the company's strengths, weaknesses, opportunities and threats; sets specific objectives; and documents decisions about targeting, positioning, products and branding, pricing, distribution, marketing communications, customer service and internal marketing. It also summarises highlights of the company's marketing programmes, forecasts, metrics and control. As you learn about the planning process, refer to this sample plan to see how a company might present and explain its chosen marketing strategies and prepare for effective and efficient implementation.

ESSENTIAL MARKETING CHECKLISTS

This new edition includes 20 checklists to lead you through the essential aspects of the planning process. Checklist topics are keyed to the material in each chapter.

Essential checklist No. 1: Situational analysis (Chapter 1)

Essential checklist No. 2: The mission statement (Chapter 1)

Essential checklist No. 3: The internal environment (Chapter 2)

Essential checklist No. 4: The external environment (Chapter 2)

Essential checklist No. 5: Analysing customers in consumer markets (Chapter 3)

Essential checklist No. 6: Analysing customers in business markets (Chapter 3)

Essential checklist No. 7: Evaluating market segments (Chapter 4)

Essential checklist No. 8: Planning for positioning (Chapter 4)

Essential checklist No. 9: Evaluating objectives (Chapter 5)

Essential checklist No. 10: Planning for products (Chapter 6)

Essential checklist No. 11: Planning for brands (Chapter 6)

Essential checklist No. 12: Pricing through the product life cycle (Chapter 7)

Essential checklist No. 13: Planning for marketing channels (Chapter 8)

Essential checklist No. 14: Planning for logistics (Chapter 8)

Essential checklist No. 15: Planning for media (Chapter 9)

Essential checklist No. 16: Planning for sales promotion (Chapter 9)

Essential checklist No. 17: Planning for customer service support (Chapter 10)

Essential checklist No. 18: Planning metrics (Chapter 11)

Essential checklist No. 19: Planning marketing budgets (Chapter 11)

Essential checklist No. 20: Evaluating implementation (Chapter 12)

REAL-WORLD VIEW OF MARKETING PLANNING TODAY

Seeing how different organisations approach marketing can provoke new thinking, provide insights into marketing situations and lead to more creative marketing plans. How does Reckitt Benckiser use marketing plans to prepare for worldwide growth (Chapter 1)? What is Experian doing to plan for meeting the needs of different business customers in different markets (Chapter 2)? How is Volkswagen using its 12 automotive brands to target specific customer groups (Chapter 4)? Why would Nuovo Trasporto Viaggiatori create three price levels for its Italo high-speed inter-city rail service in Italy (Chapter 7)? What kind of planning goes into making the communications promoting Byte Night's fundraising so successful (Chapter 11)? These and many other chapter-opening examples and chapter-ending cases reveal the contemporary realities of planning for today's dynamic global marketplace. In response to lecturer requests for more examples of business-to-business marketing, this new edition takes a closer look at the marketing activities of the Alibaba Group, Amazon Web Services, Bombardier Aerospace, Experian, FedEx, Intel, Lenovo, Microsoft and SAP.

GUIDE TO THE BOOK

Essential Guide to Marketing Planning is divided into 12 chapters, each covering a key aspect of the planning process. Chapters 1–3 introduce marketing planning, explain how to analyse the current marketing situation and discuss how to research markets and customers. Chapter 4 examines the use of segmentation, targeting and positioning. Chapter 5 looks at setting direction and objectives in the marketing plan. Chapters 6–9 focus on planning for the marketing mix: product, price, place (channels and logistics) and promotion (marketing communications and customer influence). Chapter 10 discusses planning for customer service and internal marketing to support the marketing mix. Chapter 11 explores the use of key performance indicators, metrics, forecasts, budgets and schedules to plan for measuring marketing results. Chapter 12 explains how to prepare for implementation and control of your marketing plan.

ONLINE EXTRAS

Visit the companion blog at **http://essentialmarketingplanning.blogspot.com/** for updates to cases, concepts and companies and the latest news and views in the world of marketing.

Instructors can visit **www.pearsoned.co.uk/wood-mp** to access the Instructor's Manual, which contains answers to company feature questions and case study questions plus additional resources.

Lecturer Resources

For password-protected online resources tailored to support the use of this textbook in teaching, please visit **www.pearsoned.co.uk/wood-mp**

ON THE WEBSITE

About the author

Marian Burk Wood has held vice presidential-level marketing positions in corporate and non-profit marketing with Citibank, JP Morgan Chase and the National Retail Federation. Her US book, *The Marketing Plan Handbook*, now in its fifth edition, has introduced marketing planning to thousands of students worldwide.

Wood holds an MBA in marketing from Long Island University in New York and a BA from the City University of New York. She has worked with prominent academic experts to co-author college textbooks on principles of marketing, principles of advertising and principles of management. Her special interests in marketing include social media, ethics and social responsibility, segmentation, channels and metrics.

Visit her companion blog at: **http://essentialmarketingplanning.blogspot.com/**

Acknowledgements

I am sincerely grateful to the academic reviewers who so kindly provided detailed feedback on my ideas for this new edition, offered constructive insights on previous editions and participated in reviewing my other European text, *Marketing Planning: Principles into Practice*. Thanks to Jocelyn Hayes (York Management School, University of York), John Nicholson (Hull University Business School) and Arnaz Binsardi Prahasto (Glyndwr University, Wrexham); Declan Bannon (University of Paisley Business School); Jill Brown (University of Portsmouth Business School); Noel Dennis (Teesside University); Niki Hynes (Napier University); Peter Lancaster (Sheffield Hallam University); Tony Lobo (Swinburne University of Technology); Paul Oakley (University of Brighton Business School); John Rudd (Aston Business School); Heather Skinner (Glamorgan Business School); Des Thwaites (University of Leeds); Peter Williams (Leeds Metropolitan University); Sarah Wren (North Hertfordshire College).

I greatly admire and appreciate the expertise and commitment of the many talented professionals at Pearson Education who have helped make this book so successful. A big thank you to Rachel Gear, Catharine Steers, Rufus Curnow, Mary Nisbet, Nicola Woowat, Christopher Kingston and Joy Cash.

This book is dedicated with much love to my husband Wally Wood, my sister Isabel Burk and the target market of the next generation: Amelia Biancolo, Ella Biancolo, Michael Werner, Gabriel Wood and Tobias Wood.

Marian Burk Wood

email: **marketinghandbook@hotmail.com**

blog: **http://essentialmarketingplanning.blogspot.com/**

PUBLISHER'S ACKNOWLEDGEMENTS

We are grateful to the following for permission to reproduce copyright material:

Figures

Figure 1.2 after *Strategic Marketing for Nonprofit Organizations*, 6, Pearson Education Inc. (A. Andreasen and P. Kotler 2003) 81, Prentice Hall, ANDREASEN, ALAN; KOTLER, PHILIP R, STRATEGIC MARKETING FOR NONPROFIT ORGANIZATIONS, 6th Ed., © 2003, p. 81. Reprinted and Electronically reproduced by permission of Pearson Education. Inc., Upper Saddle River, New Jersey.; Figure 2.3 adapted from *Market-based Management*, 6, Pearson (Roger J. Best 2012) 388, Prentice Hall, BEST, ROGER, MARKET-BASED MANAGEMENT, 6th Ed., (c) 2012. Reprinted and Electronically reproduced by permission of Pearson Education. Inc., Upper Saddle River, New Jersey.; Figure 6.1 from *Marketing: An Introduction*, 11th ed, Pearson Education (Armstrong, G. and Kotler, P. 2012) p. 242, ISBN-13: 978-0132744034; Figure 6.2 after *Strategic Brand Management*, 2, Pearson Education Inc. (Keller, K.L. 2003) 76, Prentice Hall, KELLER, KEVIN LANE, STRATEGIC BRAND MANAGEMENT, 2nd Ed., @ 2003. Reprinted and Electronically reproduced by permission of Pearson Education, Inc., Upper Saddle River, New Jersey.; Figure 7.1 adapted from *The Strategy and Tactics of Pricing: A Guide to Growing More Profitably*, 4, Pearson Education Inc. (Nagle, T.T. and Hogan, J. 2006) 4, Prentice Hall, NAGLE, THOMAS T.; HOGAN, JOHN, STRATEGY & TACTICS OF PRICING: GUIDE TO GROWING MORE PROFITABLY, 4th Ed., © 2006. Reprinted and Electronically reproduced by permission of Pearson Education. Inc., Upper Saddle River, New Jersey.; Figure 8.2 adapted from *Market-based Management*, 6th Ed., Pearson Education Inc. (Best, R.J. 2012) 318, ISBN-13: 978-0130387752, Reprinted and Electronically reproduced by permission of Pearson Education, Inc., Upper Saddle River, New Jersey.; Figure 9.3 after *Consumer Behavior: Buying, Having and Being*, 9th Ed., Pearson Education Inc. (Solomon, M.R. 2010) p. 257, ISBN-13: 978-0136110927, Reprinted and Electronically reproduced by permission of Pearson Education Inc., Upper Saddle River, New Jersey

Tables

Table 3.4 adapted from *Principles of Marketing*, 4e, Pearson (Kotler, P., Wang, V., Saunders, J. and Armstrong, G.) 309, Table 3.4, How buying centre participants influence purchases, adapted from Principles of Marketing, 4e, Part 1, Pearson (Kotler, P., Wang, V., Saunders, J. and Armstrong, G. 2005) 309. ISBN 10: 0273684566; Table 4.1 adapted from *Strategic and Competitive Analysis: Methods and Techniques for Analyzing Business Competition*, 1, Pearson Education Inc. (Fleischer, C.S. and Bensoussan, B. 2003) 173, Prentice Hall, FLEISHER, CRAIG S.; BENSOUSSAN, BABETTE, STRATEGIC AND COMPETITIVE ANALYSIS: METHODS AND TECHNIQUES FOR ANALYZING BUSINESS COMPETITION, 1st Ed., © 2002. Reprinted and Electronically reproduced by permission of Pearson Education, Inc., Upper Saddle River, New Jersey.; Table 4.2 adapted from *Strategic and Competitive Analysis: Methods and Techniques for Analyzing Business Competition*, 1, Pearson Education

Inc. (Fleischer, C.S. and Bensoussan, B. 2003) 174, Prentice Hall, FLEISHER, CRAIG S.; BENSOUSSAN, BABETTE, STRATEGIC AND COMPETITIVE ANALYSIS: METHODS AND TECHNIQUES FOR ANALYZING BUSINESS COMPETITION, 1st Ed., © 2002. Reprinted and Electronically reproduced by permission of Pearson Education, Inc., Upper Saddle River, New Jersey.; Table 7.1 adapted from *The Strategy and Tactics of Pricing: A Guide to Growing More Profitably*, 4, Pearson Education Inc. (Nagle, T.T. and Hogan, J. 2006) 275–77, Prentice Hall, NAGLE, THOMAS T.; HOGAN, JOHN, STRATEGY & TACTICS OF PRICING: GUIDE TO GROWING MORE PROFITABLY, 4th Ed., © 2006. Reprinted and Electronically reproduced by permission of Pearson Education. Inc., Upper Saddle River, New Jersey.; Table 11.2 from *Market-based Management*, Pearson Education Inc. (Best, R. 2013) Figure 2.8 page 47, Prentice Hall, BEST, ROGER, MARKET-BASED MANAGEMENT, 6th Ed., (c) 2012. Reprinted and Electronically reproduced by permission of Pearson Education. Inc., Upper Saddle River, New Jersey.

Text

General Displayed Text 6. adapted from *Strategic Brand Management*, 2, Pearson Education Inc. (Keller, K.L. 2003) Chapter 2, Prentice Hall, KELLER, KEVIN LANE, STRATEGIC BRAND MANAGEMENT, 2nd Ed., © 2003. Reprinted and Electronically reproduced by permission of Pearson Education, Inc., Upper Saddle River, New Jersey.

In some instances we have been unable to trace the owners of copyright material, and we would appreciate any information that would enable us to do so.

1 Introduction to marketing planning today

Learning outcomes

After studying this chapter, you will be able to:

- Outline the benefits of marketing planning
- List the seven stages of the marketing planning process
- Describe the content of a marketing plan and explain why it must be dynamic
- Discuss how the mission statement guides marketing planning

Application outcomes

After studying this chapter, you will be able to:

- Begin the first stage of marketing planning
- Analyse and prepare or improve a mission statement
- Start documenting a marketing plan

CHAPTER PREVIEW: MARKETING AT RECKITT BENCKISER

Where some people see dirt and germs, Reckitt Benckiser (www.rb.com) sees purpose and profit. The UK-based global consumer goods company specialises in products for health, hygiene and home, following its mission 'to provide innovative solutions for people to have healthier lives and happier homes'. Despite worldwide economic woes and competition from multinational giants, Reckitt's marketing plans have helped the firm grow beyond £9.5 billion in annual turnover, redefine its focus for future growth and reinforce brand loyalty for longer-term success.

Reckitt's marketing plans put particular emphasis on such best-selling products as Lysol disinfectant, Vanish laundry soap and Strepsils lozenges, which can be leveraged to support company growth. When it acquires successful brands, as it did with Durex and Scholl, Reckitt prepares special marketing plans to keep the momentum going after the change in ownership. Also, it creates special marketing plans to coordinate all activities related to the testing and introduction of new products such as the Dettol No-Touch handwash system. The head of the UK division says that Reckitt seeks to make product introductions more memorable by reinventing the product category in a way that adds value for consumers.

Reckitt's marketing plans focus on promising profit opportunities, such as expanding production and distribution in areas where increased buying power is fuelling higher demand for consumer products. Within five years, the firm expects emerging markets in Latin America, Asia and Africa to account for half of the company's annual turnover. The plans also reflect the company's commitment to sustainability targets such as slashing its products' carbon footprint and supporting its involvement with charitable groups such as Save the Children. Increasingly, Reckitt's marketing plans rely on campaigns that combine traditional media (like TV and magazines) with social media (Facebook, Twitter, YouTube) to engage and inform consumers through conversations about topics that matter – health, hygiene and home.[1]

Without marketing planning, Reckitt Benckiser would have no clear course of action for reaching out to customers, building brand loyalty and increasing profits. Yet the planning decisions that lead to growth for Reckitt will not necessarily work for Procter & Gamble, Unilever or any other competitor. Every marketing plan is therefore as unique as it is vital for the company's future. In this chapter, you'll learn about the vital role of marketing planning within today's ever-changing global marketplace, review the individual stages in the process and learn how to document a marketing plan. After you explore the three levels of planning, you'll see how a solid mission statement guides marketing planning. Take a quick look at the sample marketing plan in the Appendix for a preview of how to document your planning activities and decisions. And use this chapter's checklists to prepare for developing your own marketing plan.

THE ROLE OF MARKETING PLANNING

Marketing planning is the structured process that leads to a coordinated set of marketing decisions and actions, for a specific organisation and over a specific period, based on:

- an analysis of the current internal and external situation, including markets and customers;

- clear marketing direction, objectives, strategies and programmes for targeted customer segments;

- support through customer service and internal marketing programmes;

- management of marketing activities through implementation, evaluation and control.

The course of action that results from marketing planning is recorded in a **marketing plan**. This internal document outlines the marketplace situation and describes the marketing strategies and programmes that will support the achievement of business and organisational goals over a specified period, usually one year. Often firms create separate marketing plans for each brand and each market as well as for a new product launch or other special activities.

The benefits of marketing planning

In today's connected world, brand reputations can be won or lost with a tweet or a few seconds of video on YouTube; economic problems or severe weather conditions that originate far from home can disrupt lives, businesses and buying patterns. In other words, even though changes can occur quickly and without warning, the idea of creating a structured plan to guide your marketing efforts is more important than ever before.

Marketing planning keeps you focused on your customers, helps you determine what your organisation can do (and what it can't do) for customers, helps you examine offerings in the context of competition and the marketing environment, and sets up the rationale for allocating resources to achieve marketing efficiency and effectiveness. It provides a framework for systematically assessing different marketing possibilities, setting marketing goals and putting competition into perspective. Marketing planning, in effect, deals with the *who*, *what*, *when*, *where*, *how* and *how much* of an organisation's marketing.

However, the marketing plan is not simply an account of what you as a marketer aspire to accomplish in the coming year. Your plan must allow for measuring progress towards objectives and making adjustments if actual results vary from projections. In other words, a marketing plan must be both specific and flexible to help you prepare for the new and the unexpected: an economic crisis, new competition, evolving technology, new laws, changing regulation and other shifts that can affect marketing performance.

The dynamic marketing plan

Today's marketing environment has become so volatile that successful companies continually update their marketing plans to maintain their competitive edge and provide goods or services that customers really value. A good marketing plan must be dynamic, not only anticipating changes but also providing guidelines for how to react with customer relationships in mind. No marketing plan lasts forever; even the most effective plan must be adjusted as the marketing situation evolves. You may, in fact, want to have several alternative plans in mind that might be implemented if significant changes occur.

Consider the dramatic shifts that are bringing new urgency to the process of marketing planning. Both consumers and businesses have shown their willingness to stop buying or switch to cheaper brands at the first sign of economic trouble, forcing companies to fight harder for purchases. Some may, for instance, use discount vouchers as part of a marketing plan to attract first-time buyers, while others may use a loyalty scheme as part of a marketing plan to encourage customer loyalty. Marketing to maintain a good reputation is another key area for companies, now that consumers can quickly tell the world about positive and negative experiences by emailing, blogging, tweeting, texting or posting YouTube videos.

Marketing planning also helps organisations stay ahead of competitors by anticipating and responding to what their customers want, need and require, as the B&Q retail chain (www.diy.com) is doing.

MARKETING IN PRACTICE: B&Q

Owned by Kingfisher, Europe's largest home improvement retailer, B&Q operates more than 360 DIY stores in the UK and Ireland and competes with chains such as Homebase and Wickes. B&Q serves 3 million shoppers every week and is also growing in China, where it already has 39 stores. In 2008, B&Q began planning to implement Kingfisher's 'Delivering Value' multiyear strategy through marketing programmes aimed at achieving goals such as introducing new products to increase customer choice, testing new store formats for shopper convenience and boosting retail profit margins. Although the next few years brought challenging economic conditions and some unexpected weather patterns that dampened sales, B&Q was able to achieve these goals, double its earnings, and continue strengthening its competitive position.

In 2012, B&Q began a new multiyear cycle of marketing planning to implement Kingfisher's next long-term strategy, 'Creating the Leader'. The retailer added new goods and services for making homes greener, including a range of energy-saving devices under the iQE brand. It began offering mobile apps and other multichannel options for on-the-go shopping, and it also stepped up the use of social media to provide 'how to' instructions for DIYers. Finally, B&Q accelerated the pace of new-store openings to be ready for improved demand as the housing market recovered. Although the retailer has no control over what competitors do or how the economy fares, detailed marketing plans keep its managers focused on customer needs, profit opportunities and ongoing growth.[2]

Marketing plan analysis: In addition to the economy and competition, what other forces in the business environment should B&Q's marketers examine during the process of marketing planning?

THE MARKETING PLANNING PROCESS

The marketing plan documents decisions and actions undertaken as a result of the seven-stage marketing planning process shown in Figure 1.1. Most organisations begin this process many months before a marketing plan is scheduled to take effect. Experts warn, however, that marketing planning should be ongoing, not a once-a-year exercise. Because the marketing environment can change at any time, managers should spread analysis and planning activities throughout the year and make strategic decisions after examining important issues at length. This section gives you a brief overview of all seven stages and serves as a preview of the book.

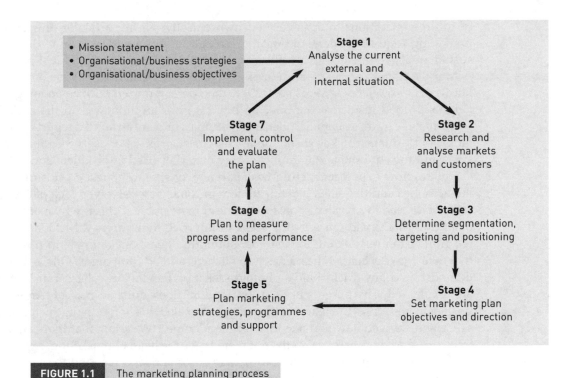

- Mission statement
- Organisational/business strategies
- Organisational/business objectives

Stage 1
Analyse the current external and internal situation

Stage 7
Implement, control and evaluate the plan

Stage 2
Research and analyse markets and customers

Stage 6
Plan to measure progress and performance

Stage 3
Determine segmentation, targeting and positioning

Stage 5
Plan marketing strategies, programmes and support

Stage 4
Set marketing plan objectives and direction

FIGURE 1.1   The marketing planning process

Stage 1: Analyse the current situation

The purpose of analysing your situation is to identify strengths, weaknesses, opportunities and threats for marketing purposes. You'll use an *internal audit* to examine the current situation within the organisation, including mission statement, resources, offerings, capabilities, important business relationships and – an important way of learning from the past – the results of earlier plans.

The mission statement is an overall guide to what the organisation wants to accomplish and where, in general terms, your marketing plan should take the organisation. To illustrate, the online grocery retailer Ocado's mission, highlighted on its website, is 'to revolutionise the way people shop forever, by giving them a uniquely innovative and greener alternative to traditional grocery shopping'. This mission identifies specific elements (such as eco-friendly shopping) that inform Ocado's marketing decisions and activities.

Using an *external audit*, you'll study trends and changes in the broad political, economic, social–cultural, technological, legal and ecological environment, and you'll analyse competitive factors. This audit should cover issues, threats and opportunities that might influence your ability to implement the marketing plan and achieve your objectives.

Due to external changes such as public pressure and internal changes such as forward-looking corporate leadership, a growing number of companies are adopting **sustainable marketing**, 'the establishment, maintenance and enhancement of customer relationships so that the objectives of the parties involved are met without compromising the ability of future generations to achieve their own objectives'.[3] In particular, this approach to marketing requires understanding the ecological, social and economic dimensions of sustainability to maintain the wellbeing of people and the planet, not just profitability.[4]

Marketing in this way entails making commitments to a broader base of **publics** (also known as *stakeholders*), groups such as stockholders, reporters, citizen action groups and neighbourhood residents that have an interest in or an influence on the organisation's performance. As an example, Unilever's executives prepare an annual report documenting global performance on key sustainability factors such as water use, greenhouse gas emissions and the environmental impact of raw materials used in products and packaging.

Publics now expect **marketing transparency**, open and honest disclosure of marketing activities and decisions that affect them in some way. Perceived lack of transparency can, in fact, lead to a harsh response from one or more publics. This is why many marketers, including McDonald's, are taking steps to improve transparency. McDonald's Canada recently began responding to customer-submitted questions online and posting videos that take viewers behind the scenes into kitchens and ad campaigns. One YouTube video demonstrated how McDonald's photographs a perfect-looking cheeseburger for its ads and explained why burgers bought locally don't look quite so perfect. Another video, posted in response to customer questions, revealed the ingredients in the Big Mac's sauce and showed how to make this burger at home.[5] 'We know that there are questions out there, and that there are myths out there,' says the head of marketing, explaining that McDonald's is using social media to engage customers and respond to their questions.[6] See **Chapter 2** for more about assessing the current situation.

Stage 2: Research and analyse markets and customers

Next you should research your markets and customers (consumers, businesses, clients or constituents). Investigate trends in market share, product demand, customer needs and perceptions, demographics, buying patterns and customer satisfaction. Who is buying or would buy the product being marketed, and why? How are buying patterns changing, and why? What is in demand and when? Where is it in demand and how is demand expected to change over time? What experiences, services and benefits do customers need, want or expect before, during and after each purchase?

During this research and analysis stage, think about what your customers might need tomorrow as well as what they need today. This will help you formulate a plan for **relationship marketing**, building mutually satisfying ongoing connections with customers and other key publics. Relationship marketing is based on the premise that when organisations look beyond the immediate transaction to build trust and meet customers' long-term needs, customers are more likely to remain loyal. Successful firms demonstrate a strong customer orientation through their marketing activities, recognising that satisfying customers will ultimately lead to satisfying shareholders and other stakeholders.[7] See **Chapter 3** for more detail.

Before you continue, take a moment to review the first checklist in this book. The questions are designed to help you consider what you'll need as you begin the marketing planning process.

ESSENTIAL CHECKLIST NO. 1:
SITUATIONAL ANALYSIS

What should you be doing to prepare for the planning process? Answer the following as you get ready for analysing your current situation, putting a tick next to each question after you've written your answer.

☐ What sources of information will help you identify and understand important developments affecting your goods or services, customers and competition? How can you obtain this information?

_____

☐ What political changes, economic issues, social–cultural changes, technological trends, legal issues and ecological considerations are likely to influence your ability to attract and retain customers?

_____

☐ How can you research your competitors' marketing activities and market share to understand your competitive strengths and weaknesses?

_____

☐ If you're marketing in more than one country, how will you uncover and monitor regional and international issues that can help or hurt your marketing efforts?

_____

☐ What insights into the marketing successes and failures of other organisations can help you anticipate or understand changes in the internal and external environment?

_____

☐ Who are your organisation's publics, and how is each important to the effective implementation of your marketing plan?

_____

Stage 3: Determine segmentation, targeting and positioning

No organisation has the resources (people, money or time) to serve every customer in every market. You will therefore use your research and customer knowledge to identify which specific subgroups can be effectively targeted through marketing. To do this, you first group customers into **segments** based on characteristics, behaviours, needs or wants that affect their demand for or usage of the product being marketed. A segment may be as small as one consumer or business customer or as large as millions of customers in multiple nations.

Next you will decide on your **targeting** approach. Will you focus on a single segment, on two or more segments or on one entire market? How will these segments be covered through marketing? For example, Toyota's Prius and Nissan's Leaf are two of many brands targeting car buyers who are particularly interested in environmentally safe vehicles that use little petrol. You also need to formulate a suitable **positioning**, which means using marketing to create a competitively distinctive place (position) for the product or brand in the mind of targeted customers. The purpose is to set your product apart from competing products in a way that is meaningful to customers. Prius appeals to its target market by being positioned as a fuel-efficient hybrid car with distinctive styling. Leaf is positioned as a fuel-efficient all-electric car with advanced technology. **Chapter 4** discusses segmentation, targeting and positioning in further detail.

Stage 4: Set marketing plan direction and objectives

The direction of a marketing plan is based on your organisation's mission statement and higher-level goals. Most use marketing plans to support a direction of growth in one of nine ways, combining offerings and markets, as shown in Figure 1.2.[8] A marketing plan for growth will define objectives in financial terms (such as higher turnover) and marketing terms (such as higher market share). High-performing firms may strive to retain or attain the role of **market leader**, which entails holding the largest market share and leading other firms in product introductions and other activities. However, instead of driving for growth, struggling companies may use their plans to sustain the current turnover, profit or market share situation.

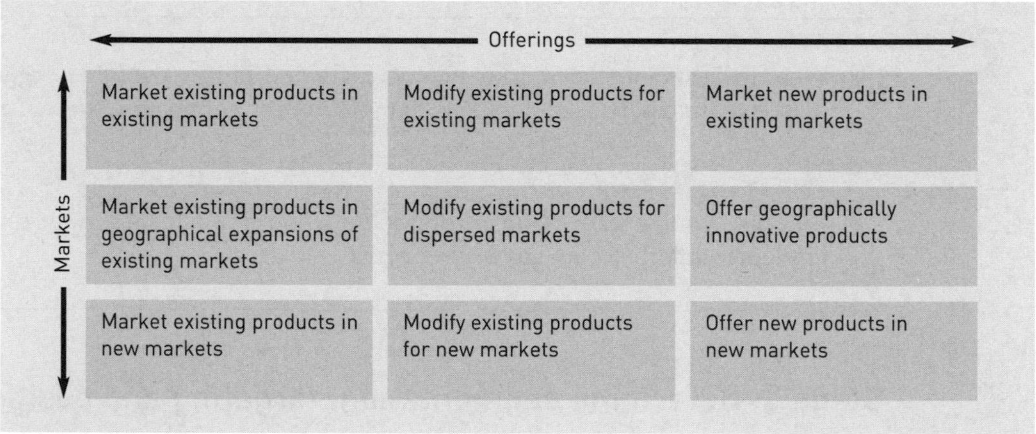

Offerings →		
Market existing products in existing markets	Modify existing products for existing markets	Market new products in existing markets
Market existing products in geographical expansions of existing markets	Modify existing products for dispersed markets	Offer geographically innovative products
Market existing products in new markets	Modify existing products for new markets	Offer new products in new markets

(Markets ↓)

FIGURE 1.2   Growth grid

Source: After *Strategic Marketing for Nonprofit Organizations*, 6, Pearson Education Inc. (A. Andreasen and P. Kotler 2003) 81, Prentice Hall, ANDREASEN, ALAN; KOTLER, PHILIP R, STRATEGIC MARKETING FOR NONPROFIT ORGANIZATIONS, 6th Ed., © 2003, p. 81. Reprinted and Electronically reproduced by permission of Pearson Education. Inc, Upper Saddle River, New Jersey.

A marketing plan can also help an established firm like Thorntons (www.thorntons. co.uk) take definite steps to improve its profitability.

MARKETING IN PRACTICE: THORNTONS

Founded in 1911, Thorntons is a familiar high-street brand famous throughout the UK for its Special Toffee sweets, among other chocolate treats. Its mission is 'to be Britain's best loved chocolate brand, making every customer smile'. Thorntons enjoys high brand awareness, yet increased competition from premium brands like Hotel Chocolat on the high end and from popularly priced chocolates on the low end have slowed its growth and hurt its profitability in recent years. Therefore, during Thorntons' centenary year, the CEO announced implementation of a marketing plan for revitalising the brand and improving profitability.

The company is closing dozens of shops each year to adjust its cost structure and support the most productive locations. It unexpectedly lost some distribution when the Clinton Cards and Birthdays stores went into administration. Now Thorntons' marketing aims to encourage buying chocolates as gifts for special occasions and family celebrations throughout the year, not just for holidays. It has launched new communications programmes to highlight its chocolate expertise, reinforce brand loyalty and demonstrate how its chocolates 'make everyday special'. Finally, with 15,000 Facebook 'likes' and 3,300 Twitter followers, Thornton is planning social media campaigns to build buzz, reward brand fans and boost future sales. Will Thorntons achieve its profit turnaround?[9]

Marketing plan analysis: What positioning should Thorntons adopt to differentiate itself from its many competitors?

Note that goals and objectives are not the same, although the words are often used interchangeably. **Goals** are longer-term targets that help a business unit (or the entire organisation) achieve overall performance and fulfil its mission; **objectives** are shorter-term performance targets that lead to goal achievement. Marketing expert Tim Ambler has emphasised that key corporate goals must be connected throughout the organisation, all the way down to the marketing plan and individual marketing programmes, if the company is to succeed.[10] In addition to financial and marketing objectives, marketers may define societal objectives, such as for social responsibility and ecological protection. Remember that you will need to allow for measuring progress towards all your objectives, as discussed below. For more about direction and objectives, see **Chapter 5**.

Stage 5: Plan marketing strategies, programmes and support

In this stage, you will plan marketing strategies and tactics to achieve the objectives you set earlier. You will look not only at how to deliver value that meets customers' needs but also at the coordination of the basic marketing tools of product, price, place and promotion within individual marketing programmes. In addition, you should determine how to support the marketing effort with customer service and internal marketing. For practical reasons, you will probably not finalise all the details of your marketing activities until your plan has been approved and funded and is ready for implementation.

Product and branding

The product offering may be a tangible good such as a television or an intangible service such as expert tax-preparation assistance. Often, however, an offering combines the tangible and the intangible, as when a mobile phone company markets phones (tangible) along with phone service (intangible) or a manufacturer markets robotic assembly equipment (tangible) and provides repair services (intangible). Tangible elements of the product include features, design, packaging, labelling and performance.

The brand is another intangible but extremely important aspect of the product offering. Every product must live up to the **brand promise**, which Philip Kotler and Kevin Keller define as 'the marketer's vision of what the brand must be and do for consumers'.[11] Other intangibles to consider in planning product strategy are benefits, quality perceptions and related services. Process elements important to product planning are the product mix/range, new product development, the product life cycle, ecological concerns and similar issues. A number of marketers are experimenting with **co-creation**, involving their customers in a highly collaborative effort to develop novel new products to satisfy needs. **Chapter 6** discusses how to plan product and brand strategy.

Price

What should you charge for your product offering? In planning price strategy, marketers must answer a number of key questions. Some are about external elements, such as the following:

- How do customers perceive the value of the good or service?
- What is the competition?
- How might market demand, channel requirements and legal or regulatory issues affect pricing?

Internal elements raise questions such as:

- How can price be used to reflect the positioning of the product, brand or organisation?
- How do costs affect revenues and profitability?
- How does the price fit with other marketing decisions and planning for other products?
- How can pricing capture value for the organisation and bring it closer to its objectives and goals?

Nestlé, for example, has created an 'affordable luxury' image for its Nespresso single-serve coffee makers and capsules (www.nespresso.com), and it charges premium prices that support its upmarket image. See **Chapter 7** for more about price and value.

MARKETING IN PRACTICE: NESPRESSO

Switzerland's Nestlé has ambitious global growth plans for its Nespresso single-serve coffee/espresso makers and replacement coffee capsules. Nespresso was a pioneer in this market and, because of its prominence and luxury brand perceptions, it has consistently enjoyed strong pricing power, with estimated profit margins exceeding 25 percent. Its marketing plans for ongoing growth include expanding to new countries, opening new branded boutiques and protecting the patents for its products as a competitive measure.

Industry analysts see no end in sight for the popularity of gourmet single-serve coffee, and Nespresso's £2.4 billion (€3.1 billion) in annual turnover puts it in a strong financial position to invest in marketing for the purpose of developing new, sophisticated machines and coffee flavours, attracting new customers and retaining the loyalty of current customers. To reduce costs and boost margins, Nestlé recently opened a third factory in Switzerland. However, Starbucks is only one of several powerful competitors making inroads in the single-serve coffee market. Will Nespresso have to change its pricing strategy to maintain its share?[12]

Marketing plan analysis: How can Nespresso plan for product or promotion decisions that will help defend against loss of share in this newly competitive situation?

Channel and logistics

Channel and logistics strategy – place strategy – is concerned with how customers gain access to the product offering, regardless of whether it is a tangible good or an intangible service. Will you market directly to your customers or make your products available through intermediaries such as wholesalers and retailers? If you market to businesses, will you go through wholesalers, distributors or agents that serve business buyers, or deal directly with some or all of your business customers? The current trend is towards **multichannel marketing**, providing a variety of distribution channels for customers to choose from when they buy goods or services at different times.

Other channel decisions involve customer preferences, number of channel members, market coverage and ecological impact. Also consider logistics such as shipping, storage, inventory management, order fulfilment and related functions. Current channel and logistical arrangements should be evaluated as part of the internal audit. Whether you're marketing for a large corporation or a small business, the needs, expectations and preferences of customers should be deciding factors in planning your channels and logistics. These topics are covered in greater detail in **Chapter 8**.

Marketing communications and influence

Marketing communications and influence strategy (also called promotion strategy) covers all the tools you use to reach customers in your targeted segments. The point is to encourage two-way communication and influence the way customers think, feel and act towards the goods, services or ideas you are marketing. Marketing in *social media* – online media such as blogs and YouTube that facilitate user interaction – has become

Table 1.1   Selected marketing communications activities of Nespresso

Communications activity	Examples of use by Nespresso
Advertising	George Clooney adverts, in-store posters, magazine ads, digital ads, billboards
Social media	Nespresso Facebook page (2 million 'likes'), Twitter account (32,000 followers), YouTube channel (2 million video views), Pinterest page
Website	Official UK brand home page (www.nespresso.com/uk/en/home)
Public relations	Sponsor of Cannes Film Festival's Critics Week, yacht racing teams, professional tennis events, show-jumping tournaments and other special events; promotes responsible recycling of used coffee capsules

increasingly popular because it can lead to *word of mouth*, which occurs when people tell other people about the brand or product.

Other tools include public relations, sales promotion, special events and experiences, personal selling and direct marketing. Given the needs, interests, perceptions, expectations and buying patterns of customers in targeted segments, most organisations allow for a variety of messages and media in their marketing plans. However, you should be sure that the content and impact of the entire promotion strategy are consistent, unified and supportive of your positioning and objectives, which is what Nespresso has done in planning activities that appeal to its target market (see Table 1.1). See **Chapter 9** for more on this topic.

Marketing support

You can plan to support your product, place, price and promotion strategies in two main ways. First, you should decide on an appropriate customer service level, in line with the chosen positioning, resource availability and customers' needs or expectations. Business customers often require service before, during and after a purchase, from tailoring product specifications to arranging installation to maintaining and repairing the product years later. For example, Munich-based Siemens, a business-to-business marketer, offers training and technical support for employees of hospitals and clinics that buy its sophisticated medical equipment. It is also helping to educate manufacturing customers and students about production advances by creating PlantVille, a social media game that invites players to try different solutions to common factory problems – including links to relevant Siemens sites, for more information.[13]

Second, you will need the commitment and cooperation of others to implement and control your plan. This requires *internal marketing*, activities designed to build relationships with colleagues and staff members backed up by personnel policies that reinforce internal commitment to the marketing plan. **Chapter 10** describes customer service and internal marketing in more detail.

Stage 6: Plan to measure progress and performance

Before implementing the marketing plan, you must decide on measures to track marketing progress and performance towards achieving your objectives. This involves developing and documenting budgets, forecasts, schedules and responsibilities for all marketing programmes. You will also forecast the effect of the marketing programmes on future turnover, profitability, market share and other measures that signal progress towards objectives. The purpose is to see whether results are better than expected, lagging expectations or just meeting projections and objectives. For perspective, it is important to put recent marketing results into context through comparisons with competitors, the overall market and the organisation's previous results.

Often marketers establish quantifiable standards (*metrics*) to measure specific marketing outcomes and activities. In many cases, these metrics look at interim performance of specific brands, individual products or product lines, geographic results, financial results, customer relationship results and so on. Deciding exactly what to measure – and how – is critical to effective implementation and control of a marketing plan. Siemens, for instance, monitors growth in turnover and profit margins by product line, product and division in each geographic region. It also tracks the number of new orders received in each month, quarter and year, by product, division and geographic region, to identify trends and pinpoint opportunities for extra marketing attention.[14] Refer to **Chapter 11** for more about planning to measure marketing progress and performance.

Stage 7: Implement, control and evaluate the plan

The real test of any marketing plan's effectiveness comes at implementation. For effective control, you will start with the objectives you have set, establish specific standards for measuring progress towards those targets, measure actual marketing performance, analyse the results and take corrective action if results are not as expected. Businesses generally apply several types of marketing control at different levels and intervals. The outcome of this stage feeds back to the beginning of the marketing planning process, paving the way for changes as needed.

Depending on your organisation and your plan, you may compare results with standards daily, weekly, monthly and quarterly; you may even compare results with standards on an hourly basis if you need to maintain extremely tight control over marketing. In addition, you and your managers should evaluate performance after all programmes are complete. See **Chapter 12** for more about planning for effective implementation and control.

Documenting a marketing plan

As you move through each stage in the marketing planning process, take time to document your decisions and actions in a written marketing plan. Every marketing plan is unique, designed specifically for the individual organisation and its current marketing situation. Although some plans may be recorded in only a few pages, larger companies generally have a formal format for presenting detailed marketing plans by unit, brand and product.

Most marketing plans consist of the main sections shown in Table 1.2 (see the sample plan in the Appendix as another example). In practice, marketers cannot write the executive summary until all other sections have been completed, because its purpose is to offer a quick overview of the plan's highlights. And when one section of the marketing plan is changed in response to competitive shifts or other environmental trends, other sections will need to be re-examined as well. Note that the exact sections and order of sections will differ from one organisation to the next.

Table 1.2   Contents of a typical marketing plan

Section	Purpose
Executive summary	To summarise the plan's objectives and main points, including what is being marketed and the market for this good or service
Current marketing situation	To explain the mission; present the results of the external audit of political, economic, social–cultural, technological, legal and ecological factors; analyse the competition; and provide background about markets, customers and current marketing activities
SWOT (strengths, weaknesses, opportunities, threats) analysis	To discuss internal strengths and weaknesses, external opportunities and threats that can affect marketing performance, and explain the organisation's response
Segmentation, targeting and positioning	To identify the segments to be targeted, and why; to explain how the product, brand or organisation will be positioned for the selected customer segment(s)
Objectives and issues	To show what the marketing plan is designed to achieve in terms of financial, marketing and societal objectives; to explain key issues that might affect the plan's implementation and success
Marketing strategy	To present the broad strategic approach that the plan will apply in providing value to achieve the objectives that have been set
Marketing programmes	To describe the set of coordinated actions that will be implemented to create, communicate and deliver value through product, pricing, place, promotion, customer service and internal marketing
Financial plans (budgets)	To back up the programmes with details about projected costs, revenue and sales forecasts, expected profit levels
Metrics and implementation controls	To indicate the organisation, responsibilities and schedule for implementation; explain metrics for measuring progress towards objectives; and include contingency plans for dealing with unexpected results and future scenarios

Now you're ready to begin your own marketing plan. The final section of th explains the first stage of the marketing planning process, how to analyse the c marketing situation. You'll continue your analysis in **Chapter 2**.

INTERNAL AUDIT: THE STARTING POINT FOR PLANNING

Plans and decisions made at the top levels of the organisation provide guidance for planning in each business unit and in the marketing function. To prepare for a thorough internal analysis, part of Stage 1 of the marketing planning process, you first need to understand the interaction among the plans at all three levels.

Three levels of planning for strategy

At the top level, planning for **organisational** (or **corporate**) **strategy** governs your organisation's overall purpose and its long-range direction and goals, establishes the range of businesses in which it will compete and shapes how it will create value for customers and other stakeholders (including shareholders). Corporate strategy includes extended plans for the long term, as far as five to ten years in the future. In turn, organisational strategy and goals provide a framework for the set of decisions made by business managers who must move their units forward towards the goals, given the organisation's resources and capabilities (see Figure 1.3).

Planning for **business strategy** covers the scope of each unit and how it will compete, what market(s) it will serve and how unit resources will be allocated and coordinated to create customer value. In establishing business strategy, senior managers must determine what portfolio of units is needed to support the organisation's overall goals and what functions should be emphasised or possibly outsourced. The business plan for one unit may span as long as three to five years.

| FIGURE 1.3 | Planning on three organisational levels |

...nning

...tfolio of business units is in place, planning for **marketing strategy** ...w each unit will use the *marketing-mix* tools of product, price, place and ...supported by customer service and internal marketing strategies – to ...tively and meet business unit objectives. Typically, the marketing plan ...rganisation's chosen marketing strategy for the coming year (but it may ...ple years).

...marketing is the organisational function closest to customers and markets, ...e pivotal role of implementing higher-level strategies while informing the ma... ...nd customer definitions of these strategies. In a customer-oriented organisation, marketing is a priority and concern of everyone at every level. Thus, marketing integrates floor-up, customer-facing knowledge of the market and the current environment with top-down development, direction and fine-tuning of organisational and business strategies. Table 1.3 illustrates decisions at the three levels of strategy, with examples showing how Reckitt Benckiser might apply them.[15]

Table 1.3	Levels of strategy	
Strategy level	**Decisions covered**	**Examples of application at Reckitt Benckiser**
Corporate	<ul><li>Purpose</li><li>Direction</li><li>Long-range goals</li><li>Focus</li><li>Value creation</li><li>Priorities</li></ul>	<ul><li>To provide innovative solutions for people to have healthier lives and happier homes</li><li>Global growth</li><li>4% annual revenue growth</li><li>Health, hygiene and home products</li><li>Brand-name, innovative products that help consumers live better and feel healthier</li><li>Growth, quality, efficiency, sustainability, consumer education</li></ul>
Business (implementing corporate strategy)	<ul><li>Unit scope</li><li>Competitive approach</li><li>Markets served</li><li>Allocation of resources</li></ul>	<ul><li>Health, hygiene and home care</li><li>Exploit strength of best-selling brands</li><li>Europe, North America, Latin America, Asia, Russia, Middle East, Africa</li><li>Invest in best-selling brands and emerging markets</li></ul>
Marketing (implementing business strategy, supporting corporate strategy)	<ul><li>Product/brand strategy</li><li>Pricing strategy</li><li>Channel/logistics strategy</li><li>Communications/influence strategy</li><li>Marketing support</li></ul>	<ul><li>Offer new product innovations that solve consumer problems</li><li>Provide benefits for which consumers will pay a brand premium</li><li>Achieve wide retail distribution throughout target markets</li><li>Use multimedia campaigns to engage and educate consumers about healthier living</li><li>Fill channel orders completely and on time; share marketing news internally to reinforce cooperation</li></ul>

Be aware that the marketing plan (prepared on the level of the marketing function) is not the same as the business plan, although the two necessarily overlap to some extent. Sir George Bull, former chairman of J. Sainsbury, once observed that focus is what distinguishes the marketing plan from the business plan. 'The business plan takes as both its starting point and its objective the business itself,' he said. In contrast, 'the marketing plan starts with the customer and works its way round to the business.'[16]

Marketing and the mission statement

Plans at all levels are made with the **mission statement** in mind. This statement explains the organisation's purpose, points the way towards a future vision of what the organisation aspires to become and drives planning at all levels. As you conduct an internal analysis of the current situation, take time to review your organisation's mission statement, because it will be an important foundation for decisions about marketing activities and resources.

A mission statement should look to the future, be credible to the organisation's publics, clarify customer priorities and set the tone for all organisation members, including marketing staff, by touching on five areas:

- *Customer focus.* Who does the organisation exist to serve? Businesses generally serve consumers, other businesses or government customers; non-profit organisations serve clients (such as patients, in the case of hospitals); government agencies serve constituents. The mission of the UK-based charity Comic Relief is 'to drive positive change through the power of entertainment' by rooting out the causes of poverty and social injustice. Clients are, therefore, people affected by poverty and social injustice.

- *Value provided.* What value will the organisation provide for its customers and other stakeholders, and how will it do so in a competitively superior way? Companies profit only when offerings provide value that customers need or want. For instance, the mission of Carnival is 'to deliver exceptional vacation experiences through the world's best-known cruise brands that cater to a variety of different lifestyles and budgets, all at an outstanding value unrivalled on land or at sea'. As expressed in this statement, customers will enjoy 'exceptional vacation experiences' at an 'outstanding value'.

- *Market scope.* Where and what will the organisation market? Defining the market scope helps management properly align structure, strategy and resources. Multinational giants such as Coca-Cola aim to operate all over the world. Other businesses, like the David Jones department store chain in Australia and Macy's in the United States, choose a specific geographic region as the scope for their marketing efforts.

- *Guiding values.* What values will guide managers and employees in making decisions and dealing with stakeholders? What does the organisation want to stand for? The DIY retail chain B&Q has identified these five key values as its top priorities: (1) customer first; (2) down to earth; (3) respect for people; (4) we can do it; and (5) nobody does it better. Notice that customers are first on the list, and the fifth value implies a competitive strength.

- *Core competencies*. What employee, process and technological capabilities give your organisation its competitive edge? These are its **core competencies** (sometimes known as *distinctive competencies*) – internal capabilities that are not easily duplicated and that differentiate the organisation from its competitors.[17] Walmart, for instance, has built the world's biggest retail business by getting the right merchandise to the right store at the right time, and at the right price. This distribution competency gives it a strong competitive advantage in the retailing industry.

Clearly, the challenge of a good mission statement is to convey all this information in as concise a manner as possible. Now continue with your marketing plan by completing Checklist No. 2. Then read **Chapter 2** for more about analysing the current marketing situation.

ESSENTIAL CHECKLIST NO. 2:
THE MISSION STATEMENT

Before you can develop a marketing plan, you need to know who the organisation exists to serve, what it expects to achieve in the long run and – in general terms – how it will compete, now and in the future. If you're preparing a plan for an existing organisation, obtain a copy of the mission statement and answer each of the questions below to evaluate both the content and the likely effect. Put a tick next to each question after you've written your answers in the space provided. If your organisation has no mission statement or if you're developing a marketing plan for a start-up or hypothetical company, use this checklist as you devise a suitable mission statement.

☐ Who will the organisation focus on as customers, clients or constituents?

_____

☐ How will it provide value for customers and other stakeholders?

_____

☐ What guiding values will the organisation adopt?

_____

☐ Does the mission statement provide appropriate direction for organisational decisions, actions and resource allocation, including marketing planning?

_____

☐ Is the mission statement credible to all publics, capable of rallying and inspiring employees and customers, and enduring to guide the organisation into the future?

_____

CHAPTER SUMMARY

Marketing planning is the structured process that leads to a coordinated set of marketing decisions and actions, for a specific organisation and period. This process consists of seven stages: (1) analyse the external and internal situation; (2) research and analyse markets and customers; (3) determine segmentation, targeting and positioning; (4) set marketing objectives and direction; (5) plan marketing strategies, programmes and support; (6) plan to measure progress; (7) implement, control and evaluate the plan. Marketing planning is used to examine opportunities and potential threats, identify and evaluate a variety of outcomes, focus on customers, assess offerings in a competitive and environmental context and then allocate resources for marketing.

The marketing plan outlines the marketplace situation and describes the marketing strategies and programmes that will support the achievement of business and organisational goals. Marketing plans must be both specific and flexible to help firms prepare for the new and the unexpected. Organisational (corporate) strategy sets the organisation's overall purpose, long-term direction, goals, businesses and approach to providing value. Business strategy sets the scope of individual units, how each will compete, the markets each will serve and how resources will be used. Marketing strategy shows how units will use the marketing mix plus service and internal marketing to achieve objectives. The mission statement outlines the organisation's fundamental purpose, the future vision of what it can become and its priorities, guiding the overall development of the marketing plan.

CASE STUDY: BURBERRY

Tweets from a luxury fashion brand that's more than 150 years old? Burberry's history may have its roots in the nineteenth century, but its brand has a twenty-first century image and is a profit leader. The once-staid British firm has more than 1 million Twitter followers, 14 million 'likes' on Facebook and 22 million YouTube views. Its Pinterest page and its brand-related websites (like www.Burberry.com and www.ArtoftheTrench.com) draw thousands of visitors every day.

Chief executive Angela Ahrendts wants to connect the brand to its customers when and where they choose. That's why Burberry spends 60 percent of its marketing budget on digital media of all kinds, including social media, mobile marketing and more. When the firm releases a new collection, it streams fashion shows live on Facebook as well as on in-store screens and media walls at Heathrow and other transportation hubs. When it introduced its new Body fragrance, it offered free samples first to Facebook fans, generating excitement and product trial. When it launched a new branded wristwatch, the first communications were delivered via mobile marketing. Mobile marketing continues in-store as well, providing shoppers with access to more detailed product information and to fashion tips.

Because retail sales constitute two-thirds of Burberry's revenues, the company has been expanding its retail presence in international markets such as Brazil, Mexico and China where demand is especially high for status-symbol clothing and accessories.

Fast-growing retail sales in these markets are helping to balance slower-growing retail sales in Europe and the United States. The company is also intensifying its new-product development efforts to increase sales of menswear and leather goods. Finally, for brand fans who want to customise their trenchcoats, Burberry Bespoke offers the opportunity to select from dozens of choices of fabrics, collars, cuffs, belts and other features – 12 million different combinations in all to make each bespoke coat one-of-a-kind.[18]

Case questions

1. Which of the nine ways to grow does Burberry appear to be using, and why?

2. What are Burberry's core competencies, and how is the firm building on them to provide value?

APPLY YOUR KNOWLEDGE

Choose a particular industry (such as biscuits or retailing) and research the mission statement and recent marketing activities of two competing businesses. Prepare a brief oral or written report summarising your comments.

- What do the mission statements say about the customer focus, value creation, market scope, guiding values and core competencies of these companies?

- For each company, how do specific marketing actions appear to relate to the stated mission? As an example, does the advertising reflect the customer focus in the mission statement?

- Now look more closely at the mission statement of one of these companies, keeping in mind the questions in Checklist No 2. What changes would you suggest to make the statement more effective as a guide for the marketing planning process or as an inspiration for managers and employees?

BUILD YOUR OWN MARKETING PLAN

By the end of this course, you will know how to work through all the stages in the marketing planning process and how to document a marketing plan. Depending on your lecturer's instructions, you will base your marketing plan on an actual organisation (as if you were one of its marketing managers), a hypothetical company or a non-profit organisation. As you complete each of these cumulative exercises, record your findings and decisions in a marketing plan. Refer to the order of topics shown in Table 1.2 and the sample marketing plan in the Appendix to see how decisions are documented.

Define the mission statement of your hypothetical organisation or locate and analyse the mission statement of the organisation you have chosen. If necessary, amend an existing organisation's mission statement or create a new one according to Checklist No. 2. What does this mission statement suggest about the organisation's purpose? Include information about the mission statement when writing about the current marketing situation in your marketing plan.

In preparation for later stages of the marketing planning process, list your ideas about the markets and customers to be researched and analysed, the product offering(s) your plan will cover, the organisation's competitive stance and its guiding values. Also look at the general direction you expect the marketing plan to take: is it likely to drive a growth strategy, sustain current turnover or support retrenching? Finally, write a few lines about what a one-year marketing plan needs to accomplish in order to lead the organisation closer to its long-term goals. Save your notes for use in completing later assignments.

ENDNOTES

1. Matthew Boyle, 'Haunting image drives Reckitt Benckiser CEO to clean up poverty', *Bloomberg*, 20 September 2012, www.bloomberg.com; David Jones, 'Reckitt sees early boost from new strategy', *Reuters*, 1 May 2012, www.reuters.com; Peter Stiff, 'Reckitt cuts its cloth in Europe and America', *Times (London)*, 9 February 2012, pp. 38–9; Paul Sonne, 'Cleaning up during the bad times', *Wall Street Journal (US)*, 17 June 2012, www.wsj.com; Loulla-Mae Eleftheriou-Smith and Rachel Barnes, 'Alan Thompson', *Marketing*, 11 January 2012, pp. 22–5; www.rb.com.

2. Alex Lawson, 'B&Q launches energy saving services', *RetailWeek*, 27 June 2012, www.retail-week. com; 'B&Q owner Kingfisher in growth drive as profits jump', *Reuters*, 22 March 2012, www.reuters. com; 'Kingfisher starts new eight-step growth plan after doubling profits in past four years', *ThisIsMoney*, 22 March 2012, www.thisismoney. co.uk; www.kingfisher.com.

3. Frances Brassington and Stephen Pettitt, *Principles of Marketing*, 3rd edn (Harlow, UK: Financial Times Prentice Hall, 2003), p. 19.

4. For more about sustainable marketing, see Diane Martin and John Schouten, *Sustainable Marketing* (Upper Saddle River, NJ: Prentice Hall, 2012).

5. Mark Brandau, 'McDonald's aims for transparency in new videos featuring food', *Nation's Restaurant News*, 13 July 2012, www.nrn.com; 'McDonalds Canada named marketer of the year for transparency campaign', *QSRweb*, 24 January 2013, www.qsrweb.com.

6. Quoted in Susan Krashinsky, 'McDonald's tries a transparent approach', *Globe and Mail (Canada)*, 20 June 2012, www.theglobeandmail.com.

7. Tim Ambler, *Marketing and the Bottom Line* (London: Financial Times Prentice Hall, 2000), pp. 19–20.

8. H. Igor Ansoff, 'Strategies for diversification', *Harvard Business Review*, September–October 1957, pp. 113–24; Ade S. Olusoga, 'Market concentration versus market diversification and internationalisation', *International Marketing Review*, vol. 10, no. 2 (1993), pp. 40–59; Alan R. Andreasen and Philip Kotler, *Strategic Marketing for Non-profit Organisations*, 6th edn (Upper Saddle River, NJ: Prentice Hall, 2003), pp. 80–1.

9. 'Thorntons sees sales rise amid cost cutting', *BBC News*, 11 July 2012, www.bbc.co.uk; Jennifer

Thompson, 'Jubilee fails to halt Thorntons sales dip', *Financial Times*, 11 July 2012, www.ft.com; Sara Luker, 'Thorntons hires Nexus Communications as it faces £2.4m loss', *PR Week UK*, 26 June 2012, www.prweek.com; www.thorntons.com.

10. Tim Ambler, 'Set clear goals and see marketing hit its target', *Financial Times*, 29 August 2002, p. 8; 'Interregna in conversation with Tim Ambler', *Interregna*, February 2009, www.interregna.com/article_tim_ambler.php.

11. Kevin Lane Keller and Philip Kotler, *Marketing Management*, 14th edn (Upper Saddle River, NJ: Prentice Hall, 2012), p. 245.

12. Haig Simonian, 'Nestlé to open third Nespresso factory', *Financial Times*, 3 May 2012, www.ft.com; Haig Simonian and Louise Lucas, 'Starbucks takes coffee wars to Nespresso', *Financial Times*, 5 March 2012, www.ft.com; Dermot Doherty and Aoife White, 'Nestlé wins backing in Europe for Nespresso system patent', *Bloomberg News*, 19 April 2012, www.bloomberg.com.

13. 'Catherine Derkosh, marketing communications director at Siemens Industry, on gamification', *BtoB Online*, 5 June 2012, www.btobonline.com; Austin

Carr, 'Siemens taps into Zynga's popularity, launches PlantVille', *Fast Company*, 24 March 2011, www.fastcompany.com.

14. 'Siemens' profits slump on project delays', *BBC*, 24 January 2012, www.bbc.co.uk.

15. Based on information on Reckitt Benckiser website, www.rb.com.

16. Quoted in Sir George Bull, 'What does the term marketing really stand for?', *Marketing*, 30 November 2000, p. 30.

17. Stephen J. Porth, *Strategic Management* (Upper Saddle River, NJ: Prentice Hall, 2003), pp. 85–6.

18. Based on information in: Lara O'Reilly, 'Burberry to put mobile first in mix', *Marketing Week*, 20 September 2012, www.marketingweek.co.uk; Charlotte Amos, 'Blooming Burberry', *The Drum*, 26 April 2012, www.thedrum.co.uk; Zoe Wood, 'Burberry targets up-and-coming luxury markets', *Guardian*, 23 May 2012, www.guardian.co.uk; 'Burberry: Putting a value on social media', *Marketing Week*, 15 February 2012, www.marketingweek.co.uk; Paul Sonne, 'Mink or Fox?' *Wall Street Journal*, 3 November 2011, www.wsj.com; www.burberry.com.

2 Analysing the current situation

Learning outcomes

After studying this chapter, you will be able to:

- Explain the purpose of internal and external audits
- Discuss how the internal and external environments affect marketing planning
- Describe the use of SWOT analysis for marketing planning

Application outcomes

After studying this chapter, you will be able to:

- Conduct an internal audit
- Conduct an external audit
- Prepare a SWOT analysis for your marketing plan

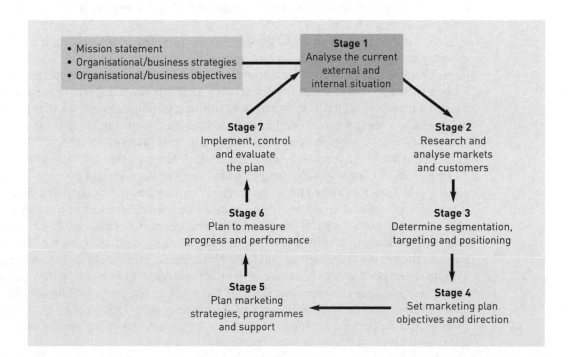

- Mission statement
- Organisational/business strategies
- Organisational/business objectives

Stage 1
Analyse the current external and internal situation

Stage 7
Implement, control and evaluate the plan

Stage 2
Research and analyse markets and customers

Stage 6
Plan to measure progress and performance

Stage 3
Determine segmentation, targeting and positioning

Stage 5
Plan marketing strategies, programmes and support

Stage 4
Set marketing plan objectives and direction

CHAPTER PREVIEW: MARKETING AT EXPERIAN

Every day, Experian generates 30,000 credit reports, processes 90 million online transactions and tracks the online activities of 25 million Internet users, all part of its mission to 'become a necessary part of every major consumer economy in the world'. With global headquarters in Dublin and a corporate office in London, Experian (www.experianplc.com) specialises in collecting and analysing data to help business customers make more informed decisions about granting credit, processing payment transactions, hiring qualified employees and building relationships with Internet users. It also markets credit score information, credit monitoring services and identity fraud protection to consumers.

The company's research, based on the data it collects and on outside surveys, yields insights for many marketing situations. For example, one Experian survey found that businesses too often fail to ask customers for mobile numbers and contact preferences. Without this information, they can't market to customers on the go via text messages or other mobile-marketing methods. On the other hand, because consumers are increasingly looking for multichannel options – including mobile purchasing and payment – Experian provides data analysis and targeting tools to help businesses meet these needs. It also works with customers that are formulating marketing plans to build on external trends that affect consumer attitudes and product demand. As an example, Experian helped the government-owned UK Royal Mint prepare to meet high demand for commemorative coins created for the London Olympics and the Queen's Diamond Jubilee. By organising the customer database, classifying customers according to interests and purchasing patterns and then analysing trends in website visits, Experian supported the Royal Mint's objectives of increasing purchasing by current customers and attracting new customers.

Experian has its own marketing plans for serving businesses in certain industries and geographic areas. During the recent recession, it targeted new UK financial services firms because its existing bank customers weren't buying as many credit reports as they had in the past. It also sought out markets like Latin America, where it sees growth in demand from financial services firms and utilities. Finally, because more than 20 percent of Experian's annual turnover of £2.9 billion (€3.7 billion) comes from the sale of credit services to consumers, the company has a separate marketing plan for reaching this audience with TV adverts and digital marketing, among other activities.[1]

This chapter continues with Stage 1 of the marketing planning process, in which you collect and interpret data about the internal and external environment. Experian, for instance, gathers and analyses a huge amount of information about developments outside the company as well as examining its own customer database. The first section of this chapter is an overview of environmental scanning and analysis for the marketing plan. In the next two sections, you'll learn about performing internal and external audits. The final section looks at how to use the data collected to evaluate your organisation's strengths, weaknesses, opportunities and threats. Use the two checklists in this chapter as a guide to planning for environmental scanning. Also look at the sample marketing plan in the Appendix for ideas about how to present the outcome of your situation analysis when you document your planning.

ENVIRONMENTAL SCANNING AND ANALYSIS

Early in the marketing planning process, you have to look at the organisation's current situation, especially within the context of the mission, higher-level plans and higher-level goals. This is accomplished through **environmental scanning and analysis**, the systematic (and ongoing) collection and interpretation of data about both internal and external factors that may affect marketing and performance. When learning about the situation inside the organisation, you'll use an **internal audit**; when learning about the situation outside the organisation, you'll use an **external audit**.

Once you gather all the relevant information, you evaluate and distil it into a critique reflecting your firm's primary strengths, weaknesses, opportunities and threats, known as the **SWOT analysis**. In addition, many marketers conduct a SWOT analysis of current or potential rivals to clarify the competitive situation. The idea is to develop a marketing plan to leverage your internal strengths, bolster your internal weaknesses, take advantage of competitors' main weaknesses and defend against competitors' strengths, as shown in Figure 2.1.

Details count in any environmental scan, but professional judgement plays a vital role as well. Use your best judgement (supported by other managers' insights, expert models and so on) to develop the most reasonable marketing plan under the circumstances. Over time, you'll develop a keener sense of how various environmental factors and trends interact and how they're likely to affect your organisation and marketing strategy. Also consider the resources and viewpoints of customers, partners, suppliers and other publics as you scan an uncertain marketing environment in search of creative opportunities and viable strategies. Having the flexibility to make changes during planning and implementation can give you an important competitive edge over organisations that do not or cannot react quickly and decisively under conditions of uncertainty.

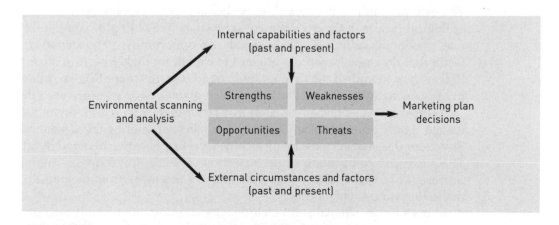

FIGURE 2.1   Environmental scanning and marketing planning

Internal audit: identifying strengths and weaknesses

The internal audit covers the mission statement (as discussed in **Chapter 1**) plus your organisation's resources and capabilities, current offerings, previous performance, business relationships and key issues. These internal factors, individually and in combination, are instrumental in the way your company fulfils its mission, serves customers and competes in the marketplace. Just as important, these factors contribute to the firm's strengths and weaknesses in using marketing to deal with opportunities and threats.

A **strength** is an internal capability or factor that can help the organisation achieve its objectives, making the most of opportunities or deflecting threats. For example, three of Rolls-Royce's great strengths are the capability to engineer high-performance car engines, the skill to hand-craft luxury bespoke vehicles for individual buyers and a long-standing worldwide reputation for quality and excellence. These strengths (which relate to what customers value) have helped propel Rolls-Royce – owned by BMW since 2003 – to its best-ever results, selling more than 3,500 vehicles worldwide.[2]

A **weakness** is an internal capability or factor that may prevent the organisation from achieving its objectives or effectively handling opportunities and threats, especially within the competitive context. The high cost of hand-crafting every vehicle is one potential weakness for Rolls-Royce, although its bespoke design and production capabilities are in demand and higher-priced customised vehicles sell well.[3] Another possible weakness is limited production capacity, which could be a problem if the lowest-priced Rolls-Royce, the Ghost, continues to be unusually popular.[4]

When auditing your internal strengths and weaknesses, search company records and databases for information such as current offerings, finances, personnel and skills, technological expertise, supplier relations, distributor connections, partnerships, previous marketing plans and results.

External audit: identifying opportunities and threats

The external audit covers political, economic, social–cultural, technological, legal and ecological factors in the environment (known as **PESTLE**) plus competitive factors that may present opportunities or pose threats. An **opportunity** is an external circumstance or factor that the organisation can attempt to exploit for higher performance. For example, Rolls-Royce identified the demographic trend towards more Russian billionaires living in Moscow as an opportunity to open a second dealership and increase sales in the city.[5]

A **threat** is an external circumstance or factor that could inhibit organisational performance, if not addressed. Many luxury carmakers are entering the same markets as Rolls-Royce, for the same reasons: rising income levels are boosting demand for upmarket cars. This increased competition could be a threat if Rolls-Royce doesn't monitor its rivals' moves and respond quickly or if Rolls-Royce veers away from its long-time strategy of marketing status-symbol cars.

Sources for an external audit include internal information about customers, suppliers, partners, market share and technical standards; customer feedback through surveys, suggestions and complaints; government, academic or syndicated studies of the market, the industry and competition; industry groups; employees, suppliers and other partners;

media and online reports; and special-interest groups. Later in this chapter you'll read more about the external audit.

SWOT analysis

Once you have data from internal and external audits, you'll prepare a SWOT analysis to make sense of what you have learned and interpret it in the context of the organisation's situation, mission and goals. The purpose of environmental scanning and SWOT analysis is to match key strengths with promising opportunities and use strengths to offset weaknesses and threats to marketing performance (see Table 2.1).

Four criteria can help you determine whether a particular internal capability, resource or factor is a strength or a weakness:[6]

1. *Previous performance.* How has the factor affected earlier performance, as measured by trends in turnover and profitability, market share, employee productivity or other appropriate standards? Are prior trends and performance likely to continue?

2. *Outcomes.* How has the factor contributed to specific outcomes defined by objectives and goals? Will the factor be likely to influence short- and long-term outcomes in the future?

3. *Competitors.* How does the factor compare with that of competitors, and is significant change likely to occur in the future?

4. *Management judgement.* How do organisational managers view the factor and what changes, if any, do they foresee in the coming months or years?

Table 2.1 The effects of strengths and weaknesses

Strength or weakness (brief description)	Internal source (resource, capability or factor)	Effect (on an opportunity or a threat and implications for marketing planning)
Strength:		
Strength:		
Weakness:		
Weakness:		

The point is not to analyse every capability, resource or factor but to single out the most important as strengths (to be employed) and weaknesses (to be counteracted). When your environmental scans identify potentially profitable opportunities or challenging threats, you'll need the proper strengths to make the most of your marketing situation and new opportunities, as London-based Virgin Atlantic Airways (www.virgin-atlantic.com) is well aware.

MARKETING IN PRACTICE: VIRGIN ATLANTIC AIRWAYS

As the second-largest long-distance UK airline, Virgin Atlantic competes with British Airways as well as with other airlines that fly to North America and beyond. Its mission is to grow a profitable airline where people love to fly and people love to work. One potential threat is that competitors often combine forces to attract passengers through code-share alliances with US, European and Asian partner airlines. Another challenge facing Virgin is that airlines need regulatory approval to gain access to additional takeoff and landing slots – and any open slots are always hotly contested by competitors.

In fact, with London's Heathrow Airport operating at maximum capacity, Virgin must make the most of its existing slots while making its case for new slots that might open as consolidation continues in the airline industry. Fortunately, one of Virgin's strengths is that it holds more than half of the early-morning arrival slots at Heathrow, an advantage for attracting North American business customers who want to arrive in time for a full day of meetings or to catch a conveniently scheduled Virgin flight to India, Africa or other destinations.

Another Virgin strength is its reputation for flair, innovation and responsiveness to customer needs and preferences. Targeting business customers and affluent consumers, the airline recently upgraded its first-class cabin seating, meals, amenities and décor, adding a technology hub for charging mobiles, tablet computers and other devices. It was also the first British airline to offer the option of making and receiving phone calls, accessing the Internet and sending or receiving texts and e-mails while crossing the Atlantic. Looking ahead, if Virgin can secure additional slots, its marketing plan calls for adding flights to China, Russia and South America, areas that are global hot-spots for business growth.[7]

Marketing plan analysis: If you were a marketer for Virgin Atlantic, how would you identify potential weaknesses relative to your competitors?

Once you've assessed your main strengths and weaknesses and your main opportunities and threats, summarise and document the results in your marketing plan.

ANALYSING THE INTERNAL ENVIRONMENT

During an internal audit, you will scan and analyse five main factors: the organisation's resources and capabilities, current offerings, previous performance, business relationships and key issues. You are looking for information that can help you understand your organisation's current situation and the strengths you can rely on when implementing a marketing plan.

| Table 2.2 | Analysing organisational resources |

Human resources: Does your company have the people, commitment and rewards to successfully implement your marketing plan? Specifically examine:	**Informational resources:** Does your company have the data, tools and access to information to successfully implement your marketing plan? Specifically examine:
<ul><li>workforce knowledge, creativity, skills, morale, experience and turnover</li><li>top management support</li><li>individual commitment, initiative and entrepreneurial spirit</li><li>recruitment, training and rewards</li></ul>	<ul><li>data capture, storage and reporting systems</li><li>analysis tools</li><li>access to timely, accurate and complete information</li><li>ability to provide customers with appropriate information throughout the buying process</li></ul>
Financial resources: Does your company have the money to successfully implement your marketing plan? Specifically examine:	**Supply resources:** Does your company have the supplies, supply systems and relationships to implement your marketing plan? Specifically examine:
<ul><li>funding for marketing activities</li><li>funding for research and testing</li><li>funding for internal support</li><li>available funding for multi-year programmes</li></ul>	<ul><li>ample availability of materials, parts, components and services</li><li>supply chain relationships</li><li>inventory management</li><li>transportation alternatives</li></ul>

Organisational resources and capabilities

As noted in **Chapter 1**, core competencies are internal capabilities that contribute to competitive superiority yet are not easily duplicated. Such capabilities are traced to the organisation's human, financial, informational and supply resources (see Table 2.2).

When planning for marketing, you and your managers must balance the investment and allocation of resources. The organisation's values, ethical standards and social responsibility position also affect this balancing act. From a practical standpoint, the internal audit helps managers determine the resources they have, the resources they can obtain and where their resources are currently committed. This is the starting point for identifying any resource gaps and determining how best to allocate resources in support of the marketing plan.

Outsourcing, strategic alliances and supply chain realignment are three ways that organisations can gain or supplement resource arrangements to bridge any gaps for added strength. A growing number of marketers are meeting some or all of their data storage and information technology needs by outsourcing to cloud computing services.

Current offerings

In this part of the internal audit, you review and analyse the goods and services currently offered so you know where you stand before making plans to move ahead. Also understand how your organisation's offerings relate to the mission and to your resources. If records are available, review the following data, looking at both historic and current trends:

- composition, sales and market share of product mix and ranges
- customer needs satisfied by features and benefits
- product pricing and profitability, contribution to overall performance
- product age and position in product life cycle
- links to other products.

Previous performance

Although past performance is never a guarantee of future performance, looking at previous results can reveal insights about internal strengths and weaknesses. The purpose is to build on past marketing experience in planning new marketing activities. At a minimum, you should analyse these performance indicators:

- prior year sales (in units and monetary terms)
- prior year profits and other financial results
- historic trends in sales and profits by product, geographic region, customer segment, etc.
- results of previous marketing plans
- customer acquisition, retention and loyalty trends and costs.

Some companies use **data mining**, sophisticated analyses of database information to uncover customer behaviour patterns and relate these to marketing activities. The Coles supermarket chain in Australia, for example, analyses purchasing data in search of patterns that will help it segment and serve specific customer groups. It also examines its customer data when deciding on new store locations and determining what merchandise to stock in each store. Finally, Coles prepares personalised discount offers based on what an individual customer has been buying, to add value and reinforce loyalty.[8]

Business relationships

Good business relationships can act as strengths, helping organisations make the most of opportunities or defend against threats and profitably satisfy customers. Among the areas of business relationships to be examined during an internal audit are:

- value added by suppliers, distributors and strategic alliance partners
- internal relationships with other units or divisions
- capacity, quality, service, commitment and costs of suppliers and channel members
- changes in business relationships over time
- level of dependence on suppliers and channel members.

The existence of a business relationship is not in and of itself a strength. Moreover, not having strong connections with vital suppliers or channel members can be a definite weakness when an organisation is seeking aggressive growth or simply struggling to survive. Yet close connections with key channel members and suppliers can be an important competitive advantage. For example, to be cost-competitive in Europe, Toyota relies on a relatively small group of suppliers that are committed to having car parts available when and where needed. On the other hand, suppliers also want to avoid the risk of relying too heavily on sales to a few large customers. That's why Toyota Boshoku Corporation, Toyota's main supplier of car seats, has been diversifying its customer base.[9] As you prepare your marketing plan, think about how your business relationships will affect your ability to serve customers and achieve objectives.

Key issues

What specific issues could interfere with the firm's ability to move towards the mission and goals, and what are the warning signs of potential problems? What specific issues are pivotal for organisational success? Take a broad look at the key issues and then dig deeper to understand the implications for your targeted customer segments, markets and products.

Start-up firms have unique issues that must be addressed during planning and early growth. Shutl, a start-up based in London (www.shutl.co.uk), determined that data management and transparency were two important issues that could affect the success of its marketing efforts.

MARKETING IN PRACTICE: SHUTL

When Tom Allason founded Shutl, a courier company that guarantees speedy, convenient delivery of online purchases from retailers such as Argos, Oasis and Maplin, he had to find an efficient, affordable way of managing information technology. Without the ability to record and track purchase information, delivery requests, courier availability and parcel location, Shutl wouldn't be able to arrange for same-day delivery within 90 minutes of purchase (or at a time chosen by the customer).

Allason decided on a cloud computing solution, outsourcing much of the technology side of the business to Amazon.com's cloud network. As a result, the £100,000 he would have spent on computers, software and servers was used, instead, for other marketing purposes. Now, just a few years after the start of operations, Shutl handles more than 1,000 daily deliveries and has the ability to make on-time deliveries to 65 percent of all UK shoppers.

The company is also focusing on maintaining a reputation for transparency and customer responsiveness. 'Being transparent about the service we provide, even when things don't go to plan, is the rod down our back that keeps us focused on providing an exceptional customer experience,' explains Allason. For this reason, Shutl invites customers to post feedback (good and bad) to its Twitter account and its Facebook page, where unedited comments will be displayed for the public to see.[10]

Marketing plan analysis: How can Shutl use its marketing plan to prepare for possible complaints about deliveries that don't arrive on time?

ESSENTIAL CHECKLIST NO. 3:
THE INTERNAL ENVIRONMENT

To formulate a realistic marketing plan, you must be knowledgeable about what your organisation has, where it has been and what it can leverage. Continue your marketing planning effort by adding a tick next to each question after writing answers in the spaces provided. If you are planning for a start-up or a hypothetical company, use this checklist to note ideas about potential weaknesses you should counter and internal strengths you'll need to support your marketing plan.

☐ Do you have appropriate human, informational, financial and supply resources for marketing?

_____

☐ What do trends in marketing results and organisational performance suggest about the effectiveness of previous plans and the content of future plans?

_____

☐ What goods and services are currently offered and how do they contribute to turnover and profits?

_____

☐ How do your offerings provide value to customers – and is this value competitively superior?

_____

☐ Are the offerings suitable for your firm's mission, goals and resources?

_____

☐ What are the trends in customer needs, acquisition, retention and loyalty?

_____

☐ How do business relationships affect capacity, quality, costs and availability?

_____

☐ What marketing research does the organisation need to support marketing planning?

_____

☐ What lessons can be applied to the marketing plan, based on the internal audit?

_____

ANALYSING THE EXTERNAL ENVIRONMENT

In contrast to the factors in the internal environment, which offer clues to strengths and weaknesses, the factors in the external environment offer clues to opportunities and threats (see Figure 2.2). These factors also suggest additional lines of inquiry for researching and analysing markets and customers (as discussed in **Chapter 3**).

Remember, the external audit is intended to help you identify trends or situations that you can exploit through marketing planning – and issues or circumstances that you should defend against through marketing planning. When you write your marketing plan, you'll summarise the most important point or points about each of these factors as you explain your organisation's current marketing situation. The following sections look at PESTLE and competitive factors in more detail. The checklist at the end of this section includes specific questions to ask when analysing the external environment.

Political factors

Depending on where your organisation is based and where it does business, political factors can lead to profitable opportunities or potential threats (or both). Political instability, as one example, can pose a threat to ongoing operations. Changes such as new political leaders or new political initiatives can also lead to new marketing possibilities. Your analysis should look at how the various political factors might affect the current marketing plan (such as in your choice of markets) and your future plans (to continue in a particular market, for instance). Political factors are often closely linked to legal factors, which are discussed later in this chapter.

Economic factors

In the interconnected global economy, recession or recovery in one region can have a cascading effect on the purchasing patterns of consumers and businesses near and

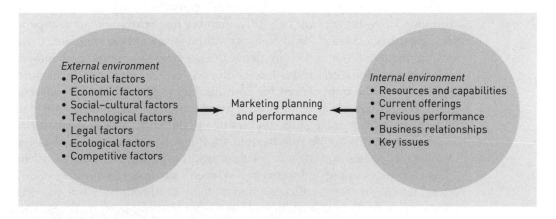

FIGURE 2.2   Factors in the external and internal environments

far. Economic factors influence customer buying power because of the effect on consumer and business income, debt and credit usage. Economic slowdowns often discourage businesses from spending heavily on upgrading their plants, for instance, or government agencies from proceeding with infrastructure improvements. Even if the home country economy is growing slowly, however, a company may create a marketing plan around opportunities in countries where the economic outlook seems more favourable.

Economic trends don't always affect different companies, industries or markets in the same way. For example, Carrefour, Europe's largest retailer, withdrew from a joint venture in Greece because it feared that shoppers would further slow their spending if the country's economy deteriorated during the recent recession and debt crisis.[11] During the same period, European luxury goods marketers such as Hugo Boss and Hermès enjoyed higher sales and profits, because they appeal to different buyers, specifically high-income consumers who can afford the latest high-fashion styles.[12] So be alert to threats and opportunities based on economic factors, and keep the economic outlook in mind when you set your marketing plan objectives (see **Chapter 5**).

Social–cultural factors

Social–cultural factors are among the most dynamic in the external environment, affecting the size and composition of markets and segments as well as customers' requirements, characteristics, attitudes and perceptions. Population shifts due to higher or lower birth rates, longer life spans and immigration can create, expand or shrink markets. Along with these shifts come changes in demand and usage of different goods and services – key changes that must be considered in marketing planning. Companies that market to businesses should look closely at trends such as the size and growth of targeted industries as measured by number of firms, number of locations or outlets, workforce size, turnover and profitability.

During your planning, examine demographic details such as gender, education, occupation, ethnic and religious composition, household size, household composition and household income, any or all of which can affect consumer purchasing and usage. Although such statistics are helpful, remember that customers are real people, not numbers; they have distinct emotions and attitudes towards companies, brands, products and buying situations, which in turn influence how they think, feel and act.

Think about the social and cultural influences on the behaviour of customers in targeted segments and the implications for your marketing plan. In the UK, for example, school proms have become big business, with female students splashing out on glamorous clothing and hairstyles, male students buying special suits and students hiring limousines or other transportation to ride in style. Clothing manufacturers such as Terani Couture, local beauty salons and car-hire services are all profiting from this social trend.[13]

As another example, in Indonesia, 7-Eleven convenience stores are open 24 hours and attract late-night crowds of consumers in their 20s through such marketing activities as offering free Wi-Fi and inviting local bands for evening performances. These customers are giving 7-Eleven's sales a big boost because they buy lots of crisps, doughnuts, soft drinks, coffee or beer as they chat, click on websites and enjoy the music hour after hour.[14]

Technological factors

Fast-changing technology has an effect on customers, suppliers, competitors, channel members, marketing techniques and organisational processes. Today, technology touches virtually every element of marketing, from digitally enhanced advertisements to packaging, research, distribution, pricing and beyond. Although the Internet has opened opportunities for consumer and business marketing worldwide, it has also raised serious questions about privacy and security, with the result that marketers in many nations must comply with legal and regulatory guidelines aimed at protecting customer data and informing website visitors about cookies and other tracking methods in use.

When examining technological factors to understand potential threats and opportunities, look at how rapidly innovations are spreading or evolving, how technology is affecting customers and others in the marketing environment, how technology is affected by or is affecting standards and regulations, how and when technology is prompting substitute or improved products, how much the industry and key competitors are investing in research and development, and how technology is affecting costs and pricing.

Social gifting – giving a virtual gift card through social media, redeemable via the recipient's mobile device – is a new trend that, thanks to technological and social–cultural factors, means opportunity for startups like Wrapp (www.wrapp.com/gb).

MARKETING IN PRACTICE: WRAPP

Founded by serial entrepreneurs in Stockholm, Sweden, Wrapp makes it easy for consumers to use social media to give virtual gift cards to friends and family. After downloading the Wrapp app, the gift-giver selects a recipient (such as a friend whose birthday is highlighted on Facebook), selects a gift card from the list of participating retailers, enters a personalised greeting and adds payment information. Wrapp notifies the recipient via text message, email or a Facebook post that a virtual gift card is available to be redeemed in the store or online. Not only does the Facebook note build buzz, it allows other friends to add money to the gift card, as well.

Wrapp makes money by charging merchants a small fee; the company also collects detailed data about gifting occasions and preferences, for future use in targeted campaigns for retailers. CEO Hjalmar Winbladh explains that Wrapp helps retailers make the most of marketing opportunities stemming from widespread use of smartphones and social networks. After a successful launch in Sweden, the company quickly expanded further into Europe, the US and Asia. In its first six months, Wrapp distributed 1 million gift cards redeemable in dozens of stores and online retail sites, including H&M, House of Fraser, Lipsy, Firebox, Gap and Sephora.

Each participating retailer also offers a limited number of free low-value gift cards each day, as an incentive for consumers to check the app frequently and get in the habit of social gifting. Why would a marketer work with Wrapp? Hardware retailer Clas Ohlson sees it as a way to increase online brand awareness and encourage visits to its high street London stores. Even the free gift cards generate incremental sales, because recipients spend four to five times more than the face value once they're in the store, according to Wrapp's research. With rival firms popping up all over Europe and North America, how long will Wrapp's innovative social gifting technology give it a competitive edge?[15]

Marketing plan analysis: If you were writing Wrapp's next marketing plan, what threats would you mention, and why?

Legal factors

Legal factors such as legislation, regulation and governmental actions can affect product purity and labelling, communications, data mining, pricing, distribution, competitive behaviour and consumer choices. Walmart, for example, wants to open small convenience stores and large general merchandise superstores in India. However, it is currently illegal for foreign retailers to operate stores that sell directly to consumers in India. For now, Walmart is continuing its marketing plans for a joint venture with Bharti Enterprises in which it operates business-to-business cash-and-carry wholesale stores.[16]

Ecological factors

Ecological factors can influence marketing in numerous ways. Manufacturers will be unable to achieve their objectives if vital raw materials such as water or minerals are unavailable for production. A steady source of non-polluting energy is problematic for businesses and non-governmental organisations in certain regions; in other areas, high energy costs pose a challenge. Further, government regulations and community attitudes are shaping how companies interact with the natural environment.

Consumers are increasingly interested in choosing brands and products that are ecologically friendly. Unfortunately, goods or services are sometimes marketed as safe for the planet even when they have little or no actual ecological impact. Customers who want to steer clear of such *greenwashing* often look for certification by groups such as Green Globe, which set specific standards for sustainability. In the travel and tourism industry, for example, Mövenpick Hotels & Resorts has achieved Green Globe certification, which reassures customers about the quality of its ecological initiatives.[17] Be sure your marketing plan covers the key ecological factors that affect your industry and your marketing efforts.

Competitive factors

All organisations, not just businesses, face competition. Charities compete with other charities for a share of donors' contributions; governments compete with each other when trying to attract businesses to create jobs, for example. As a marketer, you should examine your organisation's strength in three factors that influence competitive position: (1) differentiation advantage; (2) cost advantage; and (3) marketing advantage (see Figure 2.3).

Companies like Luxottica (spectacles) derive competitive advantage from quality, style or another point of differentiation by positioning their offerings as superior in delivering features and benefits valued by customers. Companies like Aldi (retailing) and Acer (computers) strive for cost advantage, minimising costs to keep their prices low. Companies like Shell (petrol and energy products) get a competitive edge from cost-effective marketing due to high brand awareness, extensive distribution and other efficiencies.

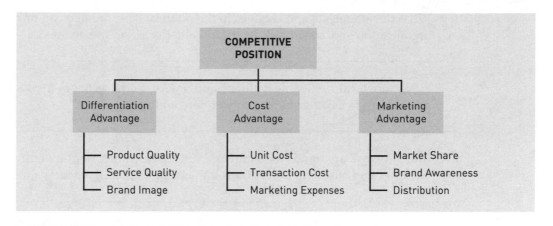

FIGURE 2.3   Factors that influence competitive position

Source: Adapted from *Market-based Management*, 6, Pearson (Roger J. Best 2012) 388, Prentice Hall, BEST, ROGER, MARKET-BASED MANAGEMENT, 6th Ed., p. 388, (c) 2012. Reprinted and Electronically reproduced by permission of Pearson Education. Inc, Upper Saddle River. New Jersey.

Another way to understand the competitive situation is to look at how easily competitors can enter or leave the market; how much power buyers and suppliers have; and whether substitutes are available for your products.[18] Easy market entry or exit increases competitive pressure, as does the availability of substitutes. Powerful buyers and suppliers can put pressure on pricing and profit margins when firms compete for orders.

Look closely at what competitors do that makes them successful (to see how you can build on these practices or ideas). Also analyse why some competitors aren't successful, so you can avoid those pitfalls. Benchmark against successful organisations in other industries so you can be innovative and gain a competitive edge in your own industry. Scan the environment for trends that might change the future competitive situation and for companies that might soon be able to satisfy your customers' needs in an entirely new or different way. Finally, focus on what your customers value as well as what your organisation needs to achieve its objectives and goals.

ESSENTIAL CHECKLIST NO. 4:
THE EXTERNAL ENVIRONMENT

As you prepare your marketing plan, you need to analyse how external factors affect your current marketing situation and how they might influence future marketing activities. Put a tick by each question below as you note your answers in the space provided. If you're writing a marketing plan for a hypothetical business, use this checklist to list what you would focus on when analysing the external environment.

☐ What developments and changes in the political environment can or will affect the organisation and, specifically, its marketing decisions and actions?

☐ How can local, regional, national and international economic conditions affect demand and customer buying power now and in the future?

☐ In what ways are trends in demographics, social values, popular culture, customer attitudes and customer perceptions influencing demand, markets and segments?

☐ How are technological innovations affecting customers, competitors, suppliers, channel partners, marketing and internal processes such as research and development?

☐ What emerging and ongoing ecological concerns may affect the organisation's materials, suppliers, energy access, processes, marketing programmes and public reputation?

☐ Which legal issues may have the most influence on your marketing activities in the short term? In the long term?

☐ What is the current competitive situation and how is it changing (or likely to change)?

☐ What are each main competitor's market share, strengths, weaknesses, opportunities, threats, resources and competitive advantages?

☐ What benchmarks can be used for competitive performance and on what basis can the organisation achieve competitive advantage?

☐ What makes successful competitors successful? What prevents unsuccessful competitors from achieving their objectives? What good ideas can be adapted from the best practices of other industries?

☐ What lessons learned through the external audit can be applied to marketing planning?

CHAPTER SUMMARY

Marketers use an internal audit to examine resources and capabilities, current offerings, past results, business relationships and key issues that affect marketing and performance. They use an external audit to understand how PESTLE (political, economic, social–cultural, technological, legal and ecological) factors as well as competitive factors might affect marketing. Three factors that affect competitive position are differentiation advantage, cost advantage and marketing advantage. To gauge whether a market is competitively attractive, look at ease of market entry and exit, buyer and supplier power and availability of substitutes for your product.

After completing the internal and external audits, analyse and distil the relevant data into a critique summarising the organisation's primary strengths, weaknesses, opportunities and threats, examined in the context of the mission and goals. Some marketers also prepare a SWOT analysis of key competitors. A SWOT analysis helps marketers match strengths with opportunities and understand how to guard against weaknesses and threats as they prepare the marketing plan.

CASE STUDY: UNIQLO

Uniqlo (www.uniqlo.com/uk/), owned by Japan's Fast Retailing, has dozens of clothing stores throughout its home country, where its colourful, affordable apparel is well known and quite popular. 'In Japan, Uniqlo is regarded as a reliable friend,' explains the company's UK chief; '80 percent of the population is within a 20-minute drive of a Uniqlo store.' Yet Japan's aging population and saturated market limit the youth-oriented brand's potential for domestic expansion. Japan's economy has also been struggling for two decades, a factor that affects buying power and consumer confidence.

After analysing the marketing situation, Uniqlo determined that countries with a younger, style-conscious population and a more robust economy would offer more potential for faster growth. So the company opened its first London store in 2001, followed by several more UK locations. After failing to make a competitive name for itself with this initial step into global expansion, Uniqlo closed most of its UK stores by 2003. By 2007, it was back with a large store in Oxford Street, the vanguard of its higher-profile approach to London retailing, where it now operates 12 stores.

Meanwhile, the company recognised that demographic and economic changes in China presented a good opportunity for expansion. In 2005, it opened two stores in Beijing – but closed them within a year, intending to conduct more intensive research into local needs. Next, Uniqlo entered the US market in 2005, when the economy was still going strong. However, its first few stores in busy suburban US shopping centres were small, and once again, the chain lacked the competitive power and distinctive brand image to attract and retain customers. Uniqlo closed three US stores in 2006 as it opened a much larger flagship store in the hip SoHo downtown area of New York City. The purpose was to make a brand statement, setting Uniqlo apart from the typical mall store selling casual clothing. It had the same objective in mind when it opened a strikingly large and modern store in Tokyo's glittering Ginza shopping district.

Now Uniqlo is searching for a sizable downtown space to open a flagship London store that will showcase the brand. It has reentered China, where turnover is growing year by year, and it's expanding throughout Asia in markets with a rising middle class, all factors that affect its ability to lower unit and marketing costs with rising volume. In line with demographic trends, Uniqlo has launched a range of children's clothing, competing against Gap Kids and other retailers. And with clever social media campaigns such as a recent Pinterest 'mosaic' featuring new tops, Uniqlo is publicising its brand-exclusive products among young audiences that want the latest in basic fashions.[19]

Case questions

1. What do Uniqlo's strengths and weaknesses appear to be?

2. Based on the factors mentioned in Figure 2.3, how would you assess Uniqlo's competitive advantages?

APPLY YOUR KNOWLEDGE

Research and analyse the forces shaping the industry of a company that is facing intense competitive pressure, such as a particular airline, food manufacturer or consumer electronics firm. Then prepare a brief oral or written report summarising your results.

- How powerful are suppliers to this industry? What are the implications for the company's business relationships?

- How powerful are buyers in this industry? What are the implications for the company's pricing decisions?

- Can customers substitute other goods or services for the company's offerings? What are the implications for customer loyalty to this company – and how can this be addressed through marketing?

- Can the company or competitors easily exit the industry? Can new rivals easily enter the industry? What are the implications for the company's marketing if environmental conditions threaten profitability?

- What differentiation, cost or marketing advantage do you see individual competitors having in this industry?

- How do you think the competitive environment is likely to affect the chosen company's marketing plan for the coming year?

BUILD YOUR OWN MARKETING PLAN

Continue the marketing planning process using the concepts and tools from this chapter, including the two checklists. Start with an internal audit of resources, offerings, previous performance, business relationships and key issues. If the organisation is a start-up, examine the recent performance of direct competitors and discuss what the trends might mean for your organisation. Next, look at relevant PESTLE and competitive factors in the external environment and analyse how these factors might affect your marketing decisions (and your competitors' marketing activities). Identify current competitors and potentially strong future competitors that you should watch as you create and implement your plan.

On the basis of your internal and external audits, prepare a SWOT analysis explaining how the main strengths and weaknesses relate to specific opportunities or threats and their implications for marketing strategy. Also consider how quickly you expect the marketing environment to evolve and how you plan to stay in touch with developments. Before you record your conclusions, think about how these latest ideas will help you develop a practical, successful marketing plan. Then enter this data in your marketing plan, with as much detail as needed to support your conclusions.

ENDNOTES

1. Michael Hunter, 'Currency movements hit Experian', *Financial Times*, 13 July 2012, www.ft.com; Adam Jones, 'Experian eyes banking newcomers', *Financial Times*, 13 July 2012, www.ft.com; Nick Goodway, 'Experian is on a high note thanks to Latin drive', *London Evening Standard*, 13 July 2012, www. standard.co.uk; www.experian.com; Matthew Chapman, 'Mobile data ignored by majority of UK business, says Experian', *Marketing*, 20 June 2012, www.marketingmagazine.co.uk; Katherine Levy, 'Experian hands £7m media account to PHD', *Campaign*, 5 July 2012, www.campaignlive.co.uk; 'Royal Mint uses Experian for 2012 campaigns', *Database Marketing*, 18 June 2012, http://www. dmarket.co.uk/a/royal-mint-uses-experian-for-2012-campaigns.

2. Christoph Rauwald, 'Rolls-Royce posts record sales', *Wall Street Journal*, 9 January 2012, www.wsj.com.

3. Mark Tisshaw, 'Rolls-Royce Wraith coupé teased-updated', *AutoCar*, 12 February 2013, www.autocar. co.uk; Anthony DeMarco, 'Bespoke Rolls-Royce Ghost sells in a day', *Forbes*, 26 August 2012, www.forbes.com.

4. Georg Kacher, 'Men and machines', *Automobile Magazine*, April 2012, p. 50.

5. Anatoly Temkin, 'Rolls-Royce sets second dealer in Russia on increasing sales', *Bloomberg Businessweek*, 28 June 2012, www.businessweek.com.

6. Mary K. Coulter, *Strategic Management in Action* (Upper Saddle River, NJ: Prentice Hall, 1998), Chapter 4.

7. Gwyn Topham, 'Virgin Atlantic planning Heathrow to Moscow flights', *Guardian*, 8 July 2012, www. guardian.co.uk; 'Virgin plans to add flights to

China', *Business Daily Update*, 15 June 2012, n.p.; Dan Thisdell, 'Branson's pickle', *Flight International*, 29 May 2012, n.p.; 'Virgin increases New York flights', *Travel & Tourism News*, 1 June 2012, n.p.; www.virgin-atlantic.com.

8. Elisabeth Sexton, 'Every click you make, they'll be watching you', *Brisbane Times*, 14 July 2012, www.brisbanetimes.com.au.

9. Anna Mukai and Masatsugu Horie, 'Toyota car-seat supplier says it gained new European client', *Bloomberg News*, 23 January 2012, www.bloomberg.com; Simon Warburton, 'Toyota Europe focuses on small supply chain to drive efficiency', *Just-Auto*, 1 July 2011, www.just-auto.com.

10. Quoted in 'Shutl champions transparency by taking customer feedback to Facebook', *Shutl press release*, 12 July 2012, www.shutl.co.uk/press-office. Other sources: 'Shutl asks customers for Facebook feedback', *Internet Retailing*, 13 July 2012, http://internetretailing.net; Stephan Lepitak, 'Maplin deal to aid Shutl growth to reach 85% of UK with service offer', 19 March 2012, www.thedrum.co.uk; Kevin J. O'Brien, 'Europe turns to the cloud', *New York Times*, 24 July 2011, www.nytimes.com.

11. 'Retailer Carrefour to sell stake in Greek joint venture', *BBC News*, 15 June 2012, www.bbc.co.uk.

12. 'Luxury brands untouched by euro zone crisis? Sales boom despite EU slump', *Economic Times (India)*, 9 February 2012, http://articles.economictimes.indiatimes.com.

13. Sally Williams, 'Fairytale ending: the rise of the British prom', *Telegraph*, 10 August 2012, www.telegraph.co.uk.

14. Sara Schonhardt, '7-Eleven finds a niche by adapting to Indonesian ways', *New York Times*, 28 May 2012, www.nytimes.com.

15. Madhumita Venkataramanan, 'Social-gifting site Wrapp is growing virally, targeted by German clones', *Wired*, 9 May 2012, www.wired.co.uk; Nivedita Bhattacharjee, 'Social gifting', *Reuters*, 30 April 2012, www.reuters.com; 'Wrapp prepares for introduction of social gifting in Japan', *China Weekly News*, 1 May 2012, n.p.; Vicki M. Young, 'Wrapp gifting service makes US debut', *WWD*, 30 April 2012, p. 6; Ronan Shields, 'Radar: Wrapp', *New Media Age Online*, 13 April 2012, n.p.; Ronan Shields, 'Brands eye social gifting as performance marketing channel', *New Media Age Online*, 24 April 2012, n.p.; Paul Skeldon, 'Social gift wrapping company Wrapp adds 13 new UK retail partners', *Internet Retailing*, 25 June 2012, http://internetretailing.net.

16. Rachit Vats, 'Walmart eyes 15 more stores in India with Bharti', *Hindustan Times*, 1 April 2012, www.hindustantimes.com.

17. Lisa A. Grimaldi, 'Mövenpick Hotels in Europe receive green certification', *Meetings and Conventions*, 21 March 2012, www.meetings-conventions.com.

18. Discussion based on theories in Michael Porter, *Competitive Advantage* (New York: Free Press, 1985), pp. 11–26.

19. Michiyo Nakamoto, 'Japan's king of casual smartens up', *Financial Times*, 15 July 2012, www.ft.com; Stephanie Clifford, 'As US retailers retreat, a Japanese chain sees an opening', *New York Times*, 22 May 2012, www.nytimes.com; Amy Corr, 'Uniqlo promotes dry mesh T-shirts with Pinterest', *Media Post*, 9 July 2012, www.mediapost.com; Imogen Fox, 'Uniqlo launches children's range', *Guardian*, 14 March 2012, www.guardian.co.uk; Chris Brook-Carter, 'Uniqlo searches for London flagship', *Retail Week*, 20 April 2012, www.retail-week.com; Tina Gaudoin, 'Uniqlo: Cheap and very cheerful', *Wall Street Journal*, 19 April 2012, www.wsj.com.

3 Analysing customers and markets

Learning outcomes

After studying this chapter, you will be able to:

- Understand why marketers examine markets according to definition, changes and share
- Explain the main influences on customer behaviour in consumer and business markets
- Describe how secondary and primary data are used in marketing planning

Application outcomes

After studying this chapter, you will be able to:

- Define and describe the market for a product
- Identify sources of information about consumer and business markets
- Calculate market share
- Analyse customer behaviour for marketing planning purposes

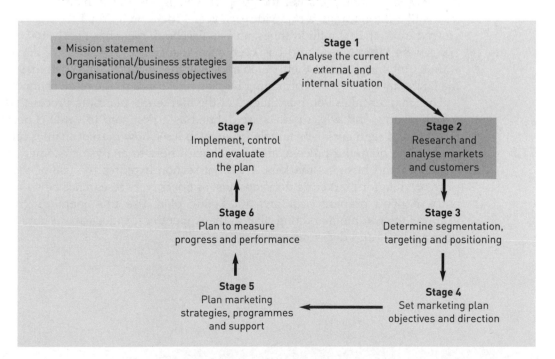

CHAPTER PREVIEW: MARKETING AT SPECSAVERS

What does Specsavers (www.specsavers.co.uk) know about its markets and customers? Headquartered in Guernsey, Specsavers and its local optician partners operate 1,400 shops in the United Kingdom, Australia, New Zealand, Scandinavia and continental Europe, with total turnover of £1.7 billion. Mary and Doug Perkins founded the company in 1984 after UK laws were changed to deregulate optometry and allow optometrists to advertise. They knew from earlier experience in the industry that consumers shopping for spectacles or contact lenses are interested in value as well as quality. Therefore, from the first day, Specsavers met this need by focusing on price and professionalism as its main competitive advantages. It also competes on the basis of style choice, because buying spectacles is a fashion decision as well as having a vision-correction purpose.

When Specsavers plans to enter new markets, it looks closely at demographics, consumer behaviour and attitudes towards competitors. Before opening its first shops in Australia, for example, Specsavers hired researchers to learn more about where consumers were currently buying eyewear, why they chose certain companies, how much they were paying, how they felt about wearing spectacles and what they thought about competitive marketing messages. The results helped Specsavers communicate its positioning as a professional provider of affordable fashion eyewear. It heavily promoted a 'two-for-one' price offer that supported its positioning and, through public relations, established high brand awareness and favourable brand attitudes on the basis of value.

Although the economic downturn slowed consumer spending in many categories, Specsavers' value positioning enabled it to attract more customers and increase sales, despite competitive pressure. Today, Specsavers is a leader in many of its markets, and it sells 12 million frames worldwide each year. Videos on its YouTube Channel have been viewed more than 3 million times, and its Facebook page has nearly 100,000 'likes'. Its Specsavers Sight Check app has been downloaded by thousands of consumers who want a quick way to test their vision and 'Ask the optician'. The chain has also become the UK's market leader in providing hearing aids through the retail channel.[1]

This chapter takes you into Stage 2 of the marketing planning process, starting with a look at how and why markets are defined as a first step towards choosing specific markets and segments to be targeted. Next you'll see how market share is calculated and used in the planning process; also, you'll learn how to analyse customer behaviour in consumer and business markets. The final section explores the use of secondary and primary data for marketing decisions, just as Specsavers researches new markets before entry. As you prepare your own marketing plan, use this chapter's checklists and examine the sample marketing plan in the Appendix for ideas about how to document your analyses and decisions.

ANALYSING CONSUMER AND BUSINESS MARKETS

People make a **market**, the group of potential customers for a good, service or other offering. The **consumer market** consists of individuals and families who buy goods and services for their own use. Specsavers' marketers are aiming to sell spectacles, contact lenses and hearing aids to the consumer market. The **business (organisational) market** consists of companies, institutions, non-governmental organisations (NGOs) and government agencies that buy goods and services for organisational use.

However, when you're marketing to businesses, remember that you're not dealing with faceless organisations, because buying decisions are, of course, made by people. Even when a company or institution develops an automatic system for reordering without human intervention, it still relies on a manager, employee or team to establish decision rules for when to buy, what to buy and from which supplier. As Figure 3.1 indicates, market analysis provides valuable background for understanding who might buy the product, what their needs are and what influences their buying behaviour – information you need to prepare an effective marketing plan.

During your preliminary analysis of consumer or business markets you'll examine three things: (1) market definition, (2) market changes and (3) market share.

Market definition

Defining the market helps you narrow the marketing focus to consumers or businesses that are qualified to be or already are buyers of a particular type of product. Within a given market, the broadest level of definition is the potential market, which has four subsets: the available, qualified available, target and penetrated markets.

The **potential market** is all the customers who may need, want or be interested in that good or service. For Specsavers, the available market would be all customers who need

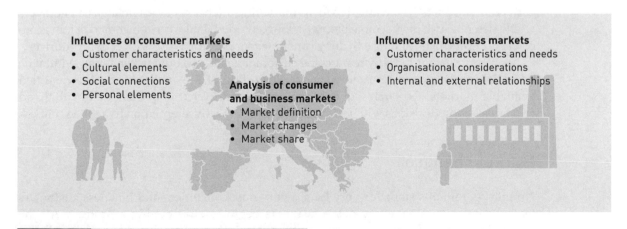

Influences on consumer markets
- Customer characteristics and needs
- Cultural elements
- Social connections
- Personal elements

Analysis of consumer and business markets
- Market definition
- Market changes
- Market share

Influences on business markets
- Customer characteristics and needs
- Organisational considerations
- Internal and external relationships

FIGURE 3.1   Consumer and business market analysis

spectacles or contact lenses to improve their vision. However, some customers in this market may be unaware of the product, some may have no access to it, some may not require its benefits, some may not be able to use it, and some may not be able to afford it. Thus, the potential market represents the *maximum* number of customers who might be interested in the product – but not the number who will *realistically* buy.

Part of the potential market is the **available market**, all the customers who are interested and have both adequate income and adequate access to the product. For Specsavers, the available market would be all customers who need vision correction and can afford spectacles or lenses and can visit a Specsavers location or its website. A subset of that is the **qualified available market**, all the customers who are qualified to buy based on product-specific criteria such as age (for alcohol and other products that may not legally be sold to under-age consumers). Car buyers need not have a driving licence, for instance, but they must be of age to sign legal contracts and, if borrowing to buy, be sufficiently credit-worthy to obtain a loan. For Specsavers, the qualified available market would be all consumers who have a vision-correction prescription or want one of the chain's opticians to examine their eyes and provide a prescription if necessary.

The **target market** is the segment of customers within the qualified available market that an organisation decides to serve. Specsavers' target market is customers with vision-correction needs who want to save money on spectacles or lenses, want many style choices and want the convenience of consulting an in-store optician. The smallest market of all is the **penetrated market**, all the customers in the target market who currently buy or have bought a specific type of product. The penetrated market for Specsavers consists of all customers in the target market who have previously purchased vision-correction products. Figure 3.2 shows how the five levels of market definition form a funnel to focus marketing activity on specific customer groups.

For planning purposes, define your potential market by more than the product. Many organisations use geography and customer description in their market definitions. 'The UK consumer market for vision-correction products' is a general description of one potential market for Specsavers. In plans to offer its products beyond UK borders, each new market would be defined geographically, such as 'the Australian consumer market for vision-correction products'. If it wanted to focus marketing attention on certain areas, Specsavers would describe each market more precisely: 'the New South Wales consumer market for vision-correction products' and 'the Sydney consumer market for vision-correction products'.

Now narrow your focus by researching customer needs and buying behaviour within the potential market, yielding a more specific definition of the available and the qualified available markets. Research will help you understand what your customers value and what marketing decisions will best support competitive differentiation in a given market.

Market changes

No market remains static for very long. Every day, consumers and business customers leave or enter an area; every day, consumers begin or stop buying a product. All the external factors in the marketing environment can influence market changes as well. For this reason, you will need to research expert projections and track overall market trends.

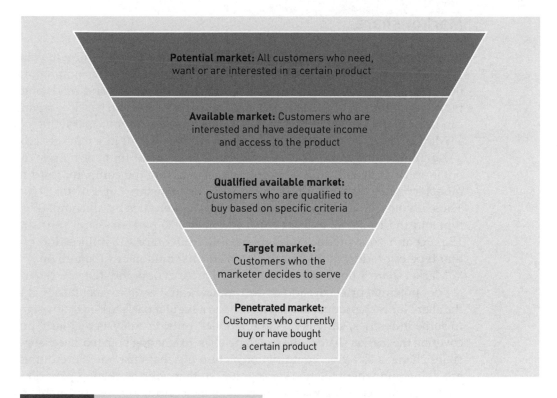

Potential market: All customers who need, want or are interested in a certain product

Available market: Customers who are interested and have adequate income and access to the product

Qualified available market: Customers who are qualified to buy based on specific criteria

Target market: Customers who the marketer decides to serve

Penetrated market: Customers who currently buy or have bought a certain product

FIGURE 3.2   Five levels of market definition

Two key changes that affect the size and nature of a market are:

- *Number of customers.* Is the consumer population (or number of businesses) increasing or decreasing, and by how much?

- *Purchases.* How many products are all customers in the industry estimated to buy in the next year and later years? How and why has the trend in purchases changed?

The purpose is to determine how changes, trends and projections are likely to affect customers in the market and the implications for your marketing decisions. For example, marketers for Philips India, a division of the Dutch corporation Philips, are projecting rapid population growth in India and economic changes that bring more consumers into the middle class. Based on this population growth, they project that hospitals, clinics and individuals will boost purchases of healthcare equipment and systems. Philips India has therefore acquired firms and invested heavily to market products for diagnosing and managing heart ailments and other conditions, earning high market share in cardio-vascular systems and revenues from the sale of medical equipment.[2]

Market share

Going beyond current and projected market size and trends, you will want to estimate your product's or brand's market share and the share held by competitors. Remember that your share will change as the market grows or shrinks and rivals enter, expand or reduce their presence, or leave. Still, market share serves as a baseline against which you can track market dynamics and measure the progress of your marketing plan results.

Market share is defined as the percentage of sales within a market accounted for by a company, brand or product, as calculated in terms of units or money (or both, if the data can be obtained). The basic formula is to divide the company's or brand's unit or monetary sales by the entire market's unit or monetary sales of that type of product. Thus, if you sell 3 million units and overall market sales by all competitors selling that type of product are 12 million units, you hold a 25 percent share. Your share would be 15 percent if your product sales totalled £15 million or €15 million and overall sales of that type of product in that market totalled £100 million or €100 million.

Market share is one of the vital signs of a product or brand that you can track over time to spot potential problems and opportunities. You'll want to calculate or at least estimate the share for each product in each market on a regular basis to detect any significant shifts. In some industries, such as cars and mobiles, outside analysts regularly publish reports covering the market share of the top companies. Examining both market changes and market share changes can give you a better picture of what customers are doing, what rivals are doing and where the market is going, so that your marketing plan does not involve attracting an increasingly large share of an ever-shrinking, less profitable market.

Marketers of web-browsing software, including Google (www.google.com), Microsoft (www.microsoft.com), Mozilla (www.mozilla.org) and Apple (www.apple.com), are very competitive with each other and constantly check reports issued by outside firms that measure market share. The 'browser wars' are important for brand reasons and because of the influence on consumers' choices of other computer- and mobile-related goods and services.

MARKETING IN PRACTICE: WEB BROWSERS

Microsoft's Internet Explorer once had a market share exceeding 90 percent. However, as competitors such as Mozilla's Firefox gained popularity, Internet Explorer lost market share little by little. Then Google introduced Chrome in 2008, using its enormous success as a search engine to lend Chrome instant recognition. Chrome changed the market-share balance just as sales of trendy Apple products such as the iPad, iPhone and Mac were on the rise, boosting Safari's share.

Beyond these broad trends, it's difficult to pinpoint the exact share of each browser because different firms use different systems to gauge usage. In spring 2012, StatCounter was reporting that Chrome's worldwide share was higher than Internet Explorer's share by less than one percentage point, with Firefox in third place and Safari as a distant fourth. This was the first report of Chrome leading the market, but it was made public just weeks after a different company, Net Applications, announced that Internet Explorer was by far the global market leader. Microsoft responded that Net Application's measurement procedure was more accurate; Google said only that market share mattered because 'everything we do lives on the web'. Two European firms reported that Internet Explorer's European market share was nearly twice that of Chrome, yet neither was tracking world-wide share.

Apart from the marketers behind the browsers, who else cares about share trends? Website developers keep an eye on the data because they aim to optimise sites for specific browsers in order to attract visitors and ensure that all features function properly. Competition regulators also follow share changes, especially when they're concerned about the competitive climate of a particular category or industry. In fact, EU competition regulators have been paying close attention to Microsoft's dominance in PC operating systems and now require the firm to offer Windows users a choice of web browsers rather than making Internet Explorer the default.[3]

Marketing plan analysis: If you were writing Google's Chrome marketing plan, what use would you make of the report that its market share was steadily increasing?

Bear in mind that changes in share are not the only indicators of competitive standing, nor do they necessarily warrant immediate attention. Companies usually include share among the metrics for measuring progress in marketing programme implementation and to signal the need for adjustments. This is discussed in **Chapters 11 and 12**.

ANALYSING CUSTOMERS IN CONSUMER MARKETS

Once you have a preliminary definition of the market, understand market changes and know your market share (or that of your main competitors), you're ready to look more closely at customer demographics, needs, buying behaviour and attitudes. What customers buy, as well as how and when they buy, can be influenced by different factors and experiences. Figure 3.3 shows the consumer decision-making process in simplified form, beginning when someone recognises a need and continuing through the post-purchase evaluation, which sometimes leads to a new round of need recognition. Marketing can influence consumer behaviour in each stage of this process. For example, your marketing might aim to stimulate need recognition, offer information about specific products and benefits related to the consumer's need, suggest criteria for evaluating competing offers, influence the timing of the purchase or reinforce the purchase as a good decision.

Although you may use aggregated data to form a picture of the average customer during your planning, technology is available to help you identify and understand customer behaviour at the individual level. To understand consumers as a prelude to developing market targeting and programmes, you should analyse characteristics and needs as well as cultural elements, social connections and personal and psychological elements (see Table 3.1).

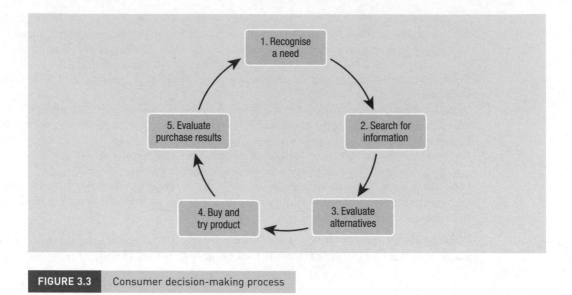

FIGURE 3.3   Consumer decision-making process

Table 3.1   Understanding behaviour in consumer markets

Customer characteristics and needs	Social connections
• Demographics such as age, occupation, family status • Problem that product will solve • Changes in stated/unstated needs • Customer-perceived value • Media-usage patterns	• Family and friends • Work associates • Organisations • Opinion leaders and influence network
Cultural elements	**Personal and psychological elements**
• Culture • Subculture • Class	• Life cycle • Lifestyle, psychographics • Motivation and attitudes

Characteristics and needs

Often some characteristic, such as gender, family status, age, education or ethnic background, affects what consumers need and buy. For example, Huggies and other disposable nappies are marketed to families with babies. Before conducting extensive marketing research, try to learn more about the characteristics of particular consumer markets from a variety of secondary sources.

As you assess consumers' needs, ask yourself the following questions:

- What problem do customers want to solve by buying a particular product?

- What are customers requesting now that they haven't requested in the past?

- What changes in need are suggested by developments revealed through internal and external audits of the business environment?

- Do customers have unstated needs and wants (such as boosting status or looking stylish) that can be uncovered through marketing research and satisfied through marketing?

Closely related is the value that consumers receive when they buy products to satisfy their needs. **Value** is defined as the difference customers perceive between the benefits they derive from a product and the total price they pay for the product. Customers perceive more value from a good or service that seems to deliver more or unique benefits for the money. *Virtual products* that exist in electronic form only – not the actual software but as digital extras purchased for social-media games or gifts – have value to the buyers because of their novelty and symbolism. When customers buy, these products also bring monetary value to their marketers. Zynga, the company behind such social games as FarmVille, derives much of its €912 million in annual turnover from players buying virtual products such as special game pieces.[4]

Cultural elements

The beliefs, customs and preferences of the culture in which consumers were raised – and the culture where they currently live – can have an influence on consumer buying behaviour. Don't make the mistake of assuming that customers everywhere have the same wants, needs and buying patterns as you do. Marketing research is a crucial way for marketers to avoid this misconception.

Within a larger culture are **subcultures**, each a discrete group that shares a particular ethnicity, religion or lifestyle. These groups can affect buying behaviour. As an example, many marketers see teens as a distinct global subculture. Consumers in this age group have much in common regardless of geography, including a shared interest in pop music and fashion. Television, social media such as YouTube and the popularity of mobile electronic devices have only intensified the commonalities of this subculture, which has an immense collective spending power (estimated at more than £7 billion in the UK alone).

College-age consumers are a specific subculture targeted by Jack Wills, the upmarket 'university outfitter' with £100 million in sales and dozens of stores in the UK. Co-founder Peter Williams wanted to create a quality fashion retail brand featuring British university styles. Now Jack Wills has stores in the US, Hong Kong and other international markets, plus a series of websites, all targeting the same subculture, supported by social media marketing on blogs, Facebook, Twitter, Soundcloud, Vimeo and Flickr.[5]

Class distinctions – more subtle in some cultures than in others – are yet another influence on consumer behaviour. Consumers in a certain class tend to buy and use products in similar ways. At the same time, consumers who want to emulate a different class – such as those who strive to move into a higher class – may adopt that class's buying or usage behaviours.

Social connections

Social connections such as family members, friends, work associates and non-work groups can influence how, what and when consumers buy. You will want to determine whether any of these connections are relevant to a particular product's purchase or usage and how they affect buying behaviour. Just as some consumers follow the buying behaviour of another class to which they aspire, others follow the buying behaviour of the social groups to which they aspire. Youngsters often imitate the clothing and accessory choices of their older siblings; employees seeking job advancement may imitate the attire of higher-level managers.

People who are especially admired or possess special skills may be seen as **opinion leaders** in a social group and therefore exert more influence over the purchasing decisions of others. Not surprisingly, marketers often single out opinion leaders for special marketing attention to promote their brands through key social connections. Athletes, musicians and actors are considered opinion leaders for fashion products and beverages, among other product categories. Thanks to social media, opinion leaders can have two-way conversations with hundreds or thousands of consumers within an **influence network** that can affect both attitudes and behaviour.[6]

Following the principle of marketing transparency, sponsorship of tweets or blogs (or any marketing activity) should be clearly disclosed. For example, just days before the 2012 Olympic Games began, Adidas sponsored a Twitter dialogue featuring influential football star David Beckham answering questions about his favourite sports memories. The hashtag #takethestage identified this as part of an ongoing Adidas campaign linked to the Olympic Games. Online and social media marketing such as this campaign are helping the company move towards its goal of increasing market share and passing Nike to become the UK market leader in sports shoes and apparel (see Table 3.2).[7]

Personal elements

The fourth category of influences in consumer markets relates to personal elements such as life cycle, lifestyle, motivation and attitudes. An adult's *life cycle* is his or her changing family status over time. People may be single, single parents, single but cohabiting (with or without children), engaged, married (with or without children), divorced (with or without children) and so on. Consumers have different needs, behaviour patterns and buying priorities in each of these life-cycle phases – which, in turn, translate into marketing opportunities.

Table 3.2	How Adidas uses online and social media marketing

Marketing element	Marketing purpose
Adidas UK home page (www.adidas.co.uk)	To demonstrate what the brand stands for, to inspire brand loyalty, to communicate product features and benefits, to facilitate purchases and to support the company's Olympic sponsorship
Adidas Twitter accounts (**@adidas**, sports-specific accounts such as **@adidasrunning**, and country-specific accounts such as **@adidasUS**)	To build a sense of community through online conversations, to show support for the Olympics, and to be able to quickly respond to customer comments and important events or issues
Adidas YouTube channel (www.youtube.com/user/adidas)	To tell the company's story, to show support for the Olympics, to link athletes and other endorsers to the brand via adverts and videos, to encourage positive brand attitudes and emotions, and to showcase special shoe and apparel styles
Adidas Facebook page (www.facebook.com/adidas)	To engage brand fans in social conversations, to promote Olympic sponsorship, to generate brand buzz and to multiply the impact of other marketing activities

Lifestyle is the pattern of living reflecting how consumers spend their time or want to spend their time. Through research, you can learn more about how lifestyle influences what and when purchases are made in your market, how purchase transactions are planned and completed, who is involved in the purchase and other aspects of consumer buying behaviour. By analysing consumer behaviour using a complex set of lifestyle variables related to activities, interests and opinions – collectively known as **psychographic characteristics** – you can learn more about what drives consumer behaviour.

Psychological factors such as motivation and attitudes are also important influences on consumer buying. **Motivation** is the internal force that drives a consumer to act in a certain way and make certain purchases as a way of satisfying needs and wants. **Attitudes** are the consumer's assessment of and emotions about a product, brand or something else, which can affect actions. Understanding how such factors drive consumer behaviour gives you a solid foundation for making decisions about who to target, where a product should be distributed and so on. Innocent Drinks (www.innocentdrinks.co.uk) successfully uses cheeky humour in marketing to influence consumers' attitudes towards its healthy, tasty products.

MARKETING IN PRACTICE: INNOCENT

Innocent's mission is to 'make delicious, natural, healthy food and drinks which help people live well and die old'. Majority-owned by Coca-Cola, the £165 million company is well known for marketing fruit smoothies, juices and vegetable dishes with 'no nasties' such as artificial ingredients (as the brand name implies). The top-selling UK smoothie brand, Innocent was the official smoothie brand of the 2012 Olympics, thanks in part to Coca-Cola's financial and marketing muscle.

Innocent's marketing mixes humour with a touch of irony to influence the attitudes of consumers who may not realise that healthy foods can be full of flavour, fun and convenient. The brand logo is simple and hand-drawn, a halo over a face, nothing like the typical corporate logo. The headquarters building is named Fruit Towers. Innocent's labels feature humorous sayings because the co-founders originally had no money for advertising and wanted to catch the attention of customers. 'So we'd write silly things, sometimes delivering a subtle message about how natural the products were but sometimes just delivering a load of nonsense,' recalls Richard Reed, one of the founders.[8]

The marketing doesn't just aim to shape attitudes, it plays up Innocent's commitment to sustainability and transparency. One promotion bundled seed packs with children's smoothies to show children how easy it is to grow their own food. Another, in partnership with Disney, included online, on-pack and TV promotions highlighting the fun of eating fruit, a key ingredient in Innocent's products. Innocent's blog and website follow the slightly cheeky tone, as do the names of its charitable projects, such as the Big Knit and Buy One, Get One Bee. Customers smile, they participate and they buy, adding to the growth as Innocent expands throughout Europe and beyond.[9]

Marketing plan analysis: Which aspects of consumer behaviour should Innocent pay special attention to when preparing a marketing plan?

ESSENTIAL CHECKLIST NO. 5:
ANALYSING CUSTOMERS IN CONSUMER MARKETS

This checklist will guide you through the stage of marketing planning in which you must research and analyse information about consumers. Answer the questions in the spaces provided, putting a tick next to each as you finish it. If your marketing plan is for a start-up or a hypothetical company, use this checklist to note where you might obtain the information you need and ideas about how to research appropriate details.

☐ What consumer needs must the product and product category address?

☐ How can customers in each consumer market be described (by demographics, geography, etc.)?

☐ How is customer behaviour affected by cultural elements such as subculture and class?

☐ How is customer behaviour affected by social connections such as family, friends and online communities?

☐ How is customer behaviour affected by personal elements such as lifestyle, motivation and attitudes?

☐ What do these influences mean for segmentation, targeting and marketing decisions?

ANALYSING CUSTOMERS IN BUSINESS MARKETS

Individuals or groups make buying decisions for businesses, government agencies and non-governmental organisations. Sometimes these decisions involve huge sums of money and months of internal review spanning multiple management layers. Business buying behaviour is generally influenced by the organisation's characteristics and needs, relationships inside and outside the organisation, and considerations unique to each organisation and its external environment (see Table 3.3).

Table 3.3 Understanding behaviour in business markets

Customer characteristics and needs	Internal and external relationships	Organisational and external considerations
• Industry classification • Turnover • Workforce size • Facilities location • Geographic focus • Customer-perceived value	• Buying centre participants • Decision process • Supplier relations • Customer relations	• Objectives • Budgets and buying cycle • Buying policies and procedures • Share and growth • Competitive situation • Other external factors

Characteristics and needs

For your marketing plan to be successful, you need to understand the unique character-istics, buying requirements and challenges of the organisations in the business markets you are considering. Try to determine the common needs and concerns of organisations in each industry and see which characteristics affect these needs (and how). One way to do this is by categorising organisations according to characteristics such as type of industry, annual turnover, number of employees, location of facilities and geographic focus. Small businesses frequently have different needs (and smaller budgets) than large businesses, for example; companies that serve localised markets have different needs than multinational corporations. Industries that are closely tied to economic conditions, such as automotive manufacturing and residential construction, often have different buying patterns depending on the strength of the economy.

The European Community's Eurostat system provides a standardised method for researching, describing and categorising statistics by industry. Similarly, the North American Industry Classification System (NAICS) provides a method for researching the characteristics of companies in specific industries in the United States, Mexico and Canada. Data organised according to UN industry standard classifications and other international and national industry standards systems are available as well.

To gather more data about industries, characteristics of businesses, non-profit organ-isations or government agencies and business products, you can consult numerous sources, including national and international trade organisations, country consulates, multinational banks, university sources, magazines, newspapers and other publications that follow international business developments.

Organisational and environmental considerations

Although a few organisations buy without budgets, most plan ahead by budgeting for certain purchases during a specified period. Thus, after gathering and analysing general data about a business market, your next step is to learn something about the size of each organisation's budget and the timing of its purchases, which can vary widely within an industry. New and fast-growing businesses are likely to make more frequent purchases than businesses that are retrenching, for instance.

Think about the company's environmental influences, including its market share situation, its objectives and its competitive situation, which can influence what, when and how much the organisation buys. US-based Microsoft (www.microsoft.com), one of the world's largest software companies, researches the automotive industry very carefully when planning for marketing to individual manufacturers.

MARKETING IN PRACTICE: MICROSOFT

Microsoft understands that the automotive industry is highly competitive and that each manufacturer wants its vehicles to have distinctive (if not exclusive) features that meet the needs of consumer and commercial buyers. One of the biggest trends is towards 'connected' vehicles that offer drivers easy, hands-free access to communications, entertainment and navigation functions. This is so important a trend that Daimler's CEO recently observed that car companies will need a 'connected' vehicle strategy to prosper in the future.

The specific problem Microsoft can address is how to help manufacturers connect these diverse in-vehicle functions (some built into the vehicle and some on the driver's mobile or other digital device) and provide a safe, reliable, driver-friendly and branded interface. For example, Microsoft worked with Ford to develop voice-dictation technology as the basis of the SYNC connectivity system, a Ford exclusive. Drivers can speak normally in any of 19 languages – geared to Ford's geographic markets – and the SYNC system will route the voice command to a mobile to make a call or to an iPod to play a song, based on Microsoft software and on wireless technology.

Connected vehicles represent an opportunity for Microsoft to work with other manufacturers. For Nissan's Leaf car, Microsoft created a Windows-based locator system so drivers can quickly find local recharging stations. Buyers of electric cars appreciate this function, which buyers of fuel-powered cars don't need. Microsoft also partnered with Nissan to develop a new information system, customisable for different geographic regions, that helps dealers manage customer relationships. By supporting dealers' marketing efforts, Nissan can make progress towards its worldwide growth goals. And because Microsoft is aware of such organisational and environmental considerations, its marketing has been successful in the automobile industry.[10]

Marketing plan analysis: Do you agree with Microsoft's marketing approach of targeting each carmaker individually? Why or why not?

Also research the buying policy and procedure, buying cycle and policies. If a multinational corporation's policy is to encourage decentralised or local buying, for example, you will have to plan for communicating with more buyers than if the policy is to centralise buying at the headquarters level. If a business insists on online buying, that policy must also be taken into account during the marketing planning process.

Budgeting and buying cycles are particularly important factors for business-to-business (B2B) marketers that sell to non-governmental organisations and government agencies. Meanwhile, growing cities and countries tend to increase their annual budgets for infrastructure improvements, creating opportunities for construction companies, telecommunications firms and other suppliers.

For large purchases in particular, business customers tend to require considerable information before narrowing their alternatives and selecting a good or service that meets their specifications. Knowing this, General Electric has been making good use of social media by posting videos and papers about industry issues and new scientific developments. The company also wants to stimulate social media dialogue to better understand business customers' needs and requirements. Not long ago, GE Energy asked its customers in the food and beverage industry to submit their most challenging problems via social media. GE Energy's employees analysed the problems and then posted their comments about potential solutions, keeping the conversation going and providing additional information for decision-makers to consider.[11]

Internal and external relationships

Many internal and external relationships can affect an organisation's buying patterns. Particularly in large organisations, a group of managers or employees may be responsible for certain purchases. Different individuals within this **buying centre** play different roles in the buying process, as shown in Table 3.4. To illustrate, when marketing its cloud computing services, Amazon.com recognises that information technology managers are generally the deciders for such corporate purchases, although executives in other departments may influence choice and budget criteria. However, not every member of the buying centre will participate in every purchase.

Another important point is that most if not all buying centre participants can access information online or via social media, making the gatekeeper function less of an obstacle than in the pre-Internet age. In addition, firms like Fujitsu, Ernst & Young and Orange are staying in touch with various buying centre participants through online or printed newsletters that deliver industry information and cover specialised topics. Ongoing communications help these firms position themselves as experts in their fields and effectively engage customers throughout the buying cycle. Applying the concept of co-creation, Fujitsu recently published a free book with ideas and content submitted by information executives who work for businesses on its advisory board.[12]

Each participant's individual situation (age, education, job position and so forth) also affects the buying decision. Thus, you should investigate relationships within the buying

Table 3.4	How buying centre participants influence purchases
Buying centre participant	**Influence on purchases**
Users	Often initiate the buying process and help define specifications.
Influencers	Often define specifications and provide information for evaluating alternatives.
Buyers	Have the formal authority to select suppliers and negotiate purchases.
Deciders	Have the formal or informal power to select or approve suppliers.
Gatekeepers	Control the flow of information to other buying centre participants.

Source: Adapted from *Principles of Marketing*, 4e, Pearson (Kotler, P., Wang, V., Saunders, J. and Armstrong, G.) 309, How buying centre participants influence purchases, adapted from Principles of Marketing, 4e, Part 1, p. 309, Pearson (Kotler, P., Wang, V., Saunders, J. and Armstrong, G. 2005) p. 309. ISBN 10: 0273684566.

centre, understand the participants and the decision process so you can market to the right participants at the right time. This is especially vital when the purchase represents a major commitment of money, time and changeover for a business customer.

Check the organisation's relations with current suppliers to find out whether long-term contracts are the norm, whether certain future purchases are already committed to current suppliers, what standards suppliers are expected to meet and how suppliers are evaluated. In some cases, a company cannot become a supplier until it has met certain criteria and been approved. Even if prior approval is not needed, you should determine what criteria the business customer uses to select suppliers so you can plan accordingly.

Clearly, cost is not the only criterion in a B2B buying decision. Staff expertise, quality, reliable delivery and other considerations can be important criteria by which buying centre participants choose among competing suppliers. In addition, by looking at how an organisation deals with its customers, you can get a sense of the value you can add to help satisfy your customers' customers.

ESSENTIAL CHECKLIST NO. 6:
ANALYSING CUSTOMERS IN BUSINESS MARKETS

If you're preparing to target a business market, this checklist will guide you through the planning in which you research and analyse information about business customers. Simply put a tick by each question, one by one, as you write answers in the spaces provided. If your marketing plan is for a start-up or a hypothetical company, use this checklist to note information you can obtain and ideas about how to research additional details, including possible data sources.

☐ What customer needs must the product and product category address?

_____

☐ How can customers in each business market be described (by demographics, buying policies, etc.)?

_____

☐ Who participates in the buying centre and what is each participant's role?

_____

☐ How does each business customer solicit, qualify and assess suppliers?

_____

☐ How do current supplier arrangements affect competition for orders?

_____

☐   What other relationships and considerations affect buying behaviour in this business market?

☐   What do these influences mean for your segmentation, targeting and marketing activities aimed at the business market?

RESEARCHING MARKETS AND CUSTOMERS

When researching markets and customers, you will usually start by consulting **secondary data**, information previously collected for another purpose. You can glean basic facts and figures from secondary research more quickly and cheaply than through **primary data**, data from studies undertaken to address specific marketing questions or situations. When using secondary research, check that the information is current, comes from a legitimate and unbiased source, can be verified through another source and can be clarified (if necessary) through contact with sources.

Primary research is particularly useful for gaining detailed knowledge about issues of great concern to customers. Retail giant Asda conducts numerous studies to understand customers' decision-making priorities. For instance, its Mumdex survey of 2,100 mothers revealed that these customers had made lifestyle changes to deal with the recent economic downturn and placed a high value on not overspending. Asda also asked thousands of customers (from all demographic groups) over a nine-month period about their attitudes towards sustainability. It found that 96 percent care about ecological issues and 70 percent say they are particularly concerned over sustainability. Such primary research helps Asda better plan its products, pricing and promotions.[13]

Online research is increasingly popular because it's not costly, it can be implemented easily and it yields results quickly. For example, some sites use a pop-up screen or follow-up email after a purchase to request that visitors complete a brief survey to provide feedback.[14] Remember, however, that the results will not be entirely representative of a product's market, because the views of many consumers and businesses that don't use the Internet or prefer not to answer online surveys are excluded from online research. Still, online surveys and analyses of unsolicited consumer comments posted on Twitter and other social media can give marketers clues to attitudes, brand reactions and purchase intentions.

Ethnographic research – observing customers' behaviour in real situations rather than in experimental surroundings – has become increasingly important for learning about needs and preferences not easily articulated. Intel, which makes computer chips and networking equipment, has dozens of researchers travelling the globe to observe how consumers use digital devices in their daily lives. By analysing the data researchers collect about how customers actually behave at home, at work or on the high street, Intel identifies everyday problems that its technology can solve and looks for clues to future products for different markets.[15]

A related technique is **behavioural tracking**, monitoring what consumers and business-people do online as they visit websites, click on ads and fill virtual shopping trolleys. The purpose is better targeting and more personalised communications. However, concern over privacy issues has led to legal and regulatory guidelines that limit how tracking is conducted and how information is shared. The EU Directive on Privacy and Electronic Communications, for example, requires websites to obtain visitors' permission to use cookies for tracking purposes.[16]

Marketers for major corporations are beginning to apply **neuromarketing**, using brain science and body responses to investigate and understand consumer reactions to marketing activities. Unilever, for example, used neuromarketing when redesigning the package and labelling for its Axe body wash. It asked consumers to wear special spectacles so that researchers could track their eye and body movements as they looked at body wash products on a virtual store shelf. Based on this eye-tracking study, Unilever modified the Axe package to be straight instead of curvy, enlarged the words on the label and placed the brand's stylised X on a bright blue background to attract attention. Researching consumer reaction to such changes through objective measurements and in a virtual setting saved Unilever time and money, speeding the redesigned product to market.[17]

Indicate any need for primary research in your marketing plan and allow for the time and money in your schedules and budgets. Also plan for research to test programmes and track marketing progress, including customer satisfaction surveys, market-share studies and promotion pre- and post-tests. These kinds of studies can yield insights to help you make decisions about segmentation, targeting, positioning and the marketing mix.

CHAPTER SUMMARY

The overall market for a particular type of good or service consists of the potential market (all customers who may be interested in that product) and, inside that, the available market (those with income and access). A narrower definition is the qualified available market (those who meet product-related criteria for buying); narrower still is the target market (which the organisation wants to serve), and narrowest of all is the penetrated market (customers who buy or have bought that type of product). Then marketers dig deeper to research and analyse market changes and market share.

During planning for consumer markets, look at (1) needs stemming, in part, from characteristics such as age; (2) national or regional culture, subculture and class; (3) social connections; and (4) personal and psychological elements. Three main influences on business markets are (1) organisational characteristics; (2) organisational and environmental considerations; and (3) internal and external relationships. Secondary data is information previously collected for a different purpose; primary data is collected to address specific questions or situations relevant to the marketing plan.

CASE STUDY: MICHELIN

France's Michelin (www.michelin.co.uk/) has increased worldwide turnover beyond €20 billion through skilful marketing of tyres (plus maps and travel guides) to both businesses and consumers. With a marketing presence in 170 countries, Michelin sells 184 million tyres every year and holds a 14.8 percent share of the global tyre market. Although the company is more than 100 years old, its marketing is very twenty-first century: The Michelin man even has his own Facebook page, Twitter account and YouTube channel, with safety and promotional messages for all audiences.

Michelin's marketers have studied the different characteristics and needs of individuals and organisations that buy tyres for cars, racing cars, SUVs, trucks, motorcycles, aircraft, agricultural vehicles and earth-moving equipment. Internal sales records show that commercial customers generally buy in higher volume during periods of economic expansion and place fewer or smaller orders during economic downturns. Customer research shows that safety, performance, cost, durability, reliability, ecological impact, compliance with regulations and effect on fuel consumption are key concerns for tyre buyers.

To be sure its tyres meet customers' needs, Michelin test-drives them on all types of vehicles, in every season and every weather situation, and on every road or off-road surface. Michelin also tests tyres in Finland under cold-weather conditions and on construction equipment under quarry conditions in Spain. Even innovative products that address customer problems sometimes run into trouble, however. When Michelin introduced PAX run-flat tyres to reduce the danger and inconvenience of punctures, few garages invested in the equipment needed to repair them. Customers complained about the difficulty of locating a local repair shop after a blowout; fewer automobile manufacturers than expected chose PAX as original equipment for their vehicles. Eventually, Michelin discontinued further development of the PAX technology and turned its attention to other products.[18]

Case questions

1. How would you define the qualified available market for Michelin's SUV tyres? What are the key qualifying criteria for this market definition?

2. If you were a Michelin executive considering a new version of PAX run-flat tyres, what research would you conduct during the planning stage? Be specific about who you would include in the research and what kinds of questions you'd need answered.

APPLY YOUR KNOWLEDGE

To reinforce your knowledge of Stage 2 of the marketing planning process, research the general definition of a particular market. You might focus on the consumer market for spectacles or mobile phones, for instance, or the business market for office furniture or specialised software. Prepare a brief oral or written report summarising your thoughts.

- How can your chosen market be described broadly in terms of product, geography and demographics?

- What characteristics relevant to the product might influence the behaviour of consumers or organisations in this market?

- What, specifically, are the main influences on buying behaviour in this market? Refer to the checklists in this chapter as you answer this question.

- How much influence do opinion leaders have on buyers in this product category? Which social media are important for influencing buyers in this market?

- What have you learned that would affect your decisions if you were preparing a marketing plan for this market?

BUILD YOUR OWN MARKETING PLAN

Continue the marketing planning process for a hypothetical organisation or an actual organisation you have chosen by broadly describing the market and the influences on customer buying behaviour. Use the two checklists in this chapter as you build your marketing plan. First, identify the five levels of market definition that apply, from the potential market to the penetrated market. Also determine the criteria by which you would consider customers to be in the available market and in the qualified available market.

Next, research the most important changes affecting this market. Also look at market share trends and the major influences on customer needs and behaviour in this consumer or business market. How do cultural elements, social connections, personal elements or psychological elements affect the consumer's buying behaviour? What social media do opinion leaders and customers in your product category typically use? If your plan is for a business market, how do customer characteristics and needs, internal and external relationships, and organisational and environmental considerations affect buying behaviour? Finally, list any primary and secondary data you would like to have to better understand your markets, and look for recent, reliable online sources of information about customers such as yours. Be sure to document what you have learned and the implications for your planning decisions.

ENDNOTES

1. 'Specsavers signs licensing deal for iPad app', *Optometry Today*, 23 January 2013, www. optometry.co.uk; 'Specsavers launches sight check app', *The Drum*, 11 July 2012, www.thedrum.co.uk; '"Incredibly tough year", but Specsavers' revenues up 11%', *Guernsey Press*, 3 July 2012, www.this-isguernsey.com; James Thompson, 'The secrets to Specsavers' super growth', *Smart Company Australia*, 16 May 2011, www.smartcompany.com.au; 'Launching the world's largest optical retailer', *Golden Target Entry 2009, University of Technology Sydney*, 2009, www.lib.uts.edu/au; www.specsavers.co.uk.

2. 'Philips India sets up healthcare manufacturing facility in Chakan', *Business Standard (India)*, 15 June 2012, www.business-standard.com/india; 'Philips to set up healthcare R&D', *Times of India*, 1 September 2010, http://articles.timesofindia. indiatimes.com; 'From chulhas to defibrillators: can Philips India be all things to all people?', *India Knowledge@Wharton*, 30 July 2009, http://knowledge. wharton.upenn.edu/india; Writankar Mukherjee, 'Philips to make India hub for medical equipment manufacturing', *The Economic Times*, 8 April 2009, http://economictimes.indiatimes.com.

3. 'Microsoft says fixing browser issue as EU opens probe', *Reuters*, 17 July 2012, www.reuters.com; Daniel Ionescu, 'Google Chrome overtakes Internet Explorer', *PC World*, 21 May 2012, www.pcworld. com; Paul McDougall, 'Internet Explorer gains market share in March', *InformationWeek*, 3 April 2012, www.informationweek.com; Carl Bialik, 'Statistically speaking: browser wars escalate', *Wall Street Journal*, 29 June 2012, www.wsj.com; Carl Bialik, 'Keeping score in the browser wars', *Wall Street Journal*, 29 June 2012, www.wsj.com.

4. Francine McKenna, 'How Zynga, Facebook and Groupon's go-to auditor rewrites accounting rules', *Forbes*, 23 April 2012, www.forbes.com; Kim-Mai Cutler, 'Zynga beats Q1 estimates', *TechCrunch*, 26 April 2012, www.techcrunch.com.

5. 'London's Kevin Tewis – Jack Wills marketing', *Chartered Institute of Marketing Greater London*, 1 April 2012, http://www.cimlondon.co.uk/blog; Julia Werdigier, 'With the eagerness of youth', *New York Times*, 1 July 2012, www.nytimes.com.

6. Tracy L. Tuten and Michael R. Solomon, *Social Media Marketing* (Upper Saddle River, NJ: Prentice Hall, 2013), p. 90.

7. 'David Beckham teams with Adidas to surprise people posing in photo booth', *The Drum*, 24 July 2012, www.thedrum.co.uk; Petah Marian, 'Sportswear brands pin hopes on Olympic performance', *Just Style*, 18 July 2012, www.just-style.com.

8. Quoted in Courtney Rubin, 'Building England's ethical, healthy and slightly cheeky beverage brand', *Inc.*, July 2010, www.inc.com.

9. Loulla-Mae Eleftheriou-Smith, 'Innocent partners with Disney to talk to kids about fruit', *Marketing*, 10 July 2012, www.marketingmagazine.co.uk; Michelle Russell, 'UK: Innocent readies kids seed campaign', *Just Drinks*, 23 February 2012, www. just-drinks.com; Ian Quinn, 'Coke puts Innocent in the Olympic Spotlight', *Grocer*, 3 December 2011, p. 5; Lara O'Reilly, 'Q&A with Innocent marketing director Thomas Delabriere', *Marketing Week*, 24 February 2011, www.marketingweek.co.uk; www.innocentdrinks.co.uk.

10. Ken Liu, 'Ford, Microsoft jointly promote sync connectivity technologies at Computex Taipei', *Taiwan Economic News*, 5 June 2012, n.p.; 'Q&A with Microsoft', *Just Auto*, 27 June 2012, www.just-auto.com; 'Microsoft and Nissan link for next-generation dealer management system', *Entertainment Closeup*, 22 December 2011, www.closeupmedia.com.

11. Christopher Bosford and Kate Maddox, 'Leading Edge focuses on new social models', *BtoB*, 16 July 2012, p. 3.

12. David Burrows, 'How to grow content marketing footprint', *Marketing Week*, 12 July 2012, p. 27.

13. 'Asda's Mumdex survey could shape future marketing decisions', *The Drum*, 23 February 2012, www.thedrum.co.uk; Julian Walker-Palin, 'Consumers are making sustainable choices, all they need is a little guidance', *Guardian*, 25 January 2012, www.guardian.co.uk.

14. Kate Hilpern, 'How to use market research tools', *The Marketer*, 29 June 2012, www.themarketer.co.uk.

15. Brendan Shanahan, 'Research gets deep', *The Australian*, 8 August 2011, www.theaustralian.com.au.

16. Sooraj Shah, 'Analysis: EU cookie law puts analytics under scrutiny', *Computing UK*, 16 July 2012, www.computing.co.uk.

17. Emily Glazer, 'The eyes have it: marketers now track shoppers' retinas', *Wall Street Journal*, 12 July 2012, www.wsj.com.

18. David Williams, 'Michelin: Tyre firm or publisher?' *The Telegraph Online*, 18 July 2012, www.telegraph.co.uk; Simon Warburton, 'Interview: Michelin marketing director Gary Guthrie', *Just Auto*, 4 July 2012, www.just-auto.com; Rita McGrath, 'Anatomy of a failed launch', *Harvard Business Review*, 13 August 2010, http://blogs.hbr.org; Ron Adner, 'Case Study: How Michelin's new tyres fell flat', *Financial Times*, 3 April 2012, www.ft.com; Chrisopher Jensen, 'Michelin giving up on PAX run-flat tire', *New York Times*, 20 April 2008, www.nytimes.com; www.michelin.com.

4 Segmenting, targeting and positioning

Learning outcomes

After studying this chapter, you will be able to:

- Explain the benefits of segmentation, targeting and positioning
- Identify segmentation variables for consumer and business markets
- Describe undifferentiated, differentiated, concentrated and individualised target marketing
- Discuss the criteria for effective positioning

Application outcomes

After studying this chapter, you will be able to:

- Apply segmentation variables in consumer and business markets
- Evaluate segments for marketing attention in your plan
- Choose a targeting approach for market coverage in your plan
- Develop a meaningful positioning for marketing planning purposes

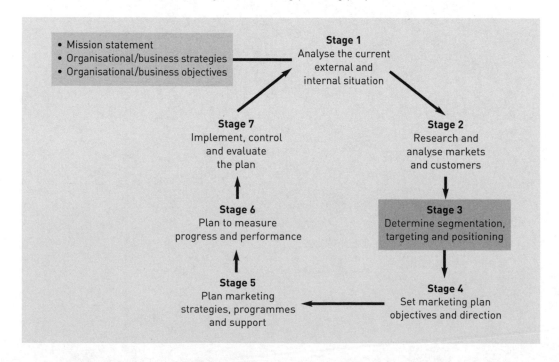

CHAPTER PREVIEW: MARKETING AT VOLKSWAGEN

Volkswagen (www.volkswagenag.com) is speeding towards its long-term goal of increasing vehicle sales to 10 million per year by 2018, thanks to the careful targeting of its twelve distinctly different automotive brands: Audi, Bentley, Bugatti, Ducati, Lamborghini, Man, Porsche, Scandia, Seat, Skoda, VW and VW Commercial. Man and VW Commercial make lorries and buses for business and municipal buyers, Ducati makes high-performance motorcycles and the others make cars and SUVs. Each model marketed under each brand has been designed to appeal to a specific group of customers.

For example, the ultra-upmarket sports car Bugatti Veyron is marketed to high-income consumers who are passionate about driving performance and appreciate the elegance and engineering of a car designed in the Grand Prix tradition. At the other extreme, Volkswagen's low-priced Skoda is marketed to price-sensitive consumers who want affordable yet reliable transportation. Skoda's combination of benefits and attributes fits the needs of first-time buyers in China and other developing countries where the company seeks higher market share. Volkswagen also knows that perceptions of quality and status can influence purchasing patterns. Its Audi and Bentley brands appeal to affluent consumers in China who want to buy luxury foreign cars with a reputation for quality and engineering. And in India, it is accelerating sales by offering stylish, mid-sized cars with high-tech features for image-conscious young buyers.[1]

As Volkswagen adds to its brand portfolio, it may one day have a vehicle to meet the needs of any and every customer. For now, the company knows it can't market to everyone, everywhere. Instead, it studies its customers, groups them according to similarities and differences, then selects specific groups for marketing attention, brand by brand – as in Stage 3 of the marketing planning process. This chapter explains how the market segmentation process works and how marketers use targeting to reach out to certain customers. Finally, you'll see how to apply positioning for competitive power. Use this chapter's two checklists as you prepare to evaluate segments for marketing attention and plan your positioning.

BENEFITS OF SEGMENTATION, TARGETING AND POSITIONING

Market segmentation involves grouping consumers or business customers within a market into smaller segments based on similarities in needs, attitudes or behaviour that marketing can address. As you saw in the opening example, Volkswagen segments its markets on the basis of income, attitudes, behaviour and other factors. By eliminating inappropriate markets and identifying promising segments for more thorough research, the company can better understand customers and more effectively respond to their needs. Because local, national and global markets are increasingly competitive these days, marketers of all sizes must know how to distinguish between different customer groups in preparation for meeting stated and unstated needs through marketing.

Segmentation also helps Volkswagen decide which segments to target for marketing activities, and in what order. Demographics indicate that the middle class is growing rapidly in China and India, for example, making those countries good places to market mid-priced cars, not just low-end budget models. Having a process for determining which customer groups should be given priority marketing attention is especially important in light of the budget pressures and competition most marketers face today. Finally, the knowledge gained during segmentation helps the firm determine how to create a meaningful and competitively distinctive position in the minds of the targeted customers (see Figure 4.1).

Segmentation is useful for marketing planning when:

- the customers within each segment have something identifiable in common;
- different segments have different responses to marketing efforts;
- the customers in segments can be reached through marketing;
- competitive advantage can be gained by focusing on segments;
- segments are sufficiently large or potentially profitable to warrant attention.

A segment may consist of millions of people, yet still be a select subset of a much larger market. Customers within each segment will have similar behaviour and needs or be seeking the same benefits from a product. Taking segmentation one step further, you may be able to distinguish **niches**, small subsegments of customers with distinct needs or requirements that can be profitably satisfied. The subsegment of customers who enjoy regionally or locally brewed ales, for example, is a relatively small part of the overall segment of beer buyers. The UK's Ilkley Brewery targets this niche with award-winning, hand-crafted ales. Founded in 2009, Ilkley Brewery is growing so rapidly that in 18 months, it nearly doubled its output and now distributes its speciality and seasonal ales through Booths, Morrisons and Harvey Nichols.[2]

Taken to the extreme, you may be able to segment a market to create niches of individual customers. In the past, marketing to such small niches would not be profitable. Now you can use technology to discern the specific needs, behaviours and responses of individual consumers or business customers. In some industries, such as jet engines, the potential size of and profit from a single order make it worthwhile to segment and target single-customer niches or, in large markets, to individualise marketing on a mass basis.

THE MARKET SEGMENTATION PROCESS

As you create your marketing plan, you'll follow three steps to segmenting a market, as Figure 4.1 indicates. The first is to choose the market to be segmented, the second is to apply appropriate segmentation variables and evaluate segments for marketing attention, and the third is to select your coverage approach for targeting chosen segments. Your decisions in all three steps depend on understanding your mission and long-term goals as well as on detailed, current information drawn from internal and external audits (see **Chapter 2**), plus your analyses of markets and customers (see **Chapter 3**).

Market and customer research

Market segmentation

1. Choose a market
2. Apply segmentation variables
3. Evaluate segments
4. Select and rank segments for marketing attention

Benefits

1. Eliminates markets that are inaccessible or inappropriate
2. Creates segments of customers with similar needs or behaviour yet different responses to marketing
3. Improves marketing efficiency
4. Identifies opportunities, threats and marketing priorities

Targeting

1. Determine target market coverage
2. Create personas for targeting

Benefits

1. Guides development of appropriate marketing activities
2. Adds a human dimension and helps marketers visualise each segment's customers

Positioning

1. Decide on point(s) of differentiation
2. Communicate positioning

Benefits

1. Highlights attributes that customers find meaningful in the competitive context
2. Reinforces differentiation, enhances consistency of marketing

Marketing activities

FIGURE 4.1   Applying segmentation, targeting and positioning

Choose the market

With your market definitions as a starting point, you begin the segmentation process by determining which markets you will investigate further and which you will eliminate. Although the specific criteria differ from organisation to organisation, you may want to consider eliminating markets based on:

- formidable legal, political, social or competitive pressures;
- extreme logistical difficulties;
- lack of purchasing power or other serious economic challenges;
- troubling ethical controversies;
- persistent ecological concerns.

For years, many marketers eliminated Vietnam from their list of viable markets because of trade barriers and other political and legal difficulties. However, once Vietnam simplified its business laws, joined the World Trade Organisation, improved its transportation infrastructure and lowered trade barriers, the country rejoined the list of markets being considered by companies around the world. Vietnam's economy has managed to grow even when other nations were experiencing economic downturns. Consumer buying power has been increasing year by year and the government is offering tax incentives for investment.

Now multinational firms are targeting Vietnamese consumers with a wide variety of goods and services. US-based Procter & Gamble sees Vietnam as particularly promising because 45 percent of the population is under 25. If P&G can encourage brand loyalty within this demographic segment, it sees significant long-term sales potential for its many personal care and household products, including Gillette razors and Ambi Pur air fresheners.[3]

Once you have eliminated inappropriate markets, look for ways to distinguish meaningful segments in your chosen markets. The point is to form consumer or business segments that are internally homogeneous yet exhibit some differences (compared with other segments) that can be addressed through marketing. If you find no differences, segmentation is pointless, because you will not need to vary your marketing approach for each segment.

Apply segmentation variables in consumer markets

In consumer markets, customer characteristics and product-related behavioural variables can be used to identify segments for planning purposes (see Table 4.1). For more specific segment definition, you should apply a combination of appropriate variables. Many customer characteristics are easy to identify and apply. However, behaviour-based, product-related approaches, which can be challenging to isolate and analyse, typically give you more insight into potentially effective marketing approaches for each consumer segment.

Table 4.1	Variables for segmenting consumer markets

Customer characteristics – a user-based approach that asks: 'Who purchases what?'

Demographic	Socioeconomic
• Age • Family size • Marital status • Gender	• Income • Class • Vocation • Education • Religion • Ethnicity
Geographic	**Lifestyle/personality**
• Global, hemispheric, national, state, city, postal code • Climate • Rural vs urban	• Attitudes/opinions • Interests • Avocations • Tastes and preferences

Product-related approaches – a behavioural approach that asks: 'Why do they purchase?'

User types	Price sensitivity
• Regular • Non-user • First-time • Potential	• Low-cost orientation • Higher-cost quality/differentiation focus
Purchase and consumption patterns	**Perceived benefits**
• Purchase occasion • Buying situation • Low, medium, high consumption • Application	• Performance • Quality • Image enhancement • Service
Brand loyalty	**Media exposure and usage**
• Loyal/satisfied • Experimenters • Unsatisfied/defectors • Unaware	• Preferred media • Multiple media usage • Time, day, occasion

Source: Adapted from *Strategic and Competitive Analysis: Methods and Techniques for Analyzing Business Competition*, 1, Pearson Education Inc. (Fleischer, C.S. and Bensoussan, B. 2003) 173, Prentice Hall, FLEISHER, CRAIG S.; BENSOUSSAN, BABETTE, STRATEGIC AND COMPETITIVE ANALYSIS: METHODS AND TECHNIQUES FOR ANALYZING BUSINESS COMPETITION, 1st Ed., p. 173, © 2002. Reprinted and Electronically reproduced by permission of Pearson Education, Inc., Upper Saddle River, New Jersey.

You can also apply geographic variables when you want to enter or increase sales in specific regions or climates, avoid specific countries or regions because of competitive challenges or other threats, or leverage your organisation's strengths for competitive advantage in those areas. Remember, however, that people are more complex and buying is motivated by numerous factors; even those who share a particular characteristic will not necessarily respond in the same way to the same marketing activities. Thus, applying non-geographic variables such as gender or vocation can reveal viable segments across geographic boundaries.

One advantage to applying variables such as consumption patterns and purchase occasion is that they are easily observed, measured and analysed. For example, Domino's uses behavioural variables such as how weather affects purchasing and how consumers use digital media to segment the British market for takeaway pizza. Extreme weather, such as heavy rain or cold temperatures, tends to increase demand for takeaway pizza, the company has found. Finding that heavy users of online and mobile media respond well to Domino's promotions, the firm offers an app that links to discount vouchers. It also conducts social-media campaigns such as cutting the price of pizza when people tweet with a designated promotional *hashtag* such as #letsdolunch.[4]

Because consumer reactions are often heavily influenced by one or more of the product-related variables listed in Table 4.1, you should apply those in addition to characteristics and other variables during your marketing planning. In many cases, understanding how and why a consumer uses or does not use a product can help you identify signs of underlying wants or needs that you will then be able to address through marketing strategies. Marketers such as Hotel Chocolat (www.hotelchocolat.co.uk) apply a variety of variables to segment their markets.

MARKETING IN PRACTICE: HOTEL CHOCOLAT

Hotel Chocolat segments the consumer market for luxury chocolates by occasion (birthdays, dinner parties, weddings, holidays, etc.), person (man, woman, child, business associate, vegan, etc.), product (hampers, packaged chocolates, etc.) and flavour preference (milk, dark, alcohol-free, etc.). It operates 62 stores plus the Hotel Chocolat luxury resort. The chief operating officer explains that customers in the firm's targeted segments are 'quite cosmopolitan, concerned with where their food comes from and willing to pay extra to make sure it's ethically sound and made only with the good stuff'.[5]

Based on this segmentation, Hotel Chocolat emphasises three points of differentiation: innovation (novel flavours and recipes), authenticity (real cocoa) and ethics (sustainably grown, ethically sourced ingredients). Before putting new products into production, the firm tests flavours and requests feedback from the 100,000 members of its Tasting Club. Hotel Chocolat changes more than 25 percent of its range every year to satisfy the needs of consumers who crave novelty and variety. Also, knowing that different segments have different purchasing patterns, it uses a multichannel marketing approach for customer convenience. Looking ahead to higher growth, the firm has begun to sell branded beauty products made with cocoa butter.[6]

Marketing plan analysis: Referring to Table 4.1, which variables would you recommend that Hotel Chocolat apply to segment the market for beauty products made with cocoa butter?

Apply segmentation variables in business markets

As in consumer markets, business markets can be segmented using both customer characteristics and product-related approaches that probe behaviour (see Table 4.2). Customer characteristics describe the organisation from the outside, whereas behavioural variables look at activities and dynamics below the surface. Generally, marketers apply both types of variables to form segments of organisational customers that are internally homogeneous but have different needs or different responses to marketing when compared with other segments.

You can apply demographics such as industry type, geography and annual turnover to narrow the dimensions of a business market before you apply behavioural variables. Business customers typically have different needs and responses from those of non-profit organisations and government agencies; likewise, larger or older organisations tend to have different needs and responses from those of smaller or newer organisations. Some organisations rely more heavily than others on certain technologies (such as e-commerce or customer contact software), another indicator that can help you segment your market. In general, look carefully at how certain characteristics reveal differences that you can build on when planning marketing activities.

You can use frequency, size, timing and method of purchasing to segment business markets, along with variables reflecting purchasing policies and authorised buyers. When you segment a business market by product-related variables, especially in combination with customer characteristics and end-user characteristics, you can uncover important needs and buying patterns. Here's how the German multinational corporation BASF (www.basf.com) segments the business market for chemical products.

Table 4.2 Variables for segmenting business markets

Customer characteristics – a user-based approach that asks: 'Who purchases what?'

• Industry type	• Company size
• Geographic	• Technology employed
• Industry position	• Business age
	• Ownership structure

Product-related approaches – a behavioural approach that asks: 'Why do they purchase?'

• Consumption patterns/usage frequency	• Relationship between seller/purchaser
• End-use application	• Psychodemographics of purchaser
• Perceived benefits	• Purchasing policies
• Goals	
• Size of purchase	

Source: Adapted from *Strategic and Competitive Analysis: Methods and Techniques for Analyzing Business Competition*, 1, Pearson Education Inc. (Fleischer, C.S. and Bensoussan, B. 2003) 174, Prentice Hall, FLEISHER, CRAIG S.; BENSOUSSAN, BABETTE, STRATEGIC AND COMPETITIVE ANALYSIS: METHODS AND TECHNIQUES FOR ANALYZING BUSINESS COMPETITION, 1st Ed., p. 174, © 2002. Reprinted and Electronically reproduced by permission of Pearson Education, Inc., Upper Saddle River, New Jersey.

MARKETING IN PRACTICE: BASF

With €73 billion in annual turnover worldwide, BASF is the world's largest chemical company. Its product portfolio includes industrial chemicals, automotive paints, packaging, plastics, coatings, additives, cleaners, crop-protection products, construction products, specialised textile coatings and oil and gas products. In the context of rapid global population growth and increased economic activity in Asia, Africa and other regions, top management recently set an ambitious revenue goal of reaching €115 billion in turnover by 2020.

As they plan marketing strategy with this goal in mind, BASF's marketers use customer characteristics such as industry type, geography and production process employed to segment the business market. They also analyse product-related variables such as consumption patterns, end-use application, perceived benefits and size of purchase when segmenting the business market. Market by market, they examine the business environment, customer needs, consumer trends and other factors that affect long-term supply and demand. They see opportunity in Asia, Africa and other regions where government and industry are investing in infrastructure and rising incomes are generating demand for consumer products.

High-growth industries are an important priority for BASF. For example, it aims to be one of the top three firms supplying battery chemicals for electric cars by 2020. This goal is based on an analysis of the segment's long-term growth, government actions supporting green vehicles and the purchasing patterns of end-users, including government buyers of vehicle fleets, taxi companies and consumers who buy cars. According to BASF's research, success in the battery chemicals segment would lead to high profit margins and high customer loyalty. Another key area is automotive paints, where the company's research allows it to segment by geography (because of regional colour preferences) and end-user behaviour (such as higher customer demand for non-petrol vehicles). BASF further segments this market according to type of vehicle (motorcycle, car, lorry and so on) which affects consumption patterns and perceived benefits.[7]

Marketing plan analysis: What role are budgets, buying cycles and competitive pressures likely to play in the way businesses respond to BASF's marketing efforts? What are the implications for the way it segments the market?

Evaluate and select segments for targeting

The next step in the segmentation process is to assess the attractiveness of each segment in terms of opportunity, environment, reach and response and see how each fits with internal considerations such as mission, image, strengths, core competencies, resources and performance. The purpose is to eliminate undesirable segments and evaluate the possible opportunities inherent in the remaining segments. Ideally, you want to be active in segments that play to your organisation's strengths and capabilities, but take care not to stretch your resources too thin. At this point, you can screen out segments with insufficient profit potential, intense competition or other complications.

After you drop unattractive or unsuitable segments from consideration, you are ready to rank the remaining segments in priority order for marketing attention, on the basis of research and analysis. You can do this in several ways. For example, you might assign relative weights to each of the evaluation criteria and calculate the total scores segment by segment. The sample ranking shown in Table 4.3 shows how you might score three segments based on the five criteria categories, along with a total score per segment. As in this sample, a segment may merit a high score for opportunity yet have a much lower score for environmental factors or another factor.

To decide which segment should be your top priority, look at the total score and, if necessary, set minimum scores for individual criteria. In the sample ranking, Segment A has the highest total score and, if the organisation does not require a minimum score of 5 or higher on all criteria, would be the highest priority. Note that Table 4.3 is a very simplified, fictitious example; organisations vary widely in their evaluation criteria, weighting and ranking systems.

Different companies use different criteria to rank segments. One criterion used by some marketers is **customer lifetime value**, the total net revenue (or profit) a particular customer relationship represents to the organisation over time. This is because research indicates that focusing marketing activities on customers in segments with the potential for higher lifetime value can significantly increase revenue.[8] Amazon, the pioneering online retailer, reportedly makes little if any profit on its Kindle e-book readers and Kindle Fire tablets. For Amazon, the real value is in the e-books, videos and other content that Kindle buyers will purchase year after year – increasing the lifetime value of each customer and reinforcing brand loyalty.[9]

The choice of criteria depends on your unique situation, your chosen market and your customer knowledge. If possible, use sensitivity analysis to adjust criteria weights under

Table 4.3	Sample segment ranking		
	Segment A	**Segment B**	**Segment C**
Opportunity	8	6	5
Environmental factors	3	5	4
Reach and response	6	4	7
Competitive advantage	7	4	3
Internal considerations	9	9	4
TOTAL SCORE	33	28	23

Note: Weighted scores range from 1 (extremely unattractive) to 10 (extremely attractive).

differing forecasts and confirm priority rankings by testing prospective strategies before moving ahead with full-scale marketing plans. Among the criteria you can use to select and rank segments for marketing attention are:

- fit with the firm's goals, strengths, resources and core competencies;
- competitive advantages;
- advantageous pricing or supply costs due to relative power of buyers or suppliers;
- sizeable profit and growth potential;
- ecological impact;
- significant potential for building long-term customer relationships.

Checklist no. 7 offers specific questions to ask when evaluating and selecting segments for marketing attention.

ESSENTIAL CHECKLIST NO. 7:
EVALUATING MARKET SEGMENTS

Before you can set objectives and plan marketing programmes, you must determine which customer segments you want to reach. This checklist will help you evaluate the various segments identified within the overall market. After you write your answers in the spaces provided, put a tick next to the questions you've answered. If your marketing plan is for a hypothetical firm, you can use this checklist as a guide to the data you'll need to gather to be able to evaluate segments.

☐ What is the current size of the segment and how is it changing?

_____

☐ What current and future sales and profit potential do you see for this segment?

_____

☐ Would marketing to this segment yield an acceptable or superior payback in customer lifetime value?

_____

☐ What is the competitive situation in this segment?

_____

☐ Can the organisation realistically capture or defend market share in this segment?

☐ How much power do buyers and suppliers in this segment have?

☐ What threats exist or could emerge to prevent success in this segment?

☐ Can customers in the segment be reached through appropriate marketing activities?

☐ Does the organisation have the strengths, competencies and resources to serve this segment?

☐ Does the segment fit with the organisation's mission, image, overall goals and sustainability situation?

Once you've selected segments for marketing attention, you're ready to make decisions about targeting.

THE TARGETING PROCESS

To plan for targeting, you must consider the market coverage approach you want to take. As shown in Figure 4.2, you can use one of four coverage approaches: undifferentiated marketing, differentiated marketing, concentrated marketing or individualised marketing.

Undifferentiated marketing

Essentially a mass-marketing approach, **undifferentiated marketing** means targeting the entire market with the same marketing mix, ignoring any segment differences. This assumes that all customers in a particular market, regardless of any differences in characteristics or behaviour, will respond in the same way to the same marketing attention. Undifferentiated marketing is less expensive than other coverage strategies, due to the lower costs of developing and implementing only one marketing mix. However, today's markets are rarely so homogeneous; even slight differences can serve as clues to underlying needs in segments where an organisation can gain competitive advantage, encourage customer loyalty and ultimately return profits.

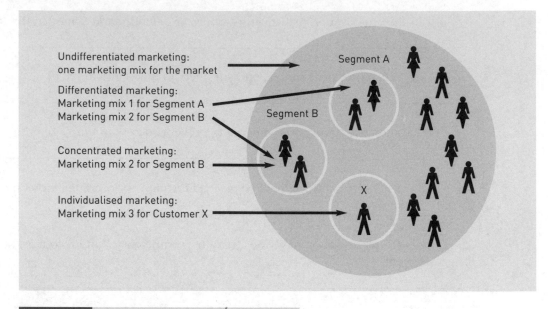

FIGURE 4.2   Segment targeting coverage strategies

Differentiated marketing

With **differentiated marketing**, you formulate a separate marketing mix for the two or more segments you choose to target. You may not target all segments in a given market, but for those you rank as priorities, you will need different marketing mixes geared to each segment's unique characteristics and behaviours. The assumption is that you can provoke a different response from each segment by using different marketing mixes. Customers benefit because their specific needs are being addressed, which increases satisfaction and encourages customer loyalty. Moreover, you can compete more effectively by tailoring the marketing mix for each segment, although this is much more costly than undifferentiated marketing and may overburden resources if not carefully managed.

Concentrated marketing

As you saw in Figure 4.2, **concentrated marketing** involves targeting one segment with one marketing mix. The idea is to compete more effectively and efficiently by understanding and satisfying one sizeable set of customers, rather than spreading organisational resources across multiple marketing activities for multiple segments. As long as the targeted segment remains attractive, this can be a profitable coverage approach. However, be aware that uncontrollable and unexpected factors such as new competition or changes in customer needs can make the targeted segment less attractive or even unfeasible over time.

Ryanair (www.ryanair.com/en), based in Dublin, has profited from its concentrated marketing approach to targeting budget-minded travellers.

MARKETING IN PRACTICE: RYANAIR

By targeting the sizable segment of price-sensitive travellers, Ryanair has become a €4 billion airline carrying 76 million passengers every year. It keeps costs down by offering few frills and charging passengers for every extra, including snacks and checked baggage. Especially during the recent global recession, when both consumers on holiday and travellers on business were eager to save money, Ryanair attracted customers in its targeted segment by promoting low, low fares.

Competing with EasyJet and other low-fare airlines, Ryanair does everything it can to minimise costs so it can meet customers' needs for low-priced air transportation. For example, the company is working with a Chinese aircraft manufacturer to design a jet for its specifications. Ryanair doesn't serve full meals and its passengers check few pieces of luggage because of the fees, so reducing the size of the galley and the hold will reduce weight and save money on fuel. The airline also wants the door to be wider so two people can enter at the same time, speeding up the boarding process and allowing the airline to get flights off the ground more quickly.

Maintaining consistent profitability is a challenge because Ryanair's fuel costs rise and fall depending on the petrol market, yet the airline hesitates to sharply increase fares. It is also spending more to attract new customers as it opens new routes where demand for budget air travel is increasing. In short, Ryanair's low fares continue to be its strongest marketing message, helping to differentiate the brand and reinforce loyalty in the intensely competitive airline industry.[10]

Marketing plan analysis: Should Ryanair target holiday travellers and business travellers with separate marketing messages? Why or why not?

Individualised marketing

You may be able to tailor marketing offers to individuals within certain targeted segments, a coverage approach known as **individualised** (or **customised**) **marketing**. Airbus, for example, can identify all the potential buyers for passenger jets and cargo planes, get to know their needs and specifications, then develop a separate marketing mix for each. The markets for commercial passenger jets and cargo planes are not so large that this is impractical, and the potential profit from each order is so great that individualised marketing makes sense for Airbus. Individualised marketing is especially important to Airbus in its competitive battle to win orders for its A350 fuel-efficient jet while arch-rival Boeing promotes its 787 Dreamliner jet. As the global economy improves, Airbus aims for higher sales to current airline customers such as Cathay Pacific and seeks to win first-time orders from airlines it hasn't served in the past.[11]

If you have the right technology, you can opt for **mass customisation** and create products and/or communications tailored to individual customers' needs on a larger scale. Australia Post, the country's postal service, is using this approach. Its app for iPhone, iPad and iPod Touch allows consumers to order their personal photos made into printed postcards. The per-card fee includes an individual message, addressing and delivery. As mail volume declines, mass customisation is one way that Australia Post can stimulate demand and cater to consumers' changing behaviour and needs.[12]

Segment personas

Marketers such as Ford Motor Company are adding a human dimension to targeting by constructing **segment personas**, fictitious yet realistic profiles representing how specific customers in targeted segments would typically buy, behave and react in a marketing situation. The idea is to think about how customers actually interact with a product (and competing products), what influences and motivates those customers, and how their needs and preferences affect their buying and consumption behaviour. Developing personas helps you avoid seeing members of a segment as faceless, nameless people in a crowd; instead, personas represent them as individuals with real needs, attitudes and behaviours, which is especially important for planning products and communications.[13]

As an example, Microsoft's Developer and Platform Evangelism Group has segmented its market and identified seven specific segments for marketing attention. It uses *Star Wars* personas to represent the personality and characteristics of each segment: Yoda is a senior executive who directs an information technology operation; Han Solo is a software or app developer; a Jedi Master is a software architect. Applying these personas to distinguish segment differences and similarities has helped the group to create effective communications for each segment audience.[14]

THE POSITIONING PROCESS

With positioning, you use marketing to create a competitively distinctive position for your product in the minds of targeted customers. You need marketing research to understand how your targeted customers perceive your organisation, product or brand and your competitors. Research can also help determine which attributes matter most to the targeted customers. Regardless of how you see your products, it is the customer's view that counts. For example, the mission of Bentley (owned by Volkswagen) is to 'build a good car, a fast car, the best in class'. The brand's positioning is based on power and performance, hand-crafted quality, distinctive design and automotive luxury, attributes that are very important to the targeted segment of affluent buyers. Even during the recession of recent years, Bentley's sales increased dramatically – especially in status-conscious China and Japan – as buyers sought out the car positioned as 'best in class'.[15]

Repositioning means using the marketing plan to change the competitively distinctive positioning of a brand in the minds of the targeted customers. To illustrate, the Howard Johnson brand, owned by the Wyndham Hotel Group, is being repositioned to replace the image of a dowdy, budget motel chain. The repositioning aims to combine nostalgia for the brand, which many American travellers remember from their childhood, with family-friendly value and modern convenience.[16]

Deciding on differentiation

Successful marketers understand the importance of deciding on points of difference that are not only competitively distinctive and advantageous but also relevant and believable. Ilkley Brewery differentiates its craft ales from competing beers on the basis of two points that its customers find advantageous, credible and relevant: innovative flavours and fresh quality.

In general, you can differentiate your offering along the lines of quality, service, image, personnel or value. Whatever your choice, a product's positioning must be based on criteria that are relevant, meaningful and desirable from the customer's perspective yet competitively distinctive. Here are three examples of effective positioning based on desirable differentiation criteria:

- *Specsavers*: affordable, stylish spectacles (value differentiation);
- *Mercedes-Benz*: well-engineered, well-appointed luxury vehicles (quality differentiation);
- *Ocado*: convenient online grocery shopping with home delivery (service differentiation).

Applying positioning

Your marketing plan must show how you'll actually carry through the positioning in your product's marketing and performance (see Checklist No. 8). Determine first whether your organisation can realistically develop and market a product that will live up to the meaningful points of difference you've chosen. Second, consider whether the points of difference can be communicated to the targeted segments. And third, be sure you can sustain the product's performance and differentiation over time.

Positioning (or repositioning) is basically the driver behind all the marketing activities you will include in your marketing plan. With differentiated marketing, you develop a positioning appropriate to each segment and apply that positioning through your marketing decisions for each segment. With concentrated marketing, you establish one positioning for the single segment you target. Remember that positioning is not a one-time decision: as markets and customers' needs change, you must be prepared to reposition a product, if necessary, for relevance, desirability and deliverability.

ESSENTIAL CHECKLIST NO. 8:
PLANNING FOR POSITIONING

Use this checklist as you make decisions about positioning or repositioning your product or brand, marking your answers in the spaces provided. If your marketing plan is for a start-up or a hypothetical company, these questions can help you develop an effective positioning. If you're planning for an existing brand, good or service, the questions are a good way to think about repositioning possibilities.

☐ What points of differentiation are meaningful to your customers and applicable to your brand or product? Be specific.

_____

☐ How can you use differentiation to position your offer as competitively distinctive, desirable and superior?

_____

☐ Is your positioning credible, relevant and realistic in the context of customers' needs, your organisation's capabilities and competing offers?

_____

☐ How can you use your marketing mix to support, communicate and deliver on your positioning?

_____

☐ If you choose differentiated marketing, how can you adapt your positioning for specific targeted segments or geographic markets?

_____

☐ What changes in customers' needs, competitive pressures or the marketing environment might cause you to undertake repositioning?

_____

CHAPTER SUMMARY

Segmentation helps marketers rule out inappropriate markets, identify specific segments for more study, and better understand customers in those segments so the organisation can respond to their needs. Evaluating segments enables the organisation to decide which groups of customers to target and in what order. The process also provides a basis for creating a meaningful and competitively distinctive position in the minds of each target segment's customers.

Marketers can segment consumer markets by user-based characteristics (demographic, geographic, socioeconomic and lifestyle/personality) and product-related behavioural variables (user types, consumption patterns and usage frequency, brand loyalty, price sensitivity, perceived benefits and more). Business markets can be segmented using customer characteristics (industry type, geographic, industry position, company size and more) and product-related behavioural variables (consumption patterns/usage frequency, end-use application, perceived benefits and more). Target-market coverage strategies include undifferentiated, differentiated, concentrated and individualised (customised) marketing. To be effective, the offer must be positioned or repositioned in a way that is competitively distinctive, relevant and credible, able to be communicated and sustainable over time.

CASE STUDY: NIKE

Even when the brand name isn't visible, consumers usually recognise anything made by Nike (www.nike.com) when they spot the well-known swoosh. Although US-based Nike is a global marketer, it profits by addressing its marketing activities to the needs, preferences, interests, lifestyles, buying behaviours and media consumption patterns of particular consumer groups. These include consumers with an active lifestyle and both professional and weekend athletes who kick footballs, dribble basketballs, run races, hit baseballs or participate in other individual or team sports.

For example, Nike designed its Flyknit shoes for sports-minded consumers seeking very flexible, very lightweight running shoes. They also appeal to consumers who prefer running shoes made from environmentally friendly materials and those who enjoy being among the first to wear the latest fashions. In other words, depending on the segment being targeted, Nike emphasises sports benefits, product performance, sustainability, style or status. Nike dominates the US market for basketball shoes, and it sponsors major players as well as the US Olympic basketball team, reinforcing its performance image among fans and consumers who like to shoot hoops. In China, Nike's second-largest market, such basketball sponsorships add to the brand's status and set it apart from other footwear and apparel marketers.

The company targets a number of segments for its Digital Sport range of technology-enabled footwear and accessories. Nike+ running shoes contain sensors synchronised to an online log, allowing runners to record and monitor their running efforts over time. The FuelBand, not for runners only, helps consumers track their physical activity, day by day. The millions of consumers who use these Digital Sport products have the option of sharing data about their performance online and learning from what other Nike customers post online, adding a social dimension that has proven very popular.

Depending on the segment being targeted, Nike will convey the brand's image and benefits using a variety of adverts, billboards, online and in-store videos, bespoke microsites, social media such as Facebook, celebrity appearances and special events. Counting the many microsites and social media accounts set up for individual products, sports and sports events, Nike's websites attract 200 million visitors every day, offering great potential for engaging customers over the long term.[17]

Case questions

1. How does Nike's decision to use differentiated marketing affect its marketing communications decisions?

2. If you were selecting criteria to rank consumer segments for Nike's basketball shoes, what specific internal and external factors would you apply and which would you put the most emphasis on?

APPLY YOUR KNOWLEDGE

Research the segmentation, targeting and positioning of a particular company active in consumer or B2B marketing, using its products, advertising, website and other activities as clues. Prepare a brief oral or written report summarising your thoughts after completing this exercise.

- Based on the organisation's marketing, what market(s) and segment(s) appear to be targeted?

- Is this company using differentiated, undifferentiated, concentrated or customised marketing? How do you know?

- What benefits are featured in the company's marketing and what customer needs are they designed to satisfy? How might the targeted segments be described in terms of needs?

- Analysing the marketing clues you have observed, what product-related variables do you think this company is using to segment its market(s), apart from benefits sought?

- In one sentence, how would you summarise the positioning this company is trying to reinforce in one of the targeted segments?

BUILD YOUR OWN MARKETING PLAN

Proceed with the marketing plan for a hypothetical organisation or an actual organisation that you have chosen. During the segmentation process for this organisation, what markets would you eliminate from consideration and why? What specific segmentation variables would you apply to the remainder of the market, and how would you expect them to create segments that make sense from a marketing perspective? What further research would support this segmentation?

What criteria would you use to evaluate the segments you identify? Given the organisation's overall goals, strengths and resources, what targeting approach would you choose? If you were constructing a persona for one of your segments, how would you describe that customer? Finally, what positioning or repositioning would you want to reinforce for the customers in each targeted segment? If these ideas are appropriate in light of your earlier decisions, document them and explain how they affect your strategy in a written marketing plan.

ENDNOTES

1. Chris Bryant, 'VW bucks trend in European car-makers', *Financial Times*, 26 July 2012, www.ft.com; 'VW's Audi affirms targets despite cloudy economy', *MarketWatch*, 31 July 2012, www.marketwatch.com; Alex Taylor III, 'Das auto giant', *Fortune*, 23 July 2012, pp. 150–155; Chancal Pal Chauhan, 'Volks-wagen's Vento overtakes Honda's City in mid-size segment', *Economic Times (India)*, 20 May 2011, http://articles.economictimes.indiatimes.com.

2. James Rush, 'Harvey Nichols joy for Ilkley Brewery', *Telegraph & Argus (Surrey)*, 9 July 2012, www.thetelegraphandargus.co.uk.

3. Shibani Mahtan, 'Vietnam still hot for American investors', *Wall Street Journal*, 31 August 2012, www.wsj.com; Lauren Coleman-Lochner, 'Emerg-ing Vietnam market draws foreign corporations', *San Francisco Chronicle*, 7 July 2012, www.sfgate.com; Don Lee, 'Multinationals take a longer view of Vietnam', *Los Angeles Times*, 11 April 2009, www.latimes.com; Michael Sheridan, 'Brits ride the Vietnam tiger', *Sunday Times*, 27 January 2008, p. 1.

4. Brenda Gohf, 'Soggy weather boosts Domino's Pizza', *Reuters*, 23 July 2012, www.reuters.com; Anh Nguyen, 'Domino's Pizza increased sales by online and social media', *CIO-IN*, 28 July 2012, www.cio.in.

5. Quoted in Beth Negus Viveiros, 'Hotel Chocolat checks into US market', *Chief Marketer*, 1 June 2009, www.chiefmarketer.com.

6. Suzanne Bearne, 'Hotel Chocolat poaches Monsoon Accessorize Roger Williams as first international director ahead of Asian expansion', *Retail Week*, 21 January 2013, www.retail-week.com; Alex Lawson, 'Hotel Chocolat boss warns against "complex" personalisation', *Retail Week*, 15 March 2012, www.retail-week.com; Alex Lawson, 'Hotel Chocolat to take dip in beauty market', *Retail Week*, 10 February 2012, www.retail-week.com; Glynn Davis, 'On the shop floor with Hotel Chocolat founder Angus Thirlwell', *The Retail Bulletin*, 29 June 2009, www.theretailbulletin.com; Beth Negus Viveiros, 'Hotel Chocolat has no reservations about US launch', *Chief Marketer*, 15 June 2009, www.chiefmarketer.com; www.hotelchocolat.co.uk.

7. Ludwig Burger and Frank Siebelt, 'Analysis: BASF to take on Asia's battery chemicals makers', *Reuters*, 16 July 2012, http://uk.reuters.com; 'Car colours shifting towards eco-tones,' *IOL Motoring (South Africa)*, 27 July 2012, www.iol.co.za; Irma Vener, 'BASF opens Nigerian office, aims to double African sales by 2020', *Engineering News*, 26 July 2012, www.engineeringnews.co.za; 'BASF ups 2020 sales goal', *Reuters*, 29 November 2011, www.reuters.com.

8. V. Kumar and Bharath Rajan, 'Profitable customer management', *Management Accounting Quarterly*, Spring 2009, pp. 1ff.

9. 'The customer lifetime value equation: Will it pay off for tech companies?', *Knowledge@Wharton*, 7 December 2011, http://knowledge.wharton.upenn.edu.

10. Dan Milmo, 'Ryanair plans to increase width of plane doors to speed up boarding', *Guardian*, 30 July 2012, www.guardian.co.uk; Nathalie Thomas, 'Ryanair suppresses price rises as recession and fuel costs hit profits', *Telegraph*, 30 July 2012, www.telegraph.co.uk; Loulla-Mae Eleftheriou-Smith, 'Ryanair profits drop 29% in first quarter despite marketing uplift', *Marketing*, 30 July 2012, www.marketingmagazine.co.uk; 'Ryanair reports 14.9m euro profit', *BBC News*, 30 January 2012, www.bbc.co.uk/news.

11. 'Airbus delays A350 XWB entry as EADS profits triple', *BBC News*, 27 July 2012, www.bbc.co.uk/news; Andrew Parker, 'Airbus sales chief warns orders "peaked"', *Financial Times*, 10 July 2012, www.ft.com.

12. 'Australia Post launches postcard app for iPhone', *Post and Parcel*, 6 July 2012, http://postandparcel.info.

13. Tim Riesterer, 'How personas can lead your messaging astray', *Marketing Profs*, 17 May 2012, www.marketingprofs.com.

14. 'The uses of research – Segmentation: Microsoft', *Marketing Week*, 20 August 2012, www.marketing-week.co.uk.

15. 'Volkswagen's record sales boost profits', *BBC News*, 26 July 2012, www.bbc.co.uk; Jonathan Welsh, 'US edges China as biggest market for Bentley cars', *Wall Street Journal*, 5 July 2012, www.wsj.com.

16. Patrick Mayock, 'Howard Johnson refresh rife with nostalgia', *Hotel News Now*, 4 April 2012, www.hotelnewsnow.com.

17. Kurt Badenhausen, 'Why Nike owns US Olympic basketball', *Forbes*, 20 July 2012, www.forbes.com; John Kell, 'Nike fiscal 4th quarter net drops 7.5% as margins fall, costs jump', *Wall Street Journal*, 28 June 2012, www.wsj.com; Scott Cendrowski, 'Nike's new marketing mojo', *Fortune*, 13 February 2012, www.fortune.com.

5 Planning direction and objectives

Learning outcomes

After studying this chapter, you will be able to:

* Explain the three broad directions that can shape a marketing plan
* Discuss how financial, marketing and societal objectives work together in a marketing plan
* Describe the characteristics of effective objectives

Application outcomes

After studying this chapter, you will be able to:

* Set a direction for your marketing plan
* Formulate your marketing plan objectives

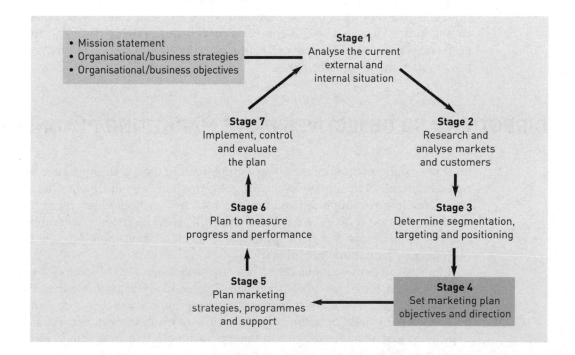

* Mission statement
* Organisational/business strategies
* Organisational/business objectives

Stage 1
Analyse the current external and internal situation

Stage 2
Research and analyse markets and customers

Stage 3
Determine segmentation, targeting and positioning

Stage 4
Set marketing plan objectives and direction

Stage 5
Plan marketing strategies, programmes and support

Stage 6
Plan to measure progress and performance

Stage 7
Implement, control and evaluate the plan

CHAPTER PREVIEW: MARKETING AT McDONALD'S

With €22.2 billion in annual turnover, 33,500 restaurants worldwide and a daily customer count of 68 million people, the US-based fast-food chain McDonald's (www.mcdonalds.com) is a marketing powerhouse wherever it does business. The company aims for consistent long-term annual sales growth of 3–5 percent by increasing sales from current units, not just by opening new units. To achieve this financial goal, McDonald's marketing plans set multiple objectives, which include increasing the number of customers who visit each restaurant, increasing the size of each transaction, introducing new foods and beverages to retain current customers and attract new customers, defending market share and strengthening customer loyalty.

McDonald's restaurants in different regions have different marketing plans for achieving these objectives. US units are promoting 'Breakfast After Midnight' to attract customers during early-morning hours; UK units are helping customers locate nearby McDonald's outlets with a mobile app; and Chinese units are attracting customers through value-priced menu items and home delivery. In addition, McDonald's marketing plans include a variety of objectives for social responsibility and sustainability, such as targets for recycling, nutrition education, philanthropy and more. Being a good corporate citizen helps McDonald's influence the way customers think and feel about its brand – very important when so many competitors are targeting the same customers.[1]

Growth is clearly the top marketing priority for McDonald's. In this chapter, you'll learn about choosing a marketing plan direction and setting objectives, which make up the fourth stage in the marketing planning process. Not all marketing plans aim for growth, which is why the chapter looks at non-growth choices as well. No matter what direction you choose, you'll also set marketing, financial and societal objectives, as discussed in this chapter. Use this chapter's checklist to evaluate your objectives; also look at the objectives in the sample marketing plan, located in the Appendix, for ideas about how to document your objectives.

DIRECTION AND OBJECTIVES DRIVE MARKETING PLANNING

Your marketing plan is not the only plan created to guide your organisation forward. As noted in **Chapter 1**, corporate-level plans are supported and implemented by business-level plans and, in turn, supported and implemented by functional-level plans for marketing, operations and so forth. As a marketer, you will formulate strategy, determine the optimal marketing-mix tools, and make programme-level decisions based on the direction and objectives of your marketing plan.

If the objectives in your marketing plan are explicit and clearly connected to higher-level objectives and long-term goals, the plan is more likely to produce the desired performance.[2] Thus, each objective, marketing strategy and marketing programme must be consistent with the plan's direction as well as with both organisational and business objectives. Just as important, when you set each objective, you should also be thinking about how your plan will allow for measuring progress towards achieving it.

MARKETING PLAN DIRECTION

Many companies set growth as the direction for each year's marketing plan, but not all organisations pursue growth. Some seek to maintain their current position, postponing growth because of adverse economic conditions, fierce competition, financial problems or for other reasons. Others retrench by selling off units or products, exiting particular markets or downsizing in other ways – often for survival purposes or to prepare for later growth. Growth and non-growth strategies, summarised in Figure 5.1, are discussed next.

Growth strategies

If your organisation wants to grow, you will choose among the four main growth strategies proposed by H. Igor Ansoff: market penetration, product development, market development, and diversification.[3] With **market penetration**, you offer existing products to customers in existing markets. This increases unit and/or monetary sales and simultaneously reinforces the brand or product's strength in each market. Food marketer Heinz, for example, is making recipes available via QR codes and mobile apps to encourage UK customers to use more of its tomato ketchup when they cook.[4]

With **product development**, you market new products or product variations to customers in existing markets. This works only when you can develop a steady stream of product innovations appropriate for the needs of customers in those markets. Taco Bell, the fast-food restaurant chain owned by Yum Brands, regularly introduces new menu items to entice customers back for new tastes. Not long ago, it launched a breakfast menu plus new burritos and side dishes, all of which helped Taco Bell increase sales in its existing US units.[5]

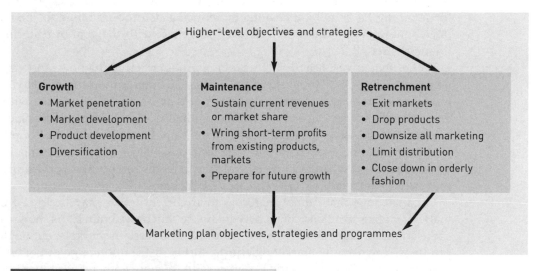

FIGURE 5.1   Choices of marketing plan direction

With **market development**, you pursue growth by marketing existing products in new markets and segments. Such a strategy builds on the popularity of established products and allows firms to expand their customer base either geographically or by segment. King.com has done this by launching popular games like Bubble Witch Saga for iPhone and iPad, replacing mouse and keyboard commands with finger movements. These changes allow King.com to expand its reach to the segment of UK customers who enjoy playing social games on mobile devices.[6]

The fourth growth strategy is **diversification**, which means marketing new products in new markets or segments. You can diversify by (1) distributing new products in new markets through existing channel arrangements, (2) initiating new marketing activities in new markets, or (3) acquiring companies to gain access to new products and new markets. South Korea's Samsung Electronics, for example, is diversifying into five new product categories for business markets: medical technology, solar cells, rechargeable batteries for hybrid electric/petrol cars, light-emitting diodes and biopharmaceuticals. Accomplished mainly through acquisitions, this diversification will help Samsung build sales and reduce its dependence on everyday products like mobiles and TVs.[7]

Non-growth strategies

Sometimes growth is not an appropriate direction. Pressured by severe economic or competitive conditions, insufficient resources, ambitious expansion, lower demand or stagnant revenues and profits, organisations may follow a maintenance strategy or even retrench. A maintenance marketing plan can be designed to keep revenues, market share or profits at current levels or at least defend against deterioration. In 2012, Canada-based BlackBerry, maker of Blackberry mobiles, needed to stabilise its market-share situation and reverse revenue declines due, in part, to strong competition from Apple iPhones and Android-compatible mobiles. Its maintenance marketing plan set objectives for retaining its 78 million customers, reducing its product range for better focus and developing new products on a delayed schedule, with the goal of restoring long-term financial strength.[8]

Rather than invest heavily in improving products, targeting new markets, developing new promotions or other marketing activities, an organisation could try to harvest short-term profits from existing products or markets and retain relationships with customers. This would conserve resources while simultaneously building a stronger foundation for later growth. The important point here, says Professor Michael Porter of Harvard University, is to plan for short- and long-term possibilities at the same time. In fact, taking a long-term view when reacting to short-term threats can present opportunities 'to make moves that you could never dream of making before'.[9]

Organisations that cannot maintain their current levels may be forced into making marketing plans to retrench or, in the extreme, to shut down entirely. As shown in Figure 5.1, some common choices here are to withdraw from certain markets, eliminate particular products, downsize all marketing efforts, shrink distribution or go out of business. After a series of profit warnings, the UK maternity retailer Mothercare prepared a three-year retrenchment plan to close unprofitable high street stores and learning centres and improve the company's retailing website. Aiming to return to profitability through these store closures, Mothercare continued opening new stores in non-UK markets, where sales are stronger and competition is less intense.[10]

And, if the retrenchment goes well, the company will soon be able to start planning for a turnaround through a new growth strategy. Guiding the organisation in a particular direction requires specific marketing plan objectives keyed to that situation, which in turn will lead to different marketing strategies and programmes.

MARKETING PLAN OBJECTIVES

Marketing plan objectives are short-term targets that, when achieved through implementation of appropriate action programmes, will bring the organisation closer to its longer-term goals. Some companies use the **Balanced Scorecard**, broad performance measures used to align strategy and objectives as a way to manage customer relationships, achieve financial targets, improve internal capabilities, prepare for future innovation and attain sustainability. In such cases, the marketing plan objectives have to be structured appropriately to support these broader measures of performance.

Types of objectives

You can set marketing plan objectives in three categories. **Financial objectives** are targets for achieving financial results through marketing strategies and programmes. **Marketing objectives** are targets for achievements in marketing relationships and activities, which in turn directly support attainment of financial objectives. **Societal objectives** are targets for accomplishing results in areas related to social responsibility; such objectives indirectly influence both marketing and financial achievements.

The choice of marketing plan objectives and specific targets will, of course, be different for every organisation. No matter what objectives you set, however, be sure you can measure progress towards your targets after you implement your plan. Otherwise, you'll have no way of knowing whether your marketing actions are having the desired result. This is where metrics must be applied, as you'll learn in **Chapter 11**, giving you information to control implementation and adjust timing or tactics as needed.

Financial objectives

Companies usually set objectives for external results such as unit, monetary, product and channel sales, plus internal requirements such as profitability, return on investment and break-even deadlines. Table 5.1 shows the focus and purpose of financial objectives commonly used by businesses. Non-governmental organisations typically set objectives for short-term and long-term fundraising as well as other financial targets. To achieve the organisation's financial objectives, you will need to coordinate other compatible

Table 5.1   Focus and purpose of financial objectives

Focus of financial objective	Purpose and examples
External results	To provide targets for outcomes of marketing activities such as: • increasing unit or monetary sales by geographic market • increasing unit or monetary sales by customer segment • increasing unit or monetary sales by product • increasing unit or monetary sales by channel • other objectives related to external results
Internal requirements	To provide targets for managing marketing to meet organisational requirements such as: • achieving break-even status • achieving profitability levels • achieving return on investment levels • other objectives related to internal requirements

objectives dealing with relationships between buyers and sellers as well as suppliers and distributors.

A company might set a financial objective for external results such as *to achieve a minimum weekly sales volume of £1,000 for each new product*. Notice that this objective is relevant (for a profit-seeking organisation), specific, time-defined and measurable. Whether it is realistic, challenging and consistent depends on the company's particular situation. A financial objective related to internal requirements might be *to achieve an average annual profit margin of 13 percent across all products*.

Because such objectives are measurable and time-defined, you can check progress and adjust your targets, your timing or your marketing if necessary. In some situations, you may change the deadline for an objective to allow more time for the marketing plan to work. Even with a later deadline, however, an objective may ultimately be unattainable. Consider Tesco's experience with its US Fresh & Easy convenience stores, founded in 2007. The US chain lost money year after year as Tesco opened new stores, paid for advertising to raise brand awareness, invested in product development and redesigned stores for local preferences. Unexpectedly intense competition and challenging economic circumstances added to the financial pressure. More than once, Tesco adjusted its marketing plan and delayed the deadline for Fresh & Easy to become profitable. Finally, in 2012, Tesco announced a strategic change when it determined that the US chain would not achieve profitability in an acceptable time period.[11]

Marketing objectives

Connections with customers and channel members are particularly critical to organisational success, which is why every marketing plan should include objectives for managing these external relationships. Looking at the life cycle of a customer relationship, the organisation would begin by approaching the customer to explore a possible relationship, establishing a relationship and adding more ties to strengthen it; reigniting customer interest if purchases plateau or loyalty wavers, saving the relationship if the customer signals intention to switch to another product or brand and restarting the relationship if the customer is open to switching back. This life cycle applies to relations with channel members as well.[12]

Many businesses establish explicit objectives for building their customer base, enhancing customers' perceptions of the brand, product or company, holding on to existing customers, increasing customer loyalty, boosting or defending market share, strengthening ties with key distributors, improving customer satisfaction, and so on, as in Table 5.2. They also set objectives for marketing that affects internal relationships. Coca-Cola, for example, aims for 100 percent employee participation in an online training course about digital and social media, knowing that this background is vital for understanding customer behaviour.[13]

In practice, you need to avoid conflicts between your marketing objectives and your financial objectives. It can be difficult to dramatically increase both market share and profitability at the same time, as one example. Therefore, determine your organisation's priorities and formulate your marketing plan accordingly. In conjunction with objectives aimed at external relationships, you may formulate objectives covering internal activities such as increasing the accuracy or speed of order fulfilment, adjusting the focus, output

Table 5.2	Focus and purpose of marketing objectives

Focus of marketing objective	Purpose and examples
External relationships	To provide targets for managing relations with customers and other publics such as: • building brand image, awareness and preference • stimulating product trial • acquiring new customers • retaining existing customers • increasing customer satisfaction and loyalty • acquiring or defending market share • expanding or defending distribution • other relationship objectives
Internal activities	To provide targets for managing specific marketing activities such as: • increasing output or speed of new product development • improving quality of goods or services • streamlining order fulfilment • managing resources to enter new markets or segments • conducting marketing research • other objectives related to internal activities

or speed of new product development, and arranging the resources for entering new segments or markets.

Planning for these activities helps lay the groundwork for achieving relationship objectives and the financial and societal objectives that depend on those relationships. Here's how the UK retailer Sainsbury's (www.sainsburys.co.uk) plans for relationship building through marketing.

MARKETING IN PRACTICE: SAINSBURY'S

As a £23 billion retailer of foods and general merchandise, Sainsbury's operates more than 550 supermarkets and 370 convenience stores throughout the UK. Its mission is to be 'the most trusted retailer, where people love to work and shop'. It competes with Tesco, Morrison, Asda and other retailers for market share, offering value for money, shopping convenience and a wide range of brand and product choices, including Sainsbury's highly popular (and profitable) private brands. The company also sells more Fairtrade ethically sourced products than any other UK retailer, which contributes to positive brand perceptions.

Sainsbury's targets employees for internal marketing because 'if you know what's going on in the business, try the products and understand what the Sainsbury's campaigns are about, you will tell customers about it', explains the director of colleague engagement. The company asks a sample of 2,000 employees for feedback every month and experiments with communications to engage employees in sharing ideas.

Targeting customers with external marketing programmes, Sainsbury's has been improving its frequent-buyer offers to reward Nectar card customers. It sees digital channels as a major opportunity and is using transactional data from its Nectar cardholders to prepare for setting objectives for mobile-based purchasing. It has also set an objective for increasing its brand credibility in the category of fashion, with quality and value as the main points of differentiation. Finally, Sainsbury's has set objectives for speeding up redesign of its own-brand products and stimulating product trial of its own-brand foods, targeting shoppers who want variety yet are concerned about pricing.[14]

Marketing plan analysis: What kind of objectives should Sainsbury's set for its internal marketing, and why?

Societal objectives

Because businesses are increasingly mindful of their responsibilities to society – and the way their actions are viewed by stakeholders – a growing number are setting societal objectives to be achieved through marketing. Such objectives are addressed in marketing plans because they help the company strengthen ties with customers (achieving marketing objectives) and increase or maintain sales (achieving financial objectives). The Swedish furniture retailer IKEA, for example, has set a long-term goal for building 50 percent of its wooden products from certified sustainable timber sources by 2017.

To reduce its use of wood, IKEA has already stopped using wooden shipping pallets, substituting recyclable cardboard pallets that weigh less (which reduces shipping costs as well as saving trees).[15]

As shown in Table 5.3, societal objectives may relate to ecological protection or to social responsibility and stakeholder relations.

Many businesses fulfil their societal objectives by donating money, goods or services to charities or good causes. This helps polish their image and demonstrates their commitment to the community and to society at large. Others integrate societal and marketing objectives. For example, in developing nations, the marketing plans for Unilever's Lifebuoy soap brand include societal objectives for reducing the number of diarrhoea-related deaths by promoting frequent hand-washing. The company has set an objective of reaching 1 billion people with this message by 2015, through communications such as mobile marketing, contests, community programmes, special packaging and other marketing activities. Sales of Lifebuoy soap have also increased as the clean-hands message reaches a wider audience.[16]

Table 5.3 Focus and purpose of societal objectives

Focus of societal objective	Purpose and examples
Ecological protection	To provide targets for managing marketing related to ecological protection and sustainability, such as: • reducing carbon footprint with eco-friendly processes, products and activities • doing business with 'green' suppliers and channel members • reducing waste by redesigning products and processes for recycling and other efficiencies • conserving natural resources • other objectives related to ecological protection
Social responsibility and relations with publics	To provide targets for managing marketing related to social responsibility and relations with publics, such as: • building a positive image as a good corporate citizen • supporting designated charities, community projects, human rights groups and others with money and marketing • encouraging employees, customers, suppliers and channel members to volunteer • engaging publics in two-way dialogue to share concerns and explain societal initiatives • other objectives related to social responsibility and relations with publics

Some companies set specific societal objectives for **cause-related marketing** (also known as *purpose marketing*), in which the brand or product is marketed through a connection to benefit a charity or other social cause. Properly implemented, such marketing initiatives have a positive effect on the cause, on customer satisfaction and on the company.[17] Be transparent about how the cause will benefit from the connection, to encourage consumer participation and avoid misunderstanding. When Selfridges (www.selfridges.com) launched Project Ocean in 2011, it worked with 22 non-governmental organisations to communicate about the cause it was supporting.

MARKETING IN PRACTICE: SELFRIDGES

'No more fish in the sea?' This was one of the straplines used during Project Ocean, a five-week cause-related marketing campaign that Selfridges developed with three objectives: (1) to raise global awareness about the potential long-term consequences of overfishing, (2) to encourage consumers to change their eating habits in favour of sustainable fish, and (3) to raise money to support marine conservation projects by the Zoological Society of London (ZSL).

At the outset, the retailer announced it would no longer sell six dozen types of endangered fish in its food halls and restaurants. It created an app to help consumers determine which fish are endangered and which are being sourced sustainably. The flagship store in London devoted its façade, plus its main windows and considerable floor space, to displays and special events about the cause. Twenty-two NGOs participated by sending experts to meet shoppers or explaining how their work protects marine life.

All of the stores' branches sold two cause-related products, a T-shirt (£10 of the purchase price went to the ZSL) and a bracelet (the entire £5 purchase price went to the ZSL). As part of the fundraising effort, shoppers could choose to donate via text message or online and then watch as their donated 'fish' joined the Project Ocean virtual ocean. In all, 17,500 customers participated in one or more campaign activities, and Selfridges met its fundraising objective within a few days. In all, it raised more than £120,000 to support marine conservation. Just as important, Selfridges inaugurated a meeting of legislators that resulted in a new sustainable fishing policy to be implemented by EU countries.[18]

Marketing plan analysis: Why was it important for buyers of Project Ocean products to know exactly how much of the purchase price was being donated to the ZSL?

To communicate their societal objectives, activities and results to stakeholders, companies including IKEA and Unilever distribute information to the media and post social responsibility and sustainability reports on their websites. Table 5.4 gives a brief listing of online sources of more information about these issues.

Table 5.4 Online sources of information about sustainability and social responsibility

Website	Focus
Gov.uk Waste and Environmental Impact (www.gov.uk/browse/business/waste-environment)	Guide to business planning for future sustainability and social responsibility actions
Centre for Business Relationships, Accountability, Sustainability and Society (www.brass.cf.ac.uk)	Research and information to help businesses plan for sustainability, social responsibility and stakeholder relations
CSR Europe (www.csreurope.org)	Online business network for sharing social responsibility and sustainability objectives, practices and successes
ENDS Europe (www.endseurope.com)	News about the latest developments in environmental issues and resource conservation for businesses
EU Ecolabel (http://ec.europa.eu/environment/ecolabel/index_en.htm)	Voluntary labelling programme that identifies goods and services meeting standards for environmental excellence
Fairtrade Foundation (www.fairtrade.org.uk)	Find out more about the non-profit organisation that licenses the Fairtrade mark in the UK
Third Sector (www.thirdsector.co.uk)	Publication covering charities, social enterprise and voluntary organisations
Wrap (www.wrap.org.uk)	Ideas and case studies showing how to reduce business's ecological impact by cutting waste and conserving natural resources

Characteristics of effective objectives

To be effective, your marketing plan objectives should be:

- *Relevant*. Be sure your objectives relate to the chosen direction and higher-level strategies and goals. Otherwise, the programmes you implement to achieve your plan's objectives will not support organisational needs. Although most businesses set objectives for revenues and profits, non-financial objectives such as those relating to corporate image are also important because they build and strengthen connections with other stakeholders.

- *Specific and measurable*. Vague targets will not help you determine what you need to accomplish and how. Simply calling for 'growth' is not enough. To be effective, your objectives should indicate, in quantitative terms, what the marketing plan is being developed to achieve. Coca-Cola, for instance, aims to double its global revenues by 2020, and it sets yearly sales objectives for stepping closer to that long-term goal.

- *Time-defined*. What is the deadline for achieving the objective? You will plan differently for objectives that must be achieved in six months compared with objectives to be achieved in 12 months. Setting an open-ended objective is like setting no objective at all, because you will lack a schedule for showing results – and it will not be accountable. Sainsbury aims to sell £1 billion in Fairtrade products by 2020, for instance – and it uses specific metrics to evaluate progress during the period leading up to the deadline.

- *Realistic*. A marketing plan geared to attaining market dominance in six months is unlikely to be realistic for any business, especially for a start-up. Thus, your marketing plan objectives should be realistic to provide purpose for marketing and to keep organisational members motivated. Also be sure your objectives make sense in the context of realistic opportunities and threats.

- *Challenging*. Realistic objectives need not be easy to attain. In fact, many marketers set aggressive yet realistic marketing plan objectives so they can expand more quickly than if their objectives resulted in incremental growth. Objectives that are too challenging, however, may discourage the marketing staff and tie up resources without achieving the desired result.

- *Consistent*. Is the objective consistent with the organisation's mission, goals, strengths, core competencies and interpretation of external opportunities and threats? Are all objectives consistent with each other? Inconsistent objectives can confuse staff members and customers, detract from the marketing effort and result in disappointing performance.

With growth as the direction, the marketing plans of Coca-Cola (www.coca-cola.co.uk) include a number of goals and objectives to help the soft-drink giant reach its long-term goals.

MARKETING IN PRACTICE: COCA-COLA

With €37 billion in annual turnover, Coca-Cola's mission is 'To refresh the world; inspire moments of optimism and happiness; create value and make a difference'. Its top long-term financial goal is to double revenues by 2020, a target intended to create value for shareholders and employees, suppliers, communities and other stakeholders. This requires year-by-year objectives for investing in new facilities, new brands and new marketing efforts to reach targeted segments and markets. In India, for example, Coca-Cola has specific objectives for opening new bottling plants, making supply-chain improvements and introducing new products, with the aim of making India one of the company's top five markets by 2020.

One of Coca-Cola's key long-term marketing goals is to build customer loyalty across its range of beverages in all markets, particularly in fast-growing nations like China, where the firm sees enormous opportunity. Another is to continually expand the product portfolio to satisfy diverse beverage needs with a range of choices, everything from water and carbonated drinks to juices, energy drinks, sports drinks, coffee and tea. In addition, its Content 2020 goal is to engage younger customers, in particular, in co-creating advertising and social-media content related to the brand. Year by year, Coca-Cola sets specific targets that will bring it closer to these goals.

It has a number of long-term societal goals, including water conservation (returning to nature or communities as much water as it uses in its beverages and production by 2020), supporting charitable causes (by donating at least 1 percent of its operating income yearly), and supporting women entrepreneurs (using Coca-Cola's value chain to help 5 million women start or grow businesses by 2020). By establishing yearly specific objectives market by market, and linking these to metrics for measuring results, Coca-Cola is moving towards the successful achievement of these societal goals.[19]

Marketing plan analysis: How would you suggest that Coca-Cola plan to evaluate yearly progress towards its long-term goals? Suggest specific metrics and explain how they might be applied.

Use Essential Checklist no. 9 to evaluate your objectives.[20]

ESSENTIAL CHECKLIST NO. 9:
EVALUATING OBJECTIVES

You must set appropriate objectives if you are to develop suitable marketing programmes for your organisation's chosen direction and current situation. This checklist will help you evaluate the financial, marketing and societal objectives you formulate. Note your comments in the spaces provided, then put a tick next to the questions as you answer each one.

☐ How is each objective relevant to the organisation's direction and long-term goals?

☐ How is each objective consistent with the organisation's mission, strengths, core competencies and competitive priorities?

☐ How is each objective appropriate for the market's opportunities and threats?

☐ Is each objective specific, time defined and measurable, so that metrics can be applied for performance evaluation?

☐ Is the objective realistic yet challenging to encourage extra effort?

☐ Does the objective conflict with any other objective or with the chosen direction?

FROM OBJECTIVES TO MARKETING-MIX DECISIONS

The objectives you set during this stage of the marketing planning process are the targets to be achieved by implementing the decisions you make about the various marketing-mix elements. This is the point at which your earlier work comes together: on the basis of your situational analysis, your market and customer research and your segmentation, targeting and positioning decisions, you will be creating product, place, price and promotion strategies and action programmes for the who, what, when, where and how of marketing.

Be aware that designing programmes to achieve some of your objectives may require marketing research support. Also note that your objectives will guide the development of customer service and internal marketing strategies to improve internal understanding of the plan and to support your marketing mix.

Chapters 6, 7, 8 and 9 discuss planning for the four marketing-mix elements; **Chapter 10** covers customer service and internal marketing. These are all part of Stage 5 in the marketing planning process.

CHAPTER SUMMARY

Higher-level strategies and goals set the direction for marketing plans that outline objectives to be achieved through marketing strategies, tactics and programmes. Many organisations prepare marketing plans for growth through market penetration (offering existing products to existing markets), product development (offering new products or variations to existing markets), market development (offering existing products to new markets or segments) or diversification (offering new products to new markets or segments). Non-growth strategies include maintenance (to sustain current levels of revenues, share or profits) and retrenchment (to prepare for a turnaround into growth or to close down entirely).

Effective objectives must be relevant, specific, time-defined, measurable, realistic yet challenging, and consistent with the current situation. Marketers also need to be sure they can identify metrics for measuring progress towards achieving the objectives they set. Financial objectives are targets for attaining financial results such as profitability through marketing strategies and programmes. Marketing objectives are targets for achievements in marketing relationships and activities. Societal objectives are targets for ecological protection or other areas of social responsibility.

CASE STUDY: HYUNDAI MOTOR COMPANY

Based in South Korea, Hyundai (www.hyundai.co.uk) creates market-by-market and product-by-product marketing plans to sell vehicles around the world. Overall, it sells

4 million vehicles each year, including 740,000 in China, 700,000 in the US, 328,000 in South Korea and 230,000 in Europe. Hyundai coordinates the financial objectives in every marketing plan with business-level objectives and long-term corporate goals. It also balances its financial objectives (such as for higher sales and profits) with marketing objectives (such as increasing brand awareness, polishing brand image, boosting market share and introducing new vehicles).

The company is adding luxury models like the Genesis and Equus to enhance its image for quality and style. It has also been able to improve its profit margin because it earns more profit on higher-priced cars than on the lower-priced cars for which it was known during its early years of global marketing. Hyundai's marketing plans also aim to reinforce the brand's credentials for technical innovation and sustainability. This is why the Veloster was featured in a Harrods window as part of South Korea's display of high-tech products. For sustainability, Hyundai developed the world's first hybrid car powered by liquefied petroleum gas, which will help it compete with Toyota, Honda and other rivals known for eco-friendly vehicles.

Hyundai's exact marketing-mix choices depend on the objectives set for each market, product and time period. Its marketing plan for introducing the Elantra hybrid in South Korea included marketing-mix activities such as media previews, dealership training and advertising to support the new-product launch. In the US, the Elantra Coupé was turned into an armoured Zombie Survival Machine for a promotion to increase brand awareness and preference among consumers attending the Comic-Con comics convention.

Recently, Hyundai's top executives decided to limit production so they can focus on improving vehicle quality and giving customers a good buying experience. Despite this limit, Hyundai's US plan included the objective of retaining a market share of 5 percent and improving profits by reducing the use of cash incentives that sell cars. As the global economy improves and Hyundai's production output increases, the company expects to discontinue the production cap, keep growing and acquire additional market share.[21]

Case questions

1. Does Hyundai's development of a hybrid car fuelled by liquefied petroleum gas represent market penetration, product development, market development or diversification? Explain.

2. As demand increases, how do you think Hyundai should balance its objectives of maintaining or improving market share, improving quality and improving profit margins?

APPLY YOUR KNOWLEDGE

Research the direction, marketing, financial and societal objectives of a particular company by examining its website, media coverage, products, advertising, packaging, financial disclosures, social responsibility reports and other aspects of its operation. Based on your findings, write a brief report or make a brief oral presentation to the class.

- Is the company pursuing a growth, maintenance or retrenchment strategy? How do you know?

- Does the company disclose any specific objectives? If so, what are they and how do they relate to the company's direction?

- Identify one specific marketing, financial or societal objective that this company has set and compare it to the characteristics in this chapter's checklist. What changes would you recommend to make this objective more effective as a target for performance?

- Look for clues about whether the objective you have identified was actually achieved (and if not, why). What metrics would you use to measure progress towards this objective if you were implementing the plan?

BUILD YOUR OWN MARKETING PLAN

Continue working on your marketing plan. Examining the organisation's current situation, environment, markets, customers and mission statement, what is an appropriate direction for your marketing plan? What marketing, financial and societal objectives will you set to move in the chosen direction? If any of these objectives conflict, which should take priority, and why? How will these objectives guide your planning for the marketing mix and marketing support? What might cause you to rethink your objectives or change the schedule for achieving them? Will you be able to measure your results to determine whether the objectives have been achieved? Take a moment to consider how the direction and objectives fit with the information already in your marketing plan and how practical they are in terms of marketing implementation. Then record your thoughts in your marketing plan.

ENDNOTES

1. Annie Gasparro, 'McDonald's loses some momentum', *Wall Street Journal*, 23 July 2012, www.wsj.com; Alicia Kelso, 'McDonald's focusing on value in slowing global economy', *QSRWeb*, 23 July 2012, www.qsrweb.com; McDonald's annual report 2011; Dan Eaton, 'McDonald's launches Breakfast after Midnight for late-night diners', *Business First (Ohio)*, 31 July 2012, www.bizjournals.com; David Moth, 'The McDonald's app clocks up 1m downloads, but is it any good?', *Econsultancy*, 2 August 2012, www.econsultancy.com; 'McDonald's Christine Xu is helping turn China into a nation of Big Mac eaters', *Advertising Age*, 22 July 2012, www.adage.com.

2. Tim Ambler, 'Set clear goals and see marketing hit its target', *Financial Times*, 29 August 2002, p. 8.

3. H. Igor Ansoff, 'Strategies for diversification', *Harvard Business Review*, September–October 1957, pp. 113–25; Philip Kotler, *Kotler on Marketing* (New York: Free Press, 1999), pp. 46–8.

4. Ishbel Macleod, 'Heinz launches augmented-reality trial for ketchup with Blippar', *The Drum*, 27 October 2011, www.thedrum.co.uk.

5. Kari Hamanaka, 'Taco Bell US sales surge', *Orange County Business Journal (US)*, 19 July 2012, www.ocbj.com.

6. Stuart Dredge, 'King.com hails mainstream potential of mobile gaming', *Guardian*, 24 September 2012, www.guardian.co.uk; John Gaudiosi, 'King.com CEO Riccardo Zacconi explains why the future of social gaming is multi-screen', *Forbes*, 31 July 2012, www.forbes.com.

7. Song Jung-a, 'Samsung eyes success in other galaxies', *Financial Times*, 6 July 2012, www.ft.com.

8. 'BlackBerry 10 handset to launch first in the UK', *BBC News*, 30 January 2013, www.bbc.co.uk; Paul Taylor, 'RIM delays new BlackBerry as losses mount', *Financial Times*, 29 June 2012, www.ft.com; Ian Austen, 'In setback, RIM delays BlackBerry's next version', *New York Times*, 28 June 2012, www.nytimes.com.

9. Quoted in 'Sound long-term strategy is key, particularly in a crisis: Harvard's Michael Porter', *Insead Knowledge*, 1 July 2009 (updated 21 December 2010), http://knowledge.insead.edu/Strategy CrisisMPorter081011.cfm.

10. Zoe Wood, 'Mothercare faces problems from Kiddicare, the new kid on the block', *Guardian*, 22 September 2012, www.guardian.co.uk; Dan Milmo, '£100m loss for Mothercare as stores close and jobs go', *Guardian*, 25 May 2012, www.guardian.co.uk; Susan Thompson and Daniel McCarthy, '830 jobs to go as Mothercare cuts back', *The Times*, 13 April 2012, p. 32; Ben Harrington, 'Strong overseas sales help Mothercare offset fall in UK', *Telegraph*, 20 July 2012, www.telegraph.co.uk.

11. Nils Pratley, 'How Tesco's Fresh & Easy became stale and difficult', *Guardian*, 5 December 2012, www.guardian.co.uk; Clare Kane, 'Tesco CEO says US business could break even this year – report', *Reuters*, 6 March 2012, http://uk.reuters.com; Elliot Zwiebach, 'Tesco pushes back break-even estimate for Fresh & Easy', *Supermarket News*, 18 April 2012, http://supermarketnews.com.

12. See Sandy D. Jap and Erin Anderson, 'Testing the life-cycle theory of inter-organisational relations: do performance outcomes depend on the path taken?', *Insead Knowledge*, February 2003, http://knowledge.insead.edu.

13. Patricia Sellers, 'Muhtar Kent's new Coke', *Fortune*, 10 May 2012, www.fortune.com.

14. Jon Severs, 'Focus on fairtrade: A Fair fight?', *The Grocer*, 8 February 2013, www.thegrocer.co.uk; 'Sainsbury's own brand relaunch 75% complete, Justin King says as Q1 figures released', *The Drum*, 14 June 2012, www.thedrum.co.uk; Andrew Cave, 'Justin King, chief executive of Sainsbury's',

Telegraph, 7 April 2012, www.telegraph.co.uk; James Thompson, 'Sainsbury's to push on with store openings', *The Independent*, 10 November 2011, www.independent.co.uk; 'The vital connection between staff and the bottom line', *Marketing Week*, 10 November 2011, p. 14; Tim Danaher, 'The Sainsbury's plan for growth', *Retail Week*, 21 April 2011, www.retail-week.com.

15. Ola Kinnander, 'Ikea's challenge to the wooden shipping pallet', *Businessweek*, 23 November 2011, www.businessweek.com; Heather King, 'Ikea's Steve Howard on bringing sustainability to the masses', *Green Biz*, 23 February 2012, www.greenbiz.com.

16. Matthew Boyle, 'Unilever wants short showers and long-term investors', *Bloomberg Businessweek*, 5 July 2012, www.businessweek.com.

17. Xueming Luo and C.B. Bhattacharya, 'Corporate social responsibility, customer satisfaction and market value', *Journal of Marketing*, October 2006, pp. 1–18.

18. 'Campaigns: CSR – Selfridges creates a sea change', *PR Week (UK)*, 10 February 2012, p. 24; Tamsin Blanchard, 'Something fishy at Selfridges', *Telegraph*, 11 May 2011, www.telegraph.co.uk; 'Selfridges launch Project Ocean', *Greenpeace UK*, 11 May 2011, www.greenpeace.org.uk; 'Cannes Lions entry: Selfridges Project Ocean', *Cannes Lions*, 2012, www.canneslions.com; 'London Selfridges removes 70 endangered fish varieties', *BBC*, 11 May 2011, www.bbc.co.uk.

19. After Marian Burk Wood, *The Marketing Plan Handbook*, 5th edn (Upper Saddle River, NJ: Pearson Prentice Hall, 2014), Chapter 5.

20. 'Coca-Cola uncaps India bottle with fizz', *Mail Today (New Delhi)*, 27 June 2012, n.p.; Nicola Clark, 'The marketing interview: James Eadie', *Marketing*, 18 January 2012, p. 22; Patricia Sellers, 'Muhtar Kent's new Coke', *Fortune*, 10 May 2012, www.fortune.com; Philip Smith, 'Global think-tank: Ivan Pollard, Coca-Cola', *PR Week (UK)*, 2 December 2011, p. 34; www.coca-cola.com.

21. Simon Mundy, 'EU drives rise in Hyundai Motor sales', *Financial Times*, 26 July 2012, www.ft.com; Lee Ji-yoon, 'Hyundai Motor sheds "cheap car" brand image', *AsiaOne*, 3 August 2012, www.asiaone.com; Amanda Remling, '"Walking Dead" creator Robert Kirkman and Hyundai build zombie survival car', *International Business Times*, 13 July 2012, www.ibtimes.com; 'Now it's the Hyundai Veloster in Harrods' window', *Cars UK*, 3 August 2012, www.carsuk.com; Alisa Priddle, 'Hyundai trying to meet demand in US despite production cap', *Detroit Free Press*, 14 July 2012, www.freep.com; Song Jung-a, 'Hyundai launches first hybrid in S Korea', *Financial Times*, July 2009, www.ft.com.

6 Planning for products and brands

Learning outcomes

After studying this chapter, you will be able to:

- Explain how product mix, product line and product life cycle affect product planning
- Understand the steps in new product development
- Discuss how product attributes provide value for customers
- Describe how to analyse and enhance brand equity

Application outcomes

After studying this chapter, you will be able to:

- Analyse a product's position in the product mix and the life cycle
- Make planning decisions about products
- Make planning decisions about brands

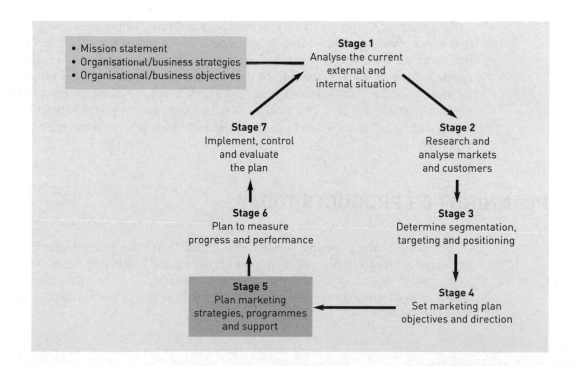

CHAPTER PREVIEW: MARKETING AT ROVIO

The Finnish company Rovio (www.rovio.com) introduced 51 mobile games – with some good but not great results – before its 52nd game, featuring green pigs and, well, angry birds, became a global phenomenon in 2009. Now Angry Birds is played by 200 million people worldwide every day, and Rovio has grown into a highly profitable €129 million company. Because the cost of downloading Angry Birds is so low, more people are inclined to try the game and continue playing when new releases are announced. For example, Angry Birds Space was downloaded 50 million times in the first 35 days of release. In all, more than 1 billion people have downloaded an Angry Birds game, and many players have paid for extras such as power-ups to improve their scores. Building on the game's popularity, Rovio has released spin-offs such as Bad Piggies, also set in the Angry Birds game world.

The company has 200 licensees producing Angry Birds-branded products, everything from T-shirts and plush toys to magnets and masks. It's also opening Angry Birds stores and theme parks in China and beyond to make the most of the brand while it's hot. 'We built the fastest-growing brand in the world using a game called Angry Birds,' states Rovio co-founder Peter Vesterbacka, who says the company's long-term goal is to make Angry Birds 'a permanent part of the pop culture.'[1]

After the success of Angry Birds, Rovio looked outside for its next big game product. The company bought a clever game called Casey's Contraptions from its developers, made some changes and introduced it as Amazing Alex. The multiyear marketing plan for Amazing Alex is similar to that used for Angry Birds: regularly release new versions of the game and special extras to attract new players and retain current players, month after month. If Amazing Alex achieves the popularity of Angry Birds, Rovio is ready to turn it into a brand empire.[2]

Rovio is profiting from its careful product and brand planning, part of stage 5 in the marketing planning process. This chapter opens with a discussion of product mix, product lines and the product life cycle, followed by an examination of new product development. Next, you'll learn how to use different attributes in devising a tangible good or intangible service that will meet your customers' needs, your organisational targets and the marketplace realities. The final section looks at how to plan for brands and brand equity. See this chapter's checklists for questions to ask when planning for products and branding.

PLANNING FOR PRODUCTS TODAY

At this point in the planning process, you understand your current situation and what each product means to the organisation in financial and marketing terms. You've also set your objectives and examined the internal and external factors that might affect your ability to reach those objectives. Now you're ready to plan your marketing mix, starting with the product.

A product may be a physical item (such as food), a service (such as vehicle repairs), a combination of tangible and intangible elements (such as a restaurant), an idea (such as better health) or a place (such as a tourist destination). Some companies, including Rovio, market a **virtual product**, a product that exists only in electronic form as a digital representation of something. More companies are looking for ways to profit from virtual products; already, 15 million people buy virtual goods from Facebook every year.[3]

For any specific product you market or plan to market, look closely at:

- the customer segment being targeted

- the needs satisfied and value provided

- trends in pricing, unit sales, market share, revenues and profits

- age and performance over time, by segment, channel and geography

- sales connections between products

- current or potential opportunities and threats related to each product

- competitive strengths, weaknesses and position

- customers' perceptions of competing products.

The point of these analyses is to determine how each product provides value to customers and your organisation. For example, Rovio's marketers know that the market for mobile games is growing rapidly, but they also see great potential for adapting their games to other platforms, such as video game consoles, and for social games, such as Angry Birds Friends for Facebook. A possible threat is increased competition from mobile games that are thriving on Facebook, such as King.com's Bubble Witch Saga and Candy Crush Saga.[4]

As a visual summary, you can create a grid matching each product to the intended target market, detail the need each product satisfies and indicate the value delivered from the customer's and organisation's perspectives (see Table 6.1). In addition, you may want to include information about each product's competitive position and strength – with the understanding that competitive circumstances can change at any time, given the volatility of today's marketplace.

Some companies are starting to produce new goods and services through *co-creation*, working closely with customers to develop innovative products; others are using **crowd-sourcing** to generate new product ideas or marketing content from concepts, designs, content or advice submitted by customers and others outside the organisation. Netflix, which streams movies and TV programmes to subscribers, is using crowdsourcing as part of an experiment with subtitles as it expands throughout Europe.[5] Volvo offers a Facebook app that allows drivers to upload photos of what's inside their cars, as a way of learning more about consumer lifestyles and preferences for storage space and other interior features.[6]

After analysing your products, you'll face decisions about managing (1) the product mix and product lines, (2) product attributes including quality and performance, features and benefits, design, packaging and labelling and branding, (3) the product life cycle

Table 6.1 Product/segment analysis grid

	Customer segment A (briefly describe)	Customer segment B (briefly describe)
Product 1 (identify)	Customer need: Value to customer: Value to organisation: Competitive situation:	Customer need: Value to customer: Value to organisation: Competitive situation:
Product 2 (identify)	Customer need: Value to customer: Value to organisation: Competitive situation:	Customer need: Value to customer: Value to organisation: Competitive situation:
Product 3 (identify)	Customer need: Value to customer: Value to organisation: Competitive situation:	Customer need: Value to customer: Value to organisation: Competitive situation:

Table 6.2 Product planning decisions

Product mix and product lines	Product attributes
• Change product line length or depth • Change product mix width • Consider cannibalisation effect • Consider limited-time and limited-edition products	• Plan level of quality and performance • Provide valued benefits through features • Design for functionality and differentiation • Create packaging and labelling • Build brand equity
Product life cycle	**New product development**
• Locate product in cycle by segment and market • Change progression through life cycle • Balance life cycles of multiple products	• Add new product categories • Expand existing lines or brands • Manage steps in process • Address ecological and ethical concerns

and (4) new product development. Table 6.2 shows these four categories of product planning decisions.

Product mix and product line decisions

When you manage the **product mix**, you're determining the assortment of product lines offered by your organisation. **Product line length** is the number of individual items in each line (or range) of related products; **product line depth** refers to the number of variations of each product within one line. Your marketing plan can cover one or more of the following activities:

- introducing new products in an existing line under the existing brand name (**line extensions** that lengthen the line);

- introducing variations of existing products in a product line (deepening the line);

- introducing new brand names in an existing product line or category (**multibrand strategy**);

- introducing new products under an existing brand (**brand extensions** that widen the mix);

- introducing new lines in other product categories (**category extensions** that widen the mix);

- eliminating a product (shortening the line);

- eliminating or adding a product line (narrowing or widening the mix).

Each decision about the product changes the way you satisfy customers in targeted segments, address opportunities, avert threats, allocate marketing resources and achieve marketing objectives. Adding new products by extending a familiar, established line or brand can minimise the risk that customers and channel partners may perceive in trying something new. Because of this familiarity, the product's introductory campaign is likely to be more efficient and may even cost less than for an entirely new brand or product in a new category. Your development costs may also be lower if you base a new product on an existing product.

Extensions that are well received will reinforce the brand, capture new customers and accommodate the variety-seeking behaviour of current customers. Extensions are not without risk, however. If you extend a line or brand, customers or channel members may become confused about the different products you offer. Remember that channel members with limited shelf or storage space may be reluctant to carry additional products. If the product doesn't succeed, perceptions of the brand or other products in the line may be affected. Also, look closely at whether you are spreading your resources too thinly and at how each product or line will contribute to organisational objectives. And if a product or line doesn't perform as well as expected, be ready to make changes or delete it.

Cannibalisation

When extending a line or creating a new product, think about the possibility of **cannibalisation**, which can occur when one of your products takes sales from another of your products. A lower-priced line extension may attract customers who previously purchased your higher-priced products, for example, which would affect your revenues. Many marketers try to minimise cannibalisation, although some, including Apple (www.apple.com), believe it's better to cannibalise their own products than risk having competitors lure customers away.

MARKETING IN PRACTICE: APPLE

Since introducing the original Macintosh computer more than 25 years ago, California-based Apple has constantly extended its product lines and expanded its product mix to include iPods, iPhones, iPads, the iTunes Store, the App Store and more. Chief executive Tim Cook observes that the pace of change in the technology world and the rate at which customers embrace new products have both increased since that first Mac. Apple sold 55 million Macs in 22 years, then sold 22 million iPods in five years and 22 million iPhones in three years. Even more amazing, Apple sold 55 million iPads in less than two years. And when it launched the iPhone5, Apple sold 5 million units during the first weekend.

When Apple first launched the iPad, some industry insiders expected the tablet to cannibalise Mac sales, just as analysts had expected the iPhone to cannibalise iPod sales (which it did). Tim Cook acknowledged then that the iPad was probably affecting Mac sales, but, referring to the highly publicised tablet buying frenzy, he added, 'if this is cannibalization, it feels pretty good'.[7] Cook noted the iPad was more likely to take sales away from competing PCs than from Macs, thus helping Apple gain more market share overall. He also commented on the iPad's *halo effect* in attracting first-time Apple customers who then buy other Apple products.

Despite increasingly intense competition, Apple has managed to maintain revenue gains and impressive profit margins. It is not only investing heavily in research and design to keep a steady flow of innovative variations in its product pipeline, it's also boosting sales by bringing its products to new markets. When Apple launched its iPad in China, the product quickly became the best-selling tablet computer by far, despite its relatively high price.[8] What's next for Apple?

Marketing plan analysis: What are the advantages and disadvantages of Apple's approach to cannibalising itself?

Limited-time and limited-edition products

Some marketers create goods or services that are marketed only during a specific period – *limited-time products* that showcase seasonal ingredients or leverage advantageous timing in another way. Although Wendy's fast-food restaurants in the United States focus on affordable hamburgers and fries, Wendy's in Japan is targeting customers with a taste for seafood and a bigger fast-food budget. It differentiates itself from competitors by introducing unusual limited-time entrées such as lobster and beef burgers and lobster sandwiches with caviar.[9]

Limited-edition products are produced just once, often in small quantities, to draw attention to a brand or to commemorate a particular event. Ferrari marked the 20th anniversary of selling its high-end sports cars in China by producing only 20 special 'Year of the Dragon' cars, priced at over €400,000 – and buyers moved quickly to reserve one before they were gone.[10] Many marketers created limited-edition products to celebrate the 2012 London Olympics. McDonald's created several limited-edition menu items for its Olympic Park restaurants, including the Wispa Gold McFlurry, an ice cream dessert featuring Cadbury Wispa pieces and Cadbury caramel sauce.[11]

Limited-time and limited-edition products get customers buzzing because they are out of the ordinary, in short supply, and suggest both urgency and exclusivity. Word of mouth about these types of products can spread quickly through social media, further increasing demand and adding to the feeling of excitement customers may experience when they are able to make this purchase.

Product life-cycle decisions

As you plan, you must make decisions about how to manage the **product life cycle**, a product's movement through the market as it passes from introduction to growth, maturity and eventual decline. Although no individual product's life cycle is entirely predictable or even necessarily sequential, the typical life cycle pictured in Figure 6.1 shows how sales and profitability can change in each part of the cycle. Corporate giants such as Unilever and Reckitt Benckiser tend to have numerous products in targeted markets at one time; each could very well be in a different part of its life cycle.

Analysing a product's life-cycle situation and using marketing activities to manage the cycle can help you plan to take advantage of anticipated ups and downs. Where is the product within its life cycle, how quickly is it progressing through each part of the cycle, and what can you consider doing to alter the cycle or to get the most out of each part? As Figure 6.1 suggests, profitability is highest during the growth part of the life cycle and tends to decrease with maturity. This is why many companies plan strategies to extend and reinvigorate products in the growth and maturity stages.

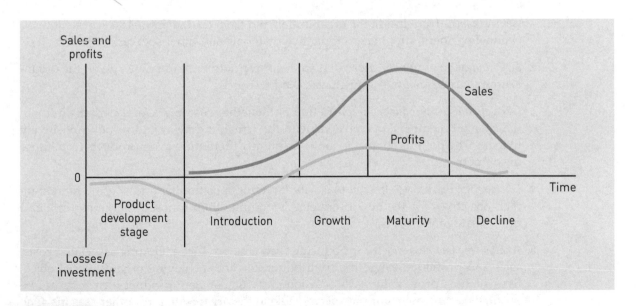

| FIGURE 6.1 | Product life cycle |

Source: Figure 6.1 from *Marketing: An Introduction*, 11th Ed., Pearson Education (Armstrong, G. and Kotler, P. 2012) p. 242, ISBN-13: 978-0132744034. Reproduced with permission from Pearson Education Ltd.

Some products are reaching maturity much faster, compressing their life cycle and creating additional marketing challenges. In a fast-moving market like mobile games, products tend to speed through growth and become mature very quickly – sometimes in a matter of months or a few years. That's why Rovio, King.com and other game-makers plan a constant stream of line extensions to keep up player enthusiasm for specific games, appeal to players who use multiple devices and wring profits from products throughout the life cycle. At the height of Angry Birds' popularity, Rovio was regularly releasing seasonal versions of the game (such as a new version for the Chinese new year) and adapting the game to other platforms. Similarly, King.com adapted its successful Bubble Witch Saga to be played on iPads, iPhones and other mobile devices.

New product development decisions

Having discovered promising opportunities during earlier stages of the planning process and analysed the life cycle of current products, you may decide to change your product mix by developing new products for targeted customer segments. Some products may open up new categories for your organisation; other products may extend existing lines or brands. Either way, product development details are usually shown in an appendix or separate document, not in the main marketing plan. However, your plan should outline the major decisions, include research or other evidence, highlight key actions and outline the product development schedule.

Here's an overview of the new product development process:

1. *Generate ideas* from inside the organisation and from customers, sales representatives, channel partners, suppliers, competitive materials and other sources.

2. *Screen ideas* to eliminate those that are inappropriate or not feasible, given the organisation's strengths, core competencies and resources.

3. *Develop and test product concepts* to find out whether customers (and perhaps influential channel members) perceive value in the remaining ideas and respond positively to them. The point is not just to innovate but to differentiate your products from those of competitors.

4. *Develop the marketing strategy* to clarify targeting, positioning and specific marketing plan objectives for the new product. Also outline the proposed marketing mix and project sales and profits.

5. *Analyse the business case* for introducing each new product, including associated costs, sales and profits, to gauge the contribution towards achieving organisational objectives such as profitability. On occasion, a particular new product idea may not be profitable on its own, but may be valuable to the organisation for other reasons. One product may lead to the purchase of other products (the way printers lead to the purchase of ink cartridges), or a product may demonstrate the firm's commitment to going green.

6. *Develop the product* to see whether the concept is practical and cost effective and meets customers' needs and expectations. Sometimes this step means reinventing the way a firm has always produced and marketed its goods or services.

7. *Test market the product*, with associated marketing strategies, to assess the likelihood of market acceptance and success. Try different marketing activities, evaluate customer response, anticipate competitors' reactions and adjust the product and marketing as needed. Intuit, which makes US bookkeeping and tax preparation software, tests 140 new product ideas every year, quickly discarding ideas that don't test well to focus on the very best product ideas.[12]

8. *Launch the product commercially*, applying the lessons learned from test marketing and from previous product introductions.

New product development doesn't end with commercialisation. You must monitor market response, including the reactions of customers, channel members and competitors. If you see that the product is not selling as well as projected, you will want to change the product or other elements of the marketing mix as needed. The most successful new product innovations result from need identification, solution identification and marketing research. At the same time, the rate of new product failure is so high that you must carefully screen ideas to avoid investing in unpromising or unneeded products.

Don't forget the ecological and ethical issues related to your product. Can eco-friendly supplies and processes be incorporated? Will the product's production or use adversely affect the natural environment? How will the new product serve your organisation's societal objectives? What ethical questions might arise (such as whether to test products on animals) and how can you address these in a satisfactory way? More buyers in more markets are looking at these aspects of a product's sustainability and social responsibility impact.

In Asia, for example, research shows that consumers in India, Vietnam and Indonesia are increasingly interested in eco-friendly products and pay attention to whether a product is recyclable and how it conserves natural resources.[13] Many European consumers prefer to buy food products made from ethically sourced Fairtrade ingredients; as a result, sales of such products have been increasing year after year.[14] Consider whether your product would have a competitive advantage or disadvantage in such situations.

Product attribute decisions

Whether you're developing new products or improving existing ones, you'll seek the optimal combination of quality and performance, features and benefits, design, packaging and labelling (see Table 6.3). You'll also face important decisions about branding, as discussed later in this chapter. You want your product to be competitively distinctive, attractive and valuable to customers while returning profits to the organisation. Be sure your product is competitively superior on features and benefits valued by customers; also check that the product supports your marketing plan objectives.

Table 6.3 Planning product attributes

	Product 1	Product 2	Product 3
Quality (customers' view) and **performance** (objective measures)			
Features and **benefits** (to satisfy customer needs)			
Design (for performance and differentiation)			
Packaging (for protection, storage and ease of use) and **labelling** (for information and marketing communication)			
Brand (to identify, differentiate and provoke response)			

Quality and performance decisions

Quality means different things to different people; this is why you should define a product's quality in terms of how well it satisfies the needs of your customers. From this perspective, a high-quality product is one that satisfies needs better than a poor-quality product. You can certainly use objective performance measures to demonstrate a product's functionality, reliability, sturdiness and lack of defects. Quality counts in services as much as it does in tangible products, although the measures may differ from service to service.

In the marketplace, customers are the final judges of quality and decide for themselves what level of quality they want and will pay for – a decision that can change depending on customers' economic situations and other factors. Tesco and other retailers have profited by offering their own branded products, ranging from basic 'value' quality at affordable prices to 'finest' quality at higher prices.[15] B2B marketers are concerned with quality and performance as well. When Rolls Royce developed an all-electric experimental Phantom car, it asked Axeon to build a powerful battery to meet the car's performance standards.[16] Before you introduce or even begin developing a new product, you have to ensure that the entire organisation is capable of consistently delivering the expected quality, given the available resources and schedule. This, too, is part of the marketing planning process.

Feature and benefit decisions

Customers buy a product not only for the **features** – specific attributes that contribute to functionality – but also for the **benefits** – the need-satisfaction outcomes they want or expect. To illustrate, Samsung's customers want mobiles to satisfy their communication needs with features for calling, texting and the Internet, all of which provide the benefit of exchanging information. Specific Samsung models offer additional features that

Table 6.4	Matching features and benefits to needs
Customer segment and need	**Feature and benefit**
Lorry fleet owners who need to monitor tyre pressure and track the location of all tyres	Sensor patch on each tyre electronically transmits pressure and identification data to owners
Farmers who need to drive tractors over fields and in uneven terrain	Large, deep tyre patterns provide more secure road grip
Professional sports car drivers who seek winning performance	Special composition tyres for speed and handling
Airlines that require durable, cost-efficient tyres	Special composition tyres for longer wear and lower maintenance costs

deliver benefits valued by customers, such as a touch screen or the ability to stream entertainment. When evaluating competing products, customers look at whether each model has the features that provide the benefits they value. In practice, you should plan for features that deliver the benefits that you know your customers value (based on marketing research).

Not all customers want or are willing to pay for the benefits provided by a particular product's features. In fact, too many features can make a product too complex or expensive for the targeted audience.[17] Different segments often have different needs and different perceptions of the value of features and benefits. Table 6.4 shows, in simplified form, how Groupe Michelin, the French tyre maker, might match features to benefits that satisfy the needs of specific customer segments. You can see how Michelin could offer value and differentiate its tyres from those of competitors such as Goodyear. Creating a similar matrix can help you pinpoint each segment's needs and identify features and benefits to satisfy those needs.

Design decisions

Directly or indirectly, customers' perceptions and buying choices are influenced to some degree by design. Moreover, your design decisions can affect the ecology as well as product performance. Therefore, as with all other product decisions, you should be sure that a product's design is consistent with your organisation's marketing, financial and societal objectives and that it fits with your other marketing mix decisions. Ideally, design decisions should create a bridge to your future vision of how the product will benefit the target market and set it apart from those of rivals. The distinctive bonnet ornaments of Rolls-Royce Motors and Jaguar are design elements that convey the cars' branding and have become associated with status, for instance.

Product design has become such a prime point of differentiation, especially for mature products like household appliances, that everyday products need not look ordinary. In fact, the pressure of global competition has prompted many marketers to devote more time and resources to product design. Apple built its business on sleek and user-friendly design, revolutionising mobiles and tablet computers with stylish and practical products. One of Apple's industrial designers says that he and his colleagues 'imagine products that don't exist and guide them to life' and that they 'obsess over details'.[18]

Design is as important for service providers such as hotels as it is for physical goods. As Whitbread (www.whitbread.co.uk) expands its Premier Inn hotels, for example, it must decide on design details for each market.

MARKETING IN PRACTICE: WHITBREAD'S PREMIER INN

Whitbread's mission is to 'grow legendary brands by building a strong customer heartbeat and innovating to stay ahead'. The Premier Inn budget hotel chain accounts for 44 percent of Whitbread's £1.8 billion annual turnover. Following a marketing plan for growth, the chain is on track to operate 65,000 hotel rooms by mid-2016, including new hotels in the UK, India and the Middle East.

In the UK, Premier Inn targets families with features like free breakfasts for children under 16, giving guests more value for their money. Some of the hotels have self-service kiosks that allow guests to avoid the queue at reception. Guests also appreciate the budget-friendly feature of 30 minutes of free Wi-Fi access every day. Another intangible feature is Premier Inn's money-back guarantee, which delivers the benefit of reassuring guests that they will be satisfied with their experience.

Whitbread is expanding into India to take advantage of opportunities created by the growth of the middle class and higher demand for domestic travel. Before it built its first Premier Inn hotels in India, it showed research participants through several prototype guest rooms to obtain feedback about the design. It learned that Indian guests prefer a closed wardrobe, rather than an open wardrobe as in its UK rooms; it also made every room large enough for a family of four. For the convenience of business travellers, every Premier Inn in India is designed with meeting rooms and a full-service restaurant. Three things Premier Inn doesn't plan to change in any market: its affordable prices, its signature purple décor and the money-back guarantee that sets the hotel apart from its competitors.[19]

Marketing plan analysis: What benefits are Premier Inn's design decisions intended to deliver to guests?

Packaging and labelling decisions

Good packaging protects tangible goods, makes their use or storage more convenient for customers and, ideally, serves societal objectives such as ecological protection. Think about how Walkers crisps are packaged to remain fresh and crispy for weeks; the company also offers packaging in various sizes for different customer needs, such as on-the-go snacks and family meals. When planning for any product to be sold in a store, be sure to consider how labelling can serve marketing functions. Labels are more than informative:

they can capture the shopper's attention, describe how product features deliver benefits, differentiate the product from competing items and reinforce brand image.

Marketing functions aside, labels must meet applicable laws and regulations wherever your products are sold. For example, only when the animals have been born and raised in the UK can meats be legally labelled as British. In Canada's Québec province, multilingual labels must include a French equivalent for every word, printed in type that is as big as or bigger than the type used for other languages. In the United States, supermarkets must label fruits, vegetables and meats to indicate the country of origin.

Use Checklist No. 10 as you proceed with planning product attributes, and be sure to consider brand planning, as discussed in the next section.

ESSENTIAL CHECKLIST NO. 10:
PLANNING FOR PRODUCTS

Now that you've set specific objectives for your marketing plan, you need to begin planning for your products. This checklist will help you think through the main issues and decisions. Write your answers in the spaces provided and put a tick next to the questions as you complete each one. If your marketing plan is for a product not yet on the market, use this checklist to consider the key decisions you'll face in planning for a successful introduction.

☐ What is the current situation of each product within its line and the overall product mix?

_____

☐ Would customers' needs and the organisation's interests be served by changing the product mix, product lines or line depth?

_____

☐ Where is each product in its life cycle and what are the implications for product planning?

_____

☐ What new products can be developed to take advantage of promising opportunities in targeted segments?

_____

☐ If you're planning a new product, how can you improve the odds of success as you move through each step in the development process?

_____

☐ How much cannibalisation might be expected from a new product introduction or line extension?

___

☐ Would a limited-edition or limited-time product be appropriate for the target market?

___

☐ What are the ecological and ethical considerations associated with each product?

___

☐ How can you use quality and performance, features and benefits, design, packaging and labelling to provide value for customers and your organisation?

___

PLANNING FOR BRANDS

Branding is a pivotal aspect of product planning because it provides identity and competitive differentiation to stimulate customer response. An unbranded product is just a commodity, indistinguishable from competing products except in terms of price. A branded product may have similar attributes to competitors' products yet be seen as distinctly different (and provoke a different customer response) because of the rational or emotional value the brand adds in satisfying the customer's needs and wants.[20]

In planning for a brand, you should identify ways to increase **brand equity**, the extra value customers perceive in a brand that ultimately builds long-term loyalty. Higher brand equity contributes to sustained competitive advantage, attracts new channel partners and reinforces current channel relationships. As you build brand equity, you educate your customers to the nuances of brand meaning in your product category. You also enhance your marketing power and wring more productivity out of your marketing activities as customers (1) become aware of your brand and its identity, (2) know what the brand stands for, (3) respond to it, and (4) want an ongoing relationship with it. The brand equity pyramid in Figure 6.2 illustrates how, at the lowest level, customers understand what your brand is about; at the peak, customers are strongly attached to the brand and interact with it.[21]

Be aware that customers in the targeted segment may know the brand, understand what it stands for and respond to it – but not want the kind of ongoing relationship that the organisation would like. The ultimate objective of brand planning is to move customers upwards through the levels of brand equity and encourage them to remain at the top, where they are likely to be loyal and even act as advocates to bring new customers to the brand. This raises the customer's lifetime value to the organisation and helps achieve your objectives. It's important to remember that companies benefit financially from brand equity, but the identity, meaning, response and relationships all derive from customer interaction with the brand.[22]

- What relationship does the customer have with the brand?

- What judgements and feelings do customers have about the brand?

- What associations do customers have with the brand?

- How aware are customers of the brand's identity?

FIGURE 6.2	Brand equity pyramid

Source: After *Strategic Brand Management*, 2, Pearson Education Inc. (Keller, K.L. 2003) 76, Prentice Hall, KELLER, KEVIN LANE, STRATEGIC BRAND MANAGEMENT, 2nd Ed., p. 76, © 2003. Reprinted and Electronically reproduced by permission of Pearson Education, Inc., Upper Saddle River, New Jersey.

Brand identity

Here, you want to make customers in the targeted segment aware of your brand's identity. A brand can consist of words, numbers, symbols and/or graphics to add salience, such as the Nike name combined with its swoosh symbol or the Nestlé name combined with the nesting bird logo. You can develop or license a brand using one or more of the approaches to naming shown in Table 6.5.

If a product doesn't perform as it should or if it attracts negative response for some other reason, the brand will suffer – a risk when you use the company name as the brand or you're participating in co-branding. When you specify co-branding in a marketing plan, look for a partner whose brand identity fits well with your brand identity and whose values are similar to your firm's values.

Bringing customers to this first level of brand equity involves decisions about the brand itself as well as other product attributes and marketing actions. For example, how can you use product packaging and labelling to convey a distinctive brand identity? Coca-Cola uses an easily recognised red-and-white logo to set its colas apart from other soft drinks. You can also build customers' awareness of the brand through advertising, in-store promotions, websites and other marketing activities that reinforce the differentiation. Customers who are unaware of a brand will not think of it when purchasing, which is why organisations often set marketing objectives for awareness. Establishing a brand identity and making customers aware of it is a prelude to creating brand meaning.

Table 6.5 Naming a brand

Approach to naming	Description	Example
Company brand (also known as manufacturer's brand or national brand)	The company name becomes the brand, thus associating the company image with the product	Virgin puts its name on all products
Family or umbrella brand	Each product in one or more lines or categories is identified as belonging to that particular brand family (or being under that brand umbrella)	Toyota puts the Lexus name on its family of luxury vehicles
Individual brand	A product is identified with a brand not shared by other products	Belu bottled water, with profits to Water Aid
Private brand	Retailers and other channel members frequently brand their own products for differentiation from manufacturers' branded products	Tesco uses Finest as one of its private brands
Co-brand	Two or more companies put their brands on one or more goods or services	Tim Hortons/Cold Stone Creamery co-branded stores

Brand meaning

The second level of brand equity is to shape the associations that customers have with your brand. What do you want the brand to stand for? What image or personality does the brand have, and is it the same as what you want to create? These are especially important points to consider when planning brand extensions. The Dutch paint company AkzoNobel wants consumers in India to make an emotional connection with its Dulux brand, so it promotes the benefit of expressing individuality through the choice of paint colour for a room or home.[23]

As customers come to understand a brand's meaning, they rely on it as a shortcut when making buying choices, which expedites the buying process and reduces the perceived risk. You can mould brand meaning through positioning and through favourable associations backed up by product performance, features that deliver value through need satisfaction, distinctive design and so on. As with brand identity, other marketing activities are involved as well. Here's a look at the branding challenges facing Lenovo (www.lenovo.com/uk/en/), the Chinese company that purchased IBM's PC division in 2005.

MARKETING IN PRACTICE: LENOVO

After purchasing all of IBM's PC products, Lenovo's chief marketing officer was deter-mined to add the Lenovo name and logo to the ThinkPad laptop, a favourite of corporate buyers. Although some Lenovo executives were concerned about hurting the ThinkPad's image or sales by adding the parent company's little-known name, this turned out to be a smart marketing decision because it helped Lenovo build a global reputation for quality, reliability and technological innovation. Today, Lenovo is a €17 billion company and one of the world's top three PC firms, as measured by market share. Unlike most of its com-petitors, Lenovo controls its own manufacturing plants, allowing the firm to react quickly to new technological advances, changes in demand and other factors.

Lenovo dominates its home country's PC market, and it became the top-selling PC brand in India by projecting a youthful image and adding the glamour of a Bollywood star's endorsement. Yet because the PC market is mature, Lenovo is looking at how to use product and brand strategy to increase sales in targeted markets. For example, identifying the educational segment as an area of opportunity, Lenovo recently developed a line of ThinkPads specifically for classroom use. This deepened the product line and differentiated Lenovo's offerings from those of its competitors. The company is also aggressively pursu-ing business customers who have computer networking needs. In addition to its growing line of servers for businesses of all sizes, Lenovo recently partnered with EMC to sell networking equipment and cloud storage services to small and medium-sized businesses.

Looking ahead, Lenovo wants to move into mobiles, tablet computers, web-enabled televisions and other products where global demand is growing. In these categories, however, formidable competitors like Apple and Samsung set themselves apart on the basis of innovative design, not yet a strength of the Lenovo brand. To compete more effectively in non-PC products, Lenovo will need to add some new associations to its brand meaning.[24]

Marketing plan analysis: How can Lenovo use new products to shape the associations that customers have of its brand?

Brand response

The third level of brand equity relates to customer response. Once customers are aware of the brand's identity and understand its meaning, they can make up their minds about the brand. Ideally, you want your customers to believe in your brand, trust it and perceive it as embodying positive qualities. You also want customers to see the brand as competitively superior and, just as important, have an emotional connection to it. Determining customer response requires marketing research, followed up by action steps either to reinforce positive responses or to turn negative (or neutral) responses into positive ones through marketing activities.

Cancer Research UK, for example, discovered that potential contributors viewed the charity as 'too clinical' and 'too scientific'. To encourage a more emotional response to the brand, the charity changed its marketing. Now its communications use a warmer tone and focus on the 'smart, brave, engaging and optimistic' scientists and contributors who support research into cancer treatment and prevention.[25]

Brand relationship

The fourth level of brand equity deals with customers' relationship to the brand. They know about the brand, know what it means to them and how they feel about it. But are they sufficiently attached to remain loyal buyers? You want to encourage strong and enduring brand relationships because loyal customers tend to buy more, resist switching to competing brands and be willing to pay a premium for the brand and recommend it to others.[26] The issue is therefore how you can use your product plan, along with other marketing-mix activities, to reinforce customers' brand preference and loyalty.

One approach is to improve or at least maintain product quality and performance to avoid disappointing customers, tarnishing the brand and discouraging customer loyalty. Another is to add products or features that better satisfy current customers' needs. A third is to continue introducing innovative or upgraded product designs, packaging and labelling consistent with the brand image. Finally, your marketing plan should allow for research to see how effective you have been in moving customers up the brand equity pyramid towards sustained customer loyalty. Use Checklist no. 11 as you plan for your brand.

ESSENTIAL CHECKLIST NO. 11:
PLANNING FOR BRANDS

Planning for brands must be carefully coordinated with planning for products. This brief checklist can help you think about your branding decisions and about how your product will support your brand. Note your answers in the spaces provided, putting a tick next to the questions as you answer them.

☐ How is the brand identified and what are the implications for its image?

_____

☐ How is the brand positioned for competitive differentiation?

_____

☐ How do product attributes support the brand image?

_____

☐ Are customers aware of the brand? If so, what does it mean to them? How can brand awareness be expanded through marketing?

_____

☐ What do customers think and feel about the brand? What relationship do they have or want with it?

☐ How can brand preference and loyalty be encouraged through marketing?

Source: Adapted from Kevin Lane Keller, *Strategic Brand Management*, 2nd edn (Upper Saddle River, NJ: Prentice Hall, 2003), Chapter 2.

CHAPTER SUMMARY

Planning for products includes decisions about the product mix (the assortment of product lines being offered), product line length (the number of items in each line) and product line depth (the number of product variations within a line). The product life cycle is a product's market movement as it progresses from introduction to growth, maturity and decline. In new product development, you will (1) generate ideas, (2) screen ideas, (3) research customer reaction, (4) develop the marketing strategy, (5) analyse the business case, (6) develop the product to determine practicality, (7) test market the product and (8) commercialise it.

Decisions must be made about product quality and performance, features and benefits, design, packaging and labelling, and branding. Quality means how well a product satisfies customer needs. Features are attributes that contribute to product functionality and deliver benefits. Design is especially important for differentiation. Packaging protects products and facilitates their use or storage. Labels provide information, attract attention, describe features and benefits, differentiate products and reinforce brand image. Branding identifies a product and differentiates it from competing products to stimulate customer response. Brand equity is the extra value customers perceive in a brand that builds long-term loyalty and boosts competitive advantage.

CASE STUDY: L'ORÉAL

L'Oréal (www.loreal.com), the world's largest cosmetics company, markets beauty products under luxury brands such as Lancôme and Yves Saint Laurent, mainstream brands such as Maybelline and Garnier, professional brands such as Matrix and Kérastase and speciality skincare brands such as Vichy. It also owns the Body Shop and Kiehl's retail chains. With €20.3 billion in annual turnover, L'Oréal is pursuing a growth strategy by managing a portfolio of products in different stages of the life cycle and planning for new products targeting consumers and beauty salons.

One of L'Oréal's fastest-growing consumer beauty brands is Kiehl's, a well-established company purchased in 2000 from its New York owner. Kiehl's is positioned as 'accessible luxury' and its namesake stores feature the brand's US-manufactured face creams and other cosmetics. Rather than promote the brand using traditional advertising, Kiehl's relies on product sampling, knowing that if customers have a positive experience with a trial-size product, they are likely to buy it.

Targeting beauty salons, L'Oréal often develops haircare products specifically for use in particular areas. For example, it created Biolage Oiltherapie for beauty salons in India and X-Tenso Care for use in beauty salons across Brazil. Twice a year, the company introduces new hair colouring products for salon use, based on the latest fashion trends. To support these new colours, L'Oréal invites thousands of professional stylists to attend special events where its trainers demonstrate new hair fashions and answer questions about product usage.

The company is extremely active in social and digital media, tracking daily mentions of its brands and analysing the content to understand how customers view its products. In its home country of France, L'Oréal has released an Instant Beauty app so that consumers can access detailed information about individual products and also see what friends recommend. It also maintains country-specific and brand-specific websites featuring celebrities such as Beyoncé Knowles and Gerard Butler as the public faces of skincare and haircare products intended to help men and women look their best in every situation.[27]

Case questions

1. In terms of the brand equity pyramid, why would L'Oréal hold special events to train professional stylists whose salons buy its professional haircare products?

2. What channel issues should L'Oréal consider when its marketing plan calls for introducing product variations such as seasonal cosmetics colours?

APPLY YOUR KNOWLEDGE

Select an organisation offering a branded good or service with which you are familiar and research its product and brand. Summarise your findings in a brief oral presentation or written report.

- From a customer's perspective, how would you describe the product's quality and performance? Do you think this perception of value matches what the marketer intended?

- How do the features deliver benefits to satisfy needs of the targeted customer segments?

- How do design, packaging and labelling contribute to your reaction, as a customer, to this product?

- Where does this product appear to be in its life cycle? How do you know?

- How would you describe this product's brand? What is the organisation doing to build brand equity?

- Would a limited-time or limited-edition version of this product be appealing to the target market and potentially profitable for the marketer? Explain your answer.

BUILD YOUR OWN MARKETING PLAN

Going back to the marketing plan you've been preparing, is your product a tangible good or an intangible service? What level of quality is appropriate (and affordable) to meet the needs of the targeted customer segments? What needs do customers satisfy through products such as yours and what features must your product have in order to deliver the expected or desired benefits? What can you do with design, packaging and labelling to add value and differentiate your product? What brand image do you want to project? How do you want customers to feel about the brand and react towards it? What can you do to encourage brand loyalty? Think about your answers in the context of your earlier ideas and decisions, then draft the product and brand sections of your marketing plan.

ENDNOTES

1. Quoted in 'Angry Birds builds nest in China', *Xinhua News Agency*, 13 June 2012, www.china.org.cn/business/2012-06/13/content_25639760.htm.

2. Kim-Mai Cutler, 'From the pig's point of view: Angry Birds-maker Rovio shows off gameplay in upcoming "Bad Piggies"', *TechCrunch*, 17 September 2012, http://techcrunch.com; 'Mobile plays lead role in growth of gaming', *Marketing Week*, 19 July 2012, p. 20; 'Rovio's golden egg: its 2011 profits', *PC Magazine Online*, 7 May 2012, www.pcmag.com; 'Rovio hopes that Amazing Alex will fly as high as Angry Birds', *Europe Intelligence Wire*, 12 July 2012, n.p.

3. Lim Yung-Hui, '1.6% of Facebook users spent over $1 billion on virtual goods', *Forbes*, 2 August 2012, www.forbes.com.

4. 'Angry Birds trilogy flying to PS3, Xbox, 3DS', *PC Magazine Online*, 10 July 2012, www.pcmag.com; 'Angry Birds Friends takes flight on Facebook', *PC Magazine Online*, 23 May 2012, www.pcmag.com; 'Mobile plays lead role in growth of gaming', *Marketing Week*, 19 July 2012, p. 20.

5. Janko Roettgers, 'Netflix experiments with crowd-sourced captioning', *GigaOm*, 30 July 2012, http://gigaom.com.

6. 'Volvo to crowdsource car designs', *Marketing Week*, 15 August 2012, www.marketingweek.co.uk.

7. Quoted in M.G. Siegler, 'Apple's Cook on iPad/ Mac relationship: '"If this is cannibalization, it feels pretty good"', *TechCrunch*, 18 January 2011, http://techcrunch.com.

8. Jennifer Saba and Sinead Carew, 'Apple sells over 5 million iPhone 5, supply constraints loom', *Reuters*, 24 September 2012, www.reuters.com; A.T. Faust III, 'Apple eclipses 70% of Chinese market', *Mashable*, 7 August 2012, http://mashable. com; Philip Elmer-DeWitt, 'Transcript: Apple CEO Tim Cook at Goldman Sachs', *Fortune*, 15 February 2012, www.fortune.com; Scott Anthony, 'Combating cannibalization concerns', *Harvard Business Review Blog Network*, 18 February 2011, http://blogs.hbr.org.

9. Eamon Murphy, 'Lobster and caviar burgers? Wendy's menu goes upscale in Japan', *Daily Finance*, 8 August 2012, www.dailyfinance.com.

10. Peter Veldes-Dapena, 'Ferrari, Rolls Royce among exotic cars selling fast in China', *CNN Money*, 4 May 2012, http://money.cnn.com.

11. Lauren Torrisi, 'McDonald's announces menu for Olympic Park', *ABC News*, 19 July 2012, http:// abcnews.go.com.

12. Andrea Meyer, 'Intuit's high-velocity experiments', *Working Knowledge*, 12 August 2012, http://workingknowledge.com.

13. Himani Chandna Gurtoo, 'The green wave', *Hindustan Times*, 8 August 2012, www.hindustantimes. com.

14. Sarah MacFarlane, 'Fairtrade global 2011 sales up 12% on year', *Reuters*, 16 July 2012, www.reuters. com.

15. Leo Hickman, 'The rise and rise of the own brand', *Guardian*, 23 May 2012, www.guardian.co.uk; Andy Barker, 'As Tesco puts Pampers in its sights, is "product" the battleground of the future?' *Research*, 25 January 2013, www.research-live.com.

16. Ross Davidson, 'Axeon "in pole position" in electric market', *Press and Journal (Scotland)*, 22 July 2011, www.pressandjournal.co.uk.

17. Roland T. Rust, Debora V. Thompson and Rebecca W. Hamilton, 'Feature Bloat', *Harvard Business School Working Knowledge*, 8 May 2006, http:// hbswk.hbs.edu.

18. Quoted in Poornima Gupta and Dan Levine, 'Apple designer: iPhone crafters are "maniacal"', *Reuters*, 1 August 2012, www.reuters.com.

19. Christopher Thompson, 'Whitbread pins hopes on the colour purple', *Financial Times*, 31 July 2012, p. 21; 'A budget for Indian tastes', *Financial Express*, 8 July 2012, n.p.; 'Whitbread's expansion strategy is proving effective', *Caterer & Hotelkeeper*, 4 May 2012, n.p.; Sudipta Dev, 'The year 2012, for most markets across the world, is being seen as a year of caution', *Express Hospitality*, 4 April 2012, n.p.; www.premierinn.com.

20. This section draws on concepts discussed in Kevin Lane Keller, *Strategic Brand Management*, 2nd edn (Upper Saddle River, NJ: Pearson Prentice Hall, 2003), Chapters 1 and 2.

21. See Donald R. Lehmann, Kevin Lane Keller and John U. Farley, 'The structure of survey-based brand metrics', *Journal of International Marketing*, vol. 16, no. 4, 2008, pp. 29–56.

22. Don E. Schultz, 'Branding geometry', *Marketing Management*, September–October 2003, pp. 8–9.

23. Arshiya Khullar, 'Dulux brand is about product innovations and consumer experience', *Pitch*, 27 July 2012, n.p.

24. Paul Mozur, 'Lenovo and EMC form partnership', *Wall Street Journal*, 1 August 2012, www.wsj.com; Loretta Chao, 'As rivals outsource, Lenovo keeps production in-house', *Wall Street Journal*, 9 July 2012, www.wsj.com; Rahul Sachitanand, 'How Shailendra Katyal took Lenovo to no. 1 position in India', *Economic Times (India)*, 31 July 2012, http://articles. economictimes.indiatimes.com; 'Lenovo targets Dell share of government, education sales', *Bloomberg News*, 6 August 2012, www.bloomberg.com.

25. Rosie Baker, 'New identity for Cancer Research has warmer tone', *Marketing Week*, 9 August 2012, p. 4; Hannah Crowne, 'Cancer Research UK seeks to embolden with rebrand', *PR Week (UK)*, 7 August 2012, www.prweek.com/uk.

26. 'Brand new; Schumpeter', *Economist* (US), 4 August 2012, p. 61.

27. Lionel Laurent, 'L'Oréal keeps targets after Q2 growth slows', *Reuters*, 26 July 2012, www.reuters.com; Richard Tyler, 'L'Oréal spreads Kiehl's across the UK', *Telegraph* (UK), 21 February 2012, www.telegraph.co.uk; Cristina Kroll, 'Growth: exports of Mexico's beauty industry boosting economy', *Global Cosmetic Industry*, May 2012, p. 24; Lucy Handley, '"Original teenagers" kick segmentation into touch', *Marketing Week*, 1 December 2011, p. 18; Lucy Handley, '"Purchasing is the point when you can start to have a conversation . . ."', *Marketing Week*, 15 March 2012, p. 41; 'L'Oréal events add colour', *Conference & Incentive Travel*, 1 February 2012, p. 52.

7   Planning for pricing

Learning outcomes

After studying this chapter, you will be able to:

- Explain how customers' perceptions of value affect price decisions
- Identify internal and external influences on pricing
- Understand pricing for new products
- Discuss how to adapt prices

Application outcomes

After studying this chapter, you will be able to:

- Analyse the influences on your pricing decisions
- Set appropriate pricing objectives
- Make planning decisions about product pricing

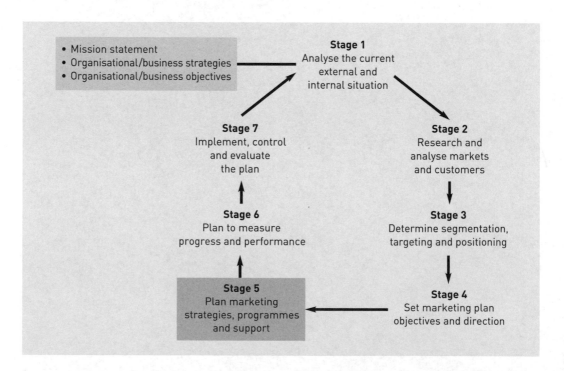

- Mission statement
- Organisational/business strategies
- Organisational/business objectives

Stage 1
Analyse the current external and internal situation

Stage 2
Research and analyse markets and customers

Stage 3
Determine segmentation, targeting and positioning

Stage 4
Set marketing plan objectives and direction

Stage 5
Plan marketing strategies, programmes and support

Stage 6
Plan to measure progress and performance

Stage 7
Implement, control and evaluate the plan

CHAPTER PREVIEW: MARKETING AT LOUIS VUITTON MOËT HENNESSEY (LVMH)

France's Louis Vuitton Moët Hennessey (www.lvmh.com) markets carefully crafted, top-quality goods and services in such categories as clothing, luggage and holiday resorts under dozens of exclusive brands. Despite unfavourable economic conditions in some markets, LVMH has increased annual turnover beyond €23 billion and is even increasing prices on some ultra-luxury products, known all over the world as status symbols.

Japan, the United States and China are the three largest markets for luxury goods, and LVMH has marketing plans for all three. In China, it reinforces its image for exclusivity by creating bespoke Louis Vuitton shoes, handbags and other products for wealthy customers willing to pay top prices for one-of-a-kind products of top quality. Other products in the Louis Vuitton range are priced up to 40 percent higher in China than in Europe because of taxes and tariffs, which is why many Chinese tourists buy overseas instead of at home. Depending on the euro's foreign exchange position, LVMH may raise prices in Europe to maintain its upmarket image and narrow the price difference between products sold in its home market and those sold elsewhere. Even the lowest-priced products in LVMH's portfolio – entry-level luxury – can't be priced too low for brand reasons.[1]

LVMH's marketers recognise that although they spend money on other marketing-mix elements (paying for product development and packaging, to give two examples), pricing is the way they make money for the company. They also know that in the marketplace, customers actually determine how much value they perceive in a Louis Vuitton handbag and how much they're willing to pay for it. Therefore, this chapter begins with a discussion of how customers perceive value and the difference between cost-based and value-based pricing. Next, you'll learn about the various external and internal influences on pricing that you must consider when preparing a marketing plan. Finally, you'll see how to handle specific pricing decisions, including setting pricing objectives, pricing new products, pricing multiple products and adapting prices.

Consult this chapter's checklist for questions to ask when pricing products during their life cycles. Also, to see how companies document their pricing strategies and activities, review the sample marketing plan in the Appendix.

UNDERSTANDING PRICE AND VALUE TODAY

Whether the price is one pound sterling, one euro or one bag of rice, customers will buy only when they perceive value – when a product's perceived benefits in meeting their needs outweigh the perceived price. Even when the price is collected in barter, customers will not complete a transaction if they perceive insufficient value. No matter how good or bad the economic circumstances, no matter what type of product you market, no matter what segments you're targeting, you can't make planning decisions about price without looking at value from your customers' perspective.

Perceptions of value

A product's value is perceived by customers according to the total benefits they receive. An individual customer may consider one benefit more important than the others, but the combination of all benefits is what provides value. Customers form value perceptions in the context of competing or substitute products that might meet their needs, on the basis of benefits such as the following:

- *Performance*. Does the product perform as it should in meeting the customer's needs? Does it perform better than competing products?

- *Features*. Does the product have all the features expected or desired to meet current needs and future or unspoken needs? How do the features compare with those of competing products?

- *Quality*. Is the product defect-free, reliable and durable compared with competing products?

- *Personal benefits*. Does the product deliver personal benefits such as status or self-expression?

- *Availability*. Is the product available whenever needed? Does the price change according to availability? How does this compare with that of competing products?

- *Service*. Does the service meet customers' expectations? Is it faster, more convenient or more personalised than that offered by competitors?

Against the total perceived benefits, customers weigh the total perceived costs (time and money) associated with the product, including the following:

- *Initial purchase price*. What time and money must the customer spend to obtain the product initially? How does the purchase price compare with competing products?

- *Maintenance and repair costs*. What is the estimated cost of maintenance over the product's life? How often is maintenance or repair generally required, and how much time or money might the customer lose while waiting for repairs or maintenance?

- *Ongoing fees*. Does the product require an annual usage charge or other fees after the initial purchase? Must the customer pay a tax to continue using or possessing the product?

- *Installation*. Does the product require installation? What is the cost in time and money for installing this product compared with competing products?

- *Search and training*. How much time must customers invest in researching this type of product, arranging the purchase and waiting for delivery or service? Do customers need training to use the product properly and, if so, what is the cost in time and money compared with competing products?

- *Ancillary products*. Does the product require the purchase of ancillary products and at what cost? How does this compare with competing products?

- *Financing*. If applicable, what is the cost of financing the purchase of this product, what is the monthly payment (if any) and how do such costs compare with those of competing products?

A growing number of consumers are clicking to hire high-end clothing, paying a fraction of the full purchase price to wear a special outfit for a special occasion. Two firms that specialise in high-fashion clothes hire are New York City's Rent the Runway (www.renttherunway.com) and Toronto's Rent frock Repeat (http://rentfrockrepeat.com).

MARKETING IN PRACTICE: HIRE IT!

Rent the Runway, founded in 2009 by Jennifer Hyman and Jenny Fleiss, is one of the pioneers of the online high-fashion hire business. US customers can browse the website, select the outfit they prefer, request it in two sizes (to ensure proper fit) and click to request delivery on a specific date, along with jewellery and other accessories if desired. Customers keep the outfit for four days (with an option to extend the hire period to eight days), then slip everything into the postage-paid package and post it back to the company. The hire fee is 15–20 percent of the outfit's full retail price; the company pays for dry-cleaning after every hiring.

In Toronto, Lisa Delorme and Kristy Wieber launched Rent frock Repeat in 2010 after deciding they would rather hire a bridesmaid's dress than buy one every time they took part in a wedding. Like Rent the Runway, Rent frock Repeat ships two sizes to each customer and allows four days per hiring, with an option to extend to eight days. So that it always has the latest fashions in stock for hire, Rent frock Repeat periodically holds a clearance sale to sell the previous season's outfits at up to 70 percent off the regular retail price.

Some designers were originally reluctant to let Rent the Runway buy their fashions, concerned that hiring them out would cannibalise their sales. Hyman and Fleiss explained that hiring would allow women to try out different looks and enjoy the experience of wearing couture styles for special occasions. Once hirers discovered which styles were most flattering, they would have the confidence and motivation to buy from their favourite designers. Designers signed up to the idea, and today Rent the Runway offers an extensive range of 24,000 luxury outfits and 12,000 accessories for hire.[2]

Marketing plan analysis: What benefits are hirers seeking from Rent the Runway and Rent frock Repeat? What costs would they avoid by hiring instead of buying?

Pricing based on value

Through research, you can determine how customers in your targeted segment(s) perceive the value of your product's total benefits and costs and the value of competing products. Then you can use this understanding of the customer's perspective to plan your pricing as well as your costs and your product design (see Figure 7.1(a)).

This is not the way marketers have traditionally planned for pricing. In the past, most started with the product and its cost, developed a pricing plan to cover costs and then looked for ways to communicate value to customer (see Figure 7.1(b)).[3] However, in today's networked world, when customers can so easily locate competitive products and

(a) Value-based pricing

Customers ⟶ Value ⟶ Price ⟶ Cost ⟶ Product

(b) Cost-based pricing

Product ⟶ Cost ⟶ Price ⟶ Value ⟶ Customers

FIGURE 7.1 Value-based pricing compared with cost-based pricing

Source: Adapted from *The Strategy and Tactics of Pricing: A Guide to Growing More Profitably*, 4, Pearson Education Inc. (Nagle, T.T. and Hogan, J. 2006) 4, Prentice Hall, NAGLE, THOMAS T.; HOGAN, JOHN, STRATEGY & TACTICS OF PRICING: GUIDE TO GROWING MORE PROFITABLY, 4th Ed., p. 4, © 2006. Reprinted and Electronically reproduced by permission of Pearson Education. Inc., Upper Saddle River, New Jersey.

compare prices online or via a mobile, you can't afford to ignore the link between value and pricing when preparing your marketing plan. IKEA (www.ikea.com) plans prices on the basis of value and never stops looking for ways to deliver more value.

MARKETING IN PRACTICE: IKEA

IKEA, known for its stylish and affordable home furnishings packed flat for customers to assemble at home, operates nearly 300 stores in 26 countries and has an annual turnover of €25 billion. Its marketers carefully research customer needs, examine value perceptions and check competitive pricing to understand the current market situation. When designing a new product, they set a target price lower than those of IKEA's rivals, estimate costs and plan features and specifications appropriate for the target price. Sustainability is a high priority as they consult with suppliers and agree costs and materials before they design the product, have it manufactured and ship it to stores.

Consider the Fagrik coffee cup, originally developed to sell at less than €1. After the Fagrik made its debut, IKEA's designers reworked the shape to fit more cups onto a single shipping pallet, and then reworked the shape a second time. With each iteration, the retailer reduced its transportation costs enough to reduce the cup's price without reducing the quality. Today, the popular cup sells for about 10 cents less than its initial price. IKEA repeats this process over and over as it examines every product to identify ways of streamlining production, sourcing, transportation and other elements that contribute to costs. During the recent recession, the company cut a large number of prices to highlight value, and shoppers responded so enthusiastically that IKEA's sales rose significantly.

As both manufacturer and distributor, IKEA is in a position to help the environment as it expands. The retailer has goals for obtaining raw materials from sustainable sources and for using energy from renewable sources. By 2017, IKEA expects to sell more wooden products made from certified sustainable timber than any other retailer in the world. It's also gone high-tech, offering apps for customers who want to view decorating videos and check product availability. IKEA's affordably priced products will soon be featured in new stores throughout Asia, Europe and beyond.[4]

Marketing plan analysis: Why would IKEA redesign a product twice to reduce the retail price by about 10 cents? Do you agree with this decision?

ANALYSING INFLUENCES ON PRICING DECISIONS

Notice how IKEA looks closely at costs and product development as well as at customer needs and other external influences when it plans for pricing. Similarly, as you prepare your marketing plan, your pricing decisions must be made with a number of internal and external influences in mind.

Internal influences

Five major internal influences can affect the decisions you make about pricing: (1) organisational and marketing plan objectives, (2) costs, (3) targeting and positioning, (4) product decisions and life cycle and (5) other marketing-mix decisions (see Figure 7.2).

Organisational and marketing plan objectives

Price and every other marketing-mix element must tie back to the objectives of the organisation and the marketing plan. Because price generates revenue, it is a particularly important ingredient for achieving sales and profitability targets as well as for meeting societal objectives. If growth and market share are your key objectives, you might lower the product's price and reduce its perceived benefits or develop an entirely new product with fewer benefits that can be marketed at a lower price. Or you might develop a new product designed to sell for less as a way of meeting customer needs.

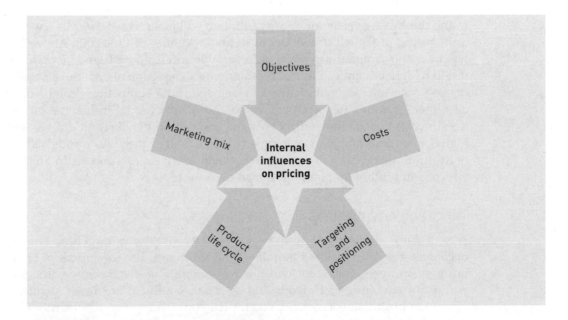

FIGURE 7.2   Internal influences on pricing decisions

Costs

Most companies price their products to cover costs, at least over the long run. In the short term, however, you may be willing to price for little or no profit when establishing a new product, competing with aggressive rivals or seeking to achieve another objective. If you compete primarily on the basis of price, you will be particularly concerned with managing variable costs and **fixed costs** (such as rent, insurance and other business expenses, which do not vary with production and sales). This keeps prices low and protects profit margins.

When you have limited control over the **variable costs** that vary with production and sales, such as the cost of raw materials and parts, you will find pricing for profit even more challenging. Although at times you may have difficulty determining a product's exact costs – especially if it has yet to be launched in the marketplace – you need cost information to calculate the **break-even point**. This is the point at which a product's revenues and costs are equal and beyond which the organisation earns more profit as more units are sold. Unless you make some change in price (which will affect demand) or variable cost, your product will not become profitable until unit volume reaches the break-even point. The equation for this calculation is

$$\text{break-even point} = \frac{\text{total fixed costs}}{\text{unit price} - \text{variable costs per unit}}$$

If, for example, a product's total fixed costs are €100,000 and one unit's variable costs are €2, the break-even point at a unit price of €6 is

$$\frac{\text{€100,000}}{\text{€6} - \text{€2}} = 25,000 \text{ units}$$

Using this break-even point, the organisation will incur losses if it sells fewer than 25,000 units priced at €6 (which works out to total revenues of €150,000). Above 25,000 units, however, the company can cover both variable and fixed costs and increase its profits as it sells a higher quantity. Figure 7.3 is a graphical depiction of break-even analysis, which doesn't take into account changes in demand, how competitors might respond, how customers perceive the product's value and other external influences on pricing. Nor does break-even analysis reflect how the cost per unit is likely to drop as you produce higher quantities and gain economies of scale. Still, it provides a rough approximation of the unit sales volume that you must achieve to cover costs and begin producing profit, which is important for planning purposes.

Targeting and positioning

Any pricing decisions should be consistent with your targeting and positioning decisions. The UK retailers Poundland and 99p Stores use low prices to target bargain-hunting shoppers, consistent with their positioning on the basis of value for money. If you're in marketing at Harrods and you target affluent customer segments with an upmarket positioning, however, you'll plan your pricing very differently from retailers that target price-sensitive consumers.

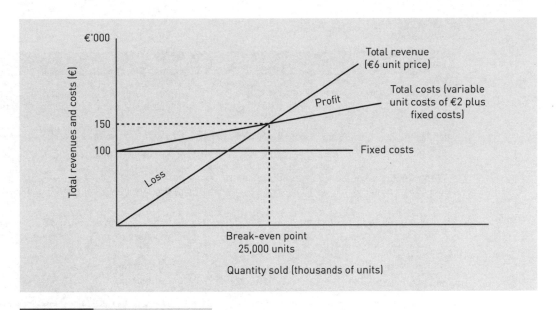

FIGURE 7.3   Break-even analysis

Product decisions and life cycle

If you look back at Figure 7.1(a), you can see that pricing decisions are closely intertwined with product decisions. More companies are developing new products after they have determined customers' perceptions of value, set target costs and set a target price, rather than starting the pricing process after initiating production. Of course, your pricing decisions will change during the product's life cycle. As discussed below, you may start with either market-skimming pricing or market-penetration pricing when launching a new product and then make changes in other stages.

By the time your product reaches the growth stage where competition is increasing, you should choose pricing strategies that support more differentiation in targeted segments or pricing strategies geared to stimulating higher demand for more economies of scale and lower costs (or a combination of both). Sales of a product in maturity will grow less rapidly even as more competitors are vying for the attention of customers, which necessitates another change in your pricing plan. Table 7.1 shows five options for pricing mature products, suggested by pricing experts Thomas Nagle and John Hogan.

Marketing-mix decisions

Beyond the product life cycle, planning for pricing is influenced by (and influences) planning for a number of marketing-mix decisions, including communications. Obviously, many producers and channel members feature pricing in their promotions to attract customer attention and compete with direct rivals. Although marketers of luxury products may not make price a visible part of their communications activities, their pricing decisions will be affected by the benefits and value they emphasise in their marketing

Table 7.1	Pricing mature products

Pricing alternatives	Purpose
Unbundle and price products individually	Compete by pricing goods and services individually rather than pricing an entire bundle
Re-examine customer price sensitivity and change price accordingly	Maintain or improve revenue and profits
Set prices based on better understanding of costs and capacity	Reflect realistic costs and earn more profit at times when demand outstrips capacity
Introduce related products	Leverage success of an existing product by adding related goods or services at a profit
Change channel pricing	Expand channel coverage while reducing channel margins

Source: Adapted from *The Strategy and Tactics of Pricing: A Guide to Growing More Profitably*, 4, Pearson Education Inc. (Nagle, T.T. and Hogan, J. 2006) 275–77, Prentice Hall, NAGLE, THOMAS T.; HOGAN, JOHN, STRATEGY & TACTICS OF PRICING: GUIDE TO GROWING MORE PROFITABLY, 4th Ed., pp. 275–77, © 2006. Reprinted and Electronically reproduced by permission of Pearson Education. Inc., Upper Saddle River, New Jersey.

communications. In short, be sure your pricing fits with the other decisions you include in your marketing plan.

Use Checklist No. 12 as you think about pricing products at different points in their life cycles.

ESSENTIAL CHECKLIST NO. 12:
PRICING THROUGH THE PRODUCT LIFE CYCLE

Whether your marketing plan is for a new product or an existing product, you'll face pricing decisions as it moves through its life cycle. The following questions are a good starting point for considering key issues in pricing at each point in any product's life cycle. Tick the questions that apply to your situation as you note your answers in the space provided.

☐ At introduction, how can pricing be used to encourage channel acceptance of a new product?

_____

☐ At introduction, what pricing approach will stimulate product trial and repeat purchasing among customers?

_____

☐ At introduction, how can pricing be used to manage initial supply and demand?

___

☐ During growth, how can pricing be used for competitive purposes?

___

☐ During growth, what pricing approach will lead to break-even and profitability?

___

☐ In maturity, how can pricing encourage customer loyalty and defend market share?

___

☐ In maturity, what pricing approach will achieve sustained profitability and other objectives?

___

☐ In maturity, what pricing approach will support expanded channel coverage?

___

☐ In decline, what pricing approach might slow the slide of unit sales and protect profits?

___

☐ In decline, how can pricing be used for profit as competitors withdraw from the market?

___

External influences

The five major external influences on pricing are (1) customers, (2) market and demand, (3) competition, (4) channel members and (5) other concerns, including legal, regulatory, ethical and sustainability considerations (see Figure 7.4).

Customers

Not all customers can or want to compare prices; not all customers are interested in buying the lowest-priced alternative. Research shows that consumers will accept a price if it is within what they consider an acceptable range for that good or service.[5] Customers may decide against buying a product that is priced unusually low because they suspect poor quality yet be willing to spend more if a product appears to offer value-added benefits, such as a prestige brand or special service. If your product is particularly innovative or

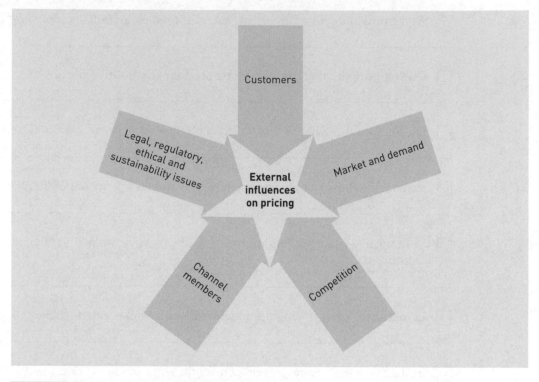

FIGURE 7.4   External influences on pricing decisions

meets unspoken customer needs, you may have to go against long-established traditions of pricing and service levels.

Business buyers in particular may feel pressure to acquire raw materials, components or services at the lowest possible prices, which in turn affects their suppliers' pricing strategies. Some business buyers and consumers constantly switch brands or suppliers in search of bargains, especially now that they can quickly and easily compare prices online. Your challenge as a marketer is to communicate your product's benefits so that customers recognise the differentiation and perceive the value in relation to the price.

Market and demand

You also need to research the **demand** for your product in the target market – how many units are likely to be sold at different prices – and the effect of price sensitivity, or the **elasticity of demand**. When your research reveals **elastic demand**, a small percentage change in price will usually produce a large change in quantity demanded. If your research reveals **inelastic demand**, a small percentage change in price will usually produce a small percentage change in quantity demanded (see Table 7.2). Keep demand in mind as you prepare your marketing plan, because pricing decisions will significantly affect your ability to achieve sales and market share objectives.

Table 7.2	Pricing and elasticity of demand	
Pricing decision	**Inelastic demand**	**Elastic demand**
Small decrease	Small increase in demand	Larger increase in demand
Small increase	Small decrease in demand	Larger decrease in demand

Note that you can actually maintain or increase revenues by raising the price when demand is inelastic or by cutting the price when demand is elastic. Still, if you price a product excessively high, you risk reducing demand; price it too low and you may spark strong demand that you cannot profitably satisfy. Yet it can be difficult to research the exact elasticity of demand for a particular product, even though you can conduct pricing experiments and analyse sales history to get data for estimating the elasticity of demand. Remember that elasticity of demand can vary widely from one segment to another and from one market to another.

Another consideration for marketers who target customers in other countries is the effect of currency fluctuations in foreign-exchange markets. Multinational corporations such as Unilever, Reckitt Benckiser and Procter & Gamble must think about the effect of foreign-exchange rates when they import or export and buy from suppliers in other regions. Currency fluctuations – especially sudden or exchange changes – can push profit margins up or down, depending on the foreign-exchange situation and the prices set in each country. If your marketing plan includes buying or selling in other nations, consider the potential implications of currency fluctuations and any restrictions on financial transfers.

Competition

Whether the product is confectionery or cars, competition exerts a strong influence on pricing decisions. Customers look at the costs and benefits of competing products when thinking about value, so be aware of what competitors are charging. However, it's risky to imitate another organisation's pricing simply for competitive reasons, because your organisation probably has very different costs, objectives and resources from those of your rival. Also, consider whether your product could face price competition from products that meet customers' needs in different ways, as when travellers can choose between air travel and rail travel. When you plan, think about the impact these substitutes might have on your pricing decisions.

Adding to the competitive pricing pressure among retailers is the growing use of *price-check apps* to compare prices on items while consumers are in a store. UK shoppers who download the RedLaser mobile app (now owned by eBay) simply scan a product code or QR code; the app looks up that item's price on eBay, in nearby stores and on other websites.[6] This has led to *showrooming*, which occurs when customers look at a product in a store, compare prices using an app and then buy online if the price is lower than in the store. Some retailers are covering up product codes in their stores to prevent shoppers from using price-check apps; others are fighting back by offering more product information and more personalised service to satisfy in-store customers.

Price wars are also part of price competition in certain industries. These reduce profit margins as prices move lower and lower. If customers become accustomed to waiting for price wars before they buy, you may have difficulty selling at what you previously considered to be normal pricing levels. Price wars often break out in the supermarket industry, where Tesco, Asda and other competitors cut prices on selected items to bring shoppers into their stores or to defend market share when a rival store opens nearby. Mobile broadband marketers have used price wars to appeal to specific customer segments and increase revenue from non-voice services. Even Boeing and Airbus, which make commercial jetliners for the world's airlines, have become involved in high-stakes price wars to retain and expand market share.[7]

Channel members

When making channel arrangements, you must ensure that wholesalers and retailers can buy at a price that will allow profitable resale to business customers or consumers. Channel members have to be able to cover the costs they incur in processing customer orders, repackaging bulk shipment lots into customer-sized lots, product storage and other operations. To make this work, think carefully about the costs and profit margins of all channel participants, along with the price perceptions of the targeted customer segment, when setting your product's price. (Note that when channel members discount selected items or participate in price wars, they typically have their own price objectives – such as defending market share.)

Even your choice of intermediaries depends on your product's price. If you market high-quality, high-priced products, you will have difficulty reaching your targeted segment through intermediaries known for stocking low-quality, low-priced products. If you market lower-quality, low-priced products, upmarket stores will not stock your products because of the mismatch with their target market. In short, carefully coordinate your channel decisions with your price decisions.

Legal, regulatory, ethical and sustainability considerations

You have to abide by local, national and regional laws and regulations when planning to price your products. Among the kinds of issues your marketing plan should cover are the following:

- *Price controls and price fixing.* Some countries control the prices of products such as prescription drugs, which limits pricing choices. Many also forbid the use of price fixing and other actions considered anti-competitive.

- *Resale price maintenance.* UK and European Union laws generally prevent marketers from insisting that channel members maintain a certain minimum price on their products. This paves the way for more competition and reinforces the need to consider pricing throughout the channel.

- *Industry regulation*. Government regulators can affect pricing in some industries by allowing or blocking the sale of certain products or bundles.

- *Government requirements*. Legal and regulatory actions can affect pricing by mandating product standards, tests or labelling; these requirements add to the costs that you will seek to recoup through product pricing.

- *Taxes and tariffs*. Prices for products sold in certain countries must include value-added tax (VAT) or sales taxes, which vary from nation to nation. In addition, import tariffs raise the price that customers pay for some products. The US government recently complained about China's import tariffs on large-engine cars such as Cadillacs, which increased the consumer price by more than 15 percent.[8]

Going beyond legal and regulatory guidelines, look at the ethical implications. Is a pharmaceutical manufacturer acting ethically when it sets high prices for a life-saving drug that patients in some areas cannot afford? Is an airline or bank acting ethically when it promotes a special price without fully and prominently explaining any restrictions and extra fees? Transparency in pricing is a key factor in building trust, so plan to let your customers know about any fees, taxes or extra charges before they buy. As challenging as such issues may be, building a reputation for ethical pricing ultimately enhances your brand's image and reinforces long-term customer loyalty.

Finally, consider sustainability issues and the effect on your costs, marketing and pricing. If your costs for green products are higher than for other products, will your customers pay a higher price? Should you accept a lower profit margin on some products when sustainability is one of your societal objectives? These types of questions should be addressed in your marketing plan.

MAKING PRICING DECISIONS

Once you understand the external and internal influences on pricing, you can set pricing objectives for the period covered by the marketing plan. If your product is new, you will decide between market-skimming and market-penetration pricing. As your product line expands, you will face decisions about pricing multiple products and you may need to plan to adapt your product's price.

Setting pricing objectives

Your objectives for pricing will be based on your organisation's objectives and those of the marketing plan. There are three categories of pricing objectives:

- *Financial objectives for pricing*. You may seek to maintain or improve profits, maintain or improve revenues, reach the break-even point by a certain date, support another product's revenues and profitability, or achieve a certain return.

- *Marketing objectives for pricing*. Here, you set relationship targets for pricing that will attract or retain customers, build or defend market share, build or change channel relations, or build brand image, awareness and loyalty.

- *Societal objectives for pricing*. You may set targets for covering the cost of using ecologically friendly materials and processes, providing reverse channels for recycling, generating cash for charitable contributions or achieving other non-business objectives.

Some marketers of software, games, apps and other products use **'freemium' pricing**, giving the basic product away free but charging for extra functionality or advanced features. This approach aims to achieve both financial and marketing objectives. One study indicates that 39 percent of UK consumers who play games on their mobiles pay for additional levels or extras that improve their standing.[9] Software companies like Adobe frequently use freemium pricing, reasoning that business users who try the product will then understand the value of paying to upgrade to a fully featured version. If only a very small percentage of a large number of users decides to pay for the upgraded product, the company will profit. Thus, the marketers must set and achieve relationship targets and financial targets to make freemium pricing successful.[10]

Pricing new products

A new product presents a special pricing challenge because you must decide whether to use **market-penetration pricing** and price relatively low for rapid acquisition of market share, or to use **market-skimming pricing**, setting a relatively high price to skim maximum revenues from the market, layer by layer. With market-penetration pricing, the price may be so low that the product is unprofitable and/or priced lower than competing products in the short term. Yet such pricing may be effective in the long run if you are determined to boost volume and gain efficiencies that will lower costs as a foundation for future profitability.

Market-penetration pricing is not appropriate for every product, which is where internal and external influences come into play. Your customers may perceive less value in a luxury product that is launched with market-penetration pricing, for example. Also, market-penetration pricing may be inappropriate for the kinds of channel members you need to use to reach targeted customer segments. Finally, such pricing may not be consistent with your promotion decisions.

Apple, maker of iPhones, iPads and Mac computers, prefers market-skimming pricing for its new products. This pricing decision supports Apple's profitability as well as its cutting-edge image for new technology, design and features. When the company introduces a new model of an existing product – such as a new iPad – it typically reduces the price of older models. This pricing decision clarifies the positioning of different products in the line and reinforces the distinction between newer and older models.

You should consider market-skimming pricing for innovative or top-quality products, to make an upmarket impression on selected customer segments that are less price sensitive and place a premium on innovation. Market-skimming pricing is common with products employing new technology such as digital radio receivers. Not only do you take in more money to help cover costs with this approach, you have the flexibility to lower prices as you monitor competitive response, attain volumes that yield economies of scale and shift to targeting more price-sensitive segments. If your initial price is too high, however, you may set customer expectations too high, slow initial sales and lower repeat sales if the product does not fulfil those expectations.

When pricing business goods and services, think about the value to your customers, how your customers prefer to pay, how pricing helps build relationships and how your product helps customers serve their customers. As technology evolves, marketers of cloud computing services, such as Amazon Web Services (http://aws.amazon.com), are taking a new look at new-product pricing.

MARKETING IN PRACTICE: AMAZON WEB SERVICES

How can a company price a product that customers use 'on demand' – when and if needed? That was one of the questions Amazon Web Services, owned by the pioneering online retailer, faced when pricing its cloud computing services (data storage capability and software applications delivered online). Cloud computing was in its infancy when Amazon began its cloud computing division in 2006, and businesses weren't accustomed to buying software products that were 'in the cloud' instead of running on their own computer systems.

Traditionally, businesses have paid for software based on the number of computers on which it runs or, for large corporations, as part of a bundle of equipment and services tailored by a technology vendor for specific business needs. In contrast, Amazon's cloud computing is priced by the month or by the hour. Customers can avoid the expense of buying equipment and software and, instead, hire data storage space or computing power from Amazon when they want to operate a website or run sophisticated computer analyses. As a business's needs change and expand, Amazon can accommodate those changes with pricing to match, because it's constantly expanding its network for customers as it expands the network for its own purposes. As a result of its flexible offerings and its pricing decisions, Amazon Web Services now has hundreds of thousands of business customers in 190 countries.

Amazon has added new functionality yet reduced the price of cloud computing, year after year after year. It has also created tiers of service, pricing the product lower for business customers who don't anticipate the need for rapid response to technical support questions, and higher for customers who must have almost immediate response. Some of Amazon's pricing plans take into consideration multiyear usage and some are geared towards entrepreneurs who need temporary storage for large databases while creating apps. How will Amazon Web Services price new products in the future?[11]

Marketing plan analysis: Do you think Amazon Web Services should price to achieve market penetration or to skim the market? Explain your answer.

Pricing multiple products

Your plan for pricing should take into account more than one product in the line or mix, any optional or complementary products and any product bundles. The way you price each product sets it apart from other products in your mix, reflecting or reinforcing customer perceptions of each product's value. You can then balance prices within the product line or mix to reach your total revenue or profit objectives.

In services, a hotel company may market deluxe hotels, convention hotels and modestly priced tourist hotels, each with its own target market, pricing objectives and room rates in line with the perceived value. Many airlines market different classes of travel, charging higher prices for first class and business class than for economy class. Each class comes with specific features and benefits such as roomier seats for comfort, differentiations that are reflected in the price.

If you offer a bundle of goods or services you must determine how to price that bundle, given the competition and customers' perceptions of the bundle's value. One advantage of bundling is that competitors can't easily duplicate every aspect of a unique, specially priced bundle. If customers do not want everything in your bundle at the price set, however, they may buy fewer products individually or look at competitive bundles. And later in a product's life cycle, you may get more benefit by unbundling and pricing each part separately.

Adapting prices

Your plan should allow for adapting prices when appropriate, either by increasing perceived value or by reducing perceived cost. Depending on local laws and regulations – and the rest of your marketing plan – some ways in which you can adapt prices include the following:

- *Discounts*. You can plan special discounts for customers who buy in large quantities or during non-peak periods, pay in cash, or assume logistical functions such as picking up products that would otherwise be delivered. Be aware of the possibility that discounting one product in a product line could cannibalise sales of other products in that line, affecting overall revenue and profit margins.

- *Allowances*. You can invite customers to trade in older products and receive credit towards purchases of newer products. You may also offer customers refunds or rebates for buying during promotional periods.

- *Extra value*. To encourage intermediaries to carry your products, you may offer small quantities free when resellers place orders during a promotional period. For consumers, you may temporarily increase the amount of product without increasing the price.

- *Periodic mark-downs*. Retailers, in particular, plan to mark down merchandise periodically, at the end of a selling season, to attract or reward shoppers or to stimulate new product trial. UK shoppers know they can get after-Christmas bargains at Boxing Day sales, for example.

- *Segmented pricing*. Depending on your segmentation decisions, your pricing can be adapted for customers of different ages (such as lower prices for children and older customers), members and non-members (such as lower prices for professional association members), different purchase locations (such as lower prices for products bought and picked up at the main plant) and time of purchase (such as lower prices for mobile phone service during non-peak periods).

Internal or external influences may prompt you to raise or lower a product's price. For example, you can use a price cut to stimulate higher demand or defend against competitive price reductions. You may want to use a price increase to deal with rising costs or product improvements that raise perceived quality and value. Whether such price adaptations achieve their objectives will depend on customer and competitor reaction.

Some marketers, especially smaller businesses, are promoting special pricing on *daily deal sites*, websites that alert subscribers to a limited number of deeply discounted offers per day. Participating businesses use deal sites to introduce themselves to new customers, with the goal of turning them into loyal customers who will buy at regular prices. In addition to broad-based deal sites such as LivingSocial, local sites have begun targeting specific consumer segments, such as mothers and seniors. Although some marketers are pleased with the results, others complain that the deep discounts hurt their profit margins. So before you plan to offer a daily deal, examine the financial aspects carefully and consider how participating will help you achieve your objectives.

Planning for prices to vary

Some marketing plans call for pricing that isn't fixed but instead varies under certain circumstances. With **dynamic pricing**, marketers vary their prices from buyer to buyer or from situation to situation. Most airlines plan for dynamic pricing, using software that aims to maximise the revenue for each flight. The software adjusts airfares depending on historical and actual demand for the flight, competition, the number of seats allocated to each class of service, the number of seats unfilled at a given time and other factors. A growing number of US sports teams, including the San Francisco Giants baseball team and the Orlando Magic basketball team, are using dynamic pricing to improve revenues. These teams charge more for seats at games against top competitors and less for games where advance ticket sales are not strong, using computer modelling to determine specific prices for each seating area.[12]

If you're preparing a marketing plan for business goods or services or for certain expensive consumer products, you should be prepared for **negotiated pricing**, in which buyer and seller negotiate and then confirm the final price and details of the offer by contract. Some business and consumer marketers use **auction pricing**, inviting buyers to submit bids to buy goods or services through a traditional auction (such as those conducted by Sotheby's) or an online auction (such as those on eBay). Auction pricing can be a good way to market excess or out-of-date stock to price-sensitive customers without affecting the fixed price set for other segments. It can also be used for special marketing situations.

CHAPTER SUMMARY

Customers perceive a product's value according to the total benefits weighed against the total costs, in the context of competitive products and prices. During the planning process, marketers must research how customers perceive the value of their product and the value of competing products and, ideally, work backwards using the perceived value to make price, cost and product decisions. Internal influences on pricing decisions are organisational and marketing plan objectives, costs, targeting and positioning, product decisions and life cycle, and other marketing-mix decisions. External influences on pricing decisions are customers, market and demand, competition, channel members, and legal, regulatory and ethical considerations.

Two approaches to pricing new products are market-penetration pricing (to capture market share quickly) and market-skimming pricing (to skim maximum revenues from each market layer). Depending on local laws and regulations and the rest of the marketing plan, marketers can adapt prices using discounts, allowances, extra value, periodic markdowns or segmented pricing. A marketing plan may not call for fixed prices but instead have prices that vary according to dynamic pricing, negotiated pricing or auction pricing.

CASE STUDY: NUOVO TRASPORTO VIAGGIATORI'S ITALO

What will travellers in Italy pay to travel between cities in speed, comfort and style? Nuovo Trasporto Viaggiatori (www.ntvspa.it/en/index.html) is finding out, with its new Italo high-speed train service inaugurated in 2012. Headed by Ferrari's chairman, Luca Cordero di Montezemolo, NTV's Italo competes with the Italian state-owned railway Trenitalia, and with airlines that serve the major cities. Travel writers have nicknamed Italo the 'Ferrari train' because it can travel at 300 kilometres per hour and the train's sleek exterior is painted a deep, glossy red. Among the free amenities for all passengers are leather seats, free Wi-Fi and at-seat sockets for charging digital devices.

Italo prices tickets at three levels. The first-class 'Club' level features the widest seats, optional three-course meals served at the seat, free coffee and newspapers and free seat-back movies or television. Club customers can reserve one of two four-seat compartments for exclusive use and use a special waiting area inside the Italo passenger lounges in Rome and Milan. The mid-priced 'Prima' is equivalent to business class, with slightly narrower seats than in Club but lots of leg room, a menu of at-seat dining options and a no-mobiles section for travellers who prefer a quiet ride. Passengers who choose the low-priced 'Smart' ticket, with fares as low as €20, get the basic amenities of leather seating and free Wi-Fi; they pay extra for snacks from vending machines and for movies. Italo also uses promotional pricing to attract travellers during off-peak periods.

As a privately operated train company, NVT must capture a sizable market share to achieve break-even and then return a profit. The company's long-term goal is to carry 9 million passengers per year and hold up to 25 percent of the market for high-speed rail travel within Italy. Competitor Trenitalia, which offers high-speed rail services under the Frecciarossa brand, is meeting the challenge by investing heavily to upgrade its passenger cars and add free Wi-Fi. Although Trenitalia has more than 30 years of experience in marketing high-speed rail services, NVT is the first competitor it has had to face in this market. NVT's marketing plan aims to attract and retain a loyal customer base of inter-city travellers, some of whom formerly used Trenitalia's rail services. Will its three-tier pricing deliver the revenue and profits the company needs in order to thrive?[13]

Case questions

1. How does NVT's three-tier pricing reflect its targeting and positioning?

2. Do you think NVT should seek to undercut Trenitalia's prices at all times, as a way of competing on price? Explain your answer.

APPLY YOUR KNOWLEDGE

Choose a particular business product (such as a tractor or technology services) and research the marketer's approach to pricing. Then write up your ideas or give an oral presentation to the class.

• What benefits does this product appear to offer to business customers?

• What initial and ongoing costs would business customers perceive in connection with buying and maintaining this product?

• If the product is new, what pricing approach is the company using to launch it? Why is this approach appropriate for the product?

• How does the price reflect the product's positioning and other marketing-mix decisions?

• How does the price of one competing or substitute product appear to reflect that product's value (from the customer's perspective)? If you were a customer, would you place a higher value on this competing product than on the product you have been researching? Why?

BUILD YOUR OWN MARKETING PLAN

Continue developing your marketing plan by making pricing decisions about a new or existing product. What pricing objectives will you set for this product? If the product is new, will you use market-skimming pricing or market-penetration pricing – and why? Which external influences are most important to the pricing of this product? How do internal influences affect your pricing decision for this product? What price will you set for this one product and in what situations would you consider adapting the price? Would dynamic, auction pricing or negotiated pricing be appropriate? Consider how these pricing decisions fit in with earlier marketing decisions and with the objectives you've set, then document them in your marketing plan.

ENDNOTES

1. Nina Sovich, 'Faster, higher, stronger: Luxury pricing goes for gold', *Reuters*, 10 August 2012, www.reuters.com; Nadya Masidlover and Laurie Burkitt, 'Labels have designs on big price tags', *Wall Street Journal*, 8 August 2012, www.wsj.com; Melanie Lee, 'Louis Vuitton lures China's super-rich with custom leather "art"', *Reuters*, 18 July 2012, www.reuters.com.

2. Lauren La Rose, 'Formal and frugal', *The Canadian Press*, 17 July 2012, www.timescolonist.com; Adrianne Pasquarelli, '40 under Forty', *Crain's New York Business*, 26 March 2012, p. F16; Lauren Drell, 'Rent the Runway', *Mashable*, 1 September 2011, www.mashable.com.

3. This section draws on concepts in Thomas T. Nagle and John E. Hogan, *The Strategy and Tactics of Pricing*, 4th edn (Upper Saddle River, NJ: Pearson Prentice Hall, 2006).

4. 'Ikea profits rise 10% as emerging markets boost sales', *BBC*, 20 January 2012, www.bbc.co.uk; James Allen, 'Three things your company can learn from a bottle of water', *Harvard Business Review Blog Network*, 7 August 2012, http://blogs.hbr.org; 'Ikea's interactive catalogue', *Ottawa Citizen (Canada)*, 10 August 2012, www.ottawacitizen.com; Heather King, 'Ikea's Steve Howard on bringing sustainability to the masses', *Green Biz*, 23 February 2012, www.greenbiz.com; Brad Tuttle, 'Everything at Ikea is getting cheaper', *Time*, 6 July 2011, www.time.com.

5. Daniel J. Howard and Roger A. Kerin, 'Broadening the scope of reference price advertising research', *Journal of Marketing*, October 2006, pp. 185–204.

6. Paul Sawyers, 'eBay's RedLaser app tops 2m UK downloads', *Next Web*, 24 February 2012, http://thenextweb.com/uk.

7. Tim Hepher, 'How plane giants descended into global "price war"', *Reuters*, 7 July 2012, www.reuters.com.

8. 'US in China car import tariff row', *BBC*, 5 July 2012, www.bbc.co.uk/news/business-18723175.

9. Charlotte McEleny, '39% of consumers pay for games every month', *New Media Age Online*, 29 June 2012, n.p.

10. Peter Cohan, 'Adobe executive's tutorial on freemium pricing', *Forbes*, 7 December 2011, www.forbes.com.

11. Mikael Riknas, 'Amazon users can track cloud-based databases with texts, emails', *Computer worldUK*, 6 February 2013, www.computerworlduk.com; 'Amazon Web Services cuts prices and revises support plans', *ComputerWorld UK*, 15 June 2012, www.computerworlduk.com; Jack Clark, 'Amazon arms developers with flash-based rentable computers', *ZDNet*, 19 July 2012, www.zdnet.com; Jack Clark, 'Amazon Web Services: Rise of the utility cloud', *ZDNet*, 6 June 2012, www.zdnet.com; 'The new software pricing model', *Knowledge@Wharton*, 9 November 2011, http://knowledge.wharton.upenn.edu; Charles Babcock, 'Amazon cuts cloud computing prices', *InformationWeek*, 6 March 2012, www.informationweek.com.

12. Mark Koba, 'How dynamic pricing is changing sports ticketing', *CNBC*, 18 July 2012, www.cnbc.com; 'Sports ticketing: The price is right', *Economist*, 9 January 2012, www.economist.com.

13. Ayesha Durgahee, 'Can Europe get its high-speed rail network together?' *CNN*, 17 April 2013, www.cnn.com; Gwyn Topham, 'Italy's Ferrari of the railways gets off to a flying start', *Guardian*, 27 April 2012, www.guardian.co.uk; Hans-Jurgen Schlamp, 'Italy introduces Ferrari on rails', *Spiegel Online*, 24 April 2012, www.spiegel.de; Philip Pullella, 'Ferrari's Montezemolo launches high-speed train', *Reuters*, 23 April 2012, www.reuters.com; Ayesha Durgahee, '"Ferrari" train driving high-speed rail renaissance', *CNN*, 22 June 2012, www.cnn.com.

8 Planning for channels and logistics

Learning outcomes

After studying this chapter, you will be able to:

- Explain the roles of the value chain, marketing channels and logistics
- Describe the various channel levels and intermediaries
- Contrast exclusive, selective and intensive distribution
- Understand the balance between logistics costs and customer services

Application outcomes

After studying this chapter, you will be able to:

- Analyse the value chain for a good or service
- Decide on the number of channel levels and members
- Analyse and plan for logistics

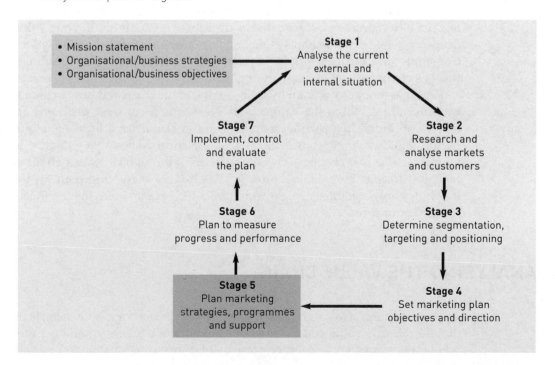

CHAPTER PREVIEW: MARKETING AT LUXOTTICA

As the world's largest eyewear company, Italy's Luxottica Group (www.luxottica. com/en/) has a definite vision of how spectacles should be marketed. The company's €6.2 billion in annual turnover comes from making and distributing eyewear under its own brands (such as Ray-Ban and Oakley) and licensed brands (such as Stella McCartney, Burberry and Prada). It operates 7,000 stores worldwide, including the global Sunglass Hut chain, the US LensCrafters chain and LC+ stores in China. In addition, Luxottica occasionally opens a temporary store, as it did when displaying a pair of A \$18,000 Bulgari sunglasses and other new designs in a Sunglass Hut store floating in Sydney Harbour for just four days.

Luxottica is also a wholesaler, selling eyewear to independent opticians and eyewear stores in 130 countries. It supports these independent retailers through loyalty programmes such as Elite Client and Advantage. In exchange for their loyalty and their buying commitments, the Elite Client and Advantage retailers receive in-depth product training and extras such as local exclusivity on certain brands or new styles. Looking ahead, Luxottica will be opening additional factories and more stores in Latin America and Asia as part of its marketing plan for aggressive growth during the coming decade.[1]

Luxottica is a good example of the marketing-mix tool of 'place', how a company profits by enabling customers to take possession of a product in a convenient place and time, in a convenient form and quantity and at an acceptable price. Not only does Luxottica operate its own retail stores, it also sells its prescription eyewear through local opticians and eyewear shops all over the world. Planning for this part of the marketing mix can be complex because these decisions must fit with your other marketing decisions while simultaneously meeting customers' needs and organisational objectives. Consumer and business products are made available through marketing channels, so this is a critical aspect of the planning process.

This chapter opens with an overview of the value chain and how to plan for flows and responsibilities within the value chain. Next, you'll consider decisions about channel levels and individual channel members; you'll also learn a little about the latest retail trends. Finally, you'll gain insights into logistical issues that must be addressed as you plan. Use this chapter's checklists to think through decisions about channels and logistics during the planning process. The sample marketing plan, in the Appendix, illustrates how a marketer might summarise and explain ideas for channels and logistics for the coming year.

ANALYSING THE VALUE CHAIN

The **value chain**, also known as the *value delivery network* or *supply chain*, is the succession of interrelated, value-added functions undertaken by the marketer with suppliers, wholesalers, retailers and other participants (including customers) to source supplies and ultimately deliver a product that fulfils customers' needs. Figure 8.1 shows a simplified value chain and explains the key areas to be analysed during the marketing planning process, including reverse channels. The point is to understand how each participant in the chain adds value to the good or service that your customers buy and use. Then your marketing plan can reflect a 'performance' view of the chain, including activities to enhance the combined efficiency and effectiveness of all partners, where possible.

Imagine Heinz as the central link of the value chain. As a producer, it is responsible for coordinating the transformation of *inputs* (beans and spices, for instance) into *outputs* (baked beans) as well as *inbound functions* that occur upstream (bringing ingredients to food-production facilities) and *outbound functions* that occur downstream (getting canned goods to stores). The value added downstream occurs within a **marketing channel** (also known as a **distribution channel**), the set of functions performed by the producer or intermediaries, such as retailers, to make a particular product available to customers. Tesco, Morrisons, Waitrose and other retailers are part of Heinz's marketing channel, buying its beans and ketchup to resell to consumers through shops and websites (all on the outbound side). Heinz also plans for a reverse channel by using recyclable plastics for its ketchup bottles.

Decisions about adding value inbound:
- How to manage suppliers and obtain materials and other inputs
- How to manage inbound physical, informational and financial flows

Decisions about adding value through the marketer's internal functions:
- How to manage flows for planning and implementation during production
- How to manage flows to transform inputs into outputs (products)
- How to manage flows through customer service and internal operations

Decisions about adding value outbound:
- How to manage outbound availability for convenient customer interactions
- How to manage distribution logistics of physical, informational and financial flows

Decisions about reverse channels:
- How to manage returns for exchange, refund, servicing or repair
- How to manage recycling and post-use disposition for sustainability

FIGURE 8.1   Areas of focus in a simplified value chain

The profitable flow of products, information and payments inbound and outbound to meet customer requirements is accomplished through **logistics**. One or more parties must handle inbound transportation of ingredients and packaging materials so Heinz can produce its foods. Heinz or one of its suppliers must maintain inventory levels of food ingredients to ensure that sufficient quantities are on hand when needed. Heinz also has to track production quantities, accept and fill retailers' orders and despatch cartons of its foods to retailers on the outbound side of the value chain.

In planning for channel and logistics decisions, you should take into account the needs and behaviour of targeted customer segments, your SWOT analysis and competitive situation, your product's positioning and your marketing plan objectives. Then consider which functions in the value chain must be accomplished and which participants should be responsible for each. These decisions lay the groundwork for adding value and meeting customers' needs at an acceptable cost to the customer and an acceptable profit to the organisation.

Also think about how technology applies to your channel and logistics situation. For example, the BBC and other entertainment providers allow consumers to view programmes on demand, downloaded or streamed when and where viewers want, depending on the provider and the customer's technology. The ability to deliver a good or service on demand is another option to consider during your channel and logistics planning. Because of the number of alternatives available to you, you should analyse a variety of channel and logistics arrangements before you make a final decision and document it in your marketing plan.

The value chain for services

If your marketing plan is for a service, be aware that your value chain should put particular focus on inbound activities, the service experience itself and outbound activities that involve the customer. Inbound functions cover supplies, information and payments related to providing the service; the service experience occurs in the central link (if delivered by your firm); and outbound functions cover service availability plus associated information and payments. Logistics for services are concerned with having the right supplies (and people) in the right place at the right time. Moreover, because services are perishable – they cannot be stored for future sale or consumption – your plan must carefully manage all flows to balance supply and demand.

Flows and responsibilities in the value chain

Think about the functions and activities that each participant in the value chain (suppliers, retailers, transportation firms and others) must perform to make your product available to customers when and where needed. Having a wide variety of supplies, materials or products immediately available at all times in all locations (or ready to be despatched quickly on demand) is the most desirable situation but is often too costly for an organisation and its customers. Yet customers are likely to be unsatisfied – and may turn to competitors – if a marketer has too few supplies or products available, the wrong quantities or models available, and/or slow or expensive transactions. When you plan your value chain, therefore, you will face difficult trade-offs between value added and cost.

Ensuring the quality and integrity of ingredients, production and packaging is a particularly vital responsibility in the value chain for food. Consumers in China have become concerned about food safety after a series of scandals involving tainted milk and questionable food additives. McDonald's recently reminded Chinese consumers of its long-standing reputation for food quality with an ad campaign focusing on its 100 percent beef burgers and other fresh ingredients.[2]

Reverse channels

Your marketing plan should consider the need for a **reverse channel**, a flow that moves backwards through the value chain to return goods for service or when worn out and to reclaim products, parts or packaging for recycling. This is particularly important if you're marketing online and want to reassure customers that they can return or exchange what they buy. In establishing reverse channels for recycling broken or outdated appliances and consumer electronics products, UK and European manufacturers and retailers must comply with legal and regulatory guidelines such as the Waste Electrical and Electronic Equipment (WEEE) Directive. This ensures that harmful materials are properly disposed of, a growing problem because consumers are upgrading mobiles, computers and other digital devices more frequently than ever before.

Properly planned and implemented, reverse channels can offer opportunities for enhancing sustainability and may help differentiate products or brands as eco-leaders. However, some companies have been accused of **greenwashing**, meaning that consumers perceive these companies as marketing products or brands on the basis of 'green' activities that have little or no actual ecological impact. Therefore, when you plan for reverse channels to handle recycling or other green activities, be sure your arrangements will lead to the desired outcome and help you reach your objectives.

Marks & Spencer has partnered with Oxfam to create a convenient reverse channel for unwanted clothing: When customers buy new clothes at M&S, they're encouraged to give the retailer at least one old or unwanted garment that is donated to Oxfam for resale in its charity stores. M&S hopes customers will adopt this 'buy one, give one' approach when they shop so that old clothes don't go to waste.[3]

PLANNING FOR CHANNELS TODAY

Depending on your organisation's situation and objectives, you can plan for a value chain that includes direct or indirect channels. With **direct channels**, you make products available directly to customers. For example, IKEA uses direct channels, marketing its furniture and homewares through its own stores, its own retail website and its own catalogues. With **indirect channels**, you work through marketing **intermediaries**, outside businesses or individuals that help producers make goods or services available to customers.

Figure 8.2 shows how goods or services would reach customers through direct and indirect channels. It also shows the three major types of intermediaries, each of which adds value in a particular way:

- **Wholesalers** buy from producers, sort and store products, create smaller lots for buyer convenience and resell to other intermediaries or to business customers. Some take on duties normally handled elsewhere in the value chain, such as monitoring a customer's inventory. Wholesalers may buy and resell consumer products or business products.

- **Retailers** are companies such as Selfridges, Amazon.com and Macy's that buy from producers and resell products, giving consumers easy and convenient access to an array of products. Many retailers also sell their own range of private-label products in their stores, on their websites and in their catalogues. Internet-only companies like Amazon and eBay are sometimes part of the channel for other retailers that want to reach customers online.

- *Representatives*, *brokers* and *agents* (such as insurance agents) bring producers together with customers but generally do not take ownership of the products they market. These intermediaries, which may represent business or consumer goods and services, add value through their knowledge of the market, customers and products.

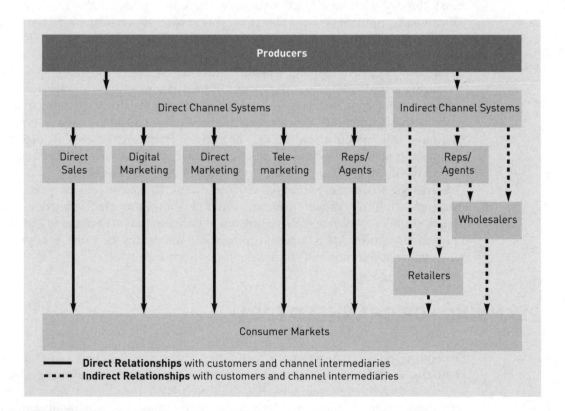

| FIGURE 8.2 | Marketing channel arrangements |

Source: Adapted from *Market-based Management*, 6th Ed., Pearson Education Inc. (Best, R.J. 2012) p. 318, ISBN-13: 978-0130387752, Reprinted and Electronically reproduced by permission of Pearson Education, Inc., Upper Saddle River, New Jersey.

Channel arrangements take time to plan and implement because you'll be working through a variety of intermediaries and each will have its own objectives and plans. Therefore, although today's business environment is highly dynamic, it usually takes time to add, eliminate or modify channels if you identify changes in your marketing situation. Also be aware of the **grey market**, which can develop when wholesalers and retailers sell a branded product when they aren't authorised to do so. The grey market isn't illegal, and the products aren't counterfeit, but it's a 'grey' area because the products weren't intended to be distributed through these intermediaries. You may need a contingency plan to deal with the possibility that your products might be sold through the grey market.

Channel length decisions

In your marketing plan, you will have to specify the number of intermediary levels you want to use for each product – in other words, the length of the channel. Longer channels have more intermediary levels separating the producer and its customers; shorter channels have fewer intermediaries. A direct channel is the shortest because there are no intermediaries and the producer deals directly with its customers through any or all of the methods shown on the left in Figure 8.2. This is appropriate when you want as much control as possible over dealings with customers and your organisation can handle all outbound functions. If your markets and segments are not well defined or you lack the resources and knowledge to work directly with customers, however, using a direct channel can be inefficient at best and ineffective at worst.

The zero-level channel can work well for both business and consumer marketers, despite differences in products, customers, prices and markets. Nippon Steel, one of the world's largest steel producers, uses direct channels to sell to construction companies, carmakers, shipbuilders and other businesses in its home country of Japan and in other markets. It recently formed a joint venture to make steel pipes in Mexico as a convenient and direct supply source for cars manufactured in North America by US, European and Japanese vehicle manufacturers.[4]

Longer channels, such as the two- and three-level indirect channels illustrated on the right in Figure 8.2, send products through a series of representatives or agents, wholesalers or retailers before they reach the final customer. Such channel arrangements allow intermediaries to add value when your company is targeting multiple or geographically dispersed markets, you have limited resources or little customer knowledge, your customers have specialised needs, or your products require training, customisation or service. Although the price paid by customers must reflect a profit for intermediaries at all levels and cover the value they add, you may find that long channels are the best way to make certain products available.

Some organisations use a direct channel for certain segments (usually business customers) and an indirect channel with one level for other segments (usually consumers). This allows more control over the typically large-volume transactions with businesses, and delegates responsibility for the higher number and smaller size of consumer transactions to intermediaries. Carmakers, for instance, use a direct channel when selling to government agencies so they can negotiate specifications, pricing and delivery; this is how Australian government agencies buy an estimated 75,000 cars and trucks each year for employee or public use.[5] In addition, carmakers use a separate, single-level (indirect) dealer channel to sell to consumers in various markets. The dealers then develop market-specific communications and promotions for consumers in their area.

Internet-based intermediaries are growing rapidly as marketers target businesses or consumers that buy electronically. Consider the success of China's Alibaba Group (http://news.alibaba.com/specials/aboutalibaba/aligroup/index.html), which operates a number of e-commerce platforms that serve as indirect channels connecting buyers and sellers. Already, more than 5 percent of China's retail sales take place digitally, and the number of transactions increases substantially every year.

MARKETING IN PRACTICE: ALIBABA GROUP

Founded in 1999, Alibaba Group owns Alibaba.com, the market leader in business-to-business e-commerce, as well as Taobao Marketplace and Tmall, two fast-growing retailing e-commerce marketplaces. Rather than taking ownership of any goods or services, Alibaba provides online space and transaction technology for wholesale and retail marketplaces. With thousands of participating companies, Alibaba's marketplaces become one-stop shopping destinations for business buyers and consumers. Alibaba makes money by charging advertising and commission fees for selling through its sites.

Every day, nearly 2 million Chinese consumers click to Alibaba's Taobao marketplace, where small retailers display merchandise for sale. Its Tmall serves as a channel for larger businesses that target consumers, such as the Japanese fashion retailer Uniqlo and the American retailer Forever 21. Tmall has also been recruiting retailers of particular products to gain category strength in competing against e-commerce rivals such as Amazon and 360Buy.com. Not long ago, it announced the signing of 1,000 online booksellers to boost the marketplace's selection of books beyond 1.3 million titles.

Some brands are testing Tmall shops as a way to gauge consumer interest and learn more about preferences in China. When US-based clothing manufacturer G-III launched a new brand, Andrew Marc, it chose Tmall as its first retailing entry in China. One way to attract attention, the company learned, was to participate in Tmall's promotions and group buying opportunities. If this test goes well, G-III plans to establish its own retail website in China and possibly expand to high street stores.[6]

Marketing plan analysis: What are the advantages and disadvantages of a retailer participating in Tmall rather than setting up its own website?

Channel member decisions

If you decide to work with at least one level of intermediary, your marketing plan should indicate how many and what type of channel members you'll need for each level in each market. These decisions depend on the market, the product and its life cycle, customer needs and behaviour, product pricing and product positioning. Table 8.1 summarises the three broad choices in number of channel members, along with the value for customers, producers and channel members.

If you use **exclusive distribution**, one intermediary will handle your product in a particular area (the way vehicle manufacturers sell through one showroom for each town or region). If you use **selective distribution**, a fairly small number of intermediaries will sell your product in the area. If you use **intensive distribution**, many intermediaries will handle your product in the area. How do you choose among these options? As the table indicates, you can enhance the luxury image of upmarket or specialised goods and services by using exclusive distribution. New products that require extensive customer

Table 8.1   Exclusive, selective and intensive distribution

	Exclusive distribution	Selective distribution	Intensive distribution
Value added for customer	• Individual attention • Knowledgeable sales help • Availability of training and other services	• Choice of outlets in each area • Some services available	• Convenient availability in many areas • Competition among outlets may lower price
Value added for producer	• Reinforces positioning of expensive or technical product • Closer cooperation and exchange of information • More control over service quality	• Ability to cover more of the market • Less dependent on a small number of channel members	• Higher unit sales • Ability to cover an area completely • Lower cost per unit
Value added for channel member	• Association with exclusive brands enhances image • Can become expert in certain product categories and lines • Can tailor services to targeted customers	• Benefit from producer's marketing support in the area • Potential to build sales volume and qualify for higher discounts	• Attract customers seeking high-volume, high-demand offerings • Enhance overall merchandise mix
Concerns for producer	• Higher cost per unit • Potentially reach fewer customers	• Medium costs, medium control	• Less control over service quality • More difficult to supervise • Possible conflict among channel members

education may be sold in exclusive or selective distribution. Also, products that require expert sales support or for which customers shop around are often marketed through selective distribution. Finally, consider intensive distribution for inexpensive, everyday products, especially impulse items, because of the opportunity to achieve higher sales volumes.

In addition, you have to select specific intermediaries for each channel. In a marketing plan for an existing product or a new entry in an existing line, you may want to reassess the value each member is providing, add more channel members to expand market coverage if needed and replace ineffective or inefficient members as necessary. As coverage increases, however, so does the possibility for conflict among channel members over customers, market coverage, pricing and other issues.

Your marketing plan should allow for educating channel members about your product's benefits and encouraging them to promote it actively. Also think about whether a particular intermediary will be a strong partner in marketing the product (and later products) in the future. Bear in mind that some retailers may stock your product online only, due to limited space in branch shops. And some retailers may give your product special consideration because they want variety in their merchandising assortment.[7]

Finally, remember the grey market, which has already been mentioned earlier in this chapter. Sometimes grey markets develop in countries where demand exists for a product but that brand has no official distributor, for example. The grey market can be especially problematic for the brand if the product is sold at extra-low prices, or in an inappropriate retail environment, for example. You may need a contingency plan to deal with the possibility that a grey market will develop for your product if you decide to limit availability or you're planning a gradual international expansion.

Retail trends

As you plan your channel strategy, you should be aware of what's happening in the retail industry. Trends can sweep through quite quickly, changing as consumers' needs and preferences change or because of business challenges and opportunities. One trend gaining momentum is **pop-up shops**, temporary stores that 'pop up' in a location for a day, a week or a few months. These are never intended to be permanent; each has a specific marketing purpose and stays open only for a limited time, which affects both planning and implementation, as well as the metrics used to evaluate results.

As you read in the opening example, Luxottica's Sunglass Hut drew attention to its high-fashion spectacles by opening a pop-up shop in Sydney Harbour for four days. The US-based retail chain Target used a one-day pop-up shop in Toronto to build positive buzz for its brand months before it opened a new high street store. The entire inventory of the pop-up shop sold out in a few hours, and Target donated that day's revenue to charity.[8] Topshop and Topman tested South African interest in their UK clothing brands by opening a three-month pop-up shop within a permanent store, the Unknown Union in Capetown.[9]

Pop-up restaurants move from one temporary location to another, attracting publicity and building brand interest. Germany's Prêt à Diner, for example, has served upmarket dinners on river banks, in skyscrapers and in historic buildings.[10] Not long ago, Electrolux sponsored a luxury pop-up restaurant on the roof of London's Royal Festival Hall to showcase its kitchen appliances.[11] A related retail trend is the popularity of food trucks, which typically park in different neighbourhoods on different days and specialise in a particular type of food, such as barbecues, tacos or cupcakes. Now entrepreneurs are marketing many types of products, including clothing and accessories, via *mobile stores* that park in various locations where customers can gather, browse and buy.[12]

A number of marketers are testing *virtual stores*, where shoppers in a transport hub or another non-store environment buy by pointing a mobile at an image that includes the product's barcode or a QR (quick response) code. Well.ca, a Canadian online retailer specialising in household, health and beauty products, recently tested a virtual store in a Toronto subway station, in partnership with Procter & Gamble. It posted billboards featuring photos of P&G products such as Tide detergent and Pantene shampoo, tagged with QR codes and prices. Shoppers first downloaded the store's app and then scanned the QR codes to buy. As a result, Well.ca sold more Tide detergent in the virtual store's first week than it had during the entire previous year.[13]

The UK retail giant Tesco (www.tesco.com) has experience with virtual stores in South Korea and is also experimenting with virtual stores closer to home.

MARKETING IN PRACTICE: TESCO

With more than £72 billion in turnover, Tesco operates 6,200 stores in 13 countries, as well as a highly successful online business. Despite this extensive network of stores, Tesco is interested in virtual stores because so many consumers now own smartphones. Its research shows that UK consumers are already buying £4.5 billion worth of goods and services via mobiles, and Tesco wants to be part of that trend, offering busy shoppers the convenience of ordering without having to visit a store.

In 2011, HomePlus, one of Tesco's retail chains, pioneered the virtual store in South Korea. It posted billboards in subway stations and bus stops around Seoul, featuring photographic displays of 500 popular grocery products, along with QR codes. Commuters used their mobiles with the HomePlus app to scan the QR codes of juices, noodles, pet foods or other items, indicate the quantity and specify a delivery time. HomePlus attracted so many new customers and increased sales so significantly that it soon expanded the project to additional commuter areas.

In 2012, Tesco opened a two-week virtual store as a test in a departure terminal of London's Gatwick Airport. Under the strapline 'Come home to a full fridge', the touch-screen displays featured full-colour product photos and ordering codes for dozens of foods and household items. Customers leaving on holiday or business could arrange for a delivery time coinciding with their return from their travels. The appeal, Tesco's director of Internet retailing explained, is that 'the virtual store blends clicks and bricks, bringing together our love of browsing with the convenience of online shopping'.[14]

Marketing plan analysis: What factors should Tesco consider when selecting a location for another virtual store?

Because many businesses are adopting *multichannel marketing*, conflict between store-based retailers and online retailers is increasing. As discussed in **Chapter 7**, some online retailers encourage shoppers to compare prices of specific items in stores and online via mobile apps, because retailers without stores are often able to sell at a lower price than store-based retailers. Increasingly, customers are examining products in local stores, comparing prices using an app and then buying online if the price is lower. This trend is known as **showrooming** because customers use the physical store as a showroom – a place to look but not buy. To combat showrooming, some store retailers are adding mobile-shopping apps, expanding their in-store services, helping customers to place orders for speedy home delivery and matching the prices of online retailers.

Checklist No. 13 will help you think about channel issues for your marketing plan.

ESSENTIAL CHECKLIST NO. 13:
PLANNING FOR MARKETING CHANNELS

A good channel strategy starts with customer research and a thorough understanding of the current marketing situation. Also consider how channel choices and changes might affect your competitive position and your organisation's ability to achieve its objectives. Tick each question below as you note your answer in the space provided.

☐ How do customers prefer or expect to gain access to the product?

_____

☐ What channels and channel members are best suited to the product, positioning and brand image?

_____

☐ What are the organisation's channel costs and will customers pay for access through these channels?

_____

☐ Are the right assortments of products available at the right time and in the right quantities, with appropriate support?

_____

☐ How much control does the organisation want over channel functions?

_____

☐ How can channel decisions be used to manage the product life cycle?

_____

☐ What geographical, ecological, legal and regulatory considerations affect channel decisions?

___

☐ How many channel levels and members are appropriate, given the organisation's situation, objectives and targeting decisions?

___

☐ Do channel members have capable sales and support staff, are they equipped to store and display the product, and are they financially sound?

___

☐ Is multichannel marketing appropriate for your good or service? What arrangements make sense for your customers and your organisation?

___

PLANNING FOR LOGISTICS TODAY

A good logistics plan can help you compete by serving customers more effectively or by saving money. This is especially important for small businesses and in fast-growing industries, where customer relationships are just being formed. Whatever your plan, you will need clear-cut, non-conflicting objectives. If your objective is to make more products available or get them to customers more quickly, expect higher costs. If your objective is to cut costs, you might have to carry less stock or use slower transportation methods, raising the possibility that some products might be out of stock for brief periods. Your logistics strategy must be realistic for your situation now and in the future, striking a balance between your customers' needs and your organisation's financial, marketing and societal objectives.

Inventory decisions

Your decisions about inventory must be made even before the first product moves into the channel. Pre-production, you should identify the stock level of parts and supplies required for the planned output. Post-production, think about how much stock of a particular product is needed outbound to meet customer demand, balanced with organisational constraints of budgets, production and storage capacity. As Figure 8.3 indicates, logistics decisions about pre- and post-production inventory, storage, transportation, order processing and fulfilment depend on whether your objectives are linked to less service (lower cost) or more service (higher cost).

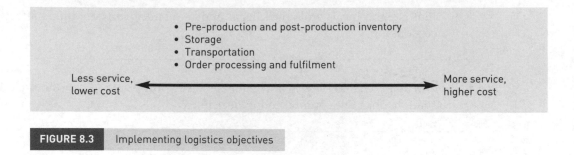

| FIGURE 8.3 | Implementing logistics objectives |

If your stocks are too low, customers will not find products when and where they want and your channel members will lose sales; if they are too high, the organisation's investment is tied up and you risk having some products going out of style, spoiling or becoming obsolete. If you're a retailer, you have to consider what shoppers will buy (and when), what your suppliers can provide (at short notice, if needed) and when you must pay your suppliers. The online retailer Amazon.com has enough experience across its product range that it can accurately predict buying habits and adjust inventory levels accordingly.

Increasingly, producers, suppliers and channel members are collaborating to forecast demand and have the right amount of stock when and where needed. Mistakes can be costly – resulting in empty shelves and disappointed customers or, just as bad, warehouses full of obsolete or overpriced products. You must be able to respond quickly when your retail partners reorder items that sell unusually well; also remember that retailers may delist products that fail to live up to their sales expectations.

Storage decisions

Where will you store materials before production and where will you store finished products until needed to fill intermediary or customer orders? How long will you store materials and finished products? Such storage decisions are based, in part, on your inventory decisions and your customers' requirements. If you promise a business customer just-in-time stock replenishment, you might store products in a nearby warehouse or distribution centre for speedy delivery on schedule. Also examine how much space is needed for storing stock at the site where customers actually gain access to the product.

Look at the product itself and typical variations in demand when planning for product storage. Is your product perishable? Is it especially large (or small) or fragile? Does it have other physical characteristics that affect storage? Are large quantities needed quickly during periods of peak demand? Is demand erratic or steady? What are the implications for your marketing plan?

Evaluate your alternatives to determine whether your organisation should maintain its own storage facilities, add or decrease storage capacity or outsource warehousing to a specialist. Recently, Woolworths in Australia invested in a new Sydney distribution centre to serve its stores in New South Wales. The firm's analysis showed that restocking its New South Wales stores from this location would save time and money – and be a greener move than restocking those stores from existing warehouses in South Australia and Queensland.[15]

Transportation decisions

In the course of planning inbound and outbound logistics, choose the means of transport that are appropriate for your product, your budget and your customers' needs and value perceptions. Choices include road transport by lorry (convenient for door-to-door shipments), rail transport (for bulky or heavy items), air transport (when time is a factor and budgets allow), water transport (when time is not a factor but cost is) and pipeline transport (for liquids and natural gases). Often products are despatched by more than one means of transport, such as lorry to water, rail or air and back to lorry.

Table 8.2 shows some of the key questions to ask when making transportation decisions for your marketing plan.

If you're a producer, your flexibility in transportation choices depends, in part, on legal and regulatory rules governing competition in pricing and schedules, as well as your balance of cost and customer service. If you are marketing transportation services, use your marketing plan to differentiate yourself from competitors through convenience, speed, special product handling or another benefit that your customers value. If you're a charity or non-governmental organisation, you may need specialised logistics to deal with accepting donated goods and services, as well as for distributing goods and services when and where needed. Deutsche Post/DHL, UPS, FedEx and other transportation firms often provide logistics expertise to supplement the plans made by NGOs.

Table 8.2 Planning for transportation

Question	Transportation choices
How quickly must products be at their destination?	Air is speediest; water is slowest
Is steady, predictable receipt of products desirable?	Pipeline allows for fairly steady transport of liquids and gases; water is least predictable
What level of transport costs is acceptable to the organisation and its customers?	Pipeline and water are least expensive; air is most expensive
Is transportation available from the point of despatch directly to the point of delivery?	Road transport offers the most convenient door-to-door delivery
How do product characteristics affect transportation options?	Water and rail easily and cost-effectively accommodate large, bulky products; lorries are often used to transport products that require a temperature-controlled environment

Some marketers outsource the process of transporting orders to specialist firms that take care of all the details. Also think about the reliability of transportation and requirements that are specific to certain products, such as maintaining a constant temperature for chilled foods throughout the distribution process.

Every marketing plan created by Hindustan Lever (www.hul.co.in), the Indian subsidiary of Unilever, addresses logistics issues such as storage, inventory and transportation.

MARKETING IN PRACTICE: HINDUSTAN LEVER

Hindustan Lever (HUL), headquartered in Mumbai, markets 35 brands in 20 product categories, including Dove soap, Pepsodent toothpaste and Kissan jams. One of its marketing objectives is to expand distribution; one financial objective is to improve product availability in stores without increasing costs; and one societal objective is to help fight rural poverty. Its channel strategy is designed to achieve all of these objectives while supporting the company's revenue growth.

A few years ago, HUL tested a logistics scheme in which its Mumbai distributors held no inventory. Instead, HUL representatives visited retailers to digitally record replenishment orders, returned to local distributors' offices and transmitted the orders to HUL. Distributors received next-day delivery and immediately transported the merchandise to individual retailers, eliminating the need to buy and store extra inventory. Although distributors had to invest in new technology, the scheme was so successful in maintaining retail in-stock positions that HUL implemented it in 42 other cities. HUL also benefits from the instant feedback on sales trends and demand levels. As India's transportation infrastructure develops, HUL can implement this scheme in additional areas.

For more than a decade, HUL has used a 'Shakti' distribution strategy to make its products available in remote rural communities through a network of entrepreneurs who sell directly to consumers and also wholesale to local shops. Today, more than 45,000 women and 30,000 men sell HUL products in very small Indian villages, often transporting products on bicycles provided by HUL. This not only adds nearly 1 million small stores to HUL's distribution network, it also enables Shakti participants to earn money. Following HUL's model, its parent company is now using the Shakti strategy to market packaged foods, personal care items and household products in Bangladesh, Nigeria and Kenya.[16]

Marketing plan analysis: Why would HUL want Shakti representatives to sell to small stores in remote villages, not just to consumers?

Order processing and fulfilment decisions

Whether you're targeting business or consumer markets, you'll have to include order processing and fulfilment in your marketing plan, with decisions about the method and timing of:

- accepting orders and billing for purchases;

- confirmation of order and available inventory;

- picking and packing products for despatch;

- documenting and tracking the contents of shipments;

- handling returns, errors and damaged goods.

Many organisations aim for better customer service through reduced order cycle time as part of their marketing plan activities. This means your customers (whether consumers or businesses) will have as short a wait as possible between placing an order and receiving delivery. Also consider whether you and your customers would benefit from paying to outsource order processing and fulfilment. For a fee, the pioneering online retailer Amazon.com will provide fulfilment functions for producers and other retailers; it stores merchandise until purchased, then packs and ships to fulfil orders placed through Amazon or through other channel members. Yet Amazon is also focused on fulfilling orders for merchandise that it sells to customers as a retailer. It recently built 18 new fulfilment centres, equipped with robotic merchandise picking systems, to be ready for peak holiday buying demand.[17]

You can use Checklist No. 14 as a guide to some of the key questions you need to ask when you plan for logistics.

ESSENTIAL CHECKLIST NO. 14:
PLANNING FOR LOGISTICS

Keep your channel strategy in mind as you think about the logistics decisions that are right for your customers, your organisation and your competitive situation. Tick each question as you answer and write notes in the space provided.

☐ What logistics arrangements would enable customers to obtain products quickly, conveniently and at an acceptable price?

_____

☐ How can logistics add more value for the customer and the organisation by boosting benefits or decreasing costs or both?

_____

☐ What influence are the organisation's SWOT and resources likely to have on logistics decisions? Can any aspect of logistics be outsourced if necessary without compromising objectives or service?

_____

☐ How can logistics be used for competitive advantage and to support positioning?

☐ What is the optimal balance of logistics costs and customer service, given the marketing plan objectives?

CHAPTER SUMMARY

The value chain (also called the value delivery network or supply chain) is the succession of interrelated, value-added functions that enables a producer to create and deliver a product that fulfils customers' needs through connections with suppliers, wholesalers, retailers and other participants. The marketing (or distribution) channel refers to the set of functions performed by the producer or by intermediaries in making a product available to customers at a profit. Marketing channels are outbound functions downstream in the value chain, closer to the customer. Logistics refers to the flow of products, information and payments inbound and outbound to meet customer requirements.

Marketers can use direct channels, in which the organisation deals directly with customers, and/or indirect channels, in which the organisation works through other businesses or individuals (intermediaries). The three major types of intermediaries are wholesalers, retailers, and representatives, brokers and agents. In a channel with one or more levels, marketers can choose exclusive, selective or intensive distribution. The main functions involved in logistics are pre- and post-production inventory, storage, transportation, order processing and fulfilment. Increasing customer service levels generally increases logistics costs, while reducing logistics costs generally reduces the level of customer service, a point to keep in mind while planning.

CASE STUDY: INDITEX

Inditex (www.inditex.com), based in La Coruña, Spain, makes and distributes clothing through eight different retail brands that operate a total of more than 5,600 stores worldwide. With annual turnover of €14 billion, Inditex is the largest clothing retailer in the world – and every year, it expands its store network by about 10 percent. The largest and best-known of Inditex's retail brands is Zara, which accounts for nearly two-thirds of the parent company's annual revenues. A glamorous flagship store on New York City's posh Fifth Avenue reinforces Zara's stylish image and showcases its ever-changing range of 'fast fashion'.

Zara has earned a reputation for moving quickly when a style takes off. Once its designers identify a new trend – with daily insights from store employees worldwide as well as from social media, art magazines, fashion shows and other sources – they can have new fashions manufactured and on display in company stores within two to four weeks. This is a never-ending process, with 18,000 new clothing products designed and distributed every year through Zara's store network in five continents. Customers stop by regularly because Zara and other Inditex stores receive small shipments of hot new merchandise all the time. If they wait too long to shop, the most popular sizes, styles and colours may be gone.

Knowing that today's most in-demand style may be unwanted tomorrow, Inditex makes much of its clothing in Spain and nearby countries to reduce the time needed to get new products into stores. Its plants use cutting-edge just-in-time systems to manage the flow of materials inbound, plan the timing of production and handle outbound details; its distribution experts use sophisticated software to track international shipments and customs documentation. Inditex is also expanding its online retailing operations to serve fashion-conscious shoppers in China, Spain, Poland and elsewhere.

As a result, Inditex has an extraordinary level of control over distribution and logistics and can restock thousands of stores worldwide very quickly. It speeds merchandise by lorry from its centrally located warehouses to its European stores for next-day delivery and sends in-demand goods by air to stores outside Europe for two-day delivery. Anticipating higher demand and a larger retail presence in China, Inditex has also opened a design centre there and makes some clothing in Asia. By controlling supply and transportation costs, and offering customers the styles they want before fads fade, Inditex has increased turnover and kept profit margins high.[18]

Case questions

1. What effect do you think Inditex's 'fast fashion' system has on the company's inventory levels, and what does this suggest about its pricing power?

2. Is Inditex using a direct or indirect channel system? How long is the channel, and why is this appropriate for Inditex?

APPLY YOUR KNOWLEDGE

Select a common consumer product, then research and analyse its value chain and its channel arrangements. Prepare a written report or an oral presentation summarising your analysis.

- Draw a diagram to show a simplified value chain for this product. Is a reverse channel necessary or desirable? Why?

- Is this product available through direct channels such as by mail or from the producer's website? How does this channel arrangement benefit customers and the organisation? What potential disadvantages can you see to this arrangement?

- Is the product available through indirect channels such as retailers? Why is this appropriate for the product, the market and the targeted customers?

- What suggestions can you make for adding channel members who fit with the product's targeting and positioning? How would you select these additional channel members?

- Is the product available through exclusive distribution? Through intensive distribution? Do you agree with this decision?

BUILD YOUR OWN MARKETING PLAN

Continue developing your marketing plan by making decisions about channel arrangements and logistics. Should you market this product directly to customers or through indirect channels or a combination? How long should your channel be, and what value will each level add? Is a reverse channel needed? Will you use intensive, selective or exclusive distribution, and why? What kinds of channel members would be most appropriate? What retail trends, if any, can you leverage for your product? Does your product require any special transportation, storage or post-purchase support? What specific customer needs should you take into account when planning logistics and how will you balance cost with customer service? Record your decisions and explain their implications in your marketing plan.

ENDNOTES

1. Xu Junqian, 'Future's so bright in optical sector', *Business Daily Update*, 18 June 2012, n.p.; Peter Marsh, 'View from the top: Andrea Guerra, chief executive of Luxottica', *Financial Times*, 28 May 2012, p. 16; John Macpherson, 'Pop up stores a boost for retail', *The Age (Melbourne, Australia)*, 30 May 2012, p. 16; 'Advantage independents', *Optician*, 16 July 2010, n.p.; www.luxottica.com.

2. Lisa Baertlein, 'China's chicken scare hit McDonald's sales: CEO', *Reuters*, 23 January 2013, www.reuters.com Laurie Burkitt, 'McDonald's to tout quality in China', *Wall Street Journal*, 29 February 2012, www.wsj.com.

3. Rebecca Smithers, 'M&S launches "schwopping" scheme', *Guardian*, 26 April 2012, www.guardian.co.uk.

4. 'Nippon Steel announces auto steel pipe venture in Mexico', *Asahi Shimbun*, 6 August 2012, http://ajw.asahi.com.

5. Paul Bastian, 'Our car industry can survive and thrive', *Herald Sun (Australia)*, 20 August 2012, http://www.heraldsun.com.au.

6. Melanie Lee, 'Alibaba Group's Jan-March net profit soars: SEC filing', *Reuters*, 10 August 2012, www.reuters.com; Lara Farrar, 'Tmall's fashion ambitions,'

WWD, 25 June 2012, p. 1; Mark Lee, 'Alibaba discounts TVs to woo 193 million Chinese online', *Bloomberg Businessweek*, 12 June 2012, www.businessweek.com; Chen Limin, 'Alibaba turns to next page', *Business Daily Update*, 13 June 2012, n.p.

7. Joanna Perry, 'A matter of choice: Is bigger product range good for shoppers?', *Retail Week*, 25 September 2009, www.retail-week.com.

8. Prithi Yelaja, 'Target pop-up store attracts 1,500 shoppers', *CBC News*, 23 February 2012, www.cbc.ca; Nicola Harrison, 'John Lewis to open first pop-up shop', *Retail Week*, 8 August 2012, www.retail-week.com.

9. Janice Kew, 'Arcadia's Topshop, Topman plan first Africa pop-up outlet', *Bloomberg News*, 9 July 2012, www.bloomberg.com.

10. David Coffer, 'World views: American trends migrate overseas', *Nation's Restaurant News*, 5 March 2012, http://nrn.com.

11. Jonathan Bacon, 'Top of the pop-ups', *Marketing Week*, 23 August 2012, www.marketingweek.co.uk.

12. 'Haute wheels: Fashion takes a cue from food trucks', *Wall Street Journal*, 31 July 2012, www.wsj.com.

13. Misty Harris, 'Virtual reality: New retail trend combines online and traditional shopping', *Canada.com*, 15 August 2012, http://o.canada.com; Dave Hale, 'Online retailers move beyond digital', *Ottawa Business Journal*, 23 April 2012, www.obj.ca.

14. Quoted in 'Fed up of coming home from holiday to an empty fridge?', *Tesco news release*, 7 August 2012, http://www.tescoplc.com/index.asp?pageid= 17&newsid=664; other sources: Maija Palmer, 'Tesco trials UK's first virtual store', *Financial Times*, 6 August 2012, www.ft.com; Anh Nguyen, 'Tesco launches virtual store at Gatwick Airport', *CIO*, 7 August 2012, www.cio.co.uk; Jason Strother, 'Shopping by phone at South Korea's virtual grocery', *BBC News*, 20 October 2011, www.bbc.co.uk; Ian Steadman, 'Tesco brings "virtual grocery stores" to the UK', *Wired*, 7 August 2012, www.wired.co.uk.

15. Blair Speedy, 'Distribution move to save Woolies millions', *Australian*, 10 August 2012, www.theaustralian.com.au.

16. Louise Lucas, 'Retail openings that bar no one', *Financial Times*, 16 August 2012, www.ft.com; Anusha Subramanian, 'Hindustan Unilever's initiative for a social cause', *Business Today*, 31 May 2011, http://businesstoday.intoday.in; Priyanka Sangani, 'Hindustan Unilever to configure distribution setup', *Economic Times*, 27 February 2009, http://articles.economictimes.indiatimes.com; Louise Lucas, 'Unilever extends "Shakti" scheme to Africa', *Financial Times*, 30 August 2011, www.ft.com; Samar Srivastava, 'Hindustan Lever rethinks rural', *Forbes India*, 1 October 2010, www.forbes.com.

17. Chad Fraser, 'Amazon.com focuses on growth', *Investing Daily*, 31 July 2012, www.investingdaily.com.

18. 'Zara owner Inditex profits rise 32%', *BBC News*, 19 September 2012, www.bbc.co.uk; Graham Keeley, 'How 50 ideas a day help to keep the customer satisfied', *The Times (London)*, 14 April 2012, p. 68; 'Fashion forward', *Economist*, 24 March 2012, www.economist.com; Sarah Butler, 'Zara's owner Inditex bucks the Spanish trend and gets bigger', *Observer*, 3 June 2012, p. 41; 'Zara owner automates', *Logistics Manager*, 4 June 2009, p. 8.

Planning for communications and influence

Learning outcomes

After studying this chapter, you will be able to:

* Understand the role of marketing in communicating with and influencing customers and other target audiences

* Outline the planning process for marketing communications and influence

* Discuss how communications tools are used to reach target audiences in support of marketing plan objectives

Application outcomes

After studying this chapter, you will be able to:

* Set communications and influence objectives consistent with marketing plan objectives

* Select appropriate communications tools

* Plan a campaign to engage with and influence target audience(s)

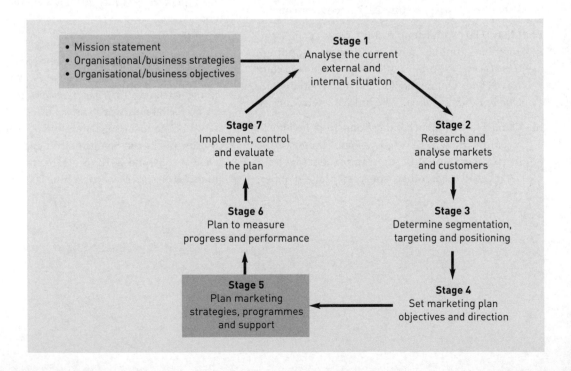

- Mission statement
- Organisational/business strategies
- Organisational/business objectives

Stage 1
Analyse the current external and internal situation

Stage 2
Research and analyse markets and customers

Stage 3
Determine segmentation, targeting and positioning

Stage 4
Set marketing plan objectives and direction

Stage 5
Plan marketing strategies, programmes and support

Stage 6
Plan to measure progress and performance

Stage 7
Implement, control and evaluate the plan

CHAPTER PREVIEW: MARKETING AT PROCTER & GAMBLE

How do you stimulate an emotional reaction to everyday products such as shampoo and disposable nappies while building positive attitudes towards the parent company? That's the challenge for marketers at Procter & Gamble (www.pg.com), the US consumer products giant with €65 billion in annual turnover and a portfolio of well-known brands such as Pantene, Pampers and Tide. Competing against Unilever, Colgate-Palmolive and other firms that market personal care and household products, P&G has traditionally made individual brands the focus of its marketing communications. However, recognising that today's consumers want to know more about the values of the companies they buy from, the head of global brand building recently added the parent company to his communication strategy.

During the 2012 Olympic Games, for example, P&G (an official sponsor) ran a multi-national campaign featuring the corporate name and 34 brand names under the theme 'Thank you, Mom' to celebrate mothers' roles in supporting their Olympic athlete children. After testing the theme with mothers worldwide, P&G engaged its audience through television and print adverts; beauty salons providing free hair styling and grooming for athletes and their families; diverse digital and social media content; and sponsorship of individual athletes. Its sponsorship activities and special events received widespread media coverage, amplifying the company's involvement and reinforcing trust in P&G and its brands. This campaign not only boosted overall sales of the featured brands, it also increased sales at the retail level for stores that used P&G's special Olympic-themed displays.[1]

Strategies for marketing communications and influence – in other words, for promotion – help you engage the people and organisations that are important to your brand or cause. P&G uses communications to influence consumers' attitudes and feelings towards its brands and corporate name, and to encourage purchasing and loyalty. In this chapter, you'll learn the basics of how to plan for communications, the most visible and creative aspects of many marketing plans, and about the need for post-implementation analysis and evaluation. You'll also be introduced to the concepts of word of mouth, buzz marketing, social media marketing, content marketing and integrated marketing communications. This chapter includes a brief overview of planning for advertising, sales promotion, personal selling, direct marketing and public relations. Two checklists in this chapter are designed to help with your planning for media and for sales promotion.

THE ROLE OF MARKETING COMMUNICATIONS AND INFLUENCE

You might have the best product on the planet, the best price or the most convenient distribution, but your marketing plan will accomplish nothing unless you have a strategy for communicating with customers and other important audiences. Until a few years ago, marketers tended to rely on one-way techniques such as advertising to get messages to broad groups of customers. Now marketers strive for two-way communications, building relationships over time by engaging specific audiences in ongoing conversations.

Targeted communications are essential to an effective *customer-influence strategy* for engaging your customers (and key publics) and influencing how these people think, feel and act towards your brand or offering. Often, the point is not to make an immediate sale but to shape attitudes and strengthen relationships with customers over an extended period, aiming for high customer lifetime value and long-term loyalty.

Increasingly, P&G and other marketers are turning to technology to stimulate word of mouth and build buzz in the short term, and then continue the conversation and the influence through social media marketing. Content marketing plays a key role in the strategies of companies that seek to differentiate themselves as experts in subjects of interest to their customers and other publics.

Word of mouth, buzz and social media marketing

Word of mouth means people telling other people about a marketing message, a particular product or another aspect of the offering or the marketing. Word of mouth has considerable credibility because it's not marketer-controlled and it reflects what people in the market think, feel and do. As a marketer, you can try to initiate positive word of mouth, and you may even reward word of mouth. However, you can't control whether your audience picks up on the message and passes it along when or as you intended. And, because word of mouth spreads in an unpredictable way, your message will probably not reach everyone in your target audience.

A more intense form of word of mouth is **buzz marketing**, in which you target opinion leaders with communications that influence them to be active in spreading brand or product information to other people. Buzz marketing can spread product or brand information especially quickly on the Internet. Yet because this is word of mouth, marketers can't control exactly what's being said, where and when the message spreads or how long it will circulate for. Often buzz about a brand will fade as quickly as it builds.

In **social media** – online media such as blogs, social networking sites and video- and photo-sharing, all of which facilitate user interaction – consumers create much of the content (in the form of text, videos, podcasts or photos) and respond to content posted by other users. The immense popularity of such sites has led to the rise of **social media marketing**, the use of social media technologies, channels and software to achieve marketing plan objectives such as increasing brand awareness, attracting website visitors and maintaining dialogues with various publics.

For many firms, social media marketing has become a priority, because research suggests that brand and product mentions in a social-media context can affect customers' attitudes and feelings and may also affect the purchasing decisions of friends within social networks.[2] Four components of social media marketing are social communities (such as business-to-business interactions on LinkedIn), social publishing (such as brand-relevant videos posted on YouTube), social commerce (such as coupons offered through Facebook) and social entertainment (such as product placement in games on Facebook).[3]

Table 9.1	Social media marketing
Social medium	**Example of marketing use**
Blog	Managing directors at John Lewis use corporate blogs to announce store openings and other news
Microblog	Intel posts messages on its various Twitter accounts to inform business customers and suppliers about new computer chip products, new technologies and other developments of interest
Photo sharing	Ford Motor Company posts photos of automotive events, new vehicle launches and other marketing activities on Flickr to engage customers
Social community	Internal: Asda encourages a sense of community with 'The Green Room', a video blog by and for the retailer's employees External: Harley-Davidson sponsors online communities for motorcyclists, including segments such as women and Latinos, to help enthusiasts connect with each other
Social networking	Panasonic maintains Facebook pages for different countries where it does business to encourage interaction with local brand fans
Video sharing	Comic Relief maintains a Red Nose Day channel on YouTube, featuring professional and consumer-generated videos to raise money for charity

Unilever's chief marketing officer observes that 'brands are now becoming conversation factors where academics, celebrities, experts and key opinion formers discuss functional, emotional and, more interestingly, social concerns,' adding: 'Of course, the conversation is no longer one way or 30 seconds.'[4] Remember, as a marketer, you aren't in control of messages that appear in social media, and you can't expect all word of mouth to be positive. See Table 9.1 for examples of how social media marketing is being used today.

For reasons of transparency and trust, you must be willing to accept some online criticism and complaints along with praise and questions. The head of social media for Coca-Cola emphasises the need to listen and respond to negative comments: 'We're getting to a point if you're not responding, you're not being seen as an authentic type of brand.'[5] To comply with fair trading regulations, be completely transparent about your company's identity when trying to spark word of mouth in any media.

Content marketing

How can a brand stand out and add value for an audience, online and off? This is the idea behind **content marketing**: marketers demonstrate thought leadership and engage or inform customers by communicating original content (such as blog posts, newsletters, how-to videos, podcasts, webcasts, webinars and games). More than three-quarters of all businesses include content marketing in their communication plans to highlight their expertise and encourage customers to contact them for more information.[6] Siemens and General Electric both produce content marketing to educate and inform industrial and municipal buyers of energy equipment and related products, which they market internationally.

Debenhams' Beauty Club blog is a good example of content marketing for consumers. The UK department store posts exclusive interviews with beauty experts, how-to videos featuring the latest techniques and other content that appeals to buyers of cosmetics and other personal care products. Consumers clearly appreciate the content: the Facebook page has more than 350,000 'likes' and the YouTube channel has more than 2 million video views.[7]

Understanding marketing communications tools

As you plan to engage your audience(s), consider how one or more of the five major marketing communications tools shown in Figure 9.1 might help you achieve your objectives. The following is a brief description; each tool is examined again later in the chapter. Think about how your audience might respond to each type of communications

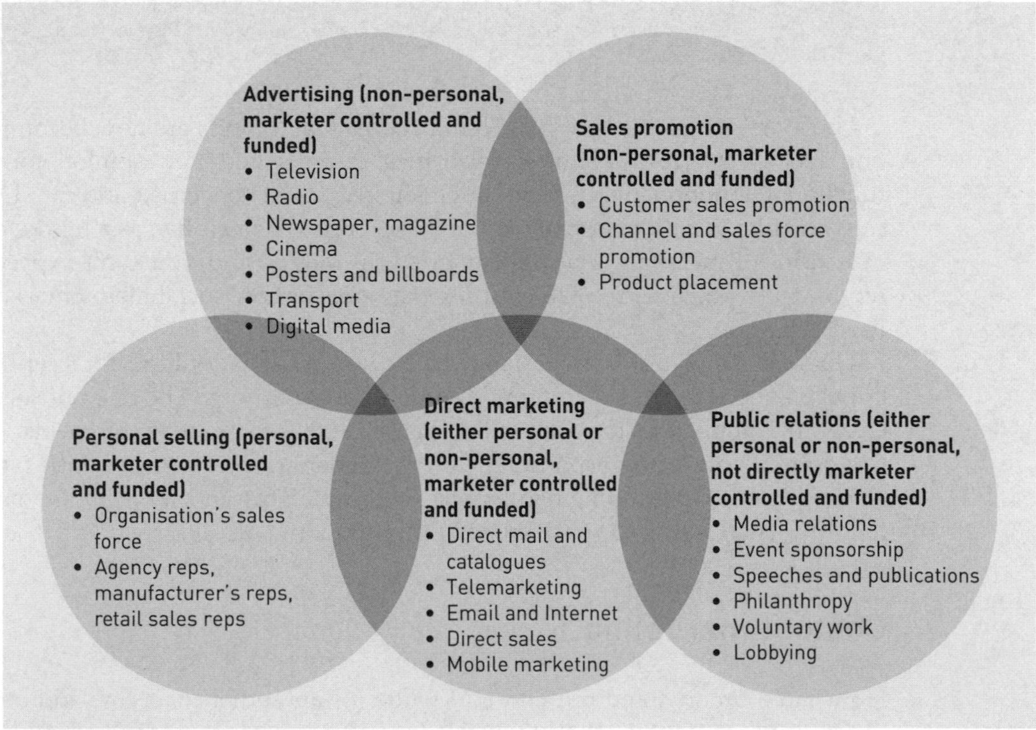

Advertising (non-personal, marketer controlled and funded)
- Television
- Radio
- Newspaper, magazine
- Cinema
- Posters and billboards
- Transport
- Digital media

Sales promotion (non-personal, marketer controlled and funded)
- Customer sales promotion
- Channel and sales force promotion
- Product placement

Personal selling (personal, marketer controlled and funded)
- Organisation's sales force
- Agency reps, manufacturer's reps, retail sales reps

Direct marketing (either personal or non-personal, marketer controlled and funded)
- Direct mail and catalogues
- Telemarketing
- Email and Internet
- Direct sales
- Mobile marketing

Public relations (either personal or non-personal, not directly marketer controlled and funded)
- Media relations
- Event sponsorship
- Speeches and publications
- Philanthropy
- Voluntary work
- Lobbying

FIGURE 9.1   Tools for marketing communications

tool, and the relative cost of creating and running a campaign that would make an impression on your audience.

Advertising

Advertising is non-personal promotion paid for by an identified sponsor. This is a cost-effective way to inform large numbers of customers or channel members about a brand or product, persuade customers or channel members about a brand's or product's merits, encourage buying and remind customers or channel members about the brand to encourage repurchase. Although television advertising remains popular, many companies see online advertising and social networking sites as less costly methods of communicating with more targeted audiences.

Sales promotion

Sales promotion consists of incentives to enhance a product's short-term value and stimulate the target audience to buy soon (or respond in another way). Although advertising is an excellent way to build brand image and awareness and bring the audience to the brink of action, sales promotion provides impetus to take action right away. You can use sales promotion to induce customers to try a new product, for example, or to encourage channel members to stock and sell a new product. The results of most promotions are easily measured by counting the number of coupons redeemed, the number of people who click on links in email newsletters or on websites, and so on. A growing number of firms are using **mobile marketing** to communicate about consumer sales promotions through text and email received on mobiles as well as through websites optimised for handset screens.

Personal selling

Personal selling – especially useful for two-way communication – can take many forms, including traditional in-person sales, Internet sales and telemarketing. Sending a sales representative to call on customers is extremely costly, whereas personal selling in most retail, telemarketing and Internet settings is less expensive. Still, companies marketing costly or complicated products to business markets may need sales representatives to learn about customers' needs, recommend solutions, explain features and benefits, answer questions, demonstrate product use and complete sales transactions. Sales reps are also key players in learning about customers and markets, as well as for building trust and strengthening relationships.

Direct marketing

With **direct marketing**, you use two-way communication to interact directly with targeted customers and stimulate direct responses, particularly purchasing, that will ultimately lead to an ongoing relationship. This communication may occur through letters and catalogues, television, radio, email, Internet and newspaper advertising, telemarketing, mobile phones or personal selling. The objective for an initial direct marketing contact might be to get a customer to ask for product information, agree to receive further messages or make a purchase. One of direct marketing's most important advantages is the ability to measure actual results in terms of purchases, requests for information and other customer responses.

Public relations

Public relations (PR) activities promote dialogue to build understanding and foster positive attitudes between the organisation and its publics. A marketing plan might call for a news conference to launch a new product, for example, or a special event to polish brand image. Because the firm doesn't directly control or pay for media mentions, and because the communication is not sales directed, PR is very believable. However, there's no guarantee that the information will reach the intended audience in the preferred form or at the preferred time, if at all. Also remember that media coverage may be positive or negative, no matter what message a marketer tries to convey.

DEVELOPING A PLAN FOR MARKETING COMMUNICATIONS AND INFLUENCE

Planning for a communications and influence campaign follows the six-step process shown in Figure 9.2.

Define the target audience

Your first planning decision is to define the audience that you'll target. This may be customers in a certain segment, people who influence buyers or users, people who are

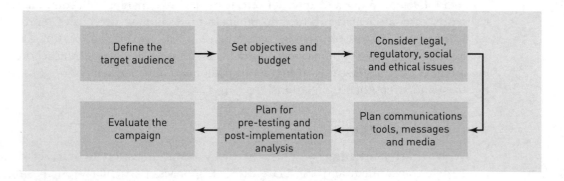

FIGURE 9.2 Planning a communications and influence campaign

currently competitors' customers, current or potential channel members, members of the general public, members of the media, government officials or regulators, or other publics.

If you target intermediaries in an effort to move or push your product through the channel to customers, you're using a **push strategy** to stir channel interest using sales promotion, advertising or other communications techniques. Manufacturers with established channel relationships often use a push strategy to induce their wholesale and retail partners to carry new products. An alternative approach is a **pull strategy**, which targets customers so they will request and buy the product from channel members. This pulls the product through the channel from producer to customer.

Nissan, for example, anticipates a significant increase in future demand for all-electric cars. Therefore, the Japanese carmaker is using email and direct mail in a pull strategy targeting two audiences: 'green' customers (who put a high priority on sustainability) and 'tech' customers (who are interested in a car's technology). The 'green' messages explain Leaf's earth-friendly benefits, while the 'tech' messages emphasise the built-in sat-nav system and other high-tech accessories. This pull strategy will grow in intensity as Nissan updates the Leaf for European buyers and introduces broader communication campaigns to influence brand preference and increase market share.[8]

In your marketing plan, define who each campaign should reach and, through research, indicate what audience members think or feel about the brand, product, organisation or idea, their attitudes and behaviour towards competitors, what kind of message, appeal, delivery and timing would be most effective, what the message should contain and how it should be conveyed. Look beyond generalities and develop a profile of a typical audience member in as much detail as possible, including age, gender, family situation, lifestyle, media preferences, product attitudes and loyalty, payment preferences, timing of buying decisions and other factors.

The purpose of careful audience definition and research is to identify nuances that will help shape the content, placement and timing of your messages. For example, the marketing director of the UK charity The National Childbirth Trust observes that 'new mums and mums-to-be are most heavily influenced by information distributed by the NHS [National Health Service] and other key sources, and by the views and experiences of friends and family, rather than broad media channels'.[9] The charity's goal is to reach 20 million UK parents of diverse backgrounds by 2020. 'Our practitioners and volunteers are training to support all parents; those from ethnic minority groups, families that are newly arrived and those who parent on their own,' explains the head of corporate communications.[10] The charity is therefore supplementing its media activities with messages aimed at getting parents involved to volunteer in local centres, raise money and help shape political and legal actions affecting parents and children.

Set the objectives and the budget

Your campaign will aim to achieve marketing objectives that move the target audience through a hierarchy of cognitive, affective and behavioural responses. A **cognitive response** refers to a customer's mental reaction, including brand awareness and knowledge of product features and benefits. An **affective response** is a customer's emotional reaction, such as being interested in or liking a product. A **behavioural response** is how the customer acts, such as by buying a product or applying for credit. Customers move through these responses in a different order, depending on how involved they are in making that type of purchase, product differentiation in that category and the influence of consumption experience (see Figure 9.3).

Usually your communications and influence objectives will relate to building long-term relationships by attracting customers' attention, communicating about the product or brand, persuading customers to seek out and buy the product once, and supporting a positive attitude leading to repeat purchases and ultimately loyalty. Specific advertising objectives may be set to complement or support objectives for personal selling, direct marketing or other tools in your plan. Panasonic UK, for example, is using social media to achieve the objective of supporting an ongoing dialogue with fans of its technology brand, not to attract a broader group of consumers.[11] You may also set sales or profit objectives, particularly when you can measure and attribute the results to a particular campaign or message. Further, you may use communications to enhance your firm's image or build brand awareness. (Review **Chapter 5** for more about setting objectives.)

The marketing communications budget is developed and allocated in the context of your organisation's overall marketing budgeting process and budget-approval process, which may be driven from the floor up or from the top down (or a combination). One floor-up option is to allocate funding according to the objectives and the cost of the tasks

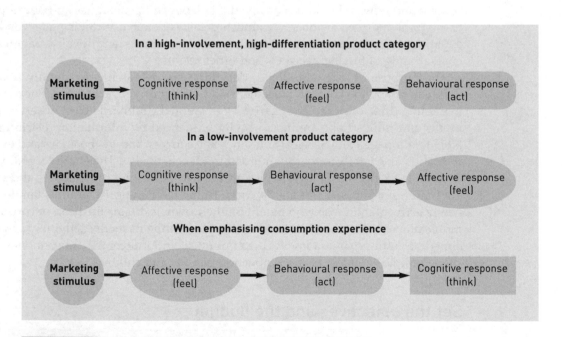

| **FIGURE 9.3** | Using communications to provoke audience response |

Source: After *Consumer Behavior: Buying, Having and Being*, 9th Ed., Pearson Education Inc. (Solomon, M.R. 2010) p. 257, ISBN-13: 978-0136110927, Reprinted and Electronically reproduced by permission of Pearson Education Inc., Upper Saddle River, New Jersey.

needed to achieve those objectives. This directly ties tasks and objectives for better accountability in terms of whether the tasks actually achieve the objectives. However, this method may lead to unrealistic budget requests and may complicate planning if particular tasks can't easily be linked to specific objectives.

Other budgeting methods include the affordability method (a top-down method based on how much the organisation can afford to spend), the percentage-of-sales method (spending a certain percentage of annual sales revenue or an average industry percentage of sales) and competitive parity (budgeting according to what rivals spend). In practice, you may use several methods to construct a preliminary budget, look closely at costs and the market situation, consider both long- and short-term objectives, and then arrive at a reasonable budget. (See **Chapter 11** for more on budgeting.)

Consider legal, regulatory, social and ethical issues

When planning, be aware of a wide range of legal, regulatory, social and ethical issues as you think creatively. On the most basic legal and ethical level, your communications should not be deceptive, distort facts or falsify product benefits. Find out whether certain types of messages are illegal and whether the rules are changing. For example, until recently, UK television networks were not allowed to accept payment for featuring branded products within programmes. Now that **product placement** is allowed, a growing number of marketers are arranging for their products or brands to appear in TV programmes (not just movies). To illustrate, the Nationwide Building Society extended its deal with ITV to show a branded ATM machine in some *Coronation Street* scenes after research showed that viewers had higher brand recall and positive brand opinions.[12]

Be aware that some industries impose self-regulation on product communications. Also take privacy into consideration. The European Union has strict rules about what personal data companies may collect and under what circumstances they are allowed to exchange such information. Retailers must first obtain permission before gathering customer data, sharing or selling it and using it for store marketing purposes. Companies must delete personal data after a set period, and they are forbidden to send personal data collected in the European Union to countries without equally strong privacy laws. New EU rules will soon require companies to obtain parents' consent for tracking the online activities of children who are 13 years old or younger.[13] Such concerns about collection, storage, use and disclosure of personal data continue to make privacy a challenging issue for marketers.

Plan for tools, messages and media

Most marketing plans employ more than one communications tool to achieve their objectives. Your exact choices depend on your target audience, objectives and budget, other marketing-mix decisions, and legal, regulatory, social and ethical considerations. They also depend on message and media strategy (discussed more fully later in this chapter). For instance, television advertising is generally more expensive than print advertising, so if you have a small budget or want to reach highly targeted audiences you may avoid television or use it sparingly. If your message involves an actual product demonstration, you will probably find radio inappropriate.

If a website or other online activity is part of your marketing plan, be prepared for **search engine optimisation (SEO)**, the process of modifying content, website characteristics and content connections to improve search engine rankings.[14] Knowing that audiences often use search engines to locate relevant product and brand information, you'll try to have your online content appear as close to the top of the search results as possible. Through SEO, you determine the keywords, tags and other elements that will help search engines find your site and rank it high in the results listing. This is essential for an effective digital pull strategy: Once the audience finds your site, they can get in touch to 'pull' more marketing their way. FedEx has used SEO to select the keywords that will attract decision makers from certain businesses and specific business departments. Its SEO experts recognise that transportation managers may search for information online using different keywords than retail managers, for example.[15] What role should SEO play in your marketing communications?

Plan for pre- and post-implementation analysis

To get the information you need for making better decisions about communications and influence, you should plan time and money for research to pre-test messages, creative approaches and use of media. The purpose is to gauge the target audience's response and have the opportunity to make changes, possibly pre-test additional elements and then launch the complete campaign. For example, you can conduct pre-tests to measure recognition (does a sample of the audience recognise what is being promoted?), recall (does the sample remember the message and what it communicated?), affective reaction (do the message, product and brand provoke positive reactions?) and behavioural intentions (are people likely to buy the product or take another action on the basis of the promotion?).

Evaluate the campaign

You should also plan for evaluating the results after full implementation of your communications and influence campaign. Did the campaign help you achieve your objectives? Also look at specific aspects of the campaign, such as whether the message or media failed to reach the target audience at times, and why; how well the audience understood the message; what the audience thought and felt about the product or brand, message and media; which messages and media were especially effective in provoking the desired audience response; how well the tools, messages and media supported the overall positioning; and how well the campaign worked with other marketing-mix strategies.

The UK charity Comic Relief (www.comicrelief.com) evaluates its marketing communications every year, using the results to help plan new campaigns.

MARKETING IN PRACTICE: COMIC RELIEF

Founded in 1985, Comic Relief has a serious purpose: to end poverty and social injustice. The London-based charity uses marketing communications to raise awareness of the issues and raise money so it can make grants to groups that work towards these goals in the UK and in Africa. With the support of UK corporate partners such as BT, the BBC, Sainsbury's, TK Maxx and British Airways, Comic Relief has raised hundreds of millions of pounds over the years by getting consumers and businesses involved in a fun way and encouraging them to make a difference through donations.

The two main fundraising events are Red Nose Day and Sport Relief, held in alternate years. In addition to accepting donations online and at fundraising sites, Comic Relief also receives millions of pounds through text message donations on Red Nose Day and Sport Relief weekend. To engage supporters, the charity also makes extensive use of social media such as Facebook, Twitter and YouTube, as well as apps to keep supporters informed of the latest news and special events.

According to research conducted by consultancy SPA Future Thinking, 95 percent of the UK population is familiar with Comic Relief's activities. Still, to be sure communications were reaching target audiences in the months leading up to Red Nose Day, the consultancy recently conducted in-depth research for the charity. More than 100 UK consumers were asked to note any interactions with Comic Relief (such as seeing a Red Nose Day ad) and indicate the influence on their behaviour, week by week. Immediately after Red Nose Day, the researchers held focus groups and used surveys to assess reactions to the campaign. The results helped Comic Relief shape its marketing plan for the following year's Sport Relief campaign. As just one example, it decided to create separate advertising messages for consumers 18–35 years old and consumers over 35.[16]

Marketing plan analysis: What two or three specific questions would you ask to learn about consumers' reaction to email messages they receive from Comic Relief? Explain how each question would help the charity improve its communications.

Integrated marketing communications

When planning a communications campaign, think about how the overall effect of the messages and media will influence customer receptivity, attention, interest and response. Also check that the content of each message is consistent with that of all other messages and with your brand's competitive points of differentiation. Be aware that customers may respond to any or all messages, regardless of media, and be prepared to react to customer responses that may be positive, negative or in between.

This is all part of **integrated marketing communications (IMC)**, coordinating content and delivery of all marketing messages in all media for an organisation, product or brand. For proper integration, carefully select communications tools and media that are appropriate for your audience and image. Consider how factors in the external marketing environment – especially social–cultural trends and technological developments – might affect your ability to get messages across to the audience and the audience's ability to understand and respond to your messages.[17]

PLANNING ADVERTISING

Planning for advertising follows the general planning pattern shown in Figure 9.2. Note that you'll generally wait to make detailed decisions until after your marketing plan is being implemented. Still, you have to plan the general direction of both message and media in order to allocate the overall budget among advertising and other communications and influence activities.

Planning messages

What will the message actually say? What will it look (and/or sound) like? These are the two main decisions in planning messages. Some messages follow a 'hard-sell' approach to induce the target audience to respond now; others take a more 'soft-sell' approach, persuading without seeming to do so. Messages targeting business customers tend to be more formal than messages targeting consumers; consumer messages are often informal and a growing number are crowdsourced or user-generated, increasing customer involvement.

Message planning is inseparable from media planning because the copy in the advertisement, the design and the creativity of its execution depend on media choice. A creative decision to show the product in action, for instance, can be executed through a visual medium such as television or the web. Creativity is, in fact, crucial for attracting attention, building awareness and shaping positive attitudes. Although not all decision details need to be finalised until the marketing plan is actually implemented, you should have some idea of message and media strategy so you can plan budgets, timing and marketing-mix coordination.

Instead of celebrities or other spokespeople, advertisers such as Toyota (www.toyota. com), Honda (www.honda.com) and McDonald's Canada (www.mcdonalds.ca) are featuring their own employees in advertising messages to give their brands more personality, enhance credibility and convey authenticity.

MARKETING IN PRACTICE: EMPLOYEES STAR IN ADVERTISING

When Toyota wanted to polish its brand image and demonstrate that its UK workforce is dedicated to car quality, the company featured employees in television and newspaper ads across Europe. Advertisements with the strapline 'Your Toyota is my Toyota' showed how each employee takes steps to ensure high quality, such as a production worker stopping the assembly line to check on a possible problem. The multinational campaign continued online with videos in which employees explain their quality responsibilities. 'We want to show this human face of Toyota, the real, authentic Toyota,' says Toyota's head of sales and marketing for Europe.[18] During a recent Super Bowl game, Toyota aired adverts of employees at one of its US Camry factories, making a similar point about personal commitment to quality.

Over the course of several years, Honda Motor has posted online videos in which top management and employees talk about pursuing (but not always achieving) very challenging goals. Also edited to air as adverts, these 'Dream the impossible' videos take viewers behind the scenes to learn more about what motivates Honda employees to strive for high ideals. 'This is not a "go out and buy a Honda" campaign,' notes the US manager for corporate advertising. The purpose is 'communicating with our customers about what our brand stands for'.[19]

When McDonald's Canada decided to create a special advert to coincide with the London Olympics, it asked employees to submit audition videos. The company asked the top contenders to attend an in-person audition and chose seven employees to perform in the 30-second commercial, choreographed by Luther Brown of *So You Think You Can Dance Canada*. Although a McBistro chicken sandwich was the product 'star', the employee stars each had their turn in the spotlight – adding their enthusiasm and talents to the message.[20]

Marketing plan analysis: Would you classify these three ads featuring employees as hard-sell or soft-sell? What are the implications for each company's marketing plan?

Planning media

Media planning has become more complex due to the multiplicity of media choices and vehicles and the resulting smaller audience sizes for each – **audience fragmentation**. You'll always have budget constraints as you seek to balance reach and frequency. **Reach** refers to the number or percentage of people in the target audience exposed to an advertisement in a particular media vehicle during a certain period. Higher reach means the message gets to more people, but this usually comes at a cost. **Frequency** is the number of times the target audience is exposed to a message in a particular media vehicle during a certain period. Higher frequency means you expose more people to your message on more occasions, again at a cost. An alternative to paying for high reach that may include people outside the target audience (which sometimes happens with television adverts, for example) is to use more precisely targeted media.

Should you plan to spend more on reach or frequency? Which media and vehicles will get your message to the right people at the right times and places? How much control do you want or need over the message and its distribution? What level of engagement and participation would you like to encourage your target audience to have with your brand and message? Considering competitive factors and audience attention factors, would non-traditional media be effective in reaching your audience?

Finally, consider how members of your targeted audience might react to higher frequency. One study, for example, revealed that UK consumers dislike repeated exposure to the same commercial messages, and 31 percent respond negatively to charity advertising in general.[21] Now some non-profit advertisers, including the National Centre for Domestic Violence, are seeking to engage consumers through interactive messages and media. The Centre invites consumers to change the screen on its digital billboard ads via mobile, allowing for consumer-controlled access to additional information and messages.[22]

Checklist No. 15 summarises planning considerations for media, including these questions.

ESSENTIAL CHECKLIST NO. 15:
PLANNING FOR MEDIA

Your marketing plan should explain the basic reasoning behind your choices of media and message, although it need not cover every detail of every communications and influence campaign. Based on the tools you will use, your budget and objectives, the marketing environment and the profile of your target audience, think about each of the following aspects of media planning. Put a tick next to each question after you've entered your answers in the space provided.

☐ What media do audience members use and prefer? Are these media available in the geographic region being targeted?

___

☐ Can the media reach the right people in appropriate numbers to deliver messages during the customers' buying cycle?

___

☐ Will the audience consider some media excessively intrusive or annoying?

___

☐ Which media will deliver the desired balance of control, cost, interactivity, credibility and personalisation?

___

☐ What media are used by competitors and how might competing messages affect audience receptivity, understanding and response?

☐ Should media be used to deliver the message continuously, intermittently or seasonally?

☐ Will the budget cover the projected cost for the desired reach and frequency?

☐ What is the expected payback based on anticipated audience reaction?

PLANNING SALES PROMOTION

Include sales promotion in your marketing plan when you want to stimulate faster response from consumers and business customers, channel members (sometimes called *the trade*) and the sales force. Although such promotions add value for only a limited time, some marketers use them as part of a longer-term strategy to strengthen relationships with the target audience. Sales promotion spending now exceeds advertising spending in a number of industries, reflecting increased competitive pressure and the need to produce immediate results.

However, because sales promotion often adds value by reducing perceived cost – lowering the product's price, in effect – over-use may heighten price sensitivity among customers, diminish brand strength and hurt profitability. Yet if competitive pressure leads to more sales promotion activity in your product category, your marketing plan should include ideas to maintain brand preference and reinforce brand image. Thus, you should set clear objectives, understand applicable laws and regulations, choose your techniques carefully, monitor implementation and evaluate results to make your sales promotion programmes successful.

Planning for customer sales promotion

Table 9.2 shows a variety of common sales promotion techniques you can use, depending on your communications objectives and strategy. Consider sales promotion to target consumers or business customers when you want to do the following:

- *Encourage product trial.* Potential customers have to try a product at least once before they can form a definite opinion and decide to buy it again (and again). Sales promotion

Table 9.2	Sales promotion techniques targeting customers

Technique	Description
Sample	Free trial of a good or service
Voucher or coupon	Certificate or special code redeemable for money off a product's price
Premium	Free or low-priced items offered to induce purchase
Sweepstake, draw, contest or game	Chance to win cash or prizes through luck, knowledge or skill
Refund or rebate	Returning part or all of a product's price to the customer
Price (or bonus) pack	Special price marked by the producer on a package (or for multiple products bought together)
Loyalty reward	Opportunity to earn gifts or cash for continuing to buy a certain offering or from a certain marketer
Point-of-purchase display or demonstration	In-shop materials promoting a product or in-shop demonstration of a good or service
Branded speciality	Everyday item such as a T-shirt or calendar bearing a brand or logo, for reminder purposes

is therefore commonly used to introduce a product and to stimulate higher sales during the maturity stage.

- *Reinforce advertising for a product or brand*. An exciting sales promotion can help customers notice and remember your advertising messages.

- *Attract interest*. Simply getting customers to visit a store or contact a manufacturer about a product can be a challenge. Some marketers use coupons, samples or other techniques in an attempt to get customers to take the first step.

- *Encourage purchase of multiple products*. Depending on your product mix, you can use sales promotion to stimulate customer purchases of two, three or even more products.

- *Encourage continued product purchase and usage*. You want to build customer loyalty, increase sales and reduce customer acquisition costs. Airlines do this with their frequent-flyer programmes; supermarkets do this with their frequent-shopper programmes.

Field marketing is used to engage the target audience by bringing sales promotion to (and sometimes taking orders from) customers 'in the field' – in stores, shopping districts and city centres, using an outside agency. Marketers often use field marketing to give away free samples of new products. The senior brand manager for the dessert company Gü, for instance, says the company distributes samples through field marketing because of the 'unique role in allowing us to have face time and direct contact with our consumers, which is still invaluable in an increasingly digital marketing ecosystem'.[23]

Beauty brands frequently use sampling to give customers an opportunity to experience products for themselves before they buy. An emerging trend is the distribution of beauty samples by subscription. Birchbox (www.birchbox.com) pioneered this type of business.

MARKETING IN PRACTICE: BIRCHBOX

Beauty marketers have found a new way to get samples into the hands of consumers: through firms like Birchbox, which sell monthly subscriptions to boxes of sample-sized items. Birchbox was founded in 2010 by two US entrepreneurs to introduce consumers to new skincare and hair care products they might not otherwise discover. They also recognised the value for the brand marketers, who want to know that the thousands of samples they give away each year reach the appropriate audience. 'From the brand side of things, we understood that the beauty industry had a need to better understand the ROI [return on investment] of sampling,' explains co-founder Hayley Barna.[24]

Birchbox gets free samples from dozens of companies, including Elizabeth Arden, Benta Berry, Juicy Couture and Kiehl's. Its customers complete an online questionnaire so they'll receive sample-sized products that fit their preferences and lifestyle, all for a monthly fee of $10. Birchbox's experts decide on a monthly theme, test and choose a small number of samples and include beauty tips and product information with that month's shipment. In addition to subscription revenue, Birchbox profits from selling full-size versions of samples included in its monthly boxes. It has expanded into sample boxes for men and occasionally includes non-beauty products as extras in a monthly box to gauge customer reaction.

Birchbox attracted more than 100,000 paying subscribers in less than two years. The company uses another sales promotion technique, loyalty rewards, to encourage subscribers to refer friends, post feedback about products and continue subscribing. Subscribers can redeem their Birchbox points to buy full-size products from the website. Now Birchbox's success has paved the way for other beauty sample subscription companies, including Memebox (in South Korea) and Glossybox (operating in 15 countries).[25]

Marketing plan analysis: What product categories do you think are most appropriate for subscription sampling boxes, and why?

Planning for channel and sales force sales promotion

Particularly when using a push strategy, you may find sales promotion effective in enlisting the support of channel members and motivating sales representatives. Specifically, you can use channel and sales force promotions to do the following:

- *Build channel commitment to a new product.* So many new products are introduced every year that channel members rarely have the space (or the money) to carry them all. Channel promotions can focus attention on a new product, encourage intermediaries to buy it, motivate the sales force to sell it and provide appropriate rewards.

- *Encourage more immediate results.* Sales promotion aimed at channel members and sales representatives offers inducements to take action during a specific time period.

- *Build relationships with channel members.* Keeping the ongoing support of major retail or wholesale businesses takes time and effort. Channel promotion offers opportunities for interactions that benefit the producer and its channel members.

- *Improve product knowledge.* Support the marketing effort by offering training and information through channel and sales force promotion.

Sales force promotions include contests (with cash or prizes as rewards for achieving sales objectives), sales meetings (for training and motivation) and special promotional material (to supplement personal sales efforts). In planning a channel promotion, you may use monetary allowances (either discounts or payments for stocking or displaying a product), limited-time discounts (for buying early in the selling season or during other specified periods), free merchandise (extra quantities provided for buying a minimum quantity or a certain product), co-operative advertising (sharing costs when a channel member advertises a particular brand or product) or trade shows (setting up a booth or room at a convention centre to demonstrate products and interact with channel members or business buyers).

Some companies are participating in virtual trade shows held on special websites. The purpose is to provide information and market goods or services to channel members or prospective customers in an innovative and entertaining yet cost-efficient way. The information technology firm EMC has held special events online as virtual product introductions, attracting thousands of views from customers worldwide and generating conversations within the company's brand community and on Facebook.[26]

As you plan for sales promotion, Checklist No. 16 may be helpful.

ESSENTIAL CHECKLIST NO. 16:
PLANNING FOR SALES PROMOTION

Whether you're planning for a consumer or business product, you're likely to use some form of sales promotion in your marketing plan. This checklist will help you think about various decisions involved in sales promotion planning. Put a tick next to each question after you've entered your answers in the space provided.

☐ Who, specifically, is the internal or external audience for your sales promotion programme?

☐ What marketing, financial and/or societal objectives do you want to achieve by targeting each audience for sales promotion activity?

☐ How much budget and how much time will you need for each programme in each market?

☐ Knowing the audience's media consumption patterns, how will you communicate about each programme in each market?

☐ In what ways can you integrate your sales promotion activities with other communications and influence programmes in your plan?

☐ What competitive issues should you consider when planning for sales promotion?

☐ When and how will you measure the results of each programme?

PLANNING PERSONAL SELLING

One of the most compelling reasons to include personal selling in a marketing plan is to establish solid relationships with new customers and maintain good relationships with the current customer base. Personal attention can make all the difference when your customers have unique problems, require customised solutions or place very large orders. It's especially important in marketing plans that target business buyers who require considerable assistance in assessing the specifications, benefits and usage requirements of expensive or complex goods and services. Through personal selling, your organisation can learn more about customers' needs and market conditions, start or strengthen customer relationships and determine how to allocate your goods or services when you have excess or limited capacity.

Be sure to coordinate personal selling with all other marketing plan decisions to achieve the desired results. SAP, which markets specialised software to businesses, uses digital banner ads and other advertising efforts to generate leads for sales follow-up.[27] This means SAP's sales force must be aware of the timing of the campaigns and ready to work on the leads they receive from the ads. SAP also highlights its products and services on the business networking site LinkedIn, posts product announcements and more on Facebook and stays in touch with 66,000 followers on Twitter (see this chapter's case study).

When planning for personal selling, consider the following factors:

- *Need*. Should your company have its own sales force or sell through retailers, agents, manufacturers' representatives or independent reps? Some online businesses offer 'live chats' with reps who can answer questions and check on product specifications or inventory levels right away.

- *Organisation*. Will you organise representatives according to geographic market, product, type of customer, size of customer or some other structure?

- *Size of force*. How many sales reps should you have, based on your objectives and current sales levels?

- *Compensation*. How will you determine sales force compensation?

- *Management*. How will you recruit, train, supervise, motivate and evaluate sales reps? How will they be educated about legal, regulatory and ethical guidelines?

- *Process*. How will you generate sales leads? How will sales personnel access information about prospects and customers? What logistical activities must be coordinated with sales transactions, and who will be responsible?

PLANNING DIRECT MARKETING

Although mail order and telemarketing are hardly new, a growing number of organisations now include these and other direct marketing techniques in their plans for communications and influence, because with better technology, marketers can target audiences more precisely, adjust messages and timing according to audience needs and build relationships cost-effectively. Direct marketing costs more than advertising in mass media, yet its interactive quality, selectivity and customisation potential may add enough flexibility to make the difference worthwhile. Just as important, you can easily measure customer response and modify the offer or the communication again and again to move customers in the desired direction and achieve your objectives.

In planning direct marketing, first decide what response you want to elicit from the target audience(s), in accordance with your objectives. Many marketers use direct marketing to generate leads for sales representatives; the desired response is to get a potential customer to indicate interest in the product by calling, emailing or sending a reply by post. Banks and mobile phone companies frequently use direct marketing – especially mailings – to attract new customers, bring former customers back and encourage current customers to buy more.

Now you're ready to select appropriate media and formulate an appropriate offer, based on research into the target audience's media and buying patterns. Different audiences and markets require different media and offers. Budget is also a consideration: digital direct marketing is growing more rapidly than door drops and direct mail, in part because of cost.[28] Be sure your direct marketing campaign fits with the product's positioning and allow time in the marketing plan schedule for testing the message and the mechanisms for response (such as a freephone number, URL, email address or postage-paid envelope). One of the advantages of direct marketing is that you can quickly see what actually works and use the results to refine your campaign or the overall marketing plan.

PLANNING PUBLIC RELATIONS

At one time or another, nearly every organisation has prepared news releases, arranged news conferences and answered questions from reporters. Yet media contact is only one aspect of this flexible and powerful tool. You can use public relations not just to convey the organisation's messages but also to build mutual understanding and maintain an ongoing dialogue between your organisation and key members of the 'public'. Moreover, your message has more credibility when conveyed by media representatives than when communicated directly by your organisation, as noted earlier.

Defining the 'public'

The 'public' in public relations may refer to people in any number of target audiences, such as customers and prospective customers, employees, channel members, suppliers, news reporters, investors and financial analysts, special interest groups, legislators and regulators, and community leaders. Each of these audiences can affect your plan's success and performance, but not all will be addressed in the same way; in fact, not all may be addressed in a single marketing plan.

In general, you can use PR to achieve one or more of the following objectives:

- *Identify and understand stakeholder concerns.* Through PR contacts such as community meetings, surveys and other methods, you can learn what your stakeholders think and feel about important issues such as your products, image, ecological record and so on. Some companies host or monitor online communities where members of the public exchange ideas and concerns about sustainability and other issues.

- *Convey the organisation's viewpoint or important information.* Knowing your target audience's views, you can adapt your organisation's position if appropriate. At the very least, you can use PR to explain your management's viewpoint or educate the public, especially vital in the midst of a crisis. Often the company website is the first place your publics will check for news and views, so be sure to post information and label links accordingly.

- *Correct misperceptions.* If one or more target audiences have misperceptions about some aspect of your organisation – such as the quality of its products – you can plan to use PR to counteract the inaccuracies by providing more information, answering questions and allowing for periodic updates.

- *Enhance the organisation's image*. Many organisations apply PR techniques to enhance their image. If an organisation has been embroiled in controversy, PR can show what management is doing to improve and how it has gone beyond minimum requirements to satisfy its publics.

- *Promote products and brands*. You can use PR to communicate the features, benefits and value of your products and promote your brands. Green Energy UK uses PR to build brand awareness and understanding of the benefits of alternative energy such as that supplied through wind and solar sources.[29]

Planning and evaluating PR activities

Your marketing plan may include a variety of PR techniques. One of the most commonly used is the news release, written and distributed to media representatives via printed document, email, weblink or *podcasting* (distributing an audio or video file via the Internet). For more significant news, you may want to call a news conference, let media reps hear management speak and hold a question-and-answer session.

Also consider whether your organisation should seek publicity through special events or special appearances. The Hong Kong Tourism Board recently held a Wine & Dine Festival in London to promote the cultural attractions and dining diversity available in Hong Kong.[30] In addition, the Hong Kong Tourism Board reaches out to travellers with communications on Facebook, Twitter and YouTube, plus free downloadable apps for self-guided tours and more.

Although it's nearly impossible to make a direct link between purchasing and PR, you can plan to evaluate how PR activities have engaged your target audience and how you've moved them in the direction of certain cognitive, affective and behavioural responses. For example, before and after a PR event, you can count how many blogs mention your product or brand, determine whether online comments are positive or negative and what commenters are talking about, count how many visitors your website attracts, note how many people buy and what/when they buy, count how many new followers you acquire on Twitter, and count how many viewers your YouTube video attracts.

Finally, dig deeper to examine what people say about your brand online. Are their comments positive or negative? What other issues are customers discussing online that are important to your product or brand? What can you learn from these discussions that will help you do a better job of engaging customers in dialogue, applying transparency, meeting their needs and influencing how they think, feel and act towards your product?

CHAPTER SUMMARY

Strategies for marketing communications and influence – for promotion – help you engage and influence the thoughts, feelings and behaviour of audiences that are important to your brand. Word of mouth, buzz marketing and social media marketing are part of the influence strategies developed by many organisations. Through content marketing, a firm can demonstrate thought leadership and engage or inform with original content that customers value. Integrated marketing communication (IMC) ensures that content and delivery of all marketing messages in all media are coordinated and consistent, and that they support the positioning and objectives of the product, brand or organisation. Communications tools include advertising, sales promotion, public relations, direct marketing and personal selling.

The steps in communications planning are to (1) define the target audience, (2) set objectives and budget, (3) consider relevant legal, regulatory, social and ethical issues, (4) select and plan for the use of specific tools, messages and media, (5) plan pre- and post-implementation analysis, and (6) evaluate the campaign. When planning advertising, consider message appeal, creativity and appropriateness for media, and balance reach and frequency in the context of the budget. Use sales promotion to stimulate faster response from customers or channel members by adding limited-time value (or reducing perceived cost). If personal selling is appropriate, consider in-person sales, Internet sales or telemarketing. Use direct marketing to build relationships with targeted audiences cost-effectively and be able to measure response. Plan for public relations to foster positive attitudes and an ongoing dialogue with key publics.

CASE STUDY: SAP

SAP (www.sap.com), the software giant with headquarters in Walldorf, Germany, serves 183,000 companies in 130 countries. Its mission is to 'help every customer become a best-run business'. SAP relies on a combination of communications tools to reach out to prospective customers and current customers. Traditionally, its communications and influence strategy has targeted key members of the buying centre, especially users, buyers, influencers and deciders connected with the information technology function within a customer's business. SAP provides initial information about its software solutions through print ads, media websites, country-specific branded websites, social media and other vehicles. Once businesses indicate interest, SAP's sales force gets involved, along with technical experts who can analyse customers' needs.

Recently, SAP decided to move beyond IT executives and target a broader audience of decision makers who serve in specific functions within corporations and businesses. The firm's TV, digital, mobile and social media campaign seeks to reach these executives 'as consumers in the places where they're seeking information,' explains the global vice-president of brand experience.[31] SAP wants these decision makers (who may be in human resources, production, sales or other departments) to visit its business innovation centre online and click for more details. This is only one example of SAP's increased emphasis on a pull strategy, engaging decision makers when and where they're interested and encouraging them to request sales contact ('pull') when they're ready to discuss their needs. Although making one-to-one contact through pull strategies takes longer than it does with push strategies, pull is less costly than push when personal selling is involved.

For the past decade, the company has also built a branded online community of 3 million customers, partners, influencers, academics and others around the world who register to participate in online discussions, blogs, how-to forums, newsletters and other content. Every day, 4,000 messages are posted in one of SAP's 15 blogs or forums, not including the many interactions on the company's LinkedIn pages, Facebook page, Twitter accounts and YouTube channel. The influence isn't just one-way (SAP influencing customers and partners) but two-way (community participants influencing SAP's policies, practices and products). It's all part of SAP's content marketing strategy, designed to make sure everyone in the buying centre has access to lots of practical information during the buying process, especially in the early stages of recognising a problem. This starts the relationship off on a positive note and builds trust to the point where SAP can later request a sales meeting (push) – or, ideally, respond to the customer's request for sales contact (pull).[32]

Case questions

1. SAP is pursuing a pull strategy by targeting decision-makers and influencers. Together with audience fragmentation, what are the implications for its communications plans?

2. If you were a business customer, would you prefer push or pull, and why? What do you think about SAP's shift to pull?

APPLY YOUR KNOWLEDGE

Choose a particular consumer or business product and find two or more advertisements, promotions, websites, social media messages or other company-controlled communications featuring that product. Analyse the company's communications and influence activities using the questions below, and then prepare a brief oral presentation or written report to explain your analysis.

- What target audience(s) do you think these communications are designed to reach?

- What cognitive, affective or behavioural response(s) might these communications provoke?

- What objectives do you think the company has set for these communications?

- How would you recommend that this firm measure results for the communications you've analysed?

- What legal, regulatory, social or ethical considerations are likely to affect this firm's planning for communications and influence?

- What specific suggestions can you offer to help this marketer do a better job of communicating with or influencing its audience(s)?

BUILD YOUR OWN MARKETING PLAN

Consider your communications and influence activities as you continue developing your marketing plan. What target audience(s) do you want to reach? What are your specific objectives for each audience? What is an appropriate budget, given the available resources, reach and frequency preferences and the chosen tools? Identify any legal, regulatory, social or ethical issues that could affect your communications and influence decisions. Will you use advertising, sales promotion, personal selling, direct marketing and/or public relations – and why? Should you try to stimulate word of mouth (possibly using social media) to achieve your objectives? How can you analyse implementation and the results? Outline one campaign, indicating objectives, target audience, general message and media decisions, approximate budget and method of measuring results. Finally, document your ideas in a written marketing plan.

ENDNOTES

1. Barney Jopson, 'P&G chief reassesses his priorities', *Financial Times*, 31 January 2013, www.ft.com; 'P&G marketing chief touts role of Facebook, Yahoo in "Thank you, Mom" campaign', *Advertising Age*, 9 August 2012, www.adage.com; Dale Buss, 'London 2012 watch: P&G hopes London halo lingers', *Brand Channel*, 9 August 2012, www.brandchannel.com; Keith Weir, 'P&G says sponsorship proving its worth', *Reuters*, 25 July 2012, www.reuters.com; Gideon Spanier, 'Gillette man must avoid close shave with Olympics', *London Evening Standard*, 11 April 2012, www.standard.co.uk.

2. Raghuram Iyengar, Sangman Han and Sunil Gupta, 'Do friends influence purchases in a social network?', *Harvard Business School Working Paper 09-123*, 21 May 2009, http://hbswk.hbs.edu.

3. Tracy L. Tuten and Michael R. Solomon, *Social Media Marketing* (Upper Saddle River, NJ: Pearson Prentice Hall, 2013), p. 7.

4. Quoted in Jack Neff, 'Lever's CMO throws down the social-media gauntlet', *Advertising Age*, 13 April 2009, p. 1.

5. Quoted in Sarah E. Needleman, 'For companies, a tweet in time can avert PR mess', *Wall Street Journal*, 3 August 2009, www.wsj.com.

6. Mikal E. Belicove, 'Why content marketing is king', *Entrepreneur*, 20 October 2011, www.entrepreneur.com.

7. Charlotte McEleny, 'Q&A: Jane Exon on Debenhams' social media strategy', *New Media Age*, 25 August 2011, www.nma.co.uk.

8. Kelvin Chan, 'Nissan chief pitches electric taxis to Hong Kong', *Bloomberg Businessweek*, 12 September 2012, www.businessweek.com; 'Nissan eyes mass market for Leaf', *Marketing Week*, 4 July 2012, www.marketingweek.co.uk; Jon Voelcker, 'Good news for Leaf fans', *Christian Science Monitor*, 17 August 2012, www.csmonitor.com.

9. Quoted in Louise Jack, 'Making your messages strike home', *Marketing Week*, 17 September 2009, www.marketingweek.co.uk.

10. Quoted in Julie Henry, 'Trust drops "evangelical" breastfeeding message', *Telegraph*, 22 January 2012, www.telegraph.co.uk.

11. Sebastian Joseph, 'Panasonic switches funds to social media', *Marketing Week*, 20 August 2012, www.marketingweek.co.uk.

12. Lara O'Reilly, 'Nationwide extends product placement deal', *Marketing Week*, 24 February 2012, www.marketingweek.co.uk; Lara O'Reilly, 'Product placement set to take off in 2013', *Marketing Week*, 13 February 2012, www.marketingweek.co.uk.

13. Thor Olavsrud, 'EU data protection regulation and cookie law – Are you ready?' *ComputerWorld UK*, 24 May 2012, www.computerworlduk.com.

14. Tracy L. Tuten and Michael R. Solomon, *Social Media Marketing* (Upper Saddle River, NJ: Pearson Prentice Hall, 2013), p. 129.

15. Elyse Dupré, 'The Evolution of FedEx SEO', *Direct Marketing News*, 21 September 2012, www.dmnews.com.

16. Charlotte Butterworth, 'Make us laugh', *Research*, March 2012, www.research-live.com; 'Sport Relief 2012 raised £7.9 million via text donations', *UK Fundraising*, 28 May 2012, www.fundraising.co.uk; 'Comic Relief tracks engagement and recall of its advertising campaign', *UK Fundraising*, 24 February 2011, www.fundraising.co.uk; www.sportrelief.com; www.rednoseday.com; www.comicrelief.com.

17. See Ilchul Kim, Dongsub Han and Don E. Schultz, 'Understanding the diffusion of integrated marketing communications', *Journal of Advertising Research*, March 2004, pp. 31–45.

18. Quoted in Andrew Peterson, 'Toyota Europe launches $26.5 million ad campaign to win back trust', *Motor Trend*, 29 April 2010, http://wot.motortrend.com.

19. Quoted in Stuart Elliott, 'For the Honda brand, a cinematic stroke', *New York Times*, 12 January 2009, www.nytimes.com.

20. Ashante Infantry, 'Why McDonald's, Red Lobster, Fisher-Price, Walmart feature real people in ads', *The Star (Toronto)*, 27 July 2012, www.thestar.com;

Helen Coster, 'Forget celebrities. Employees make compelling ad stars in tough times', *Forbes*, 17 April 2009, www.forbes.com; Johanna Beyenbach, 'The new next: it's what's on the inside that counts', *Mediapost*, 1 May 2009, www.mediapost.com; Scott Sloan, 'Georgetown workers featured in Toyota's Super Bowl ad', *Herald-Leader (Kentucky)*, 3 February 2012, www.herald-leader.com; Joe Fernandez, 'Toyota features employees in its latest reassurance push', *Marketing Week*, 7 June 2010, www.marketingweek.co.uk.

21. David Burrows, 'How brands overcome risk of rejection', *Marketing Week*, 26 July 2012, www.marketingweek.co.uk.

22. 'National Centre for Domestic Violence runs interactive billboard campaign to highlight intervention methods', *The Drum*, 7 May 2012, www.thedrum.co.uk/news/.

23. Quoted in Morag Cuddeford-Jones, 'Free samples still best way to win friends', *Marketing Week*, 27 October 2011, www.marketingweek.co.uk.

24. Quoted in 'Katia Beauchamp and Hayley Barna, Birchbox co-founders', *Advertising Age*, 4 June 2012, www.adage.com.

25. Jennifer Ryu, 'Korean firm thinks out of the box and it's a surprise hit', *The Star (Malaysia)*, 19 August 2012, http://thestar.com; Alina Dizik, 'For beauty junkies who just want to dabble', *Wall Street Journal*, 14 December 2011, www.wsj.com; Dawn Fallik, 'Beauty-box subscriptions', *Philadelphia Inquirer*, 4 April 2012, www.philly.com.

26. Karen J. Bannan, 'EMC integrates social to drive engagement', *BtoB Online*, 21 August 2012, www.btobonline.com.

27. 'Forbes' Advoice has plenty of takers, but impact on revenue is unclear', *Advertising Age*, 5 August 2012, www.adage.com.

28. Russell Parsons, 'DM leads to a quarter of all UK sales', *Marketing Week*, 31 July 2012, www.marketingweek.co.uk.

29. 'Green Energy UK appoint Punch Communications to raise awareness amongst businesses and consumers', *The Drum*, 20 August 2012, www.thedrum.co.uk.

30. John Owens, 'Hong Kong Tourism Board calls in Rooster', *PR Week UK*, 23 August 2012, www.prweek.com.

31. Quoted in Erin Dostal, 'SAP takes b-to-c approach to b-to-b marketing campaign', *Direct Marketing News*, 17 April 2012, www.dmnews.com.

32. Matthew Grant, 'Getting content strategy right: Michael Brenner on marketing smarts', *Marketing Profs*, 22 August 2012, www.marketingprofs.com; David Kiron, 'SAP: using social media for building, selling and supporting', *MIT Sloan Management Review*, 7 August 2012, http://sloanreview.mit.edu; Erin Dostal, 'SAP takes b-to-c approach to b-to-b marketing campaign', *Direct Marketing News*, 17 April 2012, www.dmnews.com; www.sap.com.

Learning outcomes

After studying this chapter, you will be able to:

- Explain why a marketing plan should include customer service and internal marketing strategies

- Understand planning for customer service and internal marketing

Application outcomes

After studying this chapter, you will be able to:

- Plan for customer service to support the marketing plan

- Plan for internal marketing to support the marketing plan

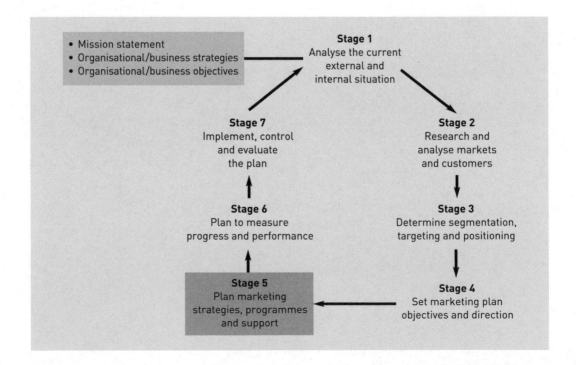

CHAPTER PREVIEW: MARKETING AT INTEL

Intel (www.intel.com) markets sophisticated computer chips, networking components and software to manufacturers and resellers of computers, mobiles, medical devices and other products. Two decades of 'Intel Inside' campaigns have built the brand into a household name, contributed to pull strategies and provided a solid foundation for reaching market share goals. To maintain momentum, its marketers plan carefully for internal marketing and service support. Intel trains its 80,000 employees to use digital and social media so they are empowered to communicate and represent the company with transparency and proficiency. Employees, vendors and suppliers are encouraged to share their insights and suggest ideas for new goods and services, a valuable dialogue that brings different viewpoints into the planning process.

As part of its marketing plan targeting resellers that customise computer and networking systems, Intel provides different levels of service through its channel partners programme. Partners receive priority technical support and expedited shipments, marketing materials and information for personal selling, loyalty rewards for purchasing, and opportunities to learn about the latest Intel offerings at conferences and in-person or online training sessions and podcasts. When they need assistance, they can live-chat with a specialist, ask or answer questions in Intel-branded online communities and 'ask an expert' for special help. Intel also designs support programmes for resellers in markets targeted for future growth, such as India, and in product categories with significant sales potential, such as digital signage. Finally, Intel's marketers have detailed plans for service recovery to keep both resellers and manufacturers satisfied.[1]

As a business-to-business marketer, Intel uses service and technical support to reinforce its brand's reputation and encourage loyalty; it uses internal marketing to establish a strong foundation for delivering quality service and making progress towards future growth. In this chapter covering stage 5 of the marketing planning process, you'll learn about the vital support role of customer service and internal marketing. You'll consider decisions that must be made when planning for customer service (including those about process and outcome); service levels; service before, during and after the purchase; service recovery; and monitoring perceptions of service. In addition, you'll think about planning for internal marketing. Use this chapter's checklist to plan for customer service support as you formulate your marketing plan.

THE ROLE OF CUSTOMER SERVICE AND INTERNAL PLANNING

Intel's marketing plan delineates its decisions about product (what equipment and software to offer), price (how much to charge), channels and logistics (such as working with resellers that customise networking systems) and communications and influence (how to connect with and affect the attitudes and behaviour of customers). All of these marketing-mix decisions are vital, yet they must also be supported by quality customer service for Intel to provide the extra value its brand represents to business buyers and to consumers who buy products with Intel components inside.

From the customer's perspective, good service is an integral part of the experience of dealing with a product or brand. In fact, respondents to a survey by the credit-card company American Express said they'd be willing to pay *more* for better service. More than half of the consumers in that survey said they'd decided against a particular purchase because of poor customer service.[2] As a result, it's best to view complaints not as annoyances but as opportunities to identify areas for improvement. Respond quickly to any complaints and give these customers tangible reasons to continue the relationship. Unsatisfactory and inconsistent customer service quality can hinder your ability to achieve marketing plan objectives, even if you've meticulously researched targeting and positioning and planned highly creative marketing activities. As you know from your own experience, people often tell others about incidents of good or bad customer service, generating positive or negative word of mouth that can help or hurt a product or brand image.

On the other hand, outstanding service can generate positive buzz and attract new customers for new or established brands alike. This is an important consideration for marketers of tangible goods as well as marketers of intangible services, especially in today's global marketplace with choices galore. Retailing and computers are exceptionally competitive industries, yet Apple stores are known for providing quality service and technical support. Every day, an estimated 50,000 customers worldwide ask for advice, request product demonstrations or seek repair services at the Genius Bar in a local Apple store.[3]

As Figure 10.1 indicates, planning for customer service supports the marketing effort outside the organisation and is, in turn, implemented with the support of the internal marketing strategy, which focuses on people and processes inside the organisation.

Marketing applications of customer service

Depending on your marketing plan, good customer service may be part of your positioning or inherent in your marketing strategy for building customer relationships and achieving the objectives you've set.

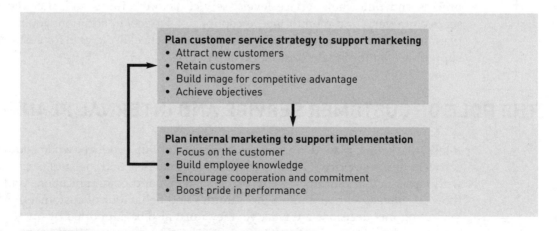

Plan customer service strategy to support marketing
- Attract new customers
- Retain customers
- Build image for competitive advantage
- Achieve objectives

Plan internal marketing to support implementation
- Focus on the customer
- Build employee knowledge
- Encourage cooperation and commitment
- Boost pride in performance

FIGURE 10.1 Customer service and internal marketing

Customer relationships

Consider how customer service can add value, helping to attract and retain customers, especially if your service level is competitively superior. Good customer service is as important in the online world as it is in any other marketing situation. These days, most manufactured goods can't be marketed without attention to quality service support (such as ensuring that orders are delivered when and where promised). Retailers often use service as part of their strategy for starting or continuing customer relationships. That's why the London department store Harrods tailors customer service for particular customer groups. For example, to serve affluent shoppers from China, it has hundreds of Mandarin-speaking employees on staff; it also offers an Android app in Mandarin to provide in-store information. These and other service extras have attracted many more Chinese tourists to Harrods than in the past – and dramatically increased sales to these shoppers.[4]

Remember, customers have many choices, so a reputation for good customer service can tip the balance when a consumer or business is deciding whether to buy from you. If your current customers remain loyal, you'll need fewer or less expensive customer acquisition programmes to meet your marketing objectives. Moreover, not having to fix a service problem saves money, which can help move you towards your financial objectives.

Good service can be a very powerful point of differentiation. Several new entrants into the UK banking industry, including Metro Bank, see friendly, efficient customer service as the key to effective competition. Metro Bank keeps its spacious branches open seven days a week and operates a 24/7 call-centre plus 24/7 online banking for customer convenience. The bank reaches out to families, with children's activities and lollipops for all. Even dogs are welcomed – with water bowls and treats.[5] The US cable company Time Warner Cable has a special premium package for subscribers willing to pay more for special services. In addition to receiving super-high-speed Internet access and other extras, these customers are served by a separate group of customer representatives and repair technicians who respond quickly to any question or technical difficulty.[6]

Marketing plan objectives

To achieve objectives such as increasing market share and enhancing brand image, look for ways to leverage good customer service as a competitive strength. Audi's UK dealers are doing this and making service more personal at the same time. When customers bring cars for maintenance or repairs, the Audi dealers offer the option of communicating with repair technicians online, rather than having to wait in the showroom or be contacted later by phone. Technicians video the problem areas on an owner's car, record narration to explain the situation and upload the video to a password-protected site, along with the estimated repair cost. Customers receive a text message alerting them that the video is ready; after viewing, they can approve or reject the repair proposal, or call for more information.[7]

Also consider how to use special customer services to increase sales in specific target segments or markets. Quality customer service can help you defend market share and establish or maintain strong ties with channel members. It will also be a particular priority if your objective is to retain or attain the role of market leader. Government agencies and municipalities need good service to satisfy citizens and attract businesses and investment. The city of Cincinnati, Ohio, has an experienced manager who does nothing but coordinate and facilitate filming of movies and television programmes in the city and surrounding suburbs, because movie projects help the local economy and introduce the city to worldwide audiences. Tax incentives help, but industry insiders say that having someone who can make things happen on schedule is an enormous advantage when trying to attract movie production companies.[8]

Marketing applications of internal marketing

Good customer service – and, in fact, effective implementation of the entire marketing plan – depends on **internal marketing**, a carefully coordinated set of policies and activities designed to build internal employee relationships and reinforce and reward internal commitment to the marketing effort and to good customer service. At the very least, internal audiences need advance notice of new promotions, new products and other marketing activities so that they are prepared when customers respond.

On a larger scale, planning for internal marketing covers decisions about hiring and training managers and employees, motivating and rewarding them for working to satisfy customers, and communicating with them about marketing plans and performance. In short, robust internal marketing lays the foundation for implementing your marketing plan and delivering good, consistent customer service.

You can use internal marketing to accomplish the following:

- *Focus on the customer*. Some employees in functions with little customer contact – such as finance or human resources – may get caught up in the daily pressures of work and lose their customer focus. Internal marketing is a good way to refocus on the customer and remind employees that their performance is essential for implementing plans that serve and satisfy customers.

- *Build employee knowledge*. Be sure employees at every level know at least the general outline of the marketing effort, are informed about the needs and expectations of targeted customers and understand what the organisation wants to achieve. This knowledge gives them the background they need to serve customers and solve any service problems. Hotel Chocolat, the UK-based luxury chocolatier, reserves a special section on its website for the 'school of chocolate', pages that educate employees about the company's special chocolate sources, products and processes.

- *Encourage organisation-wide cooperation with and commitment to the plan*. Success really is in the details. If your organisation's employees don't understand the plan or resent it, they may not give details the proper attention, let alone implement every tactic to full effect. Remember that marketing is not the only function affected by the marketing plan; manufacturing, finance and all the other departments must cooperate to achieve the objectives and you need senior management's support. Use internal marketing to build relations inside the organisation and encourage commitment among those responsible for approving the plan and making it succeed through implementation.

- *Boost pride in performance.* Internal marketing can increase employees' sense of involvement and boost their pride in performing over and above expectations. Marketing expert Kevin Lane Keller says that internal marketing encourages employees to feel they're responsible for the brand and consider what they can do to improve the customer's experiences with the brand.[9]

The next two sections highlight how you can plan for customer service and for internal marketing as you prepare your marketing plan. Many of the examples in the following pages are from service businesses, but the customer service ideas can be adapted for many situations.

PLANNING FOR CUSTOMER SERVICE

Knowing what your customers want and value, you face process decisions about how to make the customer service experience as pleasant as possible. You also face outcome decisions related to whether the customer service is delivered on time, as promised and in a satisfactory manner. Your customers will be dissatisfied if they receive the promised quality of service but find the experience of arranging for it tedious or inconvenient. Meanwhile, customers who are satisfied with both the process and the outcomes are likely to become loyal.

The specific process and outcome decisions that you will make depend on your objectives, marketing strategies, resources and capabilities. You must also consider what levels of customer service you will promise and be able to deliver, including whether self-service is appropriate, decide on the type of customer service you will offer before, during and after a purchase, formulate a process for recovering from any customer service lapses, and plan to monitor service comments (see Table 10.1).

Table 10.1 Key customer service strategy decisions

Decision	Purpose
Process	To create a satisfactory experience for customers who expect or require service delivery
Outcomes	To deliver service on time, as promised and with the expected result for customer satisfaction
Timing	To provide needed service before, during or after a purchase
Service recovery	To handle complaints, fix lapses in service delivery, anticipate potential problems and identify areas for improvement
Perception monitoring	To understand how customers perceive the organisation's customer service

Determining service levels

Few companies can afford the highest level of customer service, with completely person-alised attention immediately available on request, but then again, not every customer in every segment can afford (or will expect) such service. However, low price doesn't necessarily mean low service levels. For instance, Amazon.com's customers appreciate the low prices, on-time delivery and 30-day returns guarantee. Net-a-Porter (www.net-a-porter.com) differentiates itself on the basis of superior service as well as its assortment of upmarket fashion merchandise.

MARKETING IN PRACTICE: NET-A-PORTER

Net-a-Porter.com, founded in London in 2000, aims to provide affluent customers world-wide with the personal service, special style tips and exclusive merchandise selection they would receive in a high-street boutique. The retail website looks like an upmarket fashion magazine, with multiple photos of each item, detailed descriptions and size information, videos of the latest runway trends, and interviews with top designers. It also offers an informative email newsletter with updates about new fashion arrivals, seasonal style trends and designers' thoughts on upcoming collections.

Now owned by the luxury fashion company Richemont, Net-a-Porter's special competitive edge remains superior service. Shoppers are pampered with such extras as next-day delivery to 170 countries, elegant packaging, free style advice, personal shoppers and free returns. Those who live or work in London, New York City or Hong Kong can pay an additional fee to receive their designer purchases the same day, delivered directly to their door in the company's signature black-and-white vans. Careful attention to customer service has helped Net-a-Porter grow year after year. Its sleek new distribution centres in the US, UK and Hong Kong process and pack orders six times more efficiently than in the past.

The recent recession didn't hurt Net-a-Porter's turnover; in fact, it's attracting more customers and completing more transactions than ever before. The company now offers apps so users can browse its fashion magazine and shop at any hour, from any location, via tablet computer or mobile. Already, 30 percent of all purchases on the site are made by tablet or mobile. The company is active on Pinterest, Facebook, Twitter and YouTube, in addition to its blogs. It has also introduced a menswear site, Mr Porter, as well as an out-let site, theOutnet.com, with marked-down fashions at significant savings. Despite the discounted prices, the customer experience at theOutnet.com remains upmarket and high-fashion, with expert advice and options for posh packaging. The Outnet recently launched a local site in China.[10] What's next for Net-a-Porter?

Marketing plan analysis: What else can Net-a-Porter do to reinforce its differentiation on the basis of superior customer service?

In many industries where price competition is commonplace, there is a trend towards eliminating extras and cutting costs, often by automating service procedures. Ryanair and easyJet are two no-frills, low-fare airlines that minimise customer service costs by getting customers to buy tickets online and pay extra for in-flight food and drinks and for seat reservations. Self-service can supplement other service choices, especially during periods of peak demand. Yet companies may choose to maintain customer service levels even when they reduce prices for competitive reasons.

The level of customer service you plan should be consistent with the following elements:

- *Customer needs and expectations.* What do targeted customers want, need and expect in terms of customer service? Use marketing research to identify the service levels that would satisfy customers in each targeted segment, uncover trends in customer turnover and determine whether customers are defecting because of poor customer service. If you segment your market according to service usage and expectations, you may find promising opportunities and steer the organisation away from unprofitable segments. For instance, depending on customer requirements, price sensitivity and other factors, you may plan a high level of service to support your most expensive products and a lower level of service to support discount or clearance products or outlets.

- *Positioning and competitive strategies.* What level of service is consistent with your product's or brand's positioning? What level of service would help the product or brand compete more effectively? Net-a-Porter's positioning as a retailer of luxury fashions is carried through in the high levels of customer service that the company offers. This sets Net-a-Porter apart from competitors and also reinforces brand perceptions and loyalty.

- *Other marketing-mix decisions.* Is the product new or complicated? How is pricing likely to influence customers' expectations of customer service? Do the product's promotions promise or imply a high level of customer service? What level of customer service can your channel members deliver? How will a certain level of customer service fit in with the strategies and objectives in your marketing plan?

- *Organisational resources and strengths.* What level of customer service fits in with your organisation's financial and human resources? Is technology available to support or substitute for customer service delivery? Is good customer service delivery a particular strength? Can or should customer service be outsourced? In deciding about customer service levels, you should carefully analyse the cost–benefit trade-offs for each targeted segment.

Planning for good service throughout the relationship

Depending on your product and market, customers may have questions and require service assistance before they buy. Business buyers in particular may need help with product specifications or configuration, installation options and warranty or repair information. During the negotiation of a very large or complex business purchase, buyer and seller may agree on a certain level of post-purchase service to be delivered under contract. In negotiating such contracts, be sure you understand what your customers require and how you can meet those requirements at a profit once the purchase has been completed.[11]

If you market directly to customers, you must be prepared to provide at least some service before a purchase transaction. If you market through intermediaries, you will be relying on channel members to answer customers' questions and demonstrate features. Your marketing plan may therefore include tactics for channel training and sales promotion activities targeting wholesale or retail sales representatives. When the German carmaker BMW set a goal of increasing sales in India, it used a travelling 'dealer showroom' to bring its luxury cars to smaller cities for local test drives. The showroom was staffed by product and financing experts, all ready to answer buyers' questions.[12]

At the time or place of the purchase, your customers may want help in testing a product, completing the paperwork for a transaction, arranging for delivery or pick-up, arranging payment method or terms, taking advantage of promotions connected with purchasing, or other purchase-related service tasks. If your customer service falls short here, customers may not complete the purchase; conversely, if you deliver good customer service during the purchase transaction, you will build customer satisfaction and encourage repeat purchasing.

If you market through intermediaries, you'll plan for point-of-purchase service through activities such as product and sales training. For upmarket or technical products, however, your marketing plan may call for delivering point-of-purchase service on your own. When Apple established its own chain of retail stores, the company was aiming to control the environment in which its products are displayed and demonstrated and to control the quality of customer service delivered at the point of purchase. AT&T, which markets telecommunications services, is emphasising personalised service in its new flagship store, after studying the best practices of the Ritz Carlton hotel chain and other businesses known for superior customer service. The goal is to provide an engaging and positive experience that strengthens customer relationships.[13]

To encourage repeat business and strengthen customer relations, you'll probably have to deliver some sort of customer service after the purchase. This may include training buyers in product use, explaining maintenance or repair procedures, exchanging defective products, returning products for refunds, installing replacement parts, or other post-purchase services. Some companies use technology to detect the need for post-purchase service even before customers notice any problems. Many provide targeted customer segments with special services. When customers seek service months or years after they buy your product, you have an opportunity to reinforce their image of and loyalty to your brand. By providing the level of maintenance or repair service that customers expect, you remind them of why they selected your brand in the first place and give them yet another reason to choose your brand next time.

Because consumers have so many choices in today's marketplace, a growing number of organisations are benchmarking service leaders and looking to revitalise their approaches to serving customers. The Disney Institute (http://disneyinstitute.com) has been sharing the Walt Disney company's keys to service success since 1986. What can you learn from Disney's passion for treating customers as 'guests'?

MARKETING IN PRACTICE: WALT DISNEY

Disney is known all over the world for delivering outstanding service at its theme parks, resorts and hotels. This long-standing reputation for excellence attracts first-time customers and reinforces brand loyalty among repeat visitors. How does the company do it? First, Disney believes in communication, not only to welcome customers but also to answer their questions, explain any temporary delays and do whatever is needed to make their visit a good experience.

Second, Disney employees have been trained to cheerfully offer assistance even before customers ask for help and to show respect for every customer. For example, Disney wants parents or grandparents who wait while a child enjoys a ride or buys a toy to feel as valued and have as positive an experience as the youngster, because of their influence over purchasing decisions. Third, Disney recognises that everything contributes to satisfaction: customers expect attractive surroundings, clean facilities and other basics in addition to attentive service.

Over the years, businesses of all sizes as well as government agencies, school systems and healthcare organisations have come to the Disney Institute for training and ideas about planning for and delivering great customer service. General Motors, for example, has sent Chevrolet car dealers for Disney training so they will gain insights and inspiration for applying the 'guest' concept to serving car buyers. As another example, after Disney training, the Florida Hospital for Children took a fresh look at the hospital experience. It quickly made changes such as having staff members bend down to have conversations with children at eye-level and hanging artwork to put patients and their families at ease. The purpose was to create a friendly, caring service environment and reduce any feelings of stress that patients and families may feel.[14]

Marketing plan analysis: How might a company that produces a tangible good marketed through channel partners apply the 'guest' concept to their customer service planning?

Monitoring customer perceptions of service

Your marketing plan should provide for monitoring what customers think of your service (and your products). Be ready to analyse comments made in letters, phone calls and emails and on your company website to understand customer perceptions. Also monitor what customers (and others) say about your service and your brand elsewhere on the web by searching for comments on the following:

- *Review websites*. Review Centre, Yelp and other websites invite customers to post reviews and ratings of restaurants, shops and other establishments in many cities and towns worldwide.

- *Retail websites*. Amazon.com pioneered the idea of getting customers to rate and critique products and sellers. Now many other marketers do the same or help customers find appropriate ratings online. Accord Hotels, parent company of Sofitel and other hotel brands, links to consumer reviews posted on TripAdvisor.com.

- *YouTube*. Customers sometimes post videos online to let the world know about good or bad service experiences.

- *Blogs and miniblogs*. Many consumers, journalists and industry observers blog or tweet their complaints and compliments.

Inevitably, your monitoring will turn up a negative comment, so be ready to respond promptly by communicating with the customer and taking action to fix the problem. These are opportunities to strengthen relationships with customers and other stakeholders. In fact, inviting online reviews of customer service, product quality and other aspects of your business can build trust and enhance your reputation for transparency and customer responsiveness. Marketers like Debenhams (www.debenhams.com) have a system in place to ask customers for online reviews. It's also important to read customer comments posted on third-party review sites such as Review Centre (www.reviewcentre.com).

MARKETING IN PRACTICE: CUSTOMER REVIEWS ONLINE

Research indicates that positive customer reviews can help boost a business's revenue, while negative reviews can deter buyers from considering a brand or company. In one study of restaurants in a US city, an academic researcher discovered that if a restaurant can improve its customer review ratings by a single star (increasing its ratings average from 3 to 4, for example), sales will increase by as much as 9 percent. This is especially helpful to small restaurants, which benefit from the customer feedback as well as the potential for additional revenue.

Yet bigger firms also find online reviews a valued source of customers' opinions about goods and services. Debenhams engages shoppers by asking them to post reviews using in-store digital kiosks and/or after they've made a purchase online – and the retailer posts these reviews as written. The UK travel marketer On Holiday Group appreciates reviews posted on Google and Review Centre because it gives the company visibility and shows its transparency. The company makes a point of requesting reviews from customers who are on their way home from holiday.

However, because of the possibility that some reviews may be bogus, the Review Centre and Google (like other review sites) use special software to detect and examine suspicious posts. Another concern is that some reviewers may exaggerate their ratings to attract attention. As a result, Dr Kohei Kawamura of Edinburgh University suggests that buyers 'should discount extreme reviews more heavily when there are a larger number of reviews'.[15] Now some marketers are hiring reputation management experts to defend against negative comments they believe are unwarranted and to try to improve the position of positive information that appears in online search results.[16]

Marketing plan analysis: Should a business post a public response to a bad customer review or should it only respond privately to the customer who posted the comment? Explain your answer.

Some companies set up special online help pages for customer service. Virgin Media, which offers cable television, Internet access and mobile services to UK customers, maintains customer assistance forums and service FAQs online. It also acts quickly when customer comments and concerns are addressed to its Twitter account, whether positive or negative.[17] (See this chapter's case study for more about customer service via Twitter.) One last thought about reviews: resist the temptation to anonymously post online comments about your company's goods or services, a practice that's illegal in the UK and ethically questionable in any case.

Planning for service recovery

Because customer service may not be delivered perfectly every time, you should plan for **service recovery**: how your organisation will recover from a service lapse and satisfy customers. Service recovery offers an excellent opportunity to demonstrate understanding of customers' expectations and needs and – equally important – rebuild ties with customers through effective communication while implementing a speedy and satisfactory resolution.[18] According to one study, a sizable number of dissatisfied customers will keep buying from a company if their complaints are resolved satisfactorily. Simply responding is an important first step, because shoppers report frustration at the lack of response to complaints and negative reviews.[19] If you please customers who complain, you can turn them from potential defectors into advocates for your organisation, a good way to stimulate positive word of mouth.

Internal marketing is vital for service recovery, because employees must have the commitment, skills and authority to clarify the extent and nature of a service lapse, offer a suitable response and see that it is implemented as promised. As you plan for service recovery, focus on both process and outcome (see Figure 10.2). Customers will be more dissatisfied if you provide no convenient method for receiving complaints or fail to resolve their complaints satisfactorily. At times, customers may only want a way to express their dissatisfaction, know that their voices are heard and receive a sincere apology. In one study of online comments about a wholesaler, nearly half of the consumers who had posted negative or neutral reviews were willing to withdraw their comments after the company apologised.[20]

Be aware, however, that the number of complaints usually understates the actual number of service failures experienced by your customers, because not every dissatisfied customer will take the time to complain. Your organisation could be losing customers due to an ineffective service recovery plan, and you might never know the reason. By encouraging two-way communication with your customers and paying close attention to negative and positive comments, you'll build trust and gain valuable insights into service problems and achievement.

Be sure to seek the input of staff members who deal directly with customers when determining what tools and support you need to correct service mistakes. Also solicit suggestions from these employees for practical ways to improve delivery and prevent service lapses. And try to involve top management in service recovery, as doing so will go a long way towards proving your organisation's commitment to satisfaction and to keeping the customer relationship alive.

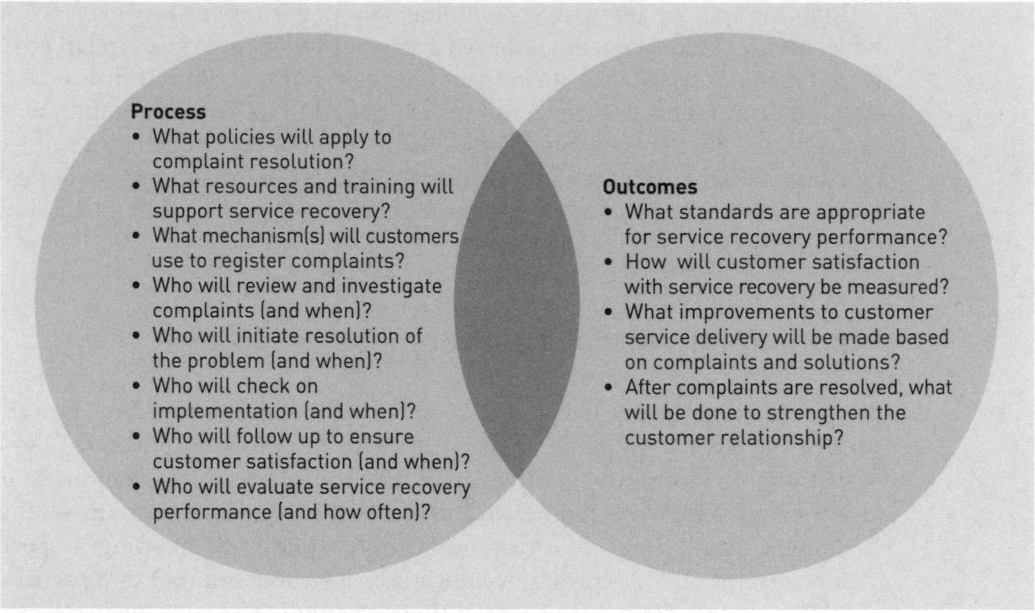

Process
- What policies will apply to complaint resolution?
- What resources and training will support service recovery?
- What mechanism(s) will customers use to register complaints?
- Who will review and investigate complaints (and when)?
- Who will initiate resolution of the problem (and when)?
- Who will check on implementation (and when)?
- Who will follow up to ensure customer satisfaction (and when)?
- Who will evaluate service recovery performance (and how often)?

Outcomes
- What standards are appropriate for service recovery performance?
- How will customer satisfaction with service recovery be measured?
- What improvements to customer service delivery will be made based on complaints and solutions?
- After complaints are resolved, what will be done to strengthen the customer relationship?

FIGURE 10.2   Planning service recovery process and outcomes

As you consider how to incorporate customer service support into your marketing plan, use Checklist No. 17.

ESSENTIAL CHECKLIST NO. 17:
PLANNING FOR CUSTOMER SERVICE SUPPORT

This checklist will guide you through the main issues to research and analyse as you plan for customer service to support your marketing activities. After you write your ideas in the spaces provided, put a tick next to the questions you've answered. If your marketing plan is for a hypothetical firm, use this checklist as a guide to the information you'd need to gather to make decisions about customer service.

☐ What level of service do targeted customers need, expect and prefer before, during and after the purchase?

_____

☐ What customer service level is reasonable and practical, based on organisational resources and objectives?

_____

☐ What competitive, industry and market considerations might affect the customer service plan?

☐ What legal, regulatory, ecological, technological, social or ethical issues might affect the customer service plan?

☐ How will you monitor customer perceptions of your service activities?

☐ How will you train and reward employees and channel members for providing good customer service?

☐ What service recovery plans and policies do you need?

PLANNING FOR INTERNAL MARKETING

Ideally, you want your internal marketing activities to engage the hearts and minds of managers and employees at every organisational level – the internal equivalent of what good external marketing seeks to achieve. First, of course, you will 'market' the marketing plan to gain senior management approval and support. Then, for the approved plan to succeed, you need internal marketing to build enthusiastic commitment among the organisation's middle managers, front-line managers and employees. This means going beyond a catchy slogan or one-time special event to develop an ongoing internal marketing strategy that you can adapt as the situation changes.

Unilever recognises that effective internal marketing is an essential foundation for external marketing. To quote the vice-president for employee engagement: 'If the employees are not embracing the brand, you'll never be able to convince the consumers.'[21] This is why Unilever sent employees boxes of samples and information about a new line of Dove personal care products for men before launching the products in Germany. The idea was to let employees know about the new products and get them to share samples with family and friends.

Although the specifics of internal marketing strategy will differ from organisation to organisation, most touch on the following:

- *Hiring and training*. Even when you are not directly involved in personnel decisions, you can influence hiring procedures to ensure that new employees have a positive attitude towards customer service. You should also influence or participate in training to build the staff's knowledge of the customer and of the marketing effort.

- *Standards*. What, exactly, constitutes performance in implementing marketing programmes? Your performance standards should be consistent with the marketing plan's (and the organisation's) objectives, with other job-related standards, with what customers want and with what you are promising and promoting.

- *Communication*. Every company can use communications for reinforcing objectives and standards, coordinating programmes and implementing responsibilities, keeping employees informed and keeping them interested and connected. You can choose any number of techniques, from printed newsletters and voicemail messages to internal websites and teleconferences. Sainsbury's, the UK grocery chain, brings employees together at special events to preview new marketing campaigns and reinforce teamwork.[22] The chain is also testing internal social networking and has been surveying 2,000 employees each month to learn their reactions to key issues.[23]

- *Participation*. Inviting participation in the planning process can encourage stronger support and commitment among those who are charged with implementation. Customer contact personnel, in particular, may be able to suggest how your proposed programmes can be improved. Lincoln Financial, a US insurance firm, recently invited four dozen employees to become internal brand influencers. They travelled the country introducing new campaigns at company facilities and encouraging colleagues to get more deeply involved.[24]

- *Monitoring and rewards*. Are employees performing up to the standards that have been set and cooperating for smooth implementation of marketing programmes? If not, what needs improvement? If so, how should you reinforce and reward good performance? Your internal marketing reward system must be consistent with the organisation's overall system of motivation, performance evaluation and rewards.

An emerging trend in internal marketing and customer service support is *gamification* – applying fun, game-like elements or rewards to engage employees and encourage them to master specific concepts or work more effectively. When the pharmaceutical firm Omnicare wanted to improve its telephone customer service, the senior director of service delivery instituted a combination education–rewards programme that awarded digital badges when employees achieved preset achievement levels. Not only did this reinforce performance, it also sparked a bit of competition as employees sought to capture additional badges.[25] As you plan, consider whether some form of gamification is appropriate for your internal marketing, and what rewards might encourage participation.

See **Chapter 12** for more about controlling marketing plan implementation.

CHAPTER SUMMARY

Customer service supports the external marketing effort and, in turn, must be supported by internal marketing focusing on people and processes inside the organisation. Customer service can help the organisation attract new customers, retain current customers, build image for competitive advantage and achieve its objectives. Internal marketing can help the organisation focus on customers, increase employee knowledge, encourage internal cooperation and commitment to marketing, and boost pride in performance.

Marketers face decisions about process (the experience customers will have in arranging for customer service) and outcomes (delivering service on time, as promised and to the customer's satisfaction). They also face decisions about the appropriate level of customer service to be promised and delivered, the delivery of customer service before, during and after a purchase, how to monitor customer comments about service, and the process of recovering from any customer service lapses.

CASE STUDY: CUSTOMER SERVICE IN 140 CHARACTERS

Social media sites have brought a new immediacy to customer service – and drawn public attention to complaints or concerns expressed by individual customers. Those conversations, once very private, are now very public: anyone can tweet about a good or bad service experience and see the complaint or compliment repeated to hundreds or thousands of people within minutes. Simply monitoring comments about service isn't enough; every marketer needs to be ready for real-time dialogue and follow-up, to satisfy customers and to prevent reputational damage.

The first step is to join the conversation by setting up a Twitter account. Some marketers have one Twitter account, while others have multiple accounts for different purposes. First Direct, a UK financial services firm, maintains a dedicated Twitter account (http://twitter.com/firstdirecthelp) for customer service and aims to respond within an hour to customers' tweets. The US carrier Delta Airlines also has a separate Twitter account for customer service (http://twitter.com/DeltaAssist), staffed by a rotating team that answers tweets around the clock. Next, have a process in place to deal with comments. When passengers post messages about OC Transpo (http://twitter.com/OC_Transpo), the public transport service in Ottawa, Canada, managers often request additional details so they can investigate more thoroughly. Just as important, they tweet a thank-you for the feedback, showing that they regard each comment as an opportunity to improve customer service.

Finally, think about how Twitter can be used to reach out to customers. When South Africa's First National Bank experienced an unexpected systems outage, the CEO used the bank's Twitter account (http://twitter.com/FNBSA) and other social media to update customers about the situation. Responsive and transparent communications 'brought people toward us, rather than pushing them from us,' says the bank's head of digital marketing and media.[26]

Case questions

1. Which of the customer-service decisions listed in Table 10.1 could include a Twitter communications component?

2. Would you recommend that a small start-up business create a separate Twitter account for customer service? Why or why not?

APPLY YOUR KNOWLEDGE

To see how customer service supports a firm's marketing mix, select a retailer with a nearby store location and an online presence. Visit one store, browse the website and then analyse this retailer's approach to customer service. Prepare a brief oral or written report summarising your analysis.

- Where on the website does the retailer place its customer service policies? Where in the store are such policies displayed? Are the policies practical and easy to understand?

- How would you describe the level of service in the store? Is it consistent with the retailer's positioning and competitive situation, its pricing and its other marketing activities?

- What customer service is offered online? Does the website invite shoppers to interact with service representatives via email, online chat, telephone or some other method?

- Are pre-purchase, point-of-purchase and/or post-purchase services offered in the store? What self-service options, if any, are available? How do these differ (if at all) from the services offered to online customers?

- How are customers invited to communicate about problems or questions?

- What changes in customer service would you suggest for this retailer? Why?

- Briefly search for online comments about this retailer. Summarise what you find and what the store's responses were, if any. What would you recommend this retailer should do to enhance and protect its service reputation online?

BUILD YOUR OWN MARKETING PLAN

Continue your marketing plan by making decisions about customer service and internal marketing. First, what is an appropriate level of customer service to support your positioning and other marketing-mix decisions? Do you know how this level of service fits with customers' needs and expectations? Does your customer service add more value than that offered by competitors? What pre-purchase, point-of-purchase and post-purchase customer service will you plan to offer and what resources will you need? Should you offer any self-service options? How will you use internal marketing to communicate the marketing plan and build commitment inside the company? How will you monitor customer perceptions of your service support? Outline a customer service or internal marketing programme, as applicable, indicating the specific audience or market being targeted and what you expect to achieve. Explain how this programme will contribute to meeting your plan's objectives.

ENDNOTES

1. S. Ronendra Singh, 'Intel to turn focus on channel partners', *Hindu Business Line*, 20 August 2012, www.thehindubusinessline.com; Erica Swallow, 'How to build a social media education for your company', *Mashable*, 18 January 2011, www.mashable.com; James Ashton, 'Computing? We've only just begun, says Intel chief', *Sunday Times*, 11 October 2009, p. 9; Ellen McGirt, 'Intel risks it all (again)', *Fast Company*, November 2009, pp. 88ff; Barbara Lippert, 'I love you, tomorrow', *Media Week*, 5 October 2009, p. 18.

2. 'As you like it: retailers explore the fine art of good customer service', *WWD*, 30 August 2012, www.wwd.com.

3. Damon Poeter, 'Report: 300 million Apple Store visitors since October', *PC Magazine*, 21 August 2012, www.pcmag.com.

4. Cecily Liu, 'UK stores try to get Chinese lovers in the mood', *China Daily*, 23 August 2012, www.chinadaily.com.cn.

5. Simon Mundy, 'Metro Bank raises £126m as it eyes IPO', *Financial Times*, 11 June 2012, p. 22; Brian Caplen, 'The new world order of retail banking', *The Banker*, 1 March 2011, n.p.

6. Alex Sherman, 'The cable guy offers more love-for a price', *Bloomberg Businessweek*, 18 February 2013, pp. 22–3; Mike Farrell, 'Cable offers "white glove" treatment', *Multichannel News*, 3 January 2011, p. 8.

7. 'New Audi Cam brings servicing online', *Motoring Research*, 13 August 2012, www.motoringresearch.com.

8. Lucy May, 'How good customer service could bring more Hollywood to Cincinnati', *Cincinnati Business Courier*, 17 August 2012, www.bizjournals.com.

9. Kevin Lane Keller, 'The classic rules remain the same', *Business World*, 18 June 2012, n.p.

10. Rachel Strugatz, 'Net-a-Porter lands in NYC', *WWD*, 26 June 2012, p. 1; Samantha Conti, 'Net-a-Porter makes move into China', *WWD*, 27 February 2012, p. 2; Rhiannon Harries, 'Discount dreamland', *Independent*, 3 May 2009, www.independent.co.uk; John Brodie, 'A winning formula for fashion retail', *Fortune*, 2 September 2009, http://money.cnn.com; www.net-a-porter.com; www.theoutnet.com.

11. Ritu Jain, 'Why customer service needs to be more than mere lip service', *Industry Week*, 18 September 2009, www.industryweek.com.

12. Asit Manohar, 'BMW launches a mobile showroom to reach the emerging markets in India', *Economic Times (India)*, 23 August 2012, http://articles.economictimes.indiatimes.com.

13. Michael V. Copeland, 'AT&T puts on the Ritz to upgrade retail experience', *Wired*, 30 August 2012, www.wired.com.

14. Brooks Barnes, 'Letting the Disney magic rub off on businesses', *International Herald Tribune*, 23 April 2012, n.p.; 'Giving health care that Disney magic', *Hamilton Spectator (Canada)*, 23 July 2011, p. C10; Stephen Williams, 'Can Chevrolet run the happiest dealerships on earth?', *Advertising Age*, 9 April 2012, p. 11; Carmine Gallo, 'How Disney works to win repeat customers', *Bloomberg Businessweek*, 1 December 2009, www.businessweek.com; Carmine Gallo, 'Customer service, the Disney way', *Forbes*, 14 April 2011, www.forbes.com.

15. Quoted in Jamie Doward, 'Online customer reviews – they're not all they're cracked up to be', *Guardian*, 25 June 2011, www.guardian.co.uk.

16. 'Big two ignore Google reviews at their peril, says Endacott', *Travel Weekly UK*, 13 August 2012, www.travelweekly.co.uk; Julia Flucht, 'Online reviews make big difference to small businesses', *Northwest Public Radio (USA)*, 6 August 2012, www.nwpr.org; Charlotte McEleny, 'The good, the bad and the useful', *Marketing Week*, July 2011,

www.marketingweek.co.uk; 'Debenhams: Customer experience driving cross-channel success', *Internet Retailing*, May 2011, http://internetretailing.net; 'Websites take on bogus reviewers', *BBC*, 16 July 2010, www.bbc.co.uk; Johnny Diaz, 'Cyber maids clean up your online image', *Sun-Sentinel (Florida)*, 10 August 2012, http://articles.sun-sentinel.com.

17. 'Social media: Battle of the brands', *Revolution*, 30 November 2011, p. 33.

18. See J. Cambra-Fierro, J. M. Berbel-Pineda, R. Ruiz-Benitez and R. Vazquez-Carrasco, 'Managing service recovery processes', *Journal of Business Economics and Management*, September 2011, pp. 503–528.

19. Gregory Smith, 'Retailers use social media to win back unhappy customers', *POPAI*, 1 April 2011, http://popai.com.

20. Douglas MacMillan, 'Why it pays to apologise', *Businessweek*, 12 October 2009, p. 22.

21. Quoted in 'Employees come first, customers second', *Marketing*, 25 July 2012, p. 26.

22. 'Brand experience: Sainsbury's, inside and out', *Conference & Incentive Travel*, 1 January 2012, p. 34.

23. 'The vital connection between staff and the bottom line', *Marketing Week*, 10 November 2011, p. 14.

24. William Ng, 'How one Fortune 250 company used internal marketing to drive engagement', *Incentive*, 13 January 2012, www.incentivemag.com.

25. Kelly Liyakasa, 'Game on!', *CRM Magazine*, May 2012, p. 28.

26. Quoted in Eleanor Seggie, 'FNB dishes out its social media secrets', *MoneyWeb (South Africa)*, 23 August 2012, http://moneyweb.co.za. Other sources: Lisa Bachelor, 'Complain on Twitter for an instant response', *Guardian*, 12 May 2012, www.guardian.co.uk; Chloe Fedio, 'When passengers tweet, OC Transpo takes notice', *Ottawa Citizen (Canada)*, 15 August 2012, www.ottawacitizen.com; Nathan Eddy, 'Facebook, Twitter popular for customer service', *eWeek*, 4 May 2012, www.eweek.com; Jack Aaronson, 'Multi-channel customer service: @DeltaAssist leads the way', *ClickZ*, 1 April 2011, www.clickz.com.

Planning metrics and performance measurement

Learning outcomes

After studying this chapter, you will be able to:

- Explain the role of key performance indicators in assessing marketing results
- Understand how metrics, forecasts, budgets and schedules measure progress towards marketing plan objectives

Application outcomes

After studying this chapter, you will be able to:

- Select metrics to measure progress towards financial, marketing and societal objectives
- Prepare for forecasting, budgeting and scheduling to support your plan

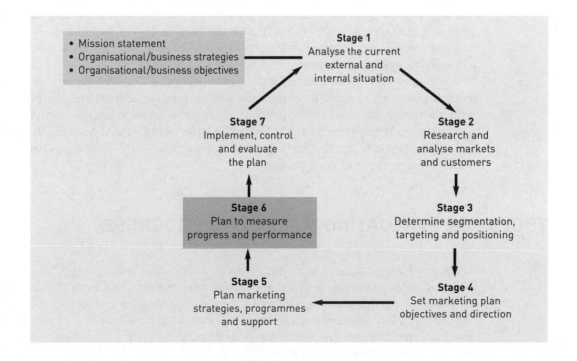

- Mission statement
- Organisational/business strategies
- Organisational/business objectives

Stage 1
Analyse the current external and internal situation

Stage 2
Research and analyse markets and customers

Stage 3
Determine segmentation, targeting and positioning

Stage 4
Set marketing plan objectives and direction

Stage 5
Plan marketing strategies, programmes and support

Stage 6
Plan to measure progress and performance

Stage 7
Implement, control and evaluate the plan

CHAPTER PREVIEW: MARKETING BYTE NIGHT

In 1998, at the height of the dot-com era, 30 people from the UK information technology industry decided to sleep rough to raise awareness about homeless children and raise money to fight the problem. These Byte Night 'sleepers' (www.bytenight.org.uk) raised nearly £35,000 for the registered charity Action for Children, which seeks to help vulnerable youngsters 'break through injustice, deprivation and inequality to fulfil their potential, shape their own destiny and experience the joy of life'. In its first 14 years, Byte Night attracted hundreds of sleepers each year and donated a total of £4.3 million to fund Action for Children activities across the UK.

For the 15th anniversary of Byte Night, organisers set a goal of recruiting 1,000 sleepers in London, the Thames Valley, Cambridge, Belfast and Scotland to participate in raising £900,000. Sleepers in each location were challenged to raise a certain amount individually or as a team. For example, the target for sleepers in London was £1,000 per person or £5,000 per team (up to five sleepers). As this 15th annual Byte Night approached, marketers counted the number of sleepers who were registered to participate month by month and compared the tally to that point during the previous year's campaign. Through traditional media and digital, mobile and social media, Byte Night publicised the cause, recruited well-known industry and celebrity supporters and explained how the charity would benefit, measuring progress at every stage. This Byte Night was the most successful in the event's history, raising £950,000 and encouraging organisers to set even more ambitious goals in the future.[1]

Byte Night must measure marketing performance to determine whether its plans are effective in attracting sleepers and charitable donations. In other words, is Byte Night achieving its objectives? The time to plan for measurement is *before* implementation, so measurement standards and checkpoints can be established in advance. If early indications show that performance is lagging or ahead of schedule, the organisation can make changes by applying marketing control (see **Chapter 12**).

In Stage 6 of the marketing planning process, you will decide how to track performance towards your marketing, financial and societal objectives. This chapter will teach you about the four tools for measuring marketing progress and performance: metrics, forecasts, budgets and schedules. See the sample plan in the Appendix for ideas about how these tools are applied in the marketing plan; review this chapter's checklists as you plan your metrics and your budgets.

TOOLS FOR EVALUATING MARKETING PROGRESS

Once implemented, how will you know whether your marketing plan is successful? Start by identifying **key performance indicators (KPIs)**, indicators that are vital (key) to effective performance, as defined by your organisation's strategic goals and your marketing plan objectives. Every organisation will have various types of KPIs that are important to the organisation and its customers, such as increases in profitability, product quality and customer satisfaction. Two of Byte Night's KPIs are the amount of money raised and the number of participating sleepers, both of which relate to the event's success.

You have to be able to make point-in-time measures and analyse trends in these measures to understand marketing performance relative to those KPIs and then be ready to adjust your marketing plan if necessary. A manufacturer, for example, might identify 'new product introduction cycle' as a KPI, knowing that the faster a product gets to market, the more quickly it can satisfy customers' needs and the more that can be sold during a given period. New products contribute to unit sales and revenue, as well as to market share and profitability, but they also matter to customers and to channel members. If measures indicate that products are not being launched as quickly as desired, marketers can take steps to improve performance on this key indicator.

Every programme and tactic in your marketing plan should contribute, if only in a small way, towards your objectives and goals. As shown in Table 11.1, you can measure marketing plan progress using these four tools:

- **Metrics** are specific numerical standards used on a regular basis to measure selected performance-related activities and outcomes. The point is to examine interim results by applying metrics measurements at set intervals and to analyse progress towards meeting marketing plan objectives. Metrics help you understand what happens as a result of your marketing and enable you to compare outcomes across various time periods.[2] Marketing expert Tim Ambler stresses that the metrics used by top management should be vital to the business, precise, consistent and comprehensive.[3]

- **Forecasts** project the estimated level of sales (for example, by product or market) and costs (for example, by product or channel) for the specific period covered by the marketing plan. By comparing actual sales and costs (or actual donations) with forecast levels, you can spot deviations and prepare to adjust your assumptions or your activities as trends develop.

Table 11.1 Measuring marketing plan performance

Tool	Description	Use
Metric	Specific numerical standard measuring an outcome that contributes to performance	Target for interim achievement against which to measure actual outcome
Forecast	Forward-looking estimate expressed in unit or monetary terms	Projected level of sales or costs against which to measure actual results
Budget	Funding allotment for specific programme or activity	Guideline for spending against which actual expenditures are measured
Schedule	Series of target dates for tasks related to a particular programme or activity	Guideline for anticipated timing against which to measure actual timing

- **Budgets** are time-defined allotments of financial resources for specific programmes, activities and products. You might, for example, prepare one overall advertising budget and allocate it across specific campaigns, programmes, products or geographic areas. After implementing the marketing plan, you check whether actual spending is above, below or at the budgeted level.

- **Schedules** are time-defined plans for coordinating and accomplishing tasks related to a specific programme or activity, such as new product development. You will prepare individual schedules showing starting and ending dates as well as responsibilities for the major tasks within a programme, plus an overall schedule reflecting the key tasks and target dates for implementing marketing plan programmes.

These tools help you know whether you're doing what you should be doing to achieve your objectives and goals. If you achieve the expected results day after day, you will move ever closer to accomplishing both short-term objectives and long-term goals. However, avoid overemphasising short-term measurements because of the risk that you might lose sight of what customers really want and what your organisation is striving to achieve. At the same time, don't wait too long to act if you identify significant shifts in competition or other elements that begin to affect the progress you expected to make towards your objectives. In short, try for a balanced perspective as you apply the metrics, forecasting, budgeting and scheduling tools discussed in the remainder of this chapter.

MEASURING PROGRESS WITH METRICS

Using metrics allows you to measure the outcomes and activities that really contribute to performance, as defined by KPIs. Organisations are concerned about holding marketing accountable for achieving the expected results, which is why the use of metrics is an important part of marketing planning. You'll need clear objectives and baseline measures against which to compare interim results and ultimate performance. Yet just because you *can* measure something doesn't mean you *should* measure it – nor should you measure everything. The key is to identify the specific metrics that apply to the most significant activities and results affecting marketing performance. Companies can use both internal and external metrics to measure progress towards objectives (see Table 11.2).

For example, the external metric of customer awareness measures progress towards the marketing objective of strengthening and expanding customer relationships: the higher the awareness, the higher the probability that prospects will become customers. In contrast, internal metrics measure results that relate to specific financial objectives such as profitability. Apply your measurements before, during and after programme implementation so you can make changes if necessary to improve performance.

Many companies use a marketing dashboard to track actual performance. A **marketing dashboard** is a computerised, easy-to-read depiction of KPI-related marketing outcomes, as measured by metrics, used to monitor progress and identify deviations from expected results. Carphone Warehouse, a leading European telecommunications retailer,

Table 11.2	Internal and external metrics for marketing	
Performance perspective	**Time horizon: forward-looking metrics**	**Time horizon: backward-looking metrics**
INTERNAL Company metrics	Company metrics applied during an operating period, such as: • Product defects • Late deliveries • Late payments • Inventory turnover	Company metrics reported at the end of an operating period, such as: • Sales revenues • Percent gross profit • Net profit before tax • Return on assets
EXTERNAL Marketing metrics	Marketing metrics applied during an operating period, such as: • Customer awareness • Customer satisfaction • Perceived performance • Intent to purchase	Marketing metrics reported at the end of an operating period, such as: • Relative market share • Market share • Customer retention • Revenue per customer

Source: *Market-based Management*, Pearson Education Inc. (Best, R. 2013) Figure 2.8 page 47, Prentice Hall, BEST, ROGER, MARKET-BASED MANAGEMENT, 6th Ed., p. 47, (c) 2012. Reprinted and Electronically reproduced by permission of Pearson Education. Inc., Upper Saddle River. New Jersey.

has implemented marketing dashboards that allow store managers to monitor performance measures such as customer satisfaction and customer retention.[4]

Selecting metrics

When you select metrics, look for measures that will help you evaluate progress throughout the course of each programme and into a new marketing plan period, so you can follow progress and assess results. See Table 11.3 for sample metrics.

When selecting metrics:

• *Match metrics to programme and marketing plan objectives.* Be sure your metrics are relevant to your objectives. A company seeking 10 percent higher sales in the coming year would check performance by regularly measuring unit or monetary sales and market share. However, if its marketers measure the number of sales leads generated but have no metric for conversion rates, they won't know the ultimate outcome of lead generation, which directly influences sales objectives. Apply metrics that will help you improve marketing performance. The UK travel company Thomas Cook measures how many customers open its email marketing messages and, of that group, how many ultimately buy what was promoted.[5] By comparing the results of messages that differ in content, offer and timing, the company can learn more about what customers respond to and change its marketing accordingly.

• *Measure activities or outcomes that show progress towards fulfilling the organisation's mission and moving in the desired direction.* Your metrics should track results that are

Table 11.3 Sample metrics for marketing plan objectives

Type of metric	Examples
Metrics to measure progress towards financial objectives	• Metrics to measure sales and profitability by unit, product line, market, channel, customer segment • Metrics to measure return on investment by product, programme, activity
Metrics to measure progress towards marketing objectives	• Metrics to measure change in customer relationships by number or percentage of new customers acquired, number or percentage of existing customers retained • Metrics to measure efficiency of support activities by product, process, personnel or facility
Metrics to measure progress towards societal objectives	• Metrics to measure change in public image by periodically assessing attitudes and perceptions of various publics • Metrics to decrease ecological impact by measuring reduction in carbon footprint, reduction in waste, increase in recycling

consistent with your mission, direction and goals. The mission of Virgin Atlantic is 'to grow a profitable airline where people love to fly and people love to work'.[6] The airline's marketers might use metrics such as increase in profitability, increase in number of passengers flown and percentage of employees retained to understand whether they are making progress towards that mission month after month.

• *Measure the non-financial and financial outcomes that can be quantified and that matter to customers.* Byte Night measures the number of sleepers and the amount of money they raise each year. Businesses typically select and measure metrics related to changes in customers' perceptions of company image, product quality and value, all of which affect customers' attitudes and behaviour. Also, they can use metrics to track the number of defectors, percentage change and reason for defections. To follow the development of customer relationships, they can track progress in acquiring customers, selling additional products to current customers, retaining customers, reactivating dormant relationships and re-establishing relations with defectors.

• *Measure appropriate internal metrics.* By tracking internal performance using metrics such as measuring order fulfilment accuracy and on-time shipping, you can quickly identify areas for improvement in processes and procedures that affect customer satisfaction and loyalty. Also consider metrics that will help you identify which of your supply-chain and channel partners are most responsive. Your internal metrics should reflect processes or outcomes that make a difference to your competitive performance or that relate to KPIs.

- *Use metrics to reinforce ongoing priorities.* You can use metrics to track the proportion of sales made to more profitable customers compared with those made to less profitable customers as a way to reinforce marketing priorities for long-term success. Also, using metrics to track the ratio of new product sales to existing product sales can show the extent to which new product innovation is fuelling growth.

The specific metrics selected depend on your organisation, its mission and objectives, your marketing plan objectives and the programmes you will implement. Most companies select metrics to measure profitability and profit margins, sales, product awareness and number of new products, among others – with profitability and sales metrics seen as the most valuable in assessing progress.[7] Other vital areas to monitor through metrics are channel and sales force performance, product portfolio performance, new product pricing, price changes and effect on profitability, and the value of individual customers and relationships.

Do look at the metrics common to your industry. Retailers, for example, track the level of merchandise loss due to theft or fraud, because reducing losses improves profits. For this reason, Stockmann, a Baltic-based retailer that operates 700 stores worldwide, measures the results of loss-prevention programmes very carefully. When Stockmann's Lindex clothes stores cut losses of clothing merchandise in half, a Lindex executive observed that the results improved gross profit margin and contributed to higher store productivity.[8]

You can select narrowly defined metrics to track progress towards particular outcomes or activities, such as the number of new products in development or the cost of responding to customer service enquiries. British Telecom (BT) has found that responding to a customer service issue through phone calls or other traditional methods costs about £12 per incident. In contrast, a Twitter response costs less than 12 pence per incident. Because of this large cost difference, BT uses metrics to monitor the proportion of service questions it resolves via traditional methods and via Twitter.[9]

Applying metrics

You will need pre-implementation numbers for every metric so you can track progress from that point forward. If possible, obtain benchmark metrics (from your industry or best-in-class organisations) against which to compare your progress. For every activity or campaign, use your marketing plan objectives as targets. Adobe Systems, which makes business software, sets ROI (return on investment) objectives for each campaign. At the close of a campaign, marketers use metrics to show top management whether the objective has been achieved.[10]

Depending on your organisation, objectives and technology, you may apply selected metrics daily, weekly, monthly, quarterly or yearly. In especially volatile markets, you may check metrics more than once a day or even on an hourly basis. Be sure to analyse the direction and rate of change in measurements taken at different intervals as well as the total progress from pre-implementation levels. This will show how quickly you are moving towards your objectives (and reveal problem areas for attention). Check your previous results to see the progress measured in comparable pre-implementation periods as a way of identifying unusual trends. By documenting your measurements, you will have historical data for comparison with future results. Also analyse your metrics in the context of competitive results whenever possible – an especially important point with measures such as market share, profitability and quality perceptions.

Remember that the metrics you apply today may not be as useful tomorrow because of environmental shifts, new competition, changes in organisational strategy or evolving customer attitudes and behaviour. For example, the number of people who click to view display ads online has dropped year by year, yet research shows that people who see such ads are more likely to visit the brand or product site than people who don't see the ads.[11] As a result, marketers test different metrics for measuring cognitive, affective and behavioural responses to communications and influence programmes in non-traditional media. Here's how Domino's UK (www.dominos.co.uk) applies metrics to its marketing programmes.

MARKETING IN PRACTICE: DOMINO'S UK

Domino's, the market-leading UK pizza delivery company, is constantly testing new recipes for marketing success. In the past few years, it has accelerated its use of digital, mobile and social media, with the idea of getting customers involved with the brand, testing new products and gauging the effectiveness of specific price offers and promotions. The company knows that investments in mobile marketing are paying off, because its metrics show that its free apps account for more than £1 million in sales every week. When Domino's offered a branded app to help sports fans follow football results – and try for prizes like discount vouchers – the app was downloaded 54,000 times in the first three weeks. Moreover, 88 percent of those who downloaded the app used it, meaning they were also seeing Domino's brand messages.

Metrics confirm that the company's online and social media marketing have also been good investments. In 1999, Domino's was the first UK delivery firm to invite Internet ordering across the country. By 2012, it was receiving more than 52 percent of its delivery orders through its website – and some of its units were receiving more than 75 percent of their orders online. The company monitors how many Facebook 'likes' its page receives (currently, nearly 1 million), how many Twitter followers it has (more than 85,000) and how many views its YouTube videos receive (more than 1.4 million). These measures relate to brand awareness and hint at engagement.

Digging deeper, Domino's counts how many Facebook fans click to order a new product (sometimes offered during the pre-launch stage) and how many comments are posted. This helps the company get ready for demand and serves as an early indicator of customer reaction. When Domino's wanted to determine the effect of its Twitter messages, it created a 'reverse auction' promotion in which it lowered the price of a lunchtime pizza each time someone tweeted the hashtag #letsdolunch. As a result, Twitter messages featuring Domino's increased by a factor of 12 on that day, and Domino's was able to see how this correlated with sales results.[12]

Marketing plan analysis: How would you suggest that Domino's use social media metrics to understand customers' attitudes towards the brand and its products?

Marketing judgement is vital for interpreting what metrics measure. Quantifiable measures are necessary but so are innovation and insight.[13] Kellogg's, which markets cereals and snacks worldwide, puts little emphasis on the number of times consumers click on its digital ads because of the difficulty of linking clicks to purchases. Instead, Kellogg's looks closely at whether its digital ads are being seen by specific audiences at particular times when they are most receptive to such messages. It also measures changes in brand awareness and purchase intentions to understand the effect of its ads.[14]

Use Checklist No. 18 as you consider suitable metrics for your marketing plan.

ESSENTIAL CHECKLIST NO. 18:
PLANNING METRICS

Your choice of metrics will determine exactly what you're able to track as you implement your marketing plan and move closer to your objectives. Be sure the metrics you choose are relevant to your organisation and the targets you've set. Also consider how often to apply your metrics so you can identify any problems quickly and make changes as needed.

☐ What metrics will help you and your management track the marketing results that relate to key performance indicators?

_____

☐ What metrics will help you track marketing results that relate to managing the life cycle of a customer relationship, including satisfaction, loyalty and retention?

_____

☐ What metrics will help you measure progress towards achieving the plan's financial, marketing and societal objectives?

_____

☐ What metrics will help you determine whether specific marketing programmes have achieved their objectives?

_____

☐ What metrics will help you track how each marketing-mix element contributes to interim performance?

_____

☐ What metrics will help you assess performance of your customer support services and internal marketing initiatives?

_____

☐ How often should you measure interim progress using each metric?

___

☐ What metrics are in general use in your industry, and why? How can you adapt them for your organisation's particular situation?

___

FORECASTING AND THE PLANNING PROCESS

The purpose of forecasting is to project future demand, sales and costs so you can make marketing decisions and coordinate internal decisions about manufacturing, finance, human resources and other functions. (Depending on the coming year's forecasts, your organisation may need to expand or reduce manufacturing capacity, change inventory levels, reallocate budgets and increase or reduce the workforce.) Forecasting is challenging because of the dynamic business environment, unpredictable competitive moves, changeable demand and other uncertainties that can affect marketing performance.

Often, forecasts will be affected by limited-time factors such as government subsidies for purchases of eco-friendly products or changing technology standards that require the purchase of new equipment or accessories. Not long ago, the end of green-car subsidies in Japan caused economists and car companies to adjust car sales forecasts for that market.[15]

Moreover, your product forecasts must take into account the interrelationships between products in the marketplace. For business markets, apply the principle of **derived demand**: the demand you forecast for a business product will be based, in part, on (derived from) the demand forecast for a related consumer product. In Indonesia, for example, 70 percent of all new-car sales are paid for with bank loans. As demand for cars increases, therefore, banks can expect demand for car loans to increase as well. In fact, to prevent a 'credit bubble' in the fast-growing Indonesian economy, the government recently set a requirement that consumers must have a down-payment of 30 percent or more when borrowing to buy a new car.[16]

Forecasts are, at best, only informed estimates, even when based on statistical data and carefully adjusted for the effect of external influences such as market growth, economic conditions, technological developments and industry trends. Still, aim to make your forecasts as accurate as possible to improve the quality of information supporting the decision-making process. You may want to develop forecasts for the most optimistic, most pessimistic and most likely situations you will face, and then, if possible, to statistically estimate the probability of each. This helps you think about the diverse ways in which your product, industry, competition and market may develop.

More companies are reforecasting future sales and costs using actual results throughout the planning and implementation period. This is especially important during periods of unusual volatility or uncertainty, such as the recent economic downturn.

Types of forecasts

What forecasts do you need for your marketing plan? Most organisations start at the macro level by forecasting industry sales by market and segment, then move to the micro level by forecasting sales for their company, sales by product, sales costs by product, and sales and costs by channel. With these forecasts in hand, you can estimate future changes in sales and costs to examine trends by product and by channel. Such analyses will show the magnitude of projected sales increases or decreases for your market, segment and individual products as well as the expected rate of change over time for sales and costs.

Market and segment sales forecasts

The first step is to project the level of overall industry sales in each market and segment for the coming months and years, using the external audit and the market analysis completed earlier in the planning process. Here you will forecast sales in the qualified available market and in your targeted segment of this market, adjusted for external influences such as expected legal restrictions and the economic outlook. Once you've forecast the size of the market, you can forecast the share you aim to achieve with your marketing plan, as well as estimating the future share for each competitor. Then bring industry sales forecasts down to the segment level to support your targeting and strategy decisions.

Bombardier Aerospace (www.bombardier.com), headquartered in Canada, forecasts industry, market and segment sales up to 20 years in advance – and publicises its forecasts to keep investors, securities analysts, suppliers and other stakeholders informed.

MARKETING IN PRACTICE: BOMBARDIER AEROSPACE

Forecasting is vitally important in an industry where firms require at least a decade and hundreds of millions of euros to research, develop, test, refine and introduce a new product. Bombardier, the world's third-largest aircraft marketer, has made its name in regional jets and business jets. It's also challenging Airbus and Boeing in the narrow-body commercial jet segment, where airlines are seeking to buy more fuel-efficient aircraft to keep costs under control. Competition from Commercial Aircraft Corporation of China (Comac), which has home-country strength, is another threat that Bombardier must bear in mind as it plans for marketing.

Bombardier prepares industry, segment and market forecasts two decades in advance, after studying factors such as the economic trends of each country where airlines are based, broad global economic indicators, projections for fuel production and consumption, population trends, the business cycle, the age of aircraft currently in airline operation and other elements that affect aircraft demand. It adjusts its market and segment forecasts every year, based on factors such as changes in the economic situation and fluctuations in the price of jet fuel. Then the company amends its marketing plans in line with these updated forecasts. For example, forecasting higher demand for business jets and commercial jets

▶

in Turkey, Bombardier has increased its trade show marketing and hired additional sales staff for this market.

Year after year, Bombardier adjusts its long-term forecasts in line with what's been happening in the business environment. Recently, it reduced its 20-year forecast for the number of small commercial jets to be sold by all industry participants, citing slower economic growth. Bombardier expects the segment of jets equipped for 100 to 149 passengers to account for two-thirds of industry demand – and has said it expects to grab a 50 percent share of this segment, thanks in part to a new jet it's introducing.[17]

Marketing plan analysis: The 20-year forecasts announced by Airbus and Boeing don't always agree with each other or with Bombardier's forecasts. Do you think Bombardier should take its competitors' forecasts into consideration when adjusting its own forecasts? Why or why not?

Company and product sales forecasts

Use your market and segment forecasts, your market and customer analyses and your knowledge of the current situation to develop sales forecasts at the company and product levels. Also factor in earlier decisions about direction, strategy and objectives when thinking about future company sales. Car manufacturers typically project industry, company and product sales three to five years in advance because of the lead time needed to design new vehicles, build or retrofit assembly facilities and plan for other operational activities. They consult forecasts from industry groups, such as the UK's Society of Motor Manufacturers and Traders, and adjust their forecasts in accordance with the latest economic indicators and other external influences. As the global economy recovered from its recent downturn, the society noted that demand was increasing and European carmakers were shifting inventory to UK dealerships because foreign exchange rates were particularly favourable for UK buyers.[18]

Most marketers prepare month-by-month sales forecasts for the coming year, although some firms prefer week-by-week forecasting and some project sales 15–18 months ahead. Manufacturers of industrial equipment and cars typically prepare monthly sales forecasts for at least two years ahead, on the basis of top-down and floor-up input, so they can plan supply acquisition and production capacity. Involving suppliers and channel members can improve accuracy and give suppliers the data they need for better forecasting to meet your organisation's needs. If your marketing plan covers at least one new product introduction, forecast those sales separately so you can measure results and track progress towards product-specific objectives. Also consider the effect that other value-chain participants could have on your product forecasts. In addition, consider the effect of seasonality and other factors that can affect sales.

Costs of sales forecasts

Now you're ready to forecast the total costs you can expect to incur for the forecast sales levels and to project when these costs will occur. This gives you an opportunity to consider the financial impact of your forecasts and revise them if necessary. Your forecasts will be more realistic if you discuss cost figures with supply-chain firms and line managers or others who are knowledgeable about the products and markets. You may need to adjust your overall cost forecasts after the marketing plan is implemented. Nonetheless, estimating these costs during the planning process helps you allocate funding to individual programmes and products.

Channel forecasts

Companies that work with multiple channels and channel members often forecast sales and costs for each, including the cost of logistics. In addition to providing benchmarks against which to measure actual channel results and costs, these forecasts give you an opportunity to reconsider your channel and logistics decisions if the costs seem too high (or surprisingly low). Even companies that own their own stores can use channel forecasts to project sales on a store-by-store basis. Ideally, you should forecast unit sales and revenue results by product and by channel (perhaps down to the store or wholesale level) so you can track progress after implementation and make changes if actual performance varies significantly from forecasts.

Direct marketers can develop forecasts for each direct channel they use. Rue La La, based in Boston, Massachusetts, an online members-only retailer, forecasts the percentage of sales it will derive from purchasers who use mobiles, those who use tablet computers and those who use desktop computers, by day of the week and by season. The retailer learned, through internal analyses, that most of its transactions on holidays are completed on mobiles, a channel where it is stronger than most Internet retailers. Now Rue La La forecasts for up to two-thirds of all holiday purchases to be completed through mobiles, and it creates plans with that channel in mind.[19]

Forecasting approaches and data sources

There are a number of approaches to forecasting sales and costs, as shown in Table 11.4. Some rely on statistical analysis or modelling, whereas others rely on expert judgement. Note that for a forecast developed with a time series or causal analysis to be at all accurate, you must have sufficient historical sales data. At the same time, historical trends can be misleading if you're entering an entirely new market, so use judgement. In fact, judgemental forecasting approaches such as the jury of executive opinion can be very valuable if applied in a systematic way. Incorporate external information and expertise to avoid too narrow an internal focus.

Some companies are supplementing executive opinion and other forecasting methods with *online prediction markets*. These operate like mock stock markets to 'crowdsource' forecasts by seeing how thousands of people (usually employees, but sometimes people outside the organisation) rate the possibilities of each predicted outcome. Each participant is given a certain amount of 'money' to invest in one or more of the predictions being considered. Like the market value of a share of stock, the value of each prediction goes up or down depending on how much money is invested in it at any given time. Using an online prediction market as input for a forecast allows management to tap the collective knowledge and experience of all the participants by seeing which predictions attract the most investment.[20]

Table 11.4 Selected approaches to forecasting

Forecasting technique	Description	Benefits/limitations
Sales force composite estimate	Judgemental approach in which sales personnel are asked to estimate future sales	Can provide valuable insights from customer-contact personnel but may introduce bias
Jury of executive opinion	Judgemental approach in which managers and sometimes channel members or suppliers are asked to estimate future sales	Combines informed judgement of many but may give too much weight to some individuals' estimates
Delphi method	Judgemental approach in which outside experts participate in successive rounds of input, leading to a consensus forecast	Minimises possibility of bias or overweighting one individual's estimates but is time consuming and accuracy depends on choice of experts
Online prediction market	Judgemental approach in which employees or invited stakeholders indicate their confidence in certain predictions through online trading in a mock stock market	Combines judgement of many people and can be an efficient forecasting method, but may involve bias towards longer-term predictions
Survey of buyer intentions	Research-based approach in which buyers in a given market are asked about their purchasing intentions	Solicits market input but may not be indicative of customers' actual behaviour
New product test marketing	Research-based approach in which a new product's sales performance in limited markets is tested and the results used to forecast future sales	Reflects actual customer input but may be affected by competition or other factors
Time series analyses	Statistical approaches in which the patterns of historical data are analysed to predict future sales, e.g. moving averages, exponential smoothing	Use actual purchase data to produce forecast estimates quickly but assume that similar buying trends will continue
Causal analyses	Methods that statistically determine the relationship between demand and the factors that affect it, e.g. regression analysis, neural networks	Provide insights into relationships between factors that affect demand but require sufficient data for analysis

In preparing forecasts, review the background information you've gathered about your markets, customers, channels and costs. Also consult industry associations, government information and financial analysts' reports when estimating future sales and costs, especially at the macro level. Before you rely on any secondary data for forecasting purposes, carefully check the source, collection method, credibility, completeness and timeliness. For a final 'reality check', compare your forecasts with the actual outcome of recent periods to identify major anomalies.

PREPARING BUDGETS AND SCHEDULES

With sales and cost forecasts complete, you can develop an overall marketing budget and, within that budget, estimate spending for specific programmes and activities in line with your marketing plan objectives. Every marketer must make hard choices because marketing budgets (and other resources) are never unlimited. As with forecasts, some marketers budget for the most optimistic, most pessimistic and most likely scenarios so they are prepared to tackle threats and opportunities.

Your organisation may set budget requirements for return on investment, limit the amount or percentage of funding that can be allocated to certain activities or products, set specific assumptions, cap cost increases, or prefer a particular budget method or format. Your marketing budget should be linked to corporate-level goals and initiatives. Enhancing brand image and preference to fuel future growth is an ongoing priority for many companies as they approve marketing budgets.

Budgeting methods

Budgets may originate in the marketing department and move upwards for review (floor up), originate at top management level and move downwards for specific allocations (top down), or be constructed through a combination of floor-up and top-down methods (see Figure 11.1). The **objective and task budget method**, a floor-up option common in large organisations, allocates marketing funding according to the cost of the tasks to be accomplished in achieving marketing plan objectives. If you can relate specific tasks to specific objectives, this method offers good accountability; however, the combined cost may result in too high a budget, given your organisation's resources. For this reason, some large corporations use the **econometric modelling method** to calculate budgets using sophisticated formulas that take into account anticipated customer response, product profitability, competitive spending, economic factors and other relevant variables.

Your organisation may use one of the top-down budgeting methods. With the **affordability budget method**, senior managers set the amount of the marketing budget on the basis of how much the organisation can afford (or will be able to afford during the period covered by the plan). Although simple, this method has no connection with market conditions, opportunities, potential profits or other factors. With the **percentage budget method**, the overall marketing budget is based on a percentage of the previous year's

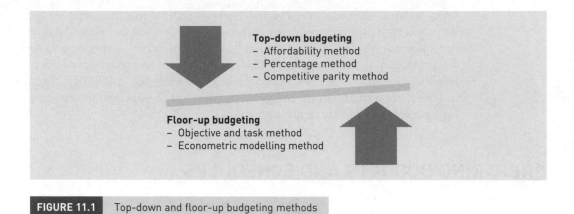

Top-down budgeting
- Affordability method
- Percentage method
- Competitive parity method

Floor-up budgeting
- Objective and task method
- Econometric modelling method

FIGURE 11.1 Top-down and floor-up budgeting methods

annual turnover, next year's expected turnover, the product's price, or an average industry percentage. Note that this method has no connection with market conditions.

With the **competitive parity budget method**, managers set a total marketing budget at least equal to that of competitors. But because no two organisations are exactly alike, mimicking another organisation's budget may be disastrous for yours. Few companies can (or should) match the annual advertising budget of Apple (€760 million) or Unilever (€5.2 billion), for example.[21] If your organisation must compete with much larger firms, you'll need to be creative about budgeting for activities that will lead you to your objectives.

The top-down budgeting methods are relatively easy to apply, but they fail to relate costs to objectives. Compared with the affordability method, the objective and task budgeting is more sophisticated, results in larger marketing budgets and is related to better profitability.[22] In practice, most marketing budgets combine top-down and floor-up methods, guided by higher-level strategic planning and product or brand-level input relative to objectives and costs. And because of economic uncertainty, among other factors, be prepared to budget for the best-case, worst-case and most likely scenarios. Complete Office, a US distributor of office supplies, generally budgets with growth in mind – but it also creates budgets that would apply in the event that sales fail to meet forecast levels.[23]

Budgets within budgets

At this point, you can create separate budgets for specific marketing activities and programmes, schedule planned expenditures and fix responsibilities for spending. This allows you to compare the actual outlays with the budgeted outlays after the marketing plan has been implemented. You will want to prepare budgets (for annual, monthly and perhaps weekly costs) covering individual marketing-mix programmes matched with appropriate objectives (such as projected profit or return on investment).

In addition, you can establish budgets within your overall budget reflecting planned expenditures by market, segment, region, business unit, product or line/category, brand, activity or responsibility. This allows examination of performance market by market, product by product and activity by activity so you and your managers can change budget priorities as appropriate. Set your budgeting priorities and make your allocation decisions based on a careful analysis of the external and internal marketing environments.

Deciding on advertising budgets can be particularly challenging because of the difficulty of measuring the direct effects of messages in mobile, digital and social media. As you saw earlier, Domino's can count the number of pizza orders, but not every marketer can determine the impact of specific messages, especially in social media. Recently, Facebook began a series of experiments to demonstrate the results of spending for ads on its pages. One test for Unilever's Suave brand found that for every $1 spent on Facebook advertising, Unilever received more than $8 in sales.[24] Marketers of every size are continuing to test so they can allocate advertising budgets for maximum impact.

As you prepare budgets for your marketing plan, consult Checklist No. 19 for ideas and note your thoughts in the spaces provided.

ESSENTIAL CHECKLIST NO. 19:
PLANNING MARKETING BUDGETS

☐ What is your overall budget for marketing?

☐ Based on the marketing-mix activities and outcomes outlined in your marketing plan, how much will you need to spend for each brand, product or product line, market or segment, function and marketing programme or campaign?

☐ At what intervals will expenditures be made, and should you be preparing weekly and monthly budgets in addition to an overall annual budget?

☐ Does your organisation have preset financial targets, such as a minimum return on investment (ROI) or a minimum profit margin for each programme or product? How does your marketing budget relate to those targets?

☐ What internal and external issues or trends might result in the need to change your overall budget or some of the budgets within your overall budget?

Planning schedules for implementation

When planning schedules for implementation, you'll estimate the start date, duration and deadlines for each programme or task to coordinate concurrent activities, prevent conflicts, obtain needed resources on time and track progress towards completion. Although you may not have to include detailed programme schedules when documenting your marketing plan for management review, you should summarise the schedule and responsibilities for major programmes. When the Ford Motor Company (www.ford.com) created a marketing plan for the launch of its redesigned Fusion model, it also developed schedules to guide preparation and implementation.

MARKETING IN PRACTICE: FORD MOTOR COMPANY

More than a year before Ford was to introduce its restyled Fusion mid-sized car, its marketers began to think about new ways to use multiple media for customer engagement. Having been successful with previous digital and social media campaigns, they wanted to create an online contest with surprises and appealing rewards. The objective was to build efficient, positive pre-launch buzz that would bring the Fusion to the attention of 10 million US car buyers even before the new model was available in local showrooms.

Although Ford's marketers wouldn't be able to measure how many people followed through with a visit to a dealer and bought a Fusion as a result of the 'Random Acts of Fusion' campaign, they would be able to measure how many people participated in the campaign. They would also be able to count how many interactions each participant had with the campaign, such as how many visits to the Fusion site, how many clicks to vote, how many comments, and where visitors went online after participating in the campaign. To gauge awareness and attitude, Ford decided to use online surveys.

As campaign planning continued, marketers set and sometimes rescheduled deadlines for contracting with celebrity spokespeople, finalising the contest's details, arranging for pre-production Fusions to be ready for test-drives and creating content for Facebook, Twitter, the website and YouTube. Four months before the Fusion's launch, Ford signed *American Idol* host Ryan Seacrest as one of three celebrity headliners, seeing his TV appearances and social media savvy as a plus for brand visibility. Marketers immediately began filming videos and producing contest-related materials. Three months before the model's launch, they released the first communications in the 'Random Acts' campaign: a Facebook teaser promotion, a television commercial, online videos and messages explaining the contest's rules and rewards. Would 'Random Acts' achieve the results that Ford's marketers projected?[25]

Marketing plan analysis: Do you agree with Ford's idea of building buzz three months before the redesigned Fusion was available in showrooms, even though the current Fusion model was still being sold? What schedule would you use in such a situation?

Remember, if tasks don't start or finish on schedule, you need to see which other tasks might be affected and try to get back on track towards the planned timing. Ford, for instance, couldn't proceed with Fusion videos and other content until it had celebrity spokespeople under contract. Also review the new timing (and cost changes, if any) with management and communicate with the major customers and suppliers who would be affected. As with budgeting and forecasting, you may want to develop schedules for the most optimistic, most pessimistic and most likely situations – and be ready to make changes in response to emerging opportunities, threats or other factors.

Meeting long-term goals requires elaborate planning and scheduling in some industries. When the Japanese carmaker Nissan created a five-year plan to capture 15 percent of the Thai market for cars by 2016, it set out detailed schedules for every step needed to achieve that goal. The company determined that it would need to introduce a total of ten new models (two per year) to meet its goals – and created separate schedules, budgets and forecasts for each model. Nissan also established year-by-year schedules for expanding its dealership and service capabilities to support its forecast sales growth. When natural disasters temporarily disrupted parts production in Japan and car production in Thailand, Nissan had to adjust its marketing schedule to allow for several weeks of delay – but the company maintained its full-year and five-year sales targets.[26]

CHAPTER SUMMARY

Key performance indicators are indicators that are vital to effective performance, as defined by the organisation's strategic goals and the marketing plan's objectives. Metrics are used to measure performance-related activities and outcomes numerically and on a regular basis. Types of metrics include internal forward-looking metrics, external forward-looking metrics, internal backward-looking metrics and external backward-looking metrics. A marketing dashboard is a computerised, easy-to-read depiction of marketing outcomes, as measured by key metrics, used to confirm progress and identify deviations from expected marketing results. Plan to apply selected metrics daily, weekly, monthly, quarterly or yearly, and review metrics regularly in light of internal and external environmental changes.

Marketers use forecasts to project the estimated level of sales and costs for the marketing plan period so they can compare actual results and identify deviations. Some prepare forecasts for the most optimistic, most pessimistic and most likely situations. Budgets are used to allot financial resources to specific programmes, activities and products and then compare actual spending to budgeted spending to pinpoint deviations. Budgets may be developed using floor-up methods, top-down methods or a combination of methods. Marketers use schedules to define the timing of tasks to plan and implement specific programmes and activities.

CASE STUDY: GOOGLE

The mission of Google (www.google.com) is to 'organise the world's information and make it universally accessible and useful'. The technology company uses metrics to measure its progress in speeding online search innovations to market, including how many of its hundreds of experiments are eventually launched and how quickly users adopt these changes. Google can monitor how many users try each new feature or service, make changes in a matter of hours and then test again to gauge viability and user response. By supercharging its rate of innovation, Google plans to maintain its market-share lead over challengers such as Microsoft's Bing search engine.

Although much of Google's revenue comes from selling advertising that appears alongside search results, its marketing initiatives extend well beyond search. Google closely monitors the market share of its Chrome web browser, designed for download and use on multiple devices, including desktop computers, mobiles and tablet computers. Its Android operating system has been installed on millions of mobiles worldwide. More recently, Google launched Google Wallet as a mobile app-based payment service, with extras such as identification verification and location-based promotions, competing against Apple and others. An innovation currently being tested is Google Glass, computerised spectacles with a display screen and processing capabilities, data storage, sat-nav features and a built-in camera.

Based on metrics of customer usage, market share, trends in technology and internal plans for future products, Google regularly discontinues existing offerings and alerts users well in advance so they can move data and consider other Google services that deliver similar benefits. When it discontinued its iGoogle home page feature, for example, it let users know 16 months in advance. The company announced its schedule for shutting down Google Video three years in advance so users had time to move their videos to the Google-owned YouTube or download for private use.

Still, search remains a central focus for Google. Some metrics used to measure the outcomes of search improvements might seem unusually exacting but Google knows they make a difference to the user's experience. After one improvement was introduced, Google engineers found that the time between search results being viewed and the user clicking on one of the links was narrowed by a tiny fraction of a second – meaning the user found a relevant result more quickly than before the improvement. 'This was a small idea,' said a Google engineer, 'but we have a real responsibility as a company to respect people's time' – in line with the company's mission.[27]

Case questions

1. Based on Table 11.2, how would you classify the metrics of market share and speed in clicking on a relevant search link if you were looking at marketing outcomes for Google's Chrome web browser? What other metrics might be relevant for Chrome?

2. Do you think schedules are useful for planning product innovations when firms find it difficult to accurately forecast the timing of major technological breakthroughs? Explain your answer.

APPLY YOUR KNOWLEDGE

Review your work researching a company's marketing, financial and societal objectives in the 'Apply your knowledge' exercise in **Chapter 5**. In a brief oral or written report, answer the following questions about measuring progress towards those objectives:

- What key performance indicators would you recommend for this company, given your knowledge of the company and its objectives?

- Does the company explain any metrics used to measure interim progress? How do they relate to the KPIs you recommend?

- Has the company revealed any of its forecasts or budgets? If so, what are they based on and how do they relate to its objectives?

- What secondary data sources would you consult if you were preparing a forecast for one of this company's products? Be specific.

- Has the company discussed any schedules for marketing activities, such as launching a new product or starting a new advertising campaign? If so, what connection do you see between the schedules and forecasts or budgets?

BUILD YOUR OWN MARKETING PLAN

Move ahead with your marketing plan by researching and estimating sales and costs, plus forecasts for industry, company and product sales, cost of sales, and sales and costs by channel. What sources will you use? Do your forecasts represent the most optimistic, most pessimistic or most likely situation? Are they appropriate for the current marketing situation? Next, develop a month-by-month marketing budget using the objective and task method and a budget for a specific programme or activity such as advertising. List any factors that would affect your budgets for the most optimistic, most pessimistic and most likely situations. Suggest two or three KPIs and identify appropriate metrics for your financial, marketing and societal objectives. Explain how, when and why you will use them to measure progress towards objectives. Document your decisions in a written marketing plan.

ENDNOTES

1. Christine Ashton, 'Thinking beyond the bottom line', *CIO UK*, 14 August 2012, www.cio.co.uk; 'Byte Night 2012: 15 years in the making', *Computer-Weekly*, 30 May 2012, www.computerweekly.com; 'Byte Night 2012: Bedding down in Belfast', *Computer-Weekly*, 13 July 2012, www.computerweekly.com; www.bytenight.org.uk/; www.actionforchildren.org.uk.

2. See Paul W. Farris, Neil T. Bendle, Phillip E. Pfeifer and David J. Reibstein, *Marketing Metrics*, 2nd edn (Upper Saddle River, NJ: FT Press, 2010), p. 1.

3. Tim Ambler, *Marketing and the Bottom Line* (London: Financial Times Prentice Hall, 2000), p. 5.

4. Fiona Briggs, 'Carphone Warehouse uses business intelligence to boost performance', *Retail Times*, 23 August 2012, www.retailtimes.co.uk.

5. Ronan Shields, 'Charities and finance top email open rates', *New Media Age Online*, 15 August 2012, n.p.

6. See www.virgin-atlantic.com/en/gb/allaboutus/missionstatement/index.jsp.

7. Tim Ambler, *Marketing and the Bottom Line* (London: Financial Times Prentice Hall, 2000), p. 163.

8. Deena M. Amato-McCoy, 'Limiting loss: apparel retailers use intelligent solutions to combat shrink', *Apparel*, June 2012, p. 38.

9. 'Marketing in social media and the complex art of measurement', *Guardian (UK)*, 21 June 2012, www.guardian.co.uk.

10. Kate Maddox, 'Forrester conference focuses on digital, social', *BtoB*, 14 May 2012, p. 3.

11. Kunur Patel, 'What to measure? Only 16 per cent of the web is clicking display ads', *Advertising Age*, 30 September 2009, www.adage.com.

12. Anh Nguyen, 'Domino's Pizza deliver strong sales from online and social media', *CIO UK*, 30 July 2012, www.cio.co.uk; 'Domino's Pizza turn to social media to support launch of Mexicano range', *The Drum*, 22 June 2012, www.thedrum.co.uk; 'Domino's Pizza sees online sales account for over half of UK delivered sales as mobile grows to a fifth of online orders', *The Drum*, 23 July 2012, www.thedrum.co.uk; John Reynolds, 'Domino's readies debut Facebook TV ad', *Marketing Magazine*, 13 March 2012, www.marketingmagazine.co.uk; Eileen Brown, 'Domino's m-commerce brings $1.6 million in sales in a single week', *ZDNet*, 29 March 2012, www.zdnet.com; Juliet Stott, 'Eight ways to adapt your content marketing strategy to mobile', *Econsultancy*, 14 February 2013, www.econsultancy.com.

13. John Nardone and Ed See, 'Free yourself from the tyranny of metrics', *Advertising Age*, 20 November 2006, p. 12.

14. Ryan Joe, 'Kellogg Company: "We don't care about clicks"', *DM News*, 21 June 2012, www.dmnews.com.

15. Andy Sharp and Keiko Ujikane, 'Japan retail sales slide with end of car subsidies looming', *Bloomberg Businessweek*, 29 August 2012, www.businessweek.com.

16. 'Stuck in fifth gear', *Economist*, 1 September 2012, p. 63.

17. Ross Marowits, 'Bombardier sees Turkey as potential "breakout market" as it attends airshow', *Edmonton Journal (Canada)*, 30 August 2012, www.edmontonjournal.com; Bertrand Marotte, 'Bombardier sees slight downturn in commercial market, sustained growth in business jets', *Globe and Mail (Canada)*, 19 June 2012, www.theglobeandmail.com; Steve Wilhelm, 'Mighty Boeing 737 has rivals on its tail – and not just Airbus', *Puget Sound Business Journal (US)*, 17 August 2012, www.bizjournals.com; Ross Marowits, 'Bombardier trims 20-year industry forecast for aircraft deliveries', *The Star (Canada)*, 19 June 2012, www.thestar.com.

18. John Reed, 'Car registrations accelerate in July', *Financial Times*, 6 August 2012, www.ft.com.

19. Larry Kavanagh, '4 ways to leverage the smartphone this holiday season', *Multichannel Merchant*, 22 August 2012, www.multichannelmerchant.com; Bill Siwicki, 'Mobile exceeds 50% of sales on a single day at e-tailer Rue La La', *Internet Retailer*, 8 May 2012, www.internetretailer.com.

20. 'Prediction markets – an uncertain future', *Economist*, 26 February 2009, www.economist.com; Jonathan Richards, 'Prediction markets: The future of decision-making', *Times Online*, 4 September 2008, http://technology.timesonline.co.uk.

21. Peter Burrows and Adam Satariano, 'Can Phil Schiller keep Apple cool?', *Bloomberg Businessweek*, 7 June 2012, www.businessweek.com; Stuart Elliott, 'Marketing budgets rise for some giants', *New York Times*, 20 February 2012, www.nytimes.com.

22. Nigel Piercy, 'The marketing budgeting process', *Journal of Marketing*, October 1987, pp. 45–59.

23. Kasey Wehrum, 'Business forecasting in a crazy, mixed-up world', *Inc.*, 1 April 2009, www.inc.com.

24. Shayndi Raice, 'Inside Facebook's push to woo big advertisers', *Wall Street Journal*, 15 August 2012, www.wsj.com.

25. Dave Guilford, 'Countdown to launch', *Automotive News*, 23 July 2012, p. 30; Dale Buss, 'Ford's Scott Monty on Ryan Seacrest, random acts of Fusion and transmedia', *BrandChannel*, 29 June 2012, www.brandchannel.com; Susan Kuchinskas, 'Ford Fusion social media effort deepens Ryan Seacrest partnership', *ClickZ*, 29 June 2012, www.clickz.com.

26. Santan Santivimolnat, 'Nissan's midterm plan a bull's-eye', *Bangkok Post*, 31 August 2012, www.bangkokpost.com; Nareerat Wiriyapong, 'Nissan eyes another eco-car in Thailand', *Bangkok Post*, 12 April 2011, www.bangkokpost.com.

27. Quoted in Robert D. Hof, 'Can Google stay on top of the web?', *Businessweek*, 12 October 2009, pp. 44–9; also: Quentin Fottrell, 'Google ups the ante in wallet wars', *MarketWatch*, 30 August 2012, www.marketwatch.com; Mark Lee, 'Google gets some rare good news in China', *Bloomberg Businessweek*, 3 September 2012, pp. 22, 24; 'Google "Spring Cleaning" continues with iGoogle shutdown', *PC Magazine Online*, 3 July 2012, n.p.; 'Google Glass launches new age of personal computing', *Computer News Middle East*, 5 July 2012, n.p.; Rob Hof, 'Google search guru Singhal: we will try outlandish ideas', *Bloomberg Businessweek*, 2 October 2009, www.businessweek.com.

Learning outcomes

After studying this chapter, you will be able to:

- Explain the role of marketing control
- Understand how marketing control works at various levels
- Discuss planning for annual, financial, productivity and strategic control

Application outcomes

After studying this chapter, you will be able to:

- Diagnose interim marketing results and plan corrective action
- Use marketing control to evaluate plan performance
- Prepare for contingency and scenario planning

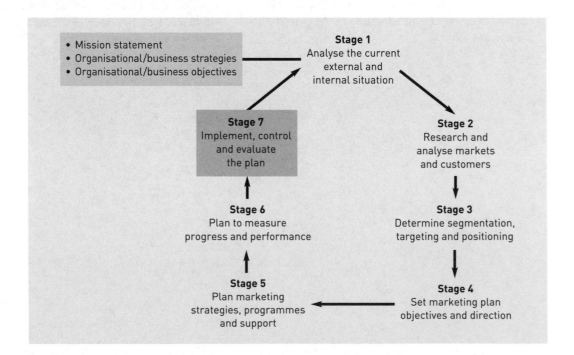

- Mission statement
- Organisational/business strategies
- Organisational/business objectives

Stage 1
Analyse the current external and internal situation

Stage 2
Research and analyse markets and customers

Stage 3
Determine segmentation, targeting and positioning

Stage 4
Set marketing plan objectives and direction

Stage 5
Plan marketing strategies, programmes and support

Stage 6
Plan to measure progress and performance

Stage 7
Implement, control and evaluate the plan

CHAPTER PREVIEW: MARKETING AT UNILEVER

From Persil and Ponds to Blue Band and Bertolli, the products of Unilever (www.unilever.com) aim to fulfil its worldwide mission of helping to 'meet everyday needs for nutrition, hygiene and wellbeing, with brands that help people look good, feel good and get more out of life'. The company has €51 billion in annual turnover and implements marketing plans for 400 brands, including a dozen billion-euro brands like Lynx/Axe, Hellmann's and Dove. Unilever sets specific marketing, financial and societal objectives, as well as multiyear targets for growth and sustainability. By 2020, it expects to double revenue while reducing its environmental footprint by 50 percent. Year by year, Unilever announces its sustainability results and explains whether it has achieved a goal, is 'on plan' towards that goal, is 'off plan' and needs corrective action, or has missed its target.

Because of Unilever's history and experience in meeting the needs of diverse segments in good and bad times, it's ready to make adjustments when needed. During the global financial crisis, it applied what it had learned from selling low-priced, small-sized packages in developing nations like India to the challenge of marketing to price-conscious shoppers in Europe. Unilever switched to selling Surf detergent in tiny pouches (at correspondingly low prices) in Spain and launched new low-priced foods under a brand created specifically for Greece. To gain a broader perspective, the firm is asking internal teams of marketing experts to review and revise strategy for key brands; it's also looking outside the organisation for innovations. Currently, more than half of the new products in Unilever's pipeline were developed with ideas or partners from outside the company. Finally, Unilever's marketers are doing more pre-testing of adverts so they can fine-tune messages and media before launching major new campaigns.[1]

Unilever's marketing-plan adjustments illustrate the importance of stage 7 in the marketing planning process, the point at which the plan is implemented, controlled and evaluated. The company knows how dynamic the marketplace can be – and it's prepared to make changes when necessary, such as shrinking package size to make products more affordable and pre-testing more ads to see what works and what doesn't. In this chapter, you'll learn about the importance of marketing control, including the levels of marketing control and the use of annual, financial, productivity and strategic control. Also, you'll consider how to use contingency planning and scenario planning for marketing purposes. The sample marketing plan in the Appendix shows how a company might apply principles of marketing control. For more ideas about planning for implementation, see the checklist later in this chapter.

PLANNING FOR MARKETING CONTROL

Marketing control is the process of setting standards and measurement intervals to gauge marketing progress, measuring interim results after implementation, comparing measurements with standards, diagnosing deviations from standards and taking corrective action if needed to achieve the planned performance. Even the best plan will be ineffective without proper implementation and the ability to respond quickly to changing circumstances; a poor plan will not be improved by superb implementation. Without marketing control, you can't determine whether your marketing plan is leading to the performance you and your organisation expect. With marketing control, you can see exactly where and when results fall short of or exceed expectations, then come to a decision about the action you will take. And if your plan is working the way it should, this process enables you to track your progress and build on your momentum.

Figure 12.1 shows how the marketing control process works. You'll start by developing standards based on your marketing plan objectives. Determine how often to measure interim results (by the day, week or month, for example). After implementation, you'll begin to measure results. Next, you'll compare these measurements with the standards you set and diagnose any deviations from expected outcomes. Are interim results better than expected? If so, see how you can transfer what you learn to other elements of the same campaign or to future campaigns. Are results lower than expected? In this case, you'll want to take corrective action (by adjusting the timing or intensity of your marketing activities, for example) to make up for the deviation from your planned results. To see whether your corrective action is effective, you'll evaluate the outcome during the next iteration of the ongoing control process, which may require you to adjust your measurement intervals or standards or both.

Marketing control is intended to help you and your managers identify the warning signs of an emerging problem early enough to take corrective action. This may entail a small change or a major decision such as discontinuing a product or increasing marketing spending. In today's volatile global economy, few companies can afford to wait an entire year to evaluate results and make decisions; that's why so many are measuring results more frequently and testing possible changes to implement before campaigns wind down.

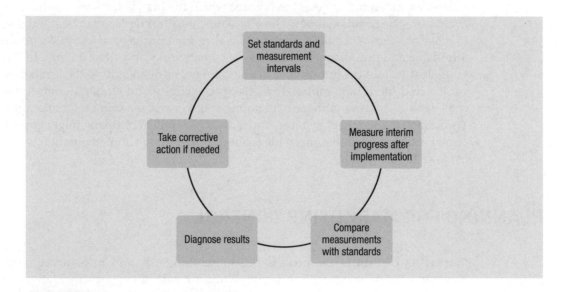

FIGURE 12.1   Applying marketing control

At times, the use of marketing control can raise ethical questions. Will marketers set less stringent standards or lower short-term sales forecasts in order to qualify for bonuses or promotions? Will they honestly and adequately explain deviations from expectations and amend or reverse their earlier decisions if necessary? Will marketers apply marketing control laxly or inconsistently if they feel pressured by senior managers to produce ever-higher quarterly results? This can lead to concentration on short-term progress to the detriment of long-term objectives and, as in several highly publicised instances, decisions to make current sales or profits look better than they actually are.

Control of marketing strategy must be coordinated with control of corporate strategy to ensure that your organisation achieves its long-term goals and short-term objectives. Tesco, for example, uses a 'steering wheel' divided into five sections (customers, communities, finance, operations and employees) to communicate its performance in each area. The purpose is to make all employees aware of the company's progress and provide guidance for their actions in supporting Tesco's movements towards its targets. 'Tesco doesn't want one leader,' the former chief executive explains, 'we want thousands of leaders who take initiative to execute the strategy.'[2]

The marketing control process

The marketing control process starts with the objectives you have already set and the detailed forecasts, budgets, schedules and metrics you have developed to track post-implementation progress towards objectives. Next, determine exactly which standards must be met to show progress at each interval of measurement. Suppose your forecast calls for selling 500 units of a product in June, your financial metrics specify an average gross profit margin of 30 percent and your advertising budget for June totals £3,000. During June you can get early indicators of progress by measuring actual results daily and weekly; at the end of June you can measure full-month results and see whether you are meeting your forecast, metrics and budget standards.

The standards and measurement intervals used for marketing control will vary from organisation to organisation. Supermarket chains such as Tesco can measure store, product category, brand and individual item sales by day, week, month, quarter and year; some track store sales by the hour for staffing purposes as much as for marketing purposes. The US convenience store chain Maverik creates scorecards for managers to use in assessing monthly and yearly performance. Results marked in green indicate that the store's performance exceeds the standards for that period; results in blue indicate that performance meets standards; results in yellow indicate that performance is slightly below standards; and results in red show that standards aren't being met. If more than 50 Maverik stores aren't meeting a particular standard, top management prepares to take chainwide corrective action and adjusts objectives if necessary.[3]

Whatever standards and intervals you choose should provide sufficient information and time to diagnose an emerging problem. You do this by comparing actual interim results with preset standards, examining the magnitude and direction of variations and calculating the rate of change from the previous period's results. Assume that your non-profit organisation actually receives £2,000 in contributions during November, although your monthly forecast standard is £2,500. Your results are 20 percent lower than the standard, which is a sizable variation. However, sharply lower November results would signal an even more problematic trend if your October contributions were 10 percent lower than the standard and your September contributions were 8 percent lower.

How can you diagnose the cause and significance of any deviations from standards? Examine your actual results and recent trends in the context of your marketing activities, previous results and overall industry results. Use internal and external audits to identify and analyse changes that may have affected your progress. Internally, you might find staffing shortages, budget cuts or operational difficulties contributed to worse-than-expected results. Externally, you might find that better-than-expected results were due, in part, to a competitor's troubles or reduced unemployment in targeted markets. Look upstream and downstream in the value chain: on the supply side, production may depend on just-in-time deliveries; on the demand side, sales may depend on demand for certain consumer products. Also look for answers by researching customer behaviour, perceptions, attitudes and relationships.

Actions based on marketing control

Depending on your interim results, you can take one of five actions. If measurements show no deviations, you can continue implementation as planned, unless you see changes in the marketing environment that might affect future performance. Even then, you may continue with your current marketing plan while you watch for a definite trend to develop. If interim results are much better than expected, you can use your diagnosis to maintain these outstanding results and enhance the implementation of other programmes.

If your actual results are much worse than expected, you can take corrective action by (1) adjusting marketing programmes, schedules or budgets, (2) adjusting the standards or measurement intervals for your metrics, or (3) changing the assumptions factored into your marketing plan, such as the prevailing economic climate or increased price competition. In turn, changing a key assumption may cause you to change your objectives or other aspects of the marketing plan (see Table 12.1).

Levels of marketing control

During plan implementation, you can apply marketing control at a number of different levels, as your organisation chooses. These levels include the following:

- *Business unit*. Is the marketing plan of a particular business unit achieving interim results as expected? How do these results compare with the results of the company's other units and with the industry in general?

Table 12.1   Responding to the diagnosis of interim results

Action	Description
Continue with implementation	Leave programmes, timing, budgets, responsibilities, metrics and measurement intervals as planned
Maintain outstanding results and enhance implementation	Use the diagnosis to find ways of sustaining superior results and enhancing the implementation of other programmes
Adjust implementation to solve a problem	Change marketing programmes, timing, budgets and/or responsibilities as suggested by diagnosis of deviation
Adjust standards or measurement intervals	Switch metrics or make other changes that will allow more accurate or timely identification of potential problems
Adjust marketing plan assumptions	Change relevant assumptions on which strategies and programmes are based to fine-tune planning and implementation

- *Marketing-mix activities.* Are the planned product, channel, pricing and communications activities achieving the desired results? Is each product meeting sales targets and other interim standards? Are sales through each channel (and channel member) up to expectations? Are advertising campaigns achieving their awareness and response objectives? Are price changes stimulating sales to the desired degree?

- *Programme.* How is each programme performing relative to the standards for interim results? Which programmes are yielding better results and which are yielding disappointing results?

- *Product or line.* Are individual products (or the entire line) meeting standards for interim progress towards objectives? Are the products or lines moving towards market share targets?

- *Segment.* What are the interim results for each customer segment being targeted?

- *Geography.* What do interim results look like for each branch or region? What area-specific elements could cause deviations in certain branches or regions?

- *Manager.* For accountability, what is the status of each manager's results compared with agreed-upon standards?

- *Brand.* Is each brand performing up to the preset standards, in financial and marketing terms? How do interim results compare with those of other brands in the portfolio and with those of competing brands?

Organisations usually apply marketing control at multiple levels, both macro and micro. Also, measurement intervals are changing now that speeding products to market has become a priority for competitive reasons. Field marketing firms often send representatives out with tablet computers, with the idea that every customer contact or store visit will be logged and tallied in real time. This gives managers immediate access to updated results so they can identify any anomalies and take action within hours if needed.[4]

Marketers also look at what competitors are doing and, if necessary, change the timing of programmes or make other changes to capture customer attention when rivals are running major campaigns. Not long ago, for example, Tesco increased the number of in-store promotions and used deeper discounts to maintain visibility when Sainsbury's, Asda, Morrisons and Waitrose were all advertising numerous promotional product deals.[5]

Consumer packaged-goods marketers such as Unilever look closely at the business unit, region, channel, product line and brand levels. 'Fast fashion' marketers such as Sweden's Hennes & Mauritz (H&M, www.hm.com/gb) give special emphasis to marketing control at the product and store level.

MARKETING IN PRACTICE: FAST FASHION

Fast fashion depends on identifying sales trends early and on quickly making and shipping more of the best-selling styles. H&M constantly monitors sales performance in its 2,600 clothing stores, replenishing stocks of popular items within a few days. H&M also operates home furnishings stores with fast-changing product assortments, unusual for that industry – which requires careful monitoring of sales to plan for timely resupply.

Zara, based in Spain, places advance orders for about half of a season's merchandise and delays ordering more until seasonal marketing is underway. Then the retailer examines each store's daily sales, listens to what stores say customers like and don't like, and tells its in-house factories exactly what to produce and in what quantities. Because the measurement interval is in days, Zara can supply up-to-the-minute styles in as little as 14 days.

Marketers for George, the fashion brand owned by the UK retailer Asda, are revamping their supply chain to reduce the amount of time needed to source clothing from suppliers. In the past, they had to place orders three or four months in advance. Today, they can respond to trends and deviations from plan performance by having new or additional products in stock within 6 weeks. Soon, response time will be down to 4 weeks, boosting George's image as a member of the fast fashion movement.[6]

Marketing plan analysis: Zara doesn't order all of its merchandise in advance. What are the implications for Zara's sales forecasting and for the possibility of markdowns?

Don't depend on only one or two levels of control; if you do, you'll get an incomplete or distorted picture of interim results and might therefore take action inappropriately. Remember, forecasts and schedules are targets; your actual results may be slightly higher or lower at each measurement interval as you move towards achieving full-year performance. When applying marketing control, you want to act soon enough to make a difference in the final outcome of your marketing plan without overreacting.

Types of marketing control

To determine the overall effectiveness of your marketing plan at its conclusion and to gauge progress while it is being implemented, you will use annual, financial, productivity and strategic control, applied at the various levels you have chosen. Table 12.2 summarises these four types of marketing control, which are discussed in more detail in the following sections.

Annual control

Annual control allows you to evaluate the current marketing plan's performance in preparation for developing next year's marketing plan. This provides an important check of what your plan has achieved and where improvements can be made, feeding back to the environmental scanning and analysis for next year. Start with a broad overview of the plan's performance. How do the full-year results match up with the primary marketing, financial and societal objectives such as increasing sales and profits, strengthening customer loyalty or improving corporate image?

Looking at performance measured by a few vital objectives can suggest strengths and weaknesses to be further investigated through internal analysis. Now look at whether other marketing plan objectives were achieved, and by what margin. Using these targets, was full-year performance below expectations, at the expected level or above expectations? At the micro level, how did each programme and marketing activity perform relative to its objectives? What can you learn from the pattern of interim progress measurements throughout the year that will help in next year's forecasting and implementation? Can line managers and others responsible for implementation and customer contact offer

Table 12.2 Annual, financial, productivity and strategic control

Annual control	Financial control
• Evaluate full-year and interim marketing plan performance • Identify ineffective or unsuitable programmes and activities • Identify ineffective or mishandled implementation	• Use financial measures to assess performance • Compare actual financial results with metrics, budgets and forecasts • Analyse profit and cost results at multiple control levels
Productivity control	**Strategic control**
• Evaluate the efficiency of marketing planning, processes and activities • Assess productivity due to higher output or lower costs • Gauge ability to transfer marketing learning and tactics	• Evaluate performance in managing the marketing function • Evaluate performance in managing key relationships • Evaluate marketing performance with regards to social responsibility and ethics

constructive feedback about the programmes, objectives, activities or anything else connected with the marketing plan?

A particular challenge is distinguishing ineffective or unsuitable programmes and activities from ineffective or mishandled implementation so you can make changes during the next planning cycle. Did a programme fail to meet objectives because its planning was flawed or because its implementation was flawed? How do the current conditions differ from those previous situations, and what conclusions can you draw? At worst, annual control will reveal poor marketing performance and the need to address bad planning or bad implementation. At best, it will indicate superior marketing performance and confirm the soundness of the plan or the implementation – or identify an unintended result brought about by the organisation's marketing.

Financial control

Businesses and non-profit organisations alike apply **financial control** to evaluate the marketing plan's interim and overall performance according to key financial measures such as sales (or contributions), profits, gross and net margin, costs and return on investment. Interim measurements show progress towards full-year objectives; full-year financial results clarify the big picture of marketing performance. You can compare actual expenditures with planned budgets, actual sales and costs with forecasts, and profit objectives with profit results at multiple levels (by product, market, segment, channel and so forth).

Productivity control

The purpose of **productivity control** is to evaluate the marketing plan's performance relative to the efficiency of key marketing processes and activities. Whereas financial control is concerned with financial measures of performance, productivity control focuses on improvements to processes and activities that either decrease costs or increase output. Different organisations apply productivity control in different ways (and at different intervals). Some common business examples include the following:

- *Overall plan productivity*. Has the current plan yielded better results with smaller-than-usual marketing budgets? Has the current plan maintained expected results without budget increases? Have implementation costs increased without corresponding increases in marketing results?

- *Communications productivity*. Without higher budgets, are advertising reach and brand/product awareness increasing over time? With lower budgets, are reach and brand/product awareness levels sustained? Which sales promotions yield the best response for the investment? If your current plan has a different combination of communications and influence programmes than in previous years, are you achieving more efficiency and effectiveness?

- *Sales force productivity*. Is the sales force contacting more prospects and making more sales without higher budgets? With lower budgets, is the sales force maintaining productivity on the same measures? Which sales people and territories are the most productive?

- *Product and development productivity.* Are more new products being generated on a stable development budget? Are more new products moving from the concept stage to commercialisation, resulting in higher sales and profit potential? Are some products more productive (yielding higher profitability relative to their costs) than others? Should some products be dropped because they are less productive?

- *Channel productivity.* Are some channels more important for long-term sales and profit productivity? Do some channels require disproportionately high investment for the level of return? Can results be maintained with lower channel costs?

- *Price productivity.* Did a price promotion stimulate revenues to offset the lower profit margin? Did a reduced price stimulate sufficient sales to bring a product to the break-even point earlier than planned? Did a price increase yield higher total profit despite lower unit sales?

- *Segment and customer productivity.* Are the marketing costs for some segments or customers too high relative to the payback? Which yield the best returns on investment? Should some be dropped because they are relatively unproductive in generating returns? Are you able to reach your targeted segments as planned? What marketing changes would allow you to target more efficiently and effectively?

Strategic control

Strategic control is used to evaluate marketing's performance in managing strategic areas such as the marketing function itself, key relationships, social responsibility and ethics. Applied annually or semi-annually, generally by marketing management and top executives, strategic control shows whether marketing is doing its job, whether the organisation is forging relationships with publics that are important, and whether social responsibility and ethics objectives are being achieved. The purpose is to assess strengths and weaknesses in these areas, identify where improvement is needed and build on success when developing marketing plans.

To assess the marketing function's performance, your organisation can conduct a **marketing audit**, a formal, detailed study of the planning process, plan implementation, personnel skills, use of resources and responsiveness. As part of the marketing audit, management should look at the skills and motivation of marketing personnel. Also consider a *brand audit* for each brand in your portfolio to determine whether your planning and implementation are having the desired effect on awareness, image, preference and loyalty.

Customer relationships are at the heart of any company's success, which is why strategic control should evaluate marketing performance in acquiring and retaining new customers, building loyalty, increasing satisfaction and supporting positive perceptions. Recently, Shell introduced attendants to pump petrol at hundreds of UK stations, aiming to differentiate its brand from self-service competitors and to reinforce customer loyalty. The company will be watching results carefully to determine whether this marketing initiative is having a positive effect on customer relationships.[7]

Finally, use strategic control to assess marketing's performance with regard to social responsibility and ethics. Is marketing effectively conveying the organisation's involvement in socially responsible causes or green initiatives? Are societal objectives being set and achieved? Are marketing decisions being made and implemented in an ethical manner? What else can marketing do to demonstrate that the firm is transparent, socially responsible and committed to strict ethical standards? Many marketers, including FedEx (www.fedex.com), make public the results of their social responsibility audits.

MARKETING IN PRACTICE: FEDEX

Every day, FedEx puts 9 million packages on a lorry, aeroplane or van for delivery to businesses and consumers worldwide. Since its first day of operation in 1971, the Tennessee-based company has expanded steadily and now operates in more than 200 countries. In addition to traditional marketing activities such as adverts and social media posts on YouTube, Facebook and Twitter, the company polishes its image as a good corporate citizen by publicising goals and results in the areas of sustainability, philanthropy and community involvement. This adds to FedEx's positive reputation and helps it compete with UPS and other rivals.

For example, FedEx announced in 2008 that by 2020, it would improve fuel efficiency and reduce emissions intensity by 20 percent. Because the company maintains a massive fleet of 90,000 vehicles plus 660 aircraft, these long-term targets can make a real difference in cutting pollution and conserving natural resources. Every year, FedEx details the steps it has taken towards these goals, such as its purchases of all-electric vehicles, hybrid-electric vehicles and other alternative fuel vehicles. The yearly reports also analyse interim progress towards goals. For instance, replacing old jets with new jets allowed FedEx to slash emissions more quickly than expected. Rather than accelerate its schedule, it raised its goal for reducing emissions by 2020. Such initiatives differentiate FedEx as a company that cares about the environment – but they also have a financial payback line. Higher fuel efficiency means lower fuel costs; less waste and more recycling means money saved.

FedEx is active in humanitarian efforts, delivering food, medicines and other supplies to areas devastated by earthquakes, hurricanes, tsunamis and other disasters. Thousands of employees do volunteer work for charities in the communities where FedEx does business. Finally, FedEx has found ways to adapt some internal sustainability programmes for consumer education. In connection with its recent Eco-drive campaign in the Philippines, the company posted a video on Facebook to share the safety and fuel-efficiency techniques that FedEx teaches its drivers.[8]

Marketing plan analysis: Why would FedEx provide so much detail about its vehicles and jets when reporting on sustainability results?

Use Checklist No. 20 as a guide to assessing the implementation of your marketing plan.

ESSENTIAL CHECKLIST NO. 20:
EVALUATING IMPLEMENTATION

When you plan for implementation, you must be ready to identify potential problems and make changes quickly if actual results vary from expected results. Also you must be prepared to gather data so you can evaluate how well the organisation did in implementing the marketing plan. These questions will start you off in the right direction when you look back on your planning and implementation activities.

☐ Were the appropriate personnel (internal and external) involved in planning and implementation?

☐ Were suitable metrics and measurement intervals selected for measuring progress towards achieving the plan's financial, marketing and societal objectives?

☐ Were marketing plan decisions made after investigating multiple options to address each opportunity, threat and competitive situation?

☐ Were marketing metrics, forecasts, schedules, budgets and implementation responsibilities clearly delineated and realistic, coordinated properly and communicated effectively?

☐ Were marketing resources, internal activities and value chain activities properly coordinated and managed during implementation?

☐ How did marketing personnel deal with interim results that deviated from standards?

☐ How can marketing planning and implementation be improved in the future?

CONTINGENCY PLANS AND SCENARIO PLANNING

You may need a **contingency plan** to be implemented in response to or anticipation of significant changes in the marketing situation that could disrupt important marketing activities. Look at your forecasts, schedules and budgets representing the most pessimistic and the most optimistic scenarios that could occur during the planning period, identify the worst-case scenarios that could be most damaging to your ability to achieve marketing plan objectives, then create plans for coping with those scenarios. Table 12.3 presents the main components of contingency planning for marketing. Note that top management may incorporate marketing contingency plans into a comprehensive organisation-wide contingency plan.

Some contingency plans deal with specific issues, while others deal with broader concerns. The decision about what to plan for depends, in part, on previous experience and on broader trends in the internal and external environments.

Table 12.3	Contingency planning for marketing
Planning action	**Purpose**
Identify emergency situations and analyse their potential consequences for marketing	To understand the marketing activities, people and operations most likely to be disrupted by each possible emergency
Consider how emergencies might affect the organisation's suppliers, wholesalers and retailers	To prepare for the possibility of disruptions due to emergency situations elsewhere in the value chain
List advance preparations that can be made to minimise disruptions and restore normality	To have materials and procedures ready in the event of an emergency
Establish warning signs of impending crises	To help recognise when an emergency is developing and provide triggers for contingency plan implementation
Assign specific actions, responsibilities and priorities for containment and customer service	To prevent the crisis from becoming more severe by organising and coordinating an effective initial response to contain the problem and continue serving customers
Create a contingency communication plan	To keep internal and external publics informed about the situation, the response and future steps
Resolve the crisis and analyse outcomes of the contingency plan	To improve the contingency planning process by eliminating ineffective actions and learning from experience for better advance preparation

MARKETING IN PRACTICE: CONTINGENCY PLANNING

Contingency plans are valuable for coping with major challenges and large-scale emergencies brought on by uncontrollable external factors such as natural disasters, epidemics, terrorism, sabotage, computer system failures, transport cuts, extreme economic conditions, unusual competitive pressures or the sudden withdrawal of a key supplier or customer. Less severe emergencies may disrupt (but not cripple) internal or external marketing activities – for an unknown period. However, a prolonged crisis may physically threaten employees, customers or suppliers, damage facilities or equipment, destroy products and supplies, and shut down channels.

During the European debt crisis, Diageo and PricewaterhouseCoopers were among the many businesses that created contingency plans to deal with the possibility that one or more countries might not retain the euro as their currency. Technology is so vital to business operations that many firms have contingency plans for outages and other problems. GoDaddy, which hosts websites, created a contingency plan in case of a significant disruption in mobile communications. Some companies create contingency plans to handle seasonal weather disruptions. The Rosewood Tucker's Point resort in Bermuda reviews and updates its contingency plans every summer, to prepare for the autumn hurricane season. Once a hurricane is forecast, the resort's managers meet every day before the storm arrives to implement the plan for rebooking guests, preventing property damage and changing marketing as needed.[9]

Marketing plan analysis: Identify two best-case scenarios for which a marketer might need a contingency.

Contingency plans may also be the outcome of a sophisticated scenario-planning process in which managers develop detailed descriptions of future situations to anticipate and plan for major shifts in external forces, industry trends, technological developments and organisational resources.[10] With **scenario planning**, marketers look beyond historical trends and short-term projections to envision broad, long-term changes in the marketing environment that could affect future performance, then prepare contingency plans for these possible situations. The purpose is to have plans ready for implementation so your organisation can adjust its activities if and when these scenarios become realities.[11] The Danish toy manufacturer Lego formulates a number of contingency plans for marketing so no matter what direction the economy moves in, the company is ready to take action. Its senior managers meet monthly to re-evaluate external conditions and discuss the situations they are most likely to face in the coming months. As a result, Lego has been able to increase sales despite global recession and mounting competition.[12]

MasterCard has an international team travelling the world to research different scenarios for growth by seeking input from the credit-card company's workforce. Using internal communications such as webcasts, the team then presents a range of scenarios to inform and inspire all employees in preparation for the different paths that the firm's future marketing initiatives might follow. Estée Lauder, which markets cosmetics, uses scenario planning to plan for rapid changes in global economic conditions and consumer demand. When considering worst-case scenarios, the chief executive asks brand managers: 'What must you have? What would you like to keep going? And what can you give up?'[13]

Be sure to examine multiple links in your organisation's value chain to pinpoint and plan for potential problems.[14] If possible, conduct a simple SWOT analysis of the key partners in your value chain to understand where they stand. Ideally, you and your suppliers and distributors should work together to develop contingency plans for situations such as the following:

- *Supply challenges*, such as insufficient or unpredictable availability of raw materials and parts

- *Transportation challenges*, such as a strike or severe weather disrupting deliveries

- *Financial challenges*, such as a reduction in credit availability

- *Personnel challenges*, such as difficulty in recruiting or retaining skilled staff

- *Communications challenges*, such as interruption of postal or telecommunications services

- *Market-by-market challenges*, such as logistical difficulties or opportunities in particular locations.

CHAPTER SUMMARY

The process of marketing control consists of (1) setting standards and measurement intervals to gauge progress towards marketing objectives, (2) measuring interim results after implementation, (3) comparing measured results with standards, (4) diagnosing any deviations and (5) taking action as needed. The purpose is to pinpoint where results are below or above expectations, understand why, and decide whether to leave the programmes and implementation unchanged, make changes to solve problems, or apply lessons learned to improve progress towards standards and, ultimately, objectives. The decisions made at the end of the process feed back to the beginning, providing feedback for changing standards, measurement intervals or even objectives.

Annual plan control is used to evaluate the current marketing plan's performance in preparation for developing next year's marketing plan. Financial control is used to evaluate the marketing plan's performance according to key financial measures such as sales and profits. Productivity control is used to evaluate the marketing plan's performance relative to the efficiency of key marketing processes and activities. Strategic control evaluates effectiveness in managing strategic areas such as the marketing function and social responsibility/ethics. Formulate contingency plans in advance to be ready to respond to potentially disruptive changes in the organisation's situation. Use scenario planning to look beyond historical trends and short-term projections and envision broad, long-term changes in the marketing environment that could significantly alter future performance.

CASE STUDY: MARKS & SPENCER

With £10 billion in annual turnover and 1,000 high-street stores spread across the UK and Europe, Marks & Spencer (M&S, www.marksandspencer.com) is well known for its clothing, home fashions and fine foods. Marketers for M&S set revenue and profit targets for one year and multiple years, then create marketing plans for the overall company, for UK and international stores, for individual products and departments and for each channel. Among the key performance indicators (KPIs) they use to evaluate marketing performance are average weekly footfall, UK market share in food products, UK market share in clothing products, growth in store space year by year, and 'mystery shopper' scores month by month.

Although the company's marketing plan targets better performance in all these KPIs, actual results don't always measure up. During the recent recession, M&S marketers developed a multiyear plan for boosting UK turnover, opening new stores and expanding multichannel marketing. By 2012, however, the UK economy was still struggling, and the company's actual sales performance was at the low end of planned levels. Diagnosing the results, M&S's executives understood that bad weather and higher petrol prices were contributing factors – and they noted that other retailers were also seeing lower footfall levels. Further analysis by product line showed that M&S had increased sales of menswear and children's clothing but it had missed sales opportunities by not ordering enough merchandise to meet seasonal demand for women's knitwear. M&S therefore lowered its sales targets, even as it invested in e-commerce initiatives, launched hundreds of new products and created new programmes to re-engage shoppers.

In addition to pursuing marketing and financial goals, M&S has set a long-term goal of becoming the world's most sustainable retailer. It introduced its Plan A sustainability strategy in 2007 and has since added new long-term targets for reducing carbon emissions and waste, using sustainable materials in its products and improving animal welfare, among other goals. Every year, M&S publicly announces its progress towards these targets and explains the corrective action it will take if actual performance doesn't match planned results.

When the company released its five-year sustainability report, for example, it highlighted its achievement of more than 100 targets, including becoming 100 percent carbon neutral and recycling 100 percent of its waste. However, M&S fell short of reaching its planned sales levels for organic foods and beverages. In addition, only 84 percent of the wood used in its wooden products was from certified sustainable sources, falling short of the 100 percent target. The company is searching for additional sources of sustainable timber so it can reach its goal. It's also looking for additional suppliers of sustainable and Fairtrade cotton so it can meet a goal of buying 50 percent of its cotton from sustainable sources. Ultimately, Plan A will help the planet and help M&S cut costs and conserve natural resources.[15]

Case questions

1. Marks & Spencer has had difficulty in finding sufficient quantities of sustainable timber and cotton to meet its goals. Should the company reduce its goals? Explain your answer.

2. What contingency plan would you recommend that Marks & Spencer consider if average weekly footfall levels remain low over an extended period?

APPLY YOUR KNOWLEDGE

Review your research and responses for the 'Apply your knowledge' exercises in **Chapters 5 and 11**. Now answer the following questions about your chosen company's marketing control. Prepare a brief written or oral report summarising your ideas.

- What revenue and profit results has this company announced in recent months? How does this performance compare with the company's forecasts and/or budgets?

- If the company's actual financial performance is different from the planned results, what corrective actions have been taken?

- Did this company recently report changes related to marketing relationships, such as market share? How do these compare with the expected performance? What marketing control steps, if any, do you think this company should take right now – and why?

- Based on what you know of this company, identify one issue that could interfere with achieving marketing plan objectives and explain how you would address this in a contingency plan.

- Is the company reporting its interim results on goals for social responsibility? What suggestions can you make for improving communication with stakeholders?

BUILD YOUR OWN MARKETING PLAN

Finalise your marketing plan by selecting the levels at which you will apply marketing control and the types of marketing control you will need to prepare for. How often will you measure results and what standards are most important for monitoring interim progress? How would you diagnose a situation in which actual expenditures exceeded budgeted costs? What corrective action might you take if actual unit sales for an important channel fell below your forecast? Should you reconsider your measurement intervals or standards if actual performance deviates significantly from your plan? Is it important to apply marketing control by segment, geography, manager and/or brand? What areas will require strategic and productivity control? What worst-case scenario might require contingency planning? Document your thoughts in a written marketing plan.

ENDNOTES

1. Matthew Boyle, 'Unilever hits record after sales growth tops expectations', *Bloomberg News*, 23 January 2013, www.businessweek.com; 'How Unilever found the balance between creativity and sales', *Advertising Age*, 9 September 2012, www.adage.com; Szu Ping Chan, 'Unilever sees "return to poverty" in Europe', *Telegraph (UK)*, 27 August 2012, www.telegraph.co.uk; Rosie Baker, 'Unilever introduces cross-discipline brand approach', *MarketingWeek*, 26 June 2012, www.marketingweek.co.uk; Joel Makower, 'Why Unilever is betting on open innovation for sustainability', *Green Biz*, 29 March 2012, www.greenbiz.com; Dean Best, 'Comment: Unilever continues pruning food business', *Just Food*, 31 July 2012, n.p.; www.unilever.com.

2. 'Earning customers' lifetime loyalty', *Balanced Scorecard Report*, March–April 2009, n.p.

3. 'Journey to peak performance', *Convenience Store News*, 1 August 2012, n.p.

4. 'The world at their fingertips', *Marketing*, 15 August 2012, p. 37.

5. Elinor Zuke, 'Tesco plays catch-up with a dramatic promotional push', *Grocer*, 19 May 2012, p. 19.

6. Petah Marian, 'George dials up fashion credentials with shorter lead times', *Just Style*, 11 May 2012, n.p.; Adrianne Pasquarelli, 'Fashion gets fast', *Crain's New York Business*, 14 May 2012, p. 1; Seth Stevenson, 'Zara gets fresh styles to stores insanely fast. How do they do it?', *Slate*, 21 June 2012, www.slate.com; Warren Shoulberg, 'H&M fast forwarding into home', *Home Textiles Today*, 13 February 2012, p. 1.

7. Guy Chazan, 'All hands to the pump for Shell', *Financial Times*, 11 July 2012, www.ft.com; David Gerrie, 'Fill her up, please', *Daily Mail*, 26 May 2012, www.dailymail.co.uk.

8. 'FedEx earns $10 for every $1 spent on recyclables', *Waste & Recycling News*, 11 September 2012, www.wasterecyclingnews.com; Bart King, 'CSR Roundup: FedEx raises bar for aircraft emissions', *Sustainable Brands*, 21 August 2012, www.sustainablebrands.com; 'FedEx Express bares eco-drive campaign', *BusinessWorld (Philippines)*, 2 April 2012, n.p.; www.fedex.com.

9. Nelson D. Schwartz, 'US companies brace for an exit from the euro by Greece', *New York Times*, 2 September 2012, www.nytimes.com; 'Diageo to trim spending in Greece', *Globe & Mail (Toronto)*, 15 May 2012, p. B9; Scott Moritz and Olga Kharif, 'RIM customers working on contingency plans', *Bloomberg Businessweek*, 9 July 2012, www.businessweek.com; Elizabeth Roberts, 'Hotels and businesses prepare for storm', *Royal Gazette Online (Bermuda)*, 6 September 2012, www.royalgazette.com.

10. See Babette E. Bensoussan and Craig Fleisher, *Analysis Without Paralysis: 10 Tools to Make Better Strategic Decisions* (Upper Saddle River, NJ: FT Press, 2008), Chapter 9.

11. 'An interview with Peter Schwartz', *Economic Times*, 16 May 2009, n.p.; Larry Lapide, 'Scenario

planning for a successful future', *Supply Chain Management Review*, October 2008, p. 8.

12. 'Managing in the fog', *The Economist*, 28 February 2009, p. 67.

13. Quoted in Matthew Boyle, 'The budget knives come out', *BusinessWeek*, 13 October 2008, p. 30; also: Reena Jana and Damian Joseph, 'Keeping employees creative in a downturn', *BusinessWeek*, 23 July 2009, www.businessweek.com.

14. Robert Handfield, 'United they'll stand', *Wall Street Journal*, 23 March 2009, p. R6.

15. Zoe Wood, 'Marks & Spencer customer poll suggests better times ahead', *Guardian*, 28 August 2012, www.guardian.co.uk; Harry Wallop, 'Women turning off Marks & Spencer fashion', *Telegraph (UK)*, 7 July 2012, www.telegraph.co.uk; Harry Wallop and Graham Ruddick, 'UK retail sales falter as Marks & Spencer misses targets', *Telegraph (UK)*, 19 May 2012, www.telegraph.co.uk; 'Marks and Spencer in first profit fall in three years', *BBC News*, 22 May 2012, www.bbc.co.uk; Rebecca Smithers, 'M&S becomes "carbon neutral"', *Guardian*, 6 June 2012, www.guardian.co.uk; www.marksandspencer.com.

Appendix
Sample marketing plan:
Lost Legends Luxury Chocolatier

The fictitious company Lost Legends Luxury Chocolatier is planning to market premium gourmet chocolates to adults in the United Kingdom and, later, in Western Europe. These markets have high per capita consumption of and spending on chocolates, and demand continues to be strong whether economic conditions are improving or deteriorating.

As this sample plan indicates, many confectionery companies target the children's chocolate sweets market. However, fewer firms are active in the adult segment and fewer still are active in upmarket chocolates. Also, our gourmet range will tap rising demand for dark chocolate products, which is forecast to grow more quickly than overall chocolate demand during this decade.

The sample plan illustrates the marketing steps that Lost Legends Luxury Chocolatier will take to launch its first products and compete with established confectionery companies. Notice how the contents, order of topics and section headings are tailored to fit the company's situation. Also notice that details (such as product-by-product pricing, detailed programme schedules and detailed budgets) are not in the main body of this sample plan, although they would be available in the appendix of an actual plan for readers who want more specifics.

EXECUTIVE SUMMARY

Lost Legends Luxury Chocolatier is a new company planning to market premium gourmet chocolates to UK adults and, later, to adults in Western Europe. In monetary terms, this market is smaller than the children's chocolate sweets market. However, confectioners offering gourmet, premium-priced chocolates under well-regarded brands can potentially earn higher profit margins by targeting specific market segments. We will target three consumer segments and three business segments at the high end of the gift, holiday and affordable personal luxury market, enhancing our positioning with superior-quality Fairtrade Marked cocoa. Our Belgian Legends product line will be introduced in September to allow time for building brand awareness and product trial prior to the Christmas period, when our seasonal Limited Edition Legends line will be featured.

Our four main financial objectives relate to first-year turnover in the UK market, a minimum level of sales for each retail outlet, achieving break-even within 16 months and aiming for 10 percent gross profit margin by the end of the second year. Our four main marketing objectives relate to first-year brand awareness among consumers and businesses, arranging for retail distribution, launching the e-commerce website and planning for new products to be introduced in the second year. Our two main societal objectives relate to supporting sustainability in a transparent manner and using recycled materials in product packaging.

Key strengths are our family recipes, patented roasting process, cost-effective hand production and glamorous history. Weaknesses include lack of brand awareness and image, limited resources and lack of channel relationships. Our marketing plan will address three major opportunities: higher demand for premium chocolates, especially dark chocolates, growing interest in treats with mystique, and growing interest in socially responsible products. The main threats we must counter are intense competition, market fragmentation and uncertain supply prices.

CURRENT MARKETING SITUATION

The company was founded by the British descendants of a nineteenth-century Bruges chocolate maker who was famous for his unusually dark and intensely flavoured chocolates. In this pre-automation era, he mixed small batches using the finest ingredients, kneaded and tempered the chocolate to achieve a smooth, refined texture and poured his confections into hand-made moulds one at a time. Dozens of his recipes were handed down from generation to generation as the family moved from Bruges to the London area, but the chocolates were never produced commercially until now. After experimenting with roasting cocoa beans and updating the recipes as they prepared for a St Valentine's Day party, two entrepreneurial family members were inspired to patent the roasting process and launch a new business. The name 'Lost Legends Luxury Chocolatier' was chosen because it captured the romance of dark, rich Belgian chocolates made in the old-fashioned way from treasured recipes.

Europe has a long tradition of chocolate making, from leading brands such as Barry Callebaut, Lindt, Nestlé, Cadbury, Perugina and Lenôtre to locally owned and operated gourmet chocolatiers. The top brands enjoy high awareness and high customer loyalty. Upmarket stores such as Harrods and Fortnum & Mason also sell private-label branded chocolates as well as domestic and imported upmarket brands, which adds to the competitive pressure. Nonetheless, a number of smaller companies are successfully targeting specific niches within the adult chocolate market by offering hand-made chocolates, exotically flavoured chocolates, Fairtrade chocolates, all-natural chocolates, lower-fat chocolates, holiday chocolates and gift chocolates. In fact, Fairtrade chocolates have gone mainstream now that Cadbury Dairy Milk, the UK's best-selling chocolate bar, is made with certified Fairtrade cocoa.

In this environment, Lost Legends Luxury Chocolatier will compete at the higher end of the gift, holiday and affordable personal luxury market. Our positioning is based on the hand-made, top-quality nature of our premium chocolates made from the finest, freshest, all-natural ingredients, our distinctive product and package differentiation, our exclusive brand image, carefully controlled production output, and highly selective distribution. Much of our marketing focus will be on our use of Fairtrade Marked cocoa, a programme ensuring that growers receive a fair price for their cocoa. By actively promoting socially responsible sourcing of top-quality cocoa (and other ingredients), we can encourage positive associations with our brand and products. We can also support the mystique aspect of our positioning by using only cocoa grown on a specific plantation renowned for the distinctive quality of the beans it produces.

MARKET SUMMARY

Worldwide annual sales of chocolate and chocolate products exceed £50 billion. Although North and South America are the largest global markets in terms of chocolate sales, sales in Europe have been slowly increasing. UK sales of chocolate exceed £4.3 billion annually and annual per capita UK consumption is estimated at 10 kg. By comparison, estimated annual per capita consumption of chocolate in Germany is 8 kg, in France 6 kg, in Spain 3 kg and in Italy 2 kg.

Five-year forecasts suggest that UK sales of all chocolates will increase by about 2 percent per year, while sales of dark chocolates will increase by 10 percent per year. Eastern Europe is expected to experience rapid growth in chocolate consumption, so we will explore opportunities there after establishing our brand and building sales in our UK home market and then in Western Europe. Fairtrade chocolate has become increasingly popular over the past 15 years, another key trend in our favour.

Looking at customer buying patterns, chocolate sales are subject to seasonality. Sales increase markedly before holiday periods such as Easter, Christmas and St Valentine's Day. Chocolate is not only a seasonal treat: one survey shows that more than half of UK consumers buy chocolate year-round without a special occasion in mind. However, sales can drop in extremely hot weather because (1) stores must keep chocolate products chilled, which reduces the opportunity for impulse purchases, and (2) customers tend to buy sweets that are less perishable and retain their quality. We plan to introduce our first products in September, building awareness and word of mouth so we can attract buyers during the critical year-end holiday period.

Consumer market

The three consumer market segments targeted by Lost Legends Luxury Chocolatier are middle- to high-income adults who (1) like (or want) to reward themselves or their families with the affordable luxury of gourmet chocolates, (2) view upmarket chocolates as a suitable gift, and (3) buy fine chocolates as a tradition for St Valentine's Day, Christmas, Easter or another holiday.

According to research, women account for the majority of purchases in this segment, and they are increasingly interested in product and packaging as expressions of pampering and personality. Although they are aware of prices, they are also loyal to their upmarket chocolate favourites. Not surprisingly, the affluent adults in our targeted segments have sophisticated tastes, high expectations and demanding standards.

We will give buyers of premium chocolate another reason to feel good about Lost Legends Luxury Chocolatier: they will be buying a brand that is socially responsible as well as top quality, an uncommon benefit combination among upmarket brands. Even before Cadbury Dairy Milk was made of Fairtrade cocoa, more than 40 percent of UK consumers had tried Fairtrade chocolates. Sales of chocolate products containing Fairtrade cocoa have increased much more rapidly than those of other Fairtrade products. This trend indicates an interest in the social responsibility aspect of chocolate products, which we will satisfy through our product and our transparency concerning ethical sourcing.

As shown in Table A.1, we plan to provide features that deliver valued benefits for the different needs of these targeted consumer segments.

Table A.1 Targeted consumer segments

Targeted segment	Characteristics and needs	Feature/benefit
Adults with middle to high income levels who buy fine chocolates for themselves or their families	• Prefer the cachet of luxury brands • Like small indulgences • Willing to splurge for themselves or loved ones • Appreciate the taste and quality of premium chocolates	• Customers can select the type and quantity of chocolates to accommodate tastes and budget • Premium brand image enhances perception of chocolates as a special treat • Fairtrade Marked cocoa balances self-indulgence with social responsibility
Adults, primarily women, with middle to high income levels who buy fine chocolates for gifts	• Seek a gift that reflects personality of giver or recipient • Seek a gift with high perceived value • Seek a gift to delight the senses • Seek a gift that is unique yet not excessively extravagant • Seek a gift with emotional associations • Seek a gift that is socially responsible	• Distinctive yet sustainable gift packaging adds to visual appeal, personality and perceived value • Top-quality, limited edition chocolates make our products unique and uncommon • Fairtrade Marked cocoa balances gift status with sense of social responsibility
Adults with middle to high income levels who buy fine chocolates for holidays	• View holidays as occasions to enjoy special treats • Have or want to create a tradition of enjoying special chocolates on certain holidays	• Seasonal/holiday packaging adds to our product's appeal for special occasions • Limited-edition range reinforces exclusivity • Fairtrade Marked cocoa combines holiday tradition with social responsibility

Business market

The business market segments targeted by Lost Legends Luxury Chocolatier consist of professionals and business people who select or give gifts (1) to clients and other business contacts, (2) to colleagues or managers on holiday occasions, and/or (3) customised by product, packaging or business logo. These segments represent a significant opportunity to build repeat purchasing and loyalty among businesses that require unique corporate gifts with wide appeal for various occasions. Many small chocolate shops accept or invite customised orders, but Lost Legends Luxury Chocolatier will aggressively target this segment and seek to build longer-term customer relationships spanning gift-giving occasions.

Table A.2 summarises the features and benefits we can deliver to satisfy the needs of these targeted segments of the business market.

Table A.2 Targeted business segments

Targeted segment	Characteristics and needs	Feature/benefit
Professionals and executives who give gifts to clients and other business contacts, or who are responsible for selecting such gifts on the firm's behalf	• Want a gift with high perceived status and value • May influence selection but not actually purchase gifts • May give gifts but not actually make the purchase • May make the purchase but not actually give the gift	• Purchasers can select the type and quantity of chocolates to accommodate budget and occasion • Premium brand image enhances perception of chocolates as a gift • Fairtrade Marked cocoa balances luxury with social responsibility
Professionals and business people who give gifts to colleagues or managers at holiday times	• Seek a gift with high perceived value • Seek a gift that is recognised as unique and exclusive • Seek a gift that is socially responsible	• Distinctive yet sustainable gift packaging adds to visual appeal and perceived value • Top-quality, limited-edition chocolates make our products unique and uncommon • Fairtrade Marked cocoa balances gift status with sense of social responsibility
Professionals and business people who give customised gifts	• Want to reinforce corporate name in a tangible, memorable way • Want to give a gift not available to the general public • Want recipients to anticipate high-quality customised gifts • Want recipients to feel good about the social responsibility aspect of the gift	• Chocolates and packaging can carry a business logo as a visual reinforcement of the corporate name • Special packaging customised for business clients reinforces the uniqueness and exclusivity of the gift • Fairtrade Marked cocoa combines holiday tradition with social responsibility

Market trends and growth

The overall European chocolate confectionery market is projected to grow modestly for the remainder of this decade, a positive trend for our product. Moreover, UK chocolate sales represent 25 percent of the total European market for chocolates, which supports our decision to launch first in the United Kingdom. Gourmet chocolate brands clearly have higher wholesale and retail value than mass-market chocolates, although per capita consumption does not match that of mass-market chocolates.

A growing number of Fairtrade chocolates have gained distribution in national chains such as Waitrose as well as in independent shops. National advertising and sales promotions support sales of Cadbury, Nestlé, Mars and other mainstream chocolate marketers, especially prior to Easter and other holidays. Chocolate products made from cocoa beans native to specific regions or plantations carry a special mystique. Two examples are chocolates marketed by Hotel Chocolat from cocoa grown in the West Indies and those marketed by Montezuma from cocoa grown in the Dominican Republic and Peru.

Further, product proliferation in the European chocolate market is adding to competitive pressure. In fact, chocolate products represent a significant fraction of all new food products introduced during any given year. Both for-profit and not-for-profit companies are introducing chocolate bars, truffles and novelties made from Fairtrade ingredients. Smaller companies are making speciality chocolate products for niche markets, such as for people who want to avoid dairy products, for diabetics, and for people who prefer natural or organic flavourings and ingredients. Established companies constantly introduce variations of truffles, bars, bonbons and other favourites to satisfy customers' variety-seeking behaviour and encourage loyalty. In many cases, companies are offering their products directly to customers through online and printed catalogues. Buzz created by social media increases awareness of upmarket chocolates, helps brand awareness and encourages product trial; because of our Fairtrade cocoa, we will be able to communicate about sustainability as well as great flavour.

Marketing research

To stay in touch with our targeted segments and track emerging market trends, we are commissioning qualitative research that will investigate perceptions, attitudes and behaviour related to premium chocolate products in general and Lost Legends Luxury Chocolatier in particular. We will use both secondary and primary research to support new product development, plan public relations activities, understand our competitive situation and monitor progress towards awareness objectives. In addition, we will commission marketing research to examine customer and channel satisfaction and identify opportunities and threats to which we must respond. Finally, we will solicit feedback through our website, Facebook page, Twitter account and manufacturer's representatives as part of our ongoing research.

CURRENT PRODUCT OFFERINGS

Initially we will offer two main product lines, both based on modern adaptations of family recipes and a proprietary cocoa bean-roasting process we recently developed. The first, Belgian Legends, features 12 dark chocolates named for Belgian cities, such as Antwerp (dark, fruity flavour) and Bruges (extra dark, sprinkled with *fleur de sel*). This product line will be available all year and both the chocolates and packaging can be customised for corporate gift giving. In subsequent years, we will add between two and four new varieties in this line and retain the best-selling eight to ten chocolates from the previous year, as measured by volume. We will also offer special packaging for three important holiday seasons: Easter, Christmas and St Valentine's Day.

Our product plan has the following advantages: (1) the product line and packaging are freshened and updated on a regular basis; (2) customers can find their favourites year after year, holiday after holiday; and (3) the product line and the names of individual chocolate varieties reflect our family's background and tradition. The plan supports steady year-round purchasing and encourages impulse and gift purchases during peak selling periods.

The second product line, Limited Edition Legends, features chocolates in one of two seasonal shapes and matching packaging: seashells for summer and snowflakes for winter. Each season we will bring back the seashell or snowflake favourites in new packaging. By restricting production and distribution of these limited-edition chocolates, and planning each seasonal announcement as a media event, similar to those for new wine vintages, we will build customer anticipation and demand. Premium chocolates have been offered in limited editions for some time, but mainstream manufacturers such as Cadbury, Nestlé and Mars have brought the practice to a wider audience by offering limited editions of well-known chocolate treats. Nestlé's Maison Cailler is offering chocolates customised for individual flavour preferences and cocoa content, sold online with the option to reorder on a regular basis.

The use of limited editions has the following advantages: (1) the temporary introduction of seasonal varieties will give sales a strong, relatively predictable boost during specific periods; (2) loyal customers will be able to buy some favourite chocolates in every season; and (3) the perceived value as a gift will be higher because these varieties are not available throughout the year. As a result, we can capture customer interest in between the peak holiday periods and fulfil consumer and corporate needs for unique, value-added gifts.

BUSINESS ENVIRONMENT

Lost Legends Luxury Chocolatier will begin operations in an environment shaped by national and regional political forces, economic uncertainty, powerful social–cultural forces, including concerns about social responsibility, new production and communications technologies, specific legal considerations, increased emphasis on sustainability, and strong competition. This section discusses how the business environment is likely to affect our marketing and performance and this is followed by a SWOT analysis of our strengths, weaknesses, opportunities and threats.

- *Political forces.* As chocolate makers, we must be knowledgeable about political conditions in the nations where we obtain our cocoa and other supplies. We must also monitor the political situation domestically and throughout Europe as we plan to expand through exporting.

- *Economic trends.* Economic conditions are not uniform throughout the European market, which will affect our ability to forecast sales and profits during the first year. Because buyers of upmarket chocolates routinely seek out new specialities, our initial sales should be strong despite the economic uncertainty. We must also monitor the economic climate in Ghana, where we source our Fairtrade Marked cocoa beans. Sharply higher demand for cocoa, particularly Fairtrade cocoa, has led to increased investment in new cocoa production methods.

- *Social–cultural trends.* The Fairtrade Marked system, designed to ensure that growers are equitably compensated for their cocoa beans, is emblematic of a larger movement towards socially responsible business operations, with which we will be associated. As consumers and business customers become more knowledgeable about the social issues connected with chocolate production, our offerings are likely to be perceived favourably. Our products take advantage of the trend towards supporting small, local brands in a world dominated by giant multinational corporations. We also recognise that attitudes towards sweets are influenced by concern about nutrition and unhealthy foods. Yet some research suggests that the flavanol in chocolate can have health benefits. Our communications will therefore suggest that fine chocolate products be enjoyed as special treats, not as a steady diet.

- *Technological trends.* Although our chocolates will be hand-produced, the special roasting process for our cocoa beans relies on new technology that we have protected through patent. Technology will enable us to communicate more efficiently and effectively with our customers, suppliers and channel partners. In addition, our automated inventory-management system will help us forecast future demand, plan for supplies, plan for production and plan for distribution to ensure that we and our intermediaries have the right products in stock when needed.

- *Ecological trends.* With a focus on sustainability, we are buying Fairtrade Marked cocoa that is grown in an ecologically sound manner. We are also planning eco-friendly packaging using recycled materials and inks that do not pollute. For transparency purposes, our communications will explain how we pursue ethical sourcing of ingredients and what we are doing to protect the environment.

- *Legal factors.* Our company must comply with all regional and national laws and regulations governing product quality, labelling, ingredients and many other aspects of the business. For example, any 'organic' chocolate product must comply with EU rules for organic certification. Similarly, our communications must comply with applicable laws in localities where we reach out to consumers and business customers.

- *Competition*. We face competition from Callebaut, Lindt, Neuhaus, Perugina, Nestlé, Cadbury and Godiva, among other major rivals. These companies have established brands and sizable advertising budgets, yet they are not immune to industry competition and the effect of economic conditions on product sales. We compete with Green & Black's, Divine and other brands specialising in Fairtrade chocolate; we also compete with Hotel Chocolat, Montezuma and other speciality chocolate makers that have upmarket shops and retail websites. Lost Legends Luxury Chocolatier will emphasise exclusivity by restricting distribution to selected shops, using our heritage and sense of social responsibility to differentiate our products, promoting our patented roasting method and our commitment to hand-made quality.

SWOT analysis

Lost Legends Luxury Chocolatier can leverage several core competencies and key strengths in addressing potentially lucrative opportunities in both consumer and business market segments. As a new and unknown company, however, we must counter a few critical weaknesses that could threaten our ability to build profitability by serving the targeted segments. Table A.3 summarises our SWOT analysis.

Strengths

Among the internal capabilities that support our ability to achieve long-term and short-term objectives are the following:

- *Unique, time-tested recipes*. No other chocolatier sells the unusually rich, flavourful chocolates we can offer, updated from dozens of original recipes developed in the Steenstraat section of Bruges – a city renowned for delicious hand-made chocolates.

Table A.3 SWOT analysis

Strengths	Weaknesses
• Unique, time-tested recipes • Patented roasting process • Cost-effective hand production • Glamorous history and heritage	• Lack of brand awareness and image • Limited resources • Lack of channel relationships
Opportunities	**Threats**
• Higher demand for premium chocolates, particularly dark chocolates • Growing interest in treats with mystique • Growing interest in socially responsible products	• Intense competition • Market fragmentation • Uncertain supply prices

- *Patented roasting process.* Our legally protected, proprietary process for roasting cocoa beans results in a distinctively rich flavour and complex aroma that add sensory appeal to the finished product.

- *Cost-effective production.* Drawing on family records and supplier connections, we have perfected a cost-effective method for producing consistently high-quality chocolates by hand.

- *Glamorous history.* Publicising the legend of our family's original recipes and generations of chocolate making will evoke vivid images of old-fashioned quality and enhance the brand's glamour.

Weaknesses

Some of the internal factors that might prevent Lost Legends Luxury Chocolatier from achieving our objectives include the following:

- *Lack of brand awareness and image.* Lost Legends Luxury Chocolatier is a new company and therefore has no brand awareness in its targeted segments. We must effectively position our brand, create a premium image and communicate product benefits in order to build positive perceptions and attract customers.

- *Limited resources.* Much of our first-year budget is committed to funding production and internal operations, leaving limited funds for paid marketing messages. We will therefore put more emphasis on social media, online marketing, special packaging, sampling, public relations and special events to generate buzz, gain brand awareness and attract buyers.

- *Lack of channel relationships.* Most of our competitors own their own shops or have long-established relationships with leading retailers serving affluent customers. We are in the process of convincing exclusive speciality shops, leading department stores and other select retailers that our products are compatible with their merchandise assortments and will be profitable to carry.

Opportunities

We plan to exploit the following key opportunities:

- *Higher demand for premium chocolates.* More people see premium gourmet chocolates as an affordable luxury and therefore buy such products for themselves and for gifts. UK customers are familiar with premium chocolates and accustomed to paying more for ultra-high-quality products, especially those made from Fairtrade ingredients. Also, corporate demand for premium chocolates is rising due to interest in status products that can be given as gifts to almost any business contact (unless restricted by religious or cultural traditions).

- *Growing interest in treats with mystique.* Research suggests that customers (both consumers and business buyers) want more than a chocolate treat – they want to know the story behind the product and share in the product's mystique. Our company's connection with the family's legendary Bruges chocolates is an intriguing story to be publicised; the unique recipes, limited-edition products and special packaging add to the mystique.

- *Growing interest in socially responsible products*. The use of Fairtrade Marked cocoa (and coffee) will appeal to consumers who like the idea of supporting socially responsible products. It will also differentiate our products from those of companies using cocoa beans not grown by Fairtrade farmers. More than two dozen companies already produce Fairtrade chocolate products for the UK market, which shows how interest has grown and suggests that competition is likely to become more intense as this niche expands.

Threats

We recognise the need to counter the following threats as we begin marketing our chocolates:

- *Intense competition and market fragmentation*. In addition to the major luxury chocolate makers with established brands, national advertising campaigns and sizable market share, many smaller, local chocolate makers are attracting loyal customers. Among the more than two dozen companies that feature Fairtrade chocolates in the UK market are Divine Chocolate, Green & Black's, Chocaid and Traidcraft. The resulting market fragmentation threatens our ability to build a solid customer base effectively and efficiently.

- *Uncertain supply prices*. Initially, we will be buying supplies in limited quantities and will not qualify for the most favourable volume discounts. Also, the price of ingredients can vary widely according to crop conditions, weather and other factors. Thus, we must allow for an extra margin when we set retail prices and recalculate break-even and profit levels as we come to know our supply prices.

Key issues

Because weather is an uncontrollable environmental factor, it has a major effect on chocolate sales and cocoa bean production. Heatwaves generally hurt sales and can affect chocolate production; cool weather allows both channel members and consumers more flexibility in storing chocolates. Lost Legends Luxury Chocolatier will forecast modest sales for the hottest summer months and be ready to increase production output if the weather is not extremely warm. Extreme weather conditions or crop diseases in Ghana will hurt cocoa bean production, making this key ingredient scarce and expensive. We must be prepared to buy from alternative Fairtrade sources if our primary growers cannot fulfil their contracts, in order to meet our first-year sales objectives. In this event, we will plan to absorb higher costs and assume smaller profit margins for a limited period to avoid raising prices.

Product and package design are becoming increasingly important drivers of gift chocolate purchasing. Some companies are targeting niche markets such as golf-ball-shaped chocolates for men who play golf. Others are packaging premium gift chocolates in keepsake boxes that communicate status and elegance. Companies that emphasise Fairtrade connections generally explain their positioning on labels and packaging. We will monitor these trends and research additional opportunities during the coming year.

MISSION, DIRECTION AND OBJECTIVES

The mission of Lost Legends Luxury Chocolatier is to make exceptional sweets that delight and inspire chocolate lovers. Our top-quality, premium chocolates are updates or variations of cherished family recipes, all produced by hand from the finest, freshest ingredients. We will use Fairtrade Marked cocoa, coffee and other ingredients from socially responsible sources, as part of our mission to inspire.

Our priority is to build our brand first in the UK market and then gradually expand our focus to other European markets. Our initial year's direction is controlled growth through the establishment of the brand, development of two main product lines and targeting adults in consumer and business segments. In the second year, we will pursue growth through both market penetration and market development. Because of ongoing plans for limited-edition chocolate products, our growth will depend on product development as well. Based on this mission and direction, we have formulated the following primary objectives for our marketing plan:

- *Financial objectives*. The main financial objectives for Lost Legends Luxury Chocolatier are to (1) achieve first-year turnover of £500,000 in the UK market, (2) achieve full-year retail sales of at least £10,000 per outlet in the retail channel, (3) reach the break-even point for UK operations within 16 months and (4) achieve 10 percent gross profit margin in our second year of operation.

- *Marketing objectives*. The main marketing objectives are to (1) generate first-year brand awareness of 35 percent within consumer segments and 40 percent within business segments, (2) place our products in 50 exclusive shops and high-end department stores located in affluent UK areas, (3) have our UK direct-sales website fully operational when the first products launch and (4) research and develop between two and four new Belgian Legends variations, based on family recipes and traditions, for introduction in the second year.

- *Societal objectives*. The main societal objectives are to (1) support socially responsible trade by buying all cocoa and coffee from Fairtrade Marked sources and (2) increase the proportion of recycled materials used in product packaging from 50 percent at start-up to 65 percent by the end of the first full year.

TARGETING AND POSITIONING DECISIONS

As shown in Table A.1 and Table A.2, we are targeting specific segments of the consumer and business markets. In demographic terms, these are adults with middle to high income levels, professionals and business people. In behavioural terms, the targeted consumer segments consist of adults who buy fine chocolates for themselves, for holidays or as gifts. The targeted business segments consist of business people who buy fine chocolates as gifts, customised or not. Because the corporate gift market is growing faster than the consumer chocolate market, and because of the potential for higher customer lifetime value and better return on investment, we will put more emphasis on the targeted business segments.

We will use differentiated marketing to reinforce the positioning of Lost Legends Luxury Chocolatier as a marketer of gourmet chocolates hand-made from 'legendary' family recipes using strictly fresh, high-quality natural ingredients drawn from socially responsible sources. This positioning sets us apart competitively and helps establish a positive, upscale image in the minds of the consumers and business customers we are targeting.

PRODUCT AND BRAND DECISIONS

Both of our initial product lines are based on updates of traditional family recipes and use our proprietary, patented cocoa bean-roasting process. The 12 chocolates in the Belgian Legends line are named for Belgian cities: Antwerp, Bruges, etc. The chocolates in the Limited Edition Legends line will be shaped like seashells (for the summer season) and snowflakes (for the winter season).

Packaging for both product lines will carry through the Belgian theme with stylised nineteenth-century artwork of the major cities on the boxes, velvet and satin ribbons, and choice of holiday or seasonal ornament to top each box. Our Lost Legends Luxury Chocolatier packaging will be instantly recognisable because of the distinctive colours and graphics. Customised orders will allow for corporate logos on each chocolate and on the ribbon and box. Limited-edition chocolates will also be individually wrapped in foil that is changed from season to season, adding to the feeling of luxury and exclusivity. Although some packaging will be retained from year to year, we will build customer anticipation by introducing elaborate new packaging for each holiday (Christmas, St Valentine's Day and Easter) and each new limited-edition range. Table A.4 summarises our main product marketing decisions.

The coming year's product development efforts will focus on researching and creating new chocolates to replace the slowest sellers in the Belgian Legends line. All new products must fit the high-quality tradition of our family recipes yet incorporate new flavours or other product elements that will trigger repeat purchasing from current customers and attract new customers. Also, every new product should take advantage of our proprietary bean-roasting process and our commitment to socially responsible sourcing of ingredients.

Table A.4 Summary of product marketing decisions

Product mix	(1) Offer the Belgian Legends range year round (2) Offer the Limited Editions Legends range seasonally, one for summer and one for winter
Product life cycle	(1) Retain the top-selling 8–10 chocolates in the Belgian Legends range each year (2) Replace the slowest-selling chocolates yearly with new flavours/variations (3) Bring back Limited Edition Legends in summer and winter to extend the growth part of the life cycle
New product development	(1) Develop at least two new Belgian Legends flavours or variations each year by updating family recipes (2) Track customer preferences, channel feedback, supplier ideas and market trends as input for new product decisions
Quality and performance	(1) Use only the finest, freshest, all-natural ingredients (2) Obtain Fairtrade Marked cocoa from a single plantation renowned for its quality (3) Hand-produce chocolates that meet highest customer standards for competitively superior taste and texture
Features and benefits	(1) Offer a range of flavours and variations to satisfy different customers' tastes, preferences and need for novelty (2) Offer year-round, holiday and customised packaging to satisfy needs for gift status (3) Use packaging materials from sustainable sources to demonstrate commitment to environmental protection
Brand	(1) Emphasise the 'legends' concept to communicate the long family heritage of gourmet, hand-made chocolates (2) Link the brand to attributes such as exclusivity, superior taste and quality, fresh, natural ingredients and socially responsible sourcing
Design and packaging	(1) Offer chocolates in distinctive shapes and combinations that convey a sense of luxury and tradition (2) Create sustainable, attractive packaging that communicates the Bruges background and tradition of our chocolates (3) Offer special seasonal packaging for the Limited Edition Legends range (4) Offer special holiday packaging for the Belgian Legends range (5) For corporate orders, design custom chocolates and packaging with company logos

The competitively distinctive 'legends' concept is central to our brand image. For brand identity purposes, the Lost Legends Luxury Chocolatier name will appear on every package, along with the name of the product line (Belgian Legends or Limited Edition Legends). Packaging, public relations and other aspects of our marketing will emphasise the 'legends' concept. We want customers to associate our brand with a decades-old family history of making top-quality chocolates by hand in the Bruges tradition, using the finest, freshest ingredients. And we want them to respond to our brand's association with social responsibility, as demonstrated through purchases of Fairtrade Marked cocoa and coffee.

(In an actual marketing plan, more information about individual products, design, packaging and new product development would be shown here, with additional detail being shown in an appendix.)

PRICING DECISIONS

We will price our two product lines differently. On the basis of our research, we will make Belgian Legends available in 200 g, 300 g and 500 g packages with introductory retail prices of £16, £22 and £32. Our wholesale prices will be 50 percent lower than the retail prices, not including quantity pricing for retailers who sell a higher volume of our products. The Limited Edition Legends range will be priced at £1 higher per package, reflecting the limited period of availability and allowing Lost Legends Luxury Chocolatier to recoup higher costs related to these seasonal products. Holiday packaging will add £2 to retail prices, depending on the package and ornaments selected. These prices support our premium positioning and the high value that our products represent.

For comparison, the following is a sample of competitive prices:

- A large UK chocolate maker offers a satin gift box with 1,800 g of assorted fine chocolates for £70 and a smaller, star-shaped satin gift box with 280 g of chocolates for £17. The company provides a special web page for corporate orders.

- A family-owned chocolate marketer sells a package of 26 mini-bars of dark chocolate for £29 and a collection of 25 truffles, total weight 325 g, for £18. Corporate gifts are priced based on quantity and customisation, available in hampers or branded packaging.

- A speciality gift company sells a 150 g box of gourmet chocolates for £9 and a 400 g box for £16. Chocolates in more deluxe packaging are priced at £22 for 300 g and £37 for 550 g.

- A mid-sized UK chocolate maker that uses organic Fairtrade ingredients sells three 150 g gourmet bars for £12 and a 500 g gift box of gourmet chocolates for £27.

Our pricing for corporate orders will be higher than the pricing for our consumer products, depending on quantity, level of customisation and delivery instructions. For customers' convenience, we will pack and address all corporate orders, include a business card or a seasonal greeting, and despatch all gifts for a nominal delivery fee. Once a corporate customer has provided names and addresses of gift recipients, we will keep the information on file and automatically provide it for updating when the customer places another order.

By aggressively pursuing these more profitable corporate orders, we expect to attain our objective of breaking even on UK operations within 16 months. However, the timing is subject to change if the cost of cocoa (or other ingredients) rises dramatically. As shown in the financial details section, our pricing is planned to support the objective of attaining 10 percent gross profit margin on our second-year turnover.

(In an actual marketing plan, more information about pricing, costs and break-even would be shown here, with additional detail included in the appendix.)

CHANNEL AND LOGISTICS DECISIONS

One of our major first-year objectives is to establish strong relationships with 50 upmarket shops that cater to affluent UK customers and have temperature-controlled storage for our chocolates. By restricting distribution to only one retail outlet in a given area of the country, we can strengthen our luxury image and more effectively reach higher-income customers. We will also use exclusive distribution to our advantage by educating store personnel about our patented roasting process, our Fairtrade Marked ingredients, our recipes and our family 'legends'. During the initial product introduction period, we will provide channel members with sample chocolates and display packaging, posters publicising the 'legends' concept, product nutrition information and literature about Fairtrade Marked sourcing.

To reinforce exclusivity, we will phase in Limited Edition Legends during each season. In the first week, only the top 20 percent of our retail outlets (measured by volume) will receive the snowflake or seashell chocolates. During the second week, the next 20 percent of the outlets will receive these seasonal chocolates. By the third week, all of our outlets will carry the product line. This approach rewards retailers that do the best job of selling our chocolates and gives their customers access to seasonal chocolates before anyone else. We will be using a push strategy to educate retail sales staff about our company and products, along with a special set of training activities that will keep sales people informed about the latest trends and motivate them to educate consumers.

We will also have our own UK direct-to-consumer website operational by the time we launch the Belgian Legends line. The site will follow the 'legends' theme in describing our company background, recipes and hand-production methods. We will allow visitors to view each product and package in a larger format and check ingredients, nutrition information and other details before buying. The site will have separate ordering pages for consumer and business buyers and allow pre-orders for seasonal and holiday offerings (to be fulfilled through retail partners). Although non-UK buyers will be able to order online for direct delivery, we will open a separate European website during our second-year expansion.

Our logistics plan includes obtaining quality ingredients (including cocoa and coffee from Fairtrade Marked sources) and packaging components on schedule and in sufficient quantities, maintaining constant, optimal product temperature and protective packaging when delivering to retail outlets, checking that retailers store and display chocolates under proper conditions, and using shipping containers that preserve product quality when fulfilling orders placed online or by corporate customers.

(In an actual marketing plan, more information about channel relationships and logistics would be shown here with additional detail included in the plan's appendix.)

MARKETING COMMUNICATIONS DECISIONS

Given the company's start-up costs, our marketing communications and influence strategy will rely less on paid advertising than on public relations and special events, sales promotion, personal selling and direct marketing (see Table A.5). Our marketing messages will use the emotional appeal of status, incorporate the 'legends' concept and be consistent with our product's upscale, superior-quality positioning. Initially, we are choosing media that will bring our messages to the attention of prospective channel members and executives who buy or influence the purchase of corporate gifts.

Consumer advertising in upmarket magazines will be considered in our second year of operation. Throughout, we will use social media to engage our channel members, business customers and consumers, to stimulate positive word of mouth and to monitor response from our target audiences. We will also have a website optimised for mobile access and will test mobile marketing campaigns during peak purchasing periods.

We are designing public relations programmes to support our financial and societal objectives and to achieve our marketing objectives of (1) generating first-year brand awareness of 35 percent within consumer segments (and 40 percent within business segments) and (2) placing our products in 50 exclusive shops and department stores. Our sales promotion programmes will encourage channel participation and reward the outside manufacturer's representatives handling our products for arranging distribution through appropriate upmarket shops and department stores. The major consumer sales promotion planned for the first year is to have UK luxury hotels and restaurants giving away product samples to their customers as an introductory 'taste' of our legendary chocolates.

Our direct marketing effort will centre on the website, with separate sections devoted to product and company information, the 'legends' behind our family recipes, corporate ordering, store locations and social responsibility activities. Visitors will be invited to email feedback, comment on our blog and subscribe to our free monthly newsletter. We will also keep a dialogue going with audiences through messages and videos posted on social media such as Twitter, Facebook and YouTube.

(In an actual marketing plan, more information about programmes, messages and schedules would be shown here, with additional detail included in the plan's appendix.)

Table A.5 Summary of decisions about marketing communications and influence

Technique	Activities
Advertising	• Targeted magazine ads to build brand awareness and acceptance among channel members and corporate customers • Channel-only advertising campaign to announce seasonal products as part of our push strategy • Use of social and mobile media to engage and influence consumers, businesses and channel members
Public relations	• Media interviews, special events, news releases and social media interaction to build brand awareness and positive word-of-mouth among consumers, businesses and channel members • Creating buzz by arranging tasting events with several celebrity opinion leaders • Communicating the 'legends' concept and associating it with the brand image • Communicating the use of Fairtrade Marked cocoa to influence public perception of our social responsibility • Through social media interaction and other methods, gathering information about each public's attitudes and perceptions to shape messages and policies
Sales promotion	• Channel sales promotion to pave the way for personal selling by manufacturer's reps, as part of our push strategy • Selective consumer sales promotion in the form of product samples distributed through luxury hotels, restaurants and shops • Sampling via vouchers downloadable from Facebook • Creating brand-building point-of-purchase displays for shops • Participating in industry trade shows • Sales force promotion to reward reps for placing our chocolate in upscale shops, as part of our push strategy
Personal selling	• Contracting with manufacturers' sales reps to visit targeted retail shops and place our products, as part of our push strategy • Arranging for periodic personal, telephone and email follow-up to gather feedback from channels and from customers • Providing ongoing training support to retail sales staff and manufacturers' reps
Direct marketing	• Encouraging corporate customers, in particular, to visit our website and order customised products • Inviting consumers to visit our website to learn more about the 'legends' concept, see our products, locate nearby shops and submit queries or comments to management • Inviting consumers to continue the dialogue by subscribing to our email newsletter, becoming Facebook fans or following us on Twitter • Testing mobile marketing campaigns to reach and influence consumers during key shopping periods

CUSTOMER SERVICE AND INTERNAL MARKETING

To support our marketing plan, we need good customer service to build positive relationships with channel members, corporate customers and consumers. We recognise that customers who buy premium chocolates expect perfection, as do our retailers. Therefore the manufacturer's representatives who call on our retailers will be allowed to replace chocolates and settle channel complaints as necessary. We are holding monthly briefing sessions to keep our reps and our employees fully informed about our products, marketing programmes, product-line performance and future plans. Further, we will keep reps and employees updated about the latest products and promotions by holding virtual training sessions every month, posting podcast messages from our owners and sending reps the monthly email newsletter one week before customers receive it. Our marketing staff will post comments and images on social media and respond quickly to social media mentions of our brand, especially if service issues are involved.

We have a separate plan for delivering pre-purchase service, post-purchase service and service recovery to our business buyers. Two employees will be responsible for answering business customers' questions before orders are placed, monitoring order fulfilment, communicating with customers about delivery schedules, tracking deliveries, contacting customers after the sale to check on satisfaction and handling any questions or complaints as quickly as possible. On the basis of our interaction with business customers, we will adjust offerings, policies and procedures to improve our service over time and build our share of this potentially profitable market. Should any complaints or concerns be posted on Twitter or other social media, we have designated an employee to respond immediately and resolve issues quickly.

(In an actual marketing plan, additional information about service support and implementation would be included here and in the plan's appendix.)

MARKETING PROGRAMMES

Given below are summaries of our main integrated marketing programmes leading up to our product introductions in September and mid-November and continuing during the year-end holiday period. Associated schedules, budgets and responsibilities are included in the appendix.

- *August.* Our push strategy will be strongest one month before the Belgian Legends product range is introduced, to prepare channel members. Employees and manufacturer's reps will visit each participating retailer to provide product training, samples and display materials. Full-page colour advertisements in major confectionery and chocolate industry magazines and online ads on selected industry websites will introduce the brand and the 'legends' concept. Simultaneously we will start our public relations efforts with media interviews, news releases and Facebook posts focusing on the 'legends' concept and the family's Bruges-style chocolate recipes. One special media event planned for August is the arrival of a shipment of Fairtrade Marked cocoa. Family members will blog about the cocoa and the importance of Fairtrade; the company will also post podcasts and YouTube videos for downloading or forwarding. In addition, we will seek to influence targeted segments and resellers through communications on Twitter and images on Pinterest.

- *September.* To launch the new product range, Lost Legends Luxury Chocolatier's founders and family members will travel to each retail outlet in an elegant horse-drawn coach and present the manager or owner with an ornate package containing all Belgian Legends varieties. This public relations event, to be covered by media outlets and taped for posting on YouTube, will focus attention on the legendary family heritage of chocolate making and the old-fashioned gourmet quality of our products. During this month participating upmarket hotels and restaurants will receive their first deliveries of Belgian Legends samples, also delivered by family members arriving by coach. Manufacturer's reps will follow up to ensure that every channel member has sufficient inventory and marketing material for the launch. Facebook fans will have the opportunity to download a voucher for one free sample plus a sample for a friend.

- *October.* We will place colour advertisements in business magazines and in the business section of London newspapers to generate response from professionals and executives who buy premium chocolate as gifts for clients, colleagues and other business contacts. All advertisements will include the Fairtrade Marked logo and a brief description of this trade programme. Our website will also be prominently featured, along with the store-location function. Our public relations programme for the month will focus on Fairtrade Marked sourcing. Our manufacturer's reps will participate in a sales contest to pre-sell the Limited Edition Legends line, which is launched in mid-November. Our first email newsletter will be sent this month, with excerpts and photos posted on Facebook. Customers and channel partners will be invited to watch a three-minute YouTube video about our unique manufacturing process, our seasonal chocolates and our use of Fairtrade cocoa.

- *November.* Our website home page will promote Christmas gifts, especially the seasonal Limited Edition Legends chocolates and special holiday packaging. Packaging will also be 'pinned' on Pinterest. Our channel promotions will highlight the Limited Edition Legends range for gift giving and encourage retailers to order early. Public relations and social-media activities will draw attention to the original family recipes on which our products are based and to the limited-edition concept. We will also send holiday samples to opinion leaders to generate buzz and influence brand perceptions and preference.

- *December.* Our website will offer suggestions for last-minute chocolate gifts for consumers and business contacts. Manufacturer's reps will visit every participating retailer to check on inventory, provide sales assistance, deliver additional display materials and provide other support as needed. Publicity and special events will showcase the 'legends' concept and our family's tradition of gourmet chocolate making. Marketing research will gauge interim awareness levels and attitudes among the targeted consumer and business segments. Our monthly email newsletter, blog posts, Facebook messages, tweets and YouTube videos will focus on the history of chocolate and chocolate gift ideas. Internally, we will be preparing for the summer line of Limited Edition Legends and for other new products.

(In an actual marketing plan, additional programme details would be shown in the appendix.)

FORECASTS AND FINANCIAL DETAILS

We are forecasting £500,000 in annual company turnover during our first full year of operation, with a minimum of £10,000 in sales per participating retail outlet. Our forecasts call for annual turnover increases of 20 percent during the next three years. We expect to reach the break-even point on UK operations within 16 months and achieve 10 percent gross profit margin by the end of our second year.

Due to constant variations in the price of ingredients such as cocoa, coffee and sugar, we can only estimate our cost of goods and then for only two or three months in advance. We will be monitoring increases in the cost of sugar and other commodities and have contingency plans in case costs move dramatically higher. In the short term, as our volume increases and we buy supplies in larger quantities, we will be able to stabilise variable costs for up to six months. Therefore, our financial projections are subject to revision during the year.

(In an actual marketing plan, additional details would be shown in the appendix.)

IMPLEMENTATION AND CONTROL

To ensure that our two product ranges are launched on time, we will adhere to weekly schedules and assign management responsibilities for supervising manufacturer's reps, coordinating sales promotion activities, and briefing the public relations, advertising, research and website experts. Three key performance indicators for evaluating the effectiveness of our marketing plan are sales trends, brand awareness and customer retention.

Among the metrics we have selected to monitor progress towards our objectives are the following:

- Unit and monetary sales (analysed daily, weekly, monthly and quarterly by product, range, channel, outlet and type of customer)

- Profitability (analysed monthly by product range, type of channel and overall sales)

- Customer perceptions of and attitudes towards brand (semi-annual research supplemented by monitoring of social media and direct customer feedback)

- Business customer retention and profitability (monthly analysis)

- Competitive standing (semi-annual research)

- Channel member participation and satisfaction (quarterly analysis)

- Image as socially responsible company (semi-annual research)

- Use of recycled materials in packaging (quarterly analysis)

- Order fulfilment speed and accuracy (monthly analysis).

We will review interim progress weekly during the first year of operation, comparing actual results with forecasts, schedules and budgets and adjusting activities if needed. We have also developed a comprehensive contingency plan to ensure a continuous supply of Fairtrade ingredients if unfavourable weather conditions or crop diseases threaten cocoa production in Ghana. A second contingency plan for repricing is ready to implement if cocoa costs increase dramatically within a short period.

(In an actual marketing plan, additional details about implementation and control would be included in the appendix, along with summaries of any contingency plans.)

Sources

Market background and environmental trends based on information from the following:
'Willy Wonka goes to Davos', *Independent*, 4 June 2012, p. 10
Sebastian Joseph, 'Mondelez to launch marketing blitz to boost sales', *Marketing Week*, 15 February 2013, www.marketingweek.co.uk
Felicity Lawrence, 'Trade, not aid', *Guardian*, 27 February 2012, p. 3
Stephen Williams, 'Is Ghana entering a sweet, golden era?', *New African*, March 2012, p. 38
Dermot Doherty, 'Nestlé bites into chocolate's $8 billion premium market', *Bloomberg*, 12 February 2012, www.bloomberg.com
Leonie Nimmo and Dan Welch, 'Chocolate revolution transforms the world's favourite treat', *Guardian Environment Blog*, 14 October 2009, www.guardian.co.uk
Stephen Baker, 'Following the luxury chocolate lover', *Businessweek*, 25 March 2009, www.businessweek.com
Carolyn Cui, 'Cocoa prices create chocolate dilemma', *Wall Street Journal*, 13 February 2009, www.wsj.com

Glossary

advertising Non-personal promotion paid for by an identified sponsor (Chapter 9)

affective response Customer's emotional reaction, such as being interested in or liking a product (Chapter 9)

affordability budget method Method in which senior managers set the total marketing budget on the basis of how much the organisation can afford or will be able to afford during the period covered by the plan (Chapter 11)

annual control Type of marketing control used to evaluate the current marketing plan's full-year performance as a foundation for creating next year's marketing plan (Chapter 12)

attitudes Consumer's assessment of and emotions about a product, brand or something else (Chapter 3)

auction pricing Approach to pricing in which buyers are invited to submit bids to buy goods or services through a traditional auction or an online auction (Chapter 7)

audience fragmentation Trend towards smaller audience sizes due to the multiplicity of media choices and vehicles (Chapter 9)

available market All the customers within the potential market who are interested, have adequate income to buy and have adequate access to the product (Chapter 3)

Balanced Scorecard Broad performance measures that help organisations align strategy and objectives to manage customer relationships, achieve financial targets, improve internal capabilities and attain sustainability (Chapter 5)

behavioural response Customer's action in response to a marketing communication, such as buying a product (Chapter 9)

behavioural tracking Monitoring what consumers and business people do online as they visit websites, click on ads and fill virtual shopping trolleys (Chapter 3)

benefits Need-satisfaction outcomes that a customer expects or wants from a product (Chapter 6)

brand equity Extra value that customers perceive in a brand, which builds long-term loyalty (Chapter 6)

brand extension Widening the product mix by introducing new products under an existing brand (Chapter 6)

brand promise Marketer's vision of what the brand must be and do for consumers (Chapter 1)

branding Giving a product a distinct identity and supporting its competitive differentiation to stimulate customer response (Chapter 6)

break-even point Point at which a product's revenues and costs are equal and beyond which the product earns more profit as more units are sold (Chapter 7)

budget Time-defined allotment of financial resources for a specific programme, activity or product (Chapter 11)

business (organisational) market Companies, institutions, non-profit organisations and government agencies that buy goods and services for organisational use (Chapter 3)

business strategy Strategy determining the scope of each unit and how it will compete, what market(s) it will serve and how unit resources will be allocated and coordinated to create customer value (Chapter 1)

buying centre Group of managers or employees that is responsible for an organisation's purchases (Chapter 3)

buzz marketing More intense form of word of mouth in which the organisation targets opinion leaders, with the aim of influencing them to spread information to other people (Chapter 9)

cannibalisation Situation in which one product takes sales from another marketed by the same organisation (Chapter 6)

category extension Widening the mix by introducing product lines in new categories (Chapter 6)

cause-related marketing Marketing a brand or product through a connection to benefit a social cause or non-profit organisation; also known as *purpose marketing* (Chapter 5)

co-creation Involving customers in a highly collaborative effort to develop novel new products to satisfy needs (Chapter 1)

cognitive response Customer's mental reaction, such as awareness of a brand or knowledge of a product's features and benefits (Chapter 9)

competitive parity budget method Method in which senior managers establish a total marketing budget at least equal to that of competitors (Chapter 11)

concentrated marketing Targeting one segment with one market mix (Chapter 4)

consumer market People and families who buy goods and services for personal use (Chapter 3)

content marketing Marketing intended to demonstrate thought leadership and engage or inform customers by communicating original content (Chapter 9)

contingency plan A plan to be implemented in response to or anticipation of a significant change in the marketing situation that could disrupt important marketing activities (Chapter 12)

core competencies Organisational capabilities that are not easily duplicated and that serve to differentiate the organisation from competitors (Chapter 1)

crowdsourcing Generating new product ideas or marketing materials from concepts, designs, content or advice submitted by customers and others outside the organisation (Chapter 6)

customer lifetime value Total net long-term revenue (or profit) an organisation estimates it will reap from a particular customer relationship (Chapter 4)

data mining Sophisticated analyses of database information used to uncover customer buying and behaviour patterns (Chapter 2)

demand How many units of a particular product will be sold at certain prices (Chapter 7)

derived demand Principle that the demand forecast for a business product ultimately derives from the demand forecast for a consumer product (Chapter 11)

differentiated marketing Targeting different segments with different marketing mixes (Chapter 4)

direct channel Marketing channel used by an organisation to make its products available directly to customers (Chapter 8)

direct marketing Use of two-way communication to engage targeted customers and stimulate a direct response that leads to a sale and an ongoing relationship (Chapter 9)

distribution channel Set of functions performed by the producer or participating intermediaries in making a particular product available to customers; also known as the *marketing channel* (Chapter 8)

diversification strategy Growth strategy in which new products are offered in new markets or segments (Chapter 5)

dynamic pricing Approach to pricing in which marketers vary prices from buyer to buyer or from situation to situation (Chapter 7)

econometric modelling method Use of sophisticated econometric models incorporating anticipated customer response and other variables to determine marketing budgets (Chapter 11)

elastic demand Relationship between change in quantity demanded and change in price, in which a small percentage change in price produces a large percentage change in demand (Chapter 7)

elasticity of demand How demand changes when a product's price changes (Chapter 7)

environmental scanning and analysis The systematic and ongoing collection and interpretation of data about internal and external factors that may affect marketing and performance (Chapter 2)

ethnographic research Observing customer behaviour in real-world situations (Chapter 3)

exclusive distribution Channel arrangement where one intermediary distributes the product in an area (Chapter 8)

external audit Examination of the situation outside the organisation, including political–legal, economic, social–cultural, technological, ecological and competitive factors (Chapter 2)

features Specific attributes that contribute to a product's functionality (Chapter 6)

field marketing Working with outside agencies on sales promotions that take place in stores, shopping districts and office locations (Chapter 9)

financial control Type of marketing control used to evaluate the current marketing plan's performance according to specific financial measures such as sales and profits (Chapter 12)

financial objectives Targets for achieving financial results such as revenues and profits (Chapter 5)

fixed costs Business costs such as rent and insurance that do not vary with production and sales (Chapter 7)

forecast Projection of the estimated level of sales and costs during the months or years covered by a marketing plan (Chapter 11)

freemium pricing Giving the basic product away free but charging for extra functionality or advanced features (Chapter 7)

frequency The number of times people in the target audience are exposed to an advertisement in a particular media vehicle during a certain period (Chapter 9)

goals Longer-term targets that help a business unit (or the organisation as a whole) achieve performance (Chapter 1)

greenwashing Perception that a company is marketing its products or brands on the basis of 'green' activities that have little or no actual ecological impact (Chapter 8)

grey market Channel situation in which wholesalers and retailers sell a branded product even though they aren't authorised to do so (Chapter 8)

indirect channel Marketing channel in which intermediaries help producers make their products available to customers (Chapter 8)

individualised (customised) marketing Tailoring marketing mixes to individual customers within targeted segments (Chapter 4)

inelastic demand Relationship between change in quantity demanded and change in price, in which a small percentage change in price produces a small percentage change in demand (Chapter 7)

influence network Network of social-media contacts in which dialogues between opinion leaders and consumers affect attitudes and behaviour (Chapter 3)

integrated marketing communications (IMC) Coordinating content and delivery of all marketing messages in all media to ensure consistency and to support the chosen positioning and objectives (Chapter 9)

intensive distribution Channel arrangement in which as many intermediaries as possible distribute the product in an area (Chapter 8)

intermediaries Businesses or individuals that specialise in distribution functions (Chapter 8)

internal audit Examination of the situation inside the organisation, including resources, offerings, previous performance, important business relationships and key issues (Chapter 2)

internal marketing Coordinated set of activities and policies designed to build employee relationships within the organisation and reinforce internal commitment to the marketing plan and to good customer service (Chapter 10)

key performance indicators (KPIs) Indicators that are vital to monitoring effective performance, as defined by the organisation's strategic goals and marketing plan objectives (Chapter 11)

lifestyle The pattern of living reflecting how consumers spend their time or want to spend their time (Chapter 3)

line extension Lengthening a product line (or range) by introducing new products (Chapter 6)

logistics Flow of products, associated information and payments through the value chain to meet customer requirements at a profit (Chapter 8)

market The group of potential buyers for a specific offering (Chapter 3)

market development strategy Growth strategy in which existing products are offered in new markets and segments (Chapter 5)

market leader Firm that holds the largest market share and leads others in new product introductions and other activities (Chapter 1)

market-penetration pricing New product pricing that aims for rapid acquisition of market share (Chapter 7)

market penetration strategy Growth strategy in which existing products are offered to customers in existing markets (Chapter 5)

market segmentation Grouping consumers or businesses within a market into segments based on similarities in needs, attitudes or behaviour that marketing can address (Chapter 4)

market share The percentage of unit or monetary sales in a particular market accounted for by one company, brand or product (Chapter 3)

market-skimming pricing New product pricing in which a high price is set to skim maximum revenues from the market, layer by layer (Chapter 7)

marketing audit Formal, detailed study of the marketing planning process and the marketing function to assess strengths, weaknesses and areas needing improvement (Chapter 12)

marketing channel Set of functions performed by the producer or participating intermediaries in making a particular product available to customers; also known as the *distribution channel* (Chapter 8)

marketing control Process of setting standards and measurement intervals to track progress towards objectives, measure post-implementation interim results, diagnose any deviations and make adjustments if needed (Chapter 12)

marketing dashboard A computerised, easy-to-read depiction of marketing outcomes, as measured by key metrics, used to confirm progress and identify deviations from expected results (Chapter 11)

marketing objectives Targets for achieving results in marketing relationships and activities (Chapter 5)

marketing plan Internal document outlining the marketplace situation, marketing strategies and programmes that will help the organisation achieve its goals and objectives during a set period, usually a year (Chapter 1)

marketing planning Structured process that leads to a coordinated set of marketing decisions and actions, for a specific period, through analysis of the current marketing situation, clear marketing direction, objectives, strategies and programmes, customer service and internal marketing support, and management of marketing activities (Chapter 1)

marketing strategy Strategy developed to determine how the marketing-mix tools of product, place, price and promotion, supported by service and internal marketing strategies, will be used to meet objectives (Chapter 1)

marketing transparency Open and honest disclosure of marketing activities and decisions that affect stakeholders in some way (Chapter 1)

mass customisation Developing products tailored to individual customers' needs on a large scale (Chapter 4)

metrics Numerical standards used to measure a performance-related marketing activity or outcome (Chapter 11)

mission statement Statement of the organisation's fundamental purpose, pointing the way towards a vision of what it aspires to become (Chapter 1)

mobile marketing Getting information, directions, vouchers or other messages to target audiences via mobile through text, email and websites optimised for handset screens (Chapter 9)

motivation Internal force driving a consumer's behaviour and purchases to satisfy needs and wants (Chapter 3)

multibrand strategy Using two or more brand names in an existing product line or category (Chapter 6)

multichannel marketing Providing a variety of distribution channels for customers to choose from when they buy goods or services at different times (Chapter 1)

negotiated pricing Approach to pricing in which buyer and seller negotiate and then confirm the final price and details of the offer by contract (Chapter 7)

neuromarketing Using brain science and body responses to investigate and understand consumer reactions to marketing activities (Chapter 3)

niches Small subsegments of customers with distinct needs or requirements (Chapter 4)

objective and task budget method Method in which money is allocated according to the total cost of the tasks to be accomplished in achieving marketing plan objectives (Chapter 11)

objectives Shorter-term performance targets that lead to the achievement of organisational goals (Chapter 1)

opinion leader Person who is especially admired or possesses special skills and therefore exerts more influence over certain purchases made by others (Chapter 3)

opportunity External circumstance or factor that the organisation aims to exploit for higher performance (Chapter 2)

organisational (corporate) strategy Strategy governing the organisation's overall purpose, long-range direction and goals, the range of businesses in which it will compete and how it will create value for customers and other publics (Chapter 1)

penetrated market All the customers in the target market who currently buy or previously bought a specific type of product (Chapter 3)

percentage budget method Method in which senior managers set the overall marketing budget on the basis of a percentage of the previous year's annual turnover, next year's expected turnover, the product's price or an average industry percentage (Chapter 11)

personal selling Personal contact for the purpose of selling, accomplished through in-person meetings, telemarketing or Internet chats (Chapter 9)

PESTLE Acronym for political, economic, social–cultural, technological, legal and ecological factors in the environment, analysed during the external audit (Chapter 2)

pop-up shops Stores that temporarily 'pop up' in a location for a brief period (Chapter 8)

positioning Use of marketing to create a competitively distinctive place (position) for the product or brand in the mind of the target market (Chapter 1)

potential market All the customers who may be interested in a particular good or service (Chapter 3)

primary data Data from research studies undertaken to address a particular situation or question (Chapter 3)

product development strategy Growth strategy in which new products or product variations are offered to customers in existing markets (Chapter 5)

product life cycle Product's movement through the market as it passes from introduction to growth, maturity and decline (Chapter 6)

product line depth Number of variations of each product within one product line (Chapter 6)

product line length Number of individual products in each product line (Chapter 6)

product mix Assortment of product lines offered by an organisation (Chapter 6)

product placement Arranging for a product or brand to appear in a TV programme or a movie for marketing purposes (Chapter 9)

productivity control Type of marketing control used to evaluate the marketing plan's performance in managing the efficiency of key marketing activities and processes (Chapter 12)

psychographic characteristics Complex set of lifestyle variables related to activities, interests and opinions that marketers study to understand the roots and drivers of consumer behaviour (Chapter 3)

public relations (PR) Promoting a dialogue to build understanding and foster positive attitudes between the organisation and its publics (Chapter 9)

publics Groups such as stockholders, reporters, citizen action groups and neighbourhood residents that are interested in or can influence the organisation's performance; also known as *stakeholders* (Chapter 1)

pull strategy Targeting customers with communications to stimulate demand and pull products through the channel (Chapter 9)

push strategy Targeting intermediaries with communications to push products through the channel (Chapter 9)

qualified available market All the customers within the available market who are qualified to buy based on product-specific criteria (Chapter 3)

quality Extent to which a good or service satisfies the needs of customers (Chapter 6)

reach The number or percentage of people in the target audience exposed to an advertisement in a particular media vehicle during a certain period (Chapter 9)

relationship marketing Marketing geared towards building ongoing relationships with customers rather than stimulating isolated purchase transactions (Chapter 1)

repositioning Changing the competitively distinctive positioning of a brand in the minds of targeted customers (Chapter 4)

retailers Intermediaries that buy from producers or wholesalers and resell to consumers (Chapter 8)

reverse channel Channel flow that moves backwards through the value chain to return goods for service or to reclaim products, parts or packaging for recycling (Chapter 8)

sales promotion Incentives to enhance a product's short-term value and stimulate the target audience to buy soon or to respond in another way (Chapter 9)

scenario planning Type of planning in which managers look beyond historical trends and short-term projections to envision broad, long-term changes in the marketing environment that could affect future performance, then prepare contingency plans to cope with these possible situations (Chapter 12)

schedule Time-defined plan for coordinating and accomplishing tasks connected to a specific programme or activity (Chapter 11)

search engine optimisation (SEO) The process of modifying content, website characteristics and content connections to improve search engine rankings of a particular website (Chapter 9)

secondary data Information collected in the past for another purpose (Chapter 3)

segment personas Fictitious yet realistic profiles representing how specific customers in targeted segments would typically buy, behave and react in a marketing situation (Chapter 4)

segments Customer groupings within a market, based on distinct needs, wants, behaviours or other characteristics that affect product demand or usage and can be effectively addressed through marketing (Chapter 1)

selective distribution Channel arrangement in which a relatively small number of intermediaries distribute a product within an area (Chapter 8)

service recovery How the organisation plans to recover from a service lapse and satisfy the customer (Chapter 10)

showrooming Situation in which customers examine goods in a nearby store but then buy online (Chapter 8)

social gifting Giving a virtual gift card through social media, redeemable via the recipient's mobile device (Chapter 2)

social media Online media such as Facebook, Twitter and YouTube that facilitate user interaction (Chapter 9)

social media marketing The use of social media technologies, channels and software to achieve specific marketing plan objectives (Chapter 9)

societal objectives Targets for achieving results in social responsibility areas (Chapter 5)

strategic control Type of marketing control used to evaluate the marketing plan's effectiveness in managing strategic areas such as the marketing function, key relationships and social responsibility/ethical performance (Chapter 12)

strength Internal capability or factor that can help the organisation achieve its objectives, capitalise on opportunities or defend against threats (Chapter 2)

subculture Discrete group within an overall culture that shares a common ethnicity, religion or lifestyle (Chapter 3)

sustainable marketing Establishing, maintaining and enhancing customer relationships to meet the objectives of the parties without compromising the ability of future generations to achieve their own objectives (Chapter 1)

SWOT analysis Evaluation of an organisation's primary strengths, weaknesses, opportunities and threats (Chapter 2)

target market All the customers within the qualified available market that an organisation intends to serve (Chapter 3)

targeting Determination of the specific market segments to be served, order of entry into the segments and coverage within segments (Chapter 1)

threat External circumstance or factor that may hinder organisational performance if not addressed (Chapter 2)

undifferentiated marketing Targeting the entire market with one marketing mix, ignoring any segment differences (Chapter 4)

value From the customers' perspective, the difference between a product's perceived total benefits and its perceived total price (Chapter 3)

value chain Sequence of interrelated, value-added actions undertaken by marketers with suppliers, channel members and other participants to create and deliver products that fulfil customer needs; also known as *supply chain* or *value delivery network* (Chapter 8)

variable costs Costs for supplies and other materials, which vary with production and sales (Chapter 7)

virtual product Product that exists in electronic form as a digital representation of something, such as a virtual gift purchased for a Facebook friend (Chapter 6)

weakness Internal capability or factor that may prevent the organisation from achieving its objectives or effectively addressing opportunities and threats (Chapter 2)

wholesalers Intermediaries that buy from producers and resell to other channel members or business customers (Chapter 8)

word of mouth People telling other people about a product, advert or some other aspect of an organisation's marketing (Chapter 9)

Index